Praise for *Don't S*

"One of the most amazing nonfiction books ~~I've ever~~
—Dave Davies (contributor, *Fresh Air*)
in his "Off Mic" blog

"I admire people like Kennedy who have taken on inner-city violence with a laser-like focus." —Alex Kotlowitz, *The American Prospect*

"Kennedy . . . argues for a crime-fighting program that makes a lot more sense than anything you're likely to hear about in Washington (or, for that matter, your local statehouse). The book reads like a thriller, but it's full of commonsense solutions to a few seemingly insurmountable problems. Reading it left us more hopeful for America's dangerous places and the millions of people who inhabit them." —Very Short List

"Fascinating . . . Kennedy's argument is solid, and he shows again and again that many of our approaches to crime are done to make an electorate feel good, without changing basic dynamics that drive the drug trade . . . Understanding and knowledge, more than guns and handcuffs, are weapons in the war on crime that last for generations." —*The Seattle Times*

"A hopeful and intelligent book." —*The Economist*

"It is rare that while reading a book I immediately want to go out and buy copies to distribute to others. But David Kennedy's *Don't Shoot* is so powerful, so convincing, and ultimately so important that anyone working to curb violence and open drug dealing in urban neighborhoods must read it." —BeyondChron.org

"In a matter-of-fact, street-smart style . . . Kennedy explains his remarkably effective strategies for combating violent crime . . . This heartfelt book shows what can happen when police, gangs, and communities come together to address some of America's most intractable social problems." —*Publishers Weekly* (starred review)

"In *Don't Shoot*, Mr. Kennedy describes the dynamics that lead to street violence and, more important, outlines his own streets-tested program for bringing the level of violence down dramatically."

—*The Wall Street Journal*

"*Don't Shoot* is a work of moral philosophy that reads like a crime novel—Immanuel Kant meets Joseph Wambaugh. It's a fascinating, inspiring, and wonderfully well-written story of one man's quest to solve a problem no one thought could be solved: the scourge of inner-city gang violence. This is a vitally important work that has the potential to usher in a new era in policing."

—John Seabrook, author of *Flash of Genius*

"[A] passionate account . . . highly readable. [Kennedy] is by turns hopeful and wry, though consistently generous to the many colleagues he's worked with in the field. He is also bracingly honest, about everything from poisoned race relations and vicious local politics to the zigzagging emotions he experiences as he immerses himself in this important work."

—*Barnes & Noble Review*

"An unlikely criminal-justice pioneer revisits his innovative, immensely successful crusade against youth homicide in America's worst neighborhoods . . . A valuable text—not just for the solution, but also for the refreshing philosophy behind it."

—*Kirkus Reviews*

"The good news about the drug- and gang-related violence epidemic is that it can be controlled and substantially reduced. As proof, you only have to read David Kennedy's wonderful new book *Don't Shoot*. Now being tried in over seventy communities, David's campaign is expanding to have the national and international impact it deserves."

—Bill Bratton, chairman of Kroll and former chief of police of the Los Angeles Police Department

"Riveting . . . Unlike so much work in urban sociology and criminology, *Don't Shoot* offers a genuine message of hope. This is the gripping story of Boston's Operation Ceasefire and the interventions it spawned across the nation. The book is part memoir, part police thriller, taking us through the ups and downs in the genesis and evolution of one of the most promising responses to urban violence and drug markets in the last two decades . . . What we need is for [Kennedy] to light a fire under the rest of us so that we also get to work, perhaps finding ways to reduce the violence in cities where Ceasefire was not successfully implemented. *Don't Shoot* may be the spark." —**Truthdig**

"Kennedy's ideas extend beyond community policing and serve to revolutionize the entire criminal justice system."
—**Garry F. McCarthy, superintendant of Chicago police**

"*Don't Shoot* is a marvelous insight into how law enforcement tracks crimes and criminals and the network that feeds them. It is revealing of how that system and the system of the gangs work in almost parallel universes. They intersect and retreat, each filling the void the other leaves. It is a poignant look at the futility of this interplay and at how more deeply etched the mistrust becomes with each generation of futility. Most of all, it offers great hope that a method has worked to save lives, change lives and civilize neighborhoods."
—***Pittsburgh Post Gazette***

"One of a small number of 'big ideas' revolutionizing crime control, especially policing and prosecution. Shame on any city, police department, or prosecutor's office that isn't learning from [Kennedy's] experience. What *Don't Shoot* documents really matters."
—**George Kelling, senior fellow at the Manhattan Institute, professor of Criminal Justice at Rutgers University, and fellow in the Kennedy School of Government at Harvard University**

Don't Shoot

Don't Shoot

One Man, a Street Fellowship,
and the End of Violence in Inner-City America

David M. Kennedy

BLOOMSBURY
NEW YORK · LONDON · NEW DELHI · SYDNEY

Published by Bloomsbury USA, New York

All papers used by Bloomsbury USA are natural, recyclable products made from wood grown in well-managed forests. The manufacturing processes conform to the environmental regulations of the country of origin.

LIBRARY OF CONGRESS CATALOGING-IN-PUBLICATION DATA

Kennedy, David M., 1958–
    Don't shoot : one man, a street fellowship, and the end of violence in inner-city America / David M. Kennedy.
        p. cm.
    Includes bibliographical references.
    ISBN: 978-1-60819-264-9 (hardback)
    1. Violence—United States—Prevention.   2. Drug abuse—United States—Prevention.   I. Title.
    HN90.V5K46 2011
    303.6'90973—dc22
2011007900

First published by Bloomsbury USA in 2011
This paperback edition published in 2012

Paperback ISBN: 978-1-60819-414-8

1 3 5 7 9 10 8 6 4 2

Typeset by Westchester Book Group
Printed in the U.S.A. by Quad / Graphics, Fairfield, Pennsylvania

To all whom we have failed so grievously.

Zina Jacque got it right, fifteen years ago. We're here to say two things. One is, we're sorry. But sorry is never enough. The second thing is, we're going to fix it.

Contents

Introduction

Timothy Thomas, a nineteen-year-old black man, a father, engaged to be married, ran from a police officer. The police officer called for backup. The chase poured into an alley. Thomas took a single round to his chest. The officer claimed he had a gun. He had no gun.

It could have been any American city, but it was in fact Cincinnati, in a poor, black, high-crime neighborhood called Over-the-Rhine. Cincinnati's racial tensions have long been rawer, and closer to the surface, than in many other places. It was the home of white Marge Schott, forced out of her ownership of the Cincinnati Reds for such things as comments about "million-dollar niggers," and of flamboyant black criminal defense lawyer Kenneth L. Lawson, who advertised his practice with posters showing him seated on a throne with a decapitated white body at his feet. The city burned during the national wave of race riots in 1967, and again in 1968 after Martin Luther King was assassinated; toxic relations between Cincinnati police and the city's black population featured in the benchmark report of the 1968 National Advisory Commission on Civil Disorders—the Kerner Commission report. Things hadn't gotten much better in the two decades since. Between then and April 7, 2001, the day Timothy Thomas was killed, there had been report after report, thirteen in all: one showing that Cincinnati's Office of Municipal Investigation found misconduct on the part of ninety-four police officers over five years, none of whom were disciplined, another surveying police officers and finding that 86 percent thought that there was racism in the department. Before Timothy Thomas, Cincinnati police had killed four black men since November of the previous year, and thirteen between 1995 and 2000.

He ran, he died, and Cincinnati burned again. Blacks squared off against the police on the streets, around city hall, around police headquarters. There was arson, gunfire, looting, tear gas. A truck driver was dragged from his rig and beaten bloody. A cop was shot; miraculously, his belt buckle deflected the round. Shots were fired into whites' homes. Mayor Charles Luken locked the city under curfew for four days; police arrested seven hundred people. Al Sharpton flew in from Africa to join Martin Luther King III and Kweisi Mfume at Thomas's funeral. Cincinnati, Mfume said, is "ground zero" for racism, the "belly of the whale." Shortly after, Harry Belafonte would walk Over-the-Rhine and declare it a third-world country.

It is practically a script, the American riot. Horrible, inexcusable, and I honestly do not know, given the reality on the ground, why it is not more common.

Timothy Thomas ran because he had fourteen outstanding warrants, most of them for traffic offenses: driving without a seat belt, driving without a license, all incurred since February 2000, twenty-one traffic charges in less than a year and a half. He had been stopped, over and over and over, in practice the only way a police officer is going to see an unworn seat belt and ask for a nonexistent license. Stopped and then ticketed: over and over and over.

"One day Tim came in the house, and he was like, 'Mom, I got two tickets . . . it's like two tickets, Mom, for the same thing," said his mother, Angela Leisure. He got two more that same day. That's what happens, said Over-the-Rhine's black residents. Police couldn't, or didn't, differentiate between the hapless, like Timothy Thomas, the serious criminals, and everybody else. "They figure they out there selling drugs, and this and that," said Tim's brother Terry. "I mean yeah, there's a few drug dealers, but you can't just point them out and say, yeah, he's a drug dealer. If you ain't seen it or know he doin' it, you can't just point him out. But that's what they was doing. They was just picking you out the crowd, like. And Tim got picked out a lot of times. But they didn't have no reason to pick him out."

I spend a lot of time with blacks in this kind of neighborhood; pretty much all the men tell this story. I spend a lot of time with blacks, not in this kind of neighborhood; most of them tell this story. I spend a lot of time with whites, not in this kind of neighborhood. I've never once heard them tell this story. I spend a lot of time with cops in this kind of neighborhood. Not long ago, in this kind of neighborhood, I rode with them. All involved knew their lines so well that when the cops pulled over and got out of their unmarked car, black kids turned around, stepped to the walls or fences in front of them, spread their legs, raised their hands above their heads, and shook their coat sleeves down to expose their wrists for the handcuffs. And that was just for the cops to *talk* to them.

"They keep asking me why did my son run," Ms. Leisure told the *New York Times*. "If you are an African male, you will run."

Over-the-Rhine was Cincinnati's most dangerous neighborhood. There are Over-the-Rhines all across America, and I have walked a vast number of them, and they are all a bit different, and they are all the same. They are poor; minority, mostly black; desperate; riven by guns and drugs and fear. They are not, any of them, *just* dangerous: When I first began my time in this world, I was amazed to find quiet, lovingly kept streets cheek by jowl with what felt to me like Beirut. It was a first sign of what I now know well: These are places full of wonderful, amazing people. I have met the finest people I have ever met here. I have met young men who live carefully, consciously righteous lives, who make their parents proud, who navigate the lethal geography that is their daily life with breathtaking focus and courage. I have met parents who turn themselves inside out to protect their children and lift them up. I have met neighborhood elders who walk freely and cleanly through streets that would make, do make—I've seen it—seasoned law enforcement quake. I've met little old ladies who think nothing of squaring off with armed drug dealers. I've met armed drug dealers who listen to them. I've met older, wiser original gangsters, sick with what they've done, desperate to make up and give back, pleading, giving, negotiating, anything they can think of, to get the young men off the corners, stopping—sometimes with their own bodies—the looming violence. I have found, where nearly all outside have written it off, rich, living *community*. From the outside, from but a little distance, all looks lost; all is very much not, a point to which we will very much return. But the bad things that go on in these neighborhoods cast long shadows, and the bad things are profoundly, indescribably, obscenely awful.

I saw it first, more than twenty-five years ago, in Nickerson Gardens. Los Angeles public housing in Watts, black, and ground zero, near enough, to the crack epidemic. I've never been so scared in my life, before or since. I was there with two imposing black LAPD officers, and my lizard hind-brain knew instantly that if they were somehow magicked away all that would ever be found of me would be my bleached bones. It was the first time I saw what I have now seen all across this great nation of ours: young black men selling drugs to the idiot white folks who drive in from outside the neighborhood and drive out again, never even getting out of their cars; the child lookouts and runners; the burnt, leathery crack monsters, many of them women, hollowed out by the pipe; old men fawning over young men for a dollar or a rock; dirt and trash and empty bottles; the cold thug bravado of the groups of young men. Older women—always the older women—locked in their apartments, afraid to go outside, afraid to go to the store, afraid of stray gunshots, afraid for their children and grandchildren, afraid *of* their children and grandchildren, afraid afraid afraid.

I was in Nickerson Gardens by happenstance; it was not the kind of place people like me get to, otherwise. I had led a pretty standard privileged, well-educated, politically aware, socially conscious, white-guy life. My parents are easterners who'd moved to Michigan, outside Detroit, where my dad was a mechanical engineer with Chrysler; my mom had given up a chance to be Margaret Mead's personal assistant to marry him and have my older and younger sister and me. (At cocktail parties, asked what she did, she'd say, "I teach American civilization.")

When I was eight, in 1967, Detroit rioted. My family had a black cleaning lady, Selina Watson, who lived downtown and who was also our friend; she and my mother were close enough that Selina had dreams in which she came into my mother's bedroom and sat on her bed and said, Something's wrong with your mother, or David, or whatever that dream was about. My mother asked her to stop telling her about them, because they invariably came true—the next day my grandmother would have a stroke, or I got hit by a car—and my mother couldn't stand the waiting. A couple of days into the riots my mother called her and said, Should Chris come get you? Selina held the phone out the window so my mother could hear the tanks outside. Don't come anywhere near here, she said. We got out of Dodge, packed up the station wagon and left early for the family summer house in Maine.

Growing up, I raged against the Vietnam War, cheered when Nixon resigned, drove fifty-five to save gas, read Gandhi. Detroit, "Murder City," twenty miles away, got barely a thought. In college, at Swarthmore, outside Philadelphia, I helped organize an antiapartheid boycott. Black Chester, poor, dangerous, was four miles away. I did some tutoring there and lost interest.

In the early 1980s, I found myself in Cambridge, Massachusetts, at Harvard's Kennedy School of Government. I wanted to be a writer and had a wonderful day job writing teaching cases for the Kennedy School faculty—real-life stories used to teach management and public policy, the way business schools use business cases. One of the Kennedy School's brightest lights, and somebody I would come to know as one of the smartest people I would ever meet, is a professor named Mark Moore. Mark is always doing a dozen things at once; among those things, he had the Kennedy School faculty chair in criminal justice and directed the Program in Criminal Justice Policy and Management; he worked on juvenile justice, firearms, drugs and alcohol, violent offenders, corrections. He and a small circle of colleagues were launching a project on policing. Would I like to write the cases? We talked. He gave me some things to read and had me sit in on his team's planning for something they called the Executive Session on Policing. The general thrust was clear. Research and field experience had led them to think that the basic model of modern policing was bankrupt. They thought something better could be developed and were beginning a several-year undertaking to do that. There were new ideas in the air they were interested in, something called "community policing," something called "problem-oriented policing." Mark's team had already started cultivating police contacts who were putting them into practice in the field, and selected some first things they wanted to look at. Going and looking would be my job.

I said yes. It sounded interesting, I was quite enjoying Mark and his thinking, and the first trip was to London. I was in.

London was fun. The story was the London Metropolitan Police Force's response to the Brixton riot of 1981, a full-fledged antipolice race riot. I spent several days at New Scotland Yard hearing about how god-awful Brixton was, finally got there on my own, and discovered what felt to me like a vibrant multicultural neighborhood, fish-and-chip shops side by side with Jamaican jerk houses, reggae pulsing from shop doors. I went back and told the Met's commissioner, the wonderfully patrician Sir Kenneth Newman, that if I could make America's worst neighborhoods like Brixton, I'd get the Nobel Peace Prize. He chuckled and invited me to dinner in his private dining room, where we sat at a table that had come down from Admiral Nelson. I stayed off Russell Square, ate my first tandoori shrimp, drank real beer. Echo & the Bunnymen had "Bring on the Dancing Horses" on the radio, still one of my favorite songs. Brilliant.

The second trip was to Los Angeles.

That was different.

Freshmen philosophy classes get asked to debate, if you could go back in history and kill Hitler, would that be moral? Give me the guy who invented crack, a rusty bayonet, and a wayback machine, and get out of my way.

Los Angeles was *Blade Runner*. I know now that in most police forces a "man with a gun" call is a major deal, something rare; everybody in the area drops what they're doing and rushes to the scene. In Los Angeles, riding patrol, we were getting "man with an Uzi" from dispatch. *Regularly.* The week before I got there, somebody had put a rifle round through the driveshaft to the tail rotor of an LAPD helicopter and brought it down. "This is usually where I say, They shoot at us a lot," the air wing commander told me before I went up, "and you'll see muzzle flashes, but don't worry, they never hit us—but I can't say that anymore." The section of shaft, bullet hole drilled neatly through, was on display in the flight room.

South Central L.A. was surreal to someone like me, raised in the Midwest and on the East Coast. L.A. is low-rise; it goes out, not up. Single-family houses, nice lawns, Beach Boys sunshine, and whole neighborhoods with windows and doors behind iron bars. I watched, from the air, LAPD metro cars chasing gangbangers through the alleys that ran behind the houses. A husband in one of the drug areas hid his wife under a rug in his back seat when he left home; if both of them were seen leaving, their house would be scavenged clean before they returned. It was the first time I heard the term "rock house"—someplace where anybody could wander up, knock on the door, and buy rock cocaine—crack. When I headed west to L.A., the *New York Times* was just starting to write about this new drug called crack. In L.A., it was *on*.

I went to Nickerson Gardens because LAPD was trying a new foot-patrol experiment to see if the same officers, in the same area, getting to know the people and local action, could make a difference. The place is huge, almost sixty acres, a small town of low-rise stucco-and-concrete townhouse apartments, sun-bleached and pale. I didn't know it then, but I was just across the line from Compton, which some think really was ground zero for crack. It could truly have been the most dangerous place in America, on that particular day. I spent the day walking with the two of them. One was tough and compact, didn't say much, ranged out like a hunting dog working the trail for game: check this door, a look around the corner, double back for a word with that group of young men, flick forward again. Every once in a while he'd slide by for a quick word with his partner, off again. I stayed with the partner—big, talkative, friendly. He was a magnet for the little kids; they flocked, he joked, handed out baseball cards. Stopped and talked to the older women. Nodded to the young men, clustered, watchful, all sinew and hard eyes.

All the day, he schooled me. It was like walking with a field biologist who knows every root and branch and bird and butterfly; you're not really in the same forest they are. The cars come in from that way, see the kid walking up to the window, he's serving them. Those old men sitting at the card table, they're watching the heroin stash, it's buried over there, the dealers pay them off. We have to watch those traffic lights at rush hour, all the cars get ripped off. That guy, he's a heroin junkie, old, they can last forever if they keep eating, it's like the heroin preserves them; crack, though, it burns them up fast. I don't think I ever got more than eighteen inches from him. If you could have seen the fear and tension—*fear-vision goggles*—everything would have glowed white-hot. The *buildings* would have glowed. It was like watching time-lapse photography, the gorgeous flower blooming, the clouds scudding over, but what was unfolding was the end of the world. You could *see* it.

It was making a difference, what they were doing. As bad as it was, it had recently been a whole lot worse. All day long, as we walked and stopped, older black women said, thank God you're here. I can come outside again.

I felt like I had to do something. I took the two of them to dinner. I felt like I had to say something. Thank you, I told them, awkwardly. I know I didn't belong there. Thank you for taking care of me. The quiet one started to laugh. I was humiliated. No, you don't get it, he said. It's not you, I'm not laughing at you. Those kids who were coming up all day long? To get the baseball cards? The dealers were sending them. They wanted to know who you were. They never see a white guy in a suit. So all day long, out there, what I was telling people? *Fed.* You've done us a big favor. Things are going to be really quiet for a couple of weeks.

I had an absolutely visceral response to Nickerson Gardens. It was not reasoned, not moral, not mediated. It was

This is not okay. People should not have to live like this. This is wrong.

Somebody needs to do something.

It seized me in a way none of my other writing jobs had. I did more fieldwork for Mark Moore. Tampa, where I turned a corner in College Hill in my rental car and, for the first time, had a teenager on a banana-seat bicycle cruise by and check me out. Drug market lookout. First time of many. Went through my first door: Form up at dawn under an overpass, coffee and shuffling feet, entry briefing, raid vehicles streaming to the house, *out out out* blast through the door *police police police down down everybody down* I'm maybe the fifth through, cops coursing through the side rooms *clear clear* a man and a woman sitting cuffed against the wall in the living room paralyzed in shock. Not long after, I sat at Tampa police headquarters with the narcotics commander while he worked with the feds to make sure that the gram of marijuana—a joint, maybe a sample—the postal inspectors had just found in a letter made it into the house of the addressee before they took it, so he could seize the house. "People think I'm in the drug business," he said. "I'm not. I'm in the take-everything-you-own business." The command staff all drove luxury cars seized from dealers.

In Houston, where a whole apartment complex called Link Valley had been taken over, the drug traffic was so heavy dealers used light wands to direct it, like airline ground crews. Dealers drove off landlords by main force, there were six homicides in one year, jonesing buyers broke into sixty-six-year-old Gloria Pastor's home in an adjoining neighborhood, robbed it, killed her. On to East New York, in Brooklyn, where whole precincts were taken over by dealers and you could buy kilos of powder without getting out of your car. The Dominicans run the weight trade, my DEA guides said, they're tough, drove the Colombians out. Entire apartment buildings gone, each unit a stash house or a cook room, dealers stringing wires from the rear windows so they could slide out the back when the cops came in the front. I sat in a Hispanic shopkeeper's little office. We need *big black cops*, she said, cops these guys will *listen* to. They've got to turn the cops *loose*. My daughter can't walk down the street. Some of the cops turned themselves loose: One of them crimped a wire, staged an entry, went in a front door, dealer goes out the back window, *splat*. I walked Anacostia in southeast Washington D.C., gunshot survivors, young men with canes and walkers—leg injuries, spinal-cord injuries, the paraplegics and quadra-plegics don't get out so much—thick on the sidewalk. Our nation's capital. Colostomy bags, if you could see them. Lots and lots of colostomy bags, this world. There were craters in the buildings where they'd taken rounds.

I hit drug markets all over the country, flew to wonderful cities and dove into their worst corners, parallel worlds of violence and fear and despair, became a connoisseur of drug markets. It's becoming fashion-able these days to say that crack sparked a "moral panic": that it was never really that bad, that the public and political and law enforcement response was just a fevered overreaction. The argument goes something like this. Crack is just cocaine, pharmacologically; smoking it makes it hit harder and sharper, but otherwise, no big difference. Survey work shows that whites and blacks both use and sell cocaine in roughly equal numbers, and nobody started treating white neighborhoods like battle zones, so obviously that's just racism. The worst media excesses—one hit turns ordinary people into hopeless addicts, crack babies are ruined for life—turned out not to be true. The political bidding war to penalize crack was misbegotten—college basketball star Len Bias, whose cocaine-overdose death two days after being drafted by the Boston Celtics in 1986 helped drive Congress to enact, among other things, the notorious federal crack/powder disparity, actually died from using powder, not crack—and hugely disproportionate, given that crack was objectively not all that serious. Cocaine was slick when Hollywood hipsters snorted it, a demon drug when black kids smoked it. Drug warriors knowingly exaggerated its dangers; politicians took advantage for their own ends. The fever, hypocrisy, and racism has brought us where we are today, with black neighborhoods on lockdown and black drug users swelling the prisons. Crack was just never that big a deal.

There's a very strong case to be made for each of those predicates. As for the conclusion, it's nice to have a scholarly background; it gives one a subtle and refined perspective to bring to bear on empirical claims. The correct, judicious, judgment to be rendered in this case is

Bullshit.

Crack blew through America's poor black neighborhoods like the Four Horsemen of the Apocalypse had traded their steeds for supercharged bulldozers. It is now genuinely true, I think, that you had to be there. The moral panic crowd wishes all the evidence away: The cops aren't to be trusted, so their views don't count; the arrests were biased, so the numbers don't count; the newspaper reporters spun anecdotes, not systematic research, so their stories don't count; the tales of horror were overblown and hysterical, so they don't count. I was there. I've been there ever since. There are out-of-control drug markets all over the country; they're spreading. When I started it was all core urban stuff, but not anymore: It's been moving into the small towns for years. More than anything else, the moral panic nonsense misses the mark because it's all about *use*. Crack use, drug use, has never been the real drug problem.

Crack *markets*, drug *markets*, are the problem. I'd rather be in a crack market than be, say, held at gunpoint, or have boiling oil poured on me. Short of that, things don't get much worse.

I wrote it all up, huddled with Mark and his crew, sat in on his Executive Session, got to know the chiefs of police of L.A. and New York and Houston; Ed Meese, attorney general of the United States; Herman Goldstein, the father of problem-oriented policing; George Kelling, the father of broken-windows policing, other top academics nationally; Frank Hartmann, the executive director of the Program in Criminal Justice and genius moderator for the Executive Sessions; amazing law enforcement people from England and Australia. There was reason, real reason, to be hopeful. The core idea behind the new policing was that there were fundamentally more effective ways to go after important crime problems. The Kennedy School Executive Session, and police scholars nationally, worked out a whole architecture to retool policing in accordance with the new "community" and "problem-oriented" ideas. The police could work with new partners, bring different resources to bear from neighborhoods and businesses and city government. They could be analytic about their work, use tools other than arrest, do more than just chase calls and take reports. The future was visible. It won't happen overnight, was the thought. Give it, oh, five years.

The substance, the details, don't matter. It didn't take. American policing was not transformed. Whatever the new ideas' potential, it simply was not realized. There were isolated success stories on the street; you could see it really was possible to do things differently. There were a few departments that came pretty close to actually redesigning themselves. But it wasn't enough. Nobody went all the way. Most departments, most of the time, continued to do what they'd always done: drive around in cars, answer 911 calls, investigate crimes after they'd already happened. I watched from the sidelines in increasing desperation.

Meanwhile, crack had lit the fuse of America's youth-homicide epidemic, and the violence was spiking. Homicide, anywhere, everywhere, is overwhelmingly about young men. In America, homicide is overwhelmingly about poor young black men, and overwhelmingly about poor young black men and handguns. Criminologists stratify populations: A standard move is to look at young men's high-risk years, about eighteen to twenty-four. Before crack, things were getting better. The homicide victimization rate for eighteen-to-twenty-four-year-old blacks had actually been *declining*, from about 97 per 100,000 population in 1980—the tail end of the heroin epidemic—to about 68 per 100,000 in 1984. Then, beginning in 1985, it skyrocketed, to over 180 per 100,000 in 1993: an increase of more than *250 percent*. (Homicide deaths among eighteen-to-twenty-four-year-old whites went from 16.2 per 100,000 to 17.2 per 100,000.) There were headlines every day: young black men killing each other over drug turf, over sneakers, over a hard look—*mean mugging*—over nothing at all.

But that's over, of course. Everybody knows crime is down these days, it's a national success story. America's homicide rate hit almost 10 per 100,000 in the peak years; it's now about half that. But not for black men. Black men are dying, overwhelmingly by gunshot, at a horrendous pace. In 2005, black men aged eighteen to twenty-four were murdered at a rate of 102 per 100,000 (white men of the same age: 12.2 per 100,000). Recent data show that, even as homicide overall continues to decline, black men are dying *more*. Between 2000 and 2007, the gun homicide rate for black men aged fourteen to seventeen went up 40 percent; eighteen to twenty-four, up 18 percent; twenty-five and over, up almost 27 percent. And it's not just the big cities anymore. It's moving to the small cities, the towns, places that never dreamt they'd be dealing with this. The biggest increase in black killing, fourteen-to-twenty-four-year-old men from 2000 to 2007, was in cities between fifty and a hundred thousand: up a full third. Whites far outnumber blacks in the population, but the black homicide rate is so high that there are, in absolute numbers, more bodies: over 2,200 black men eighteen to twenty-four in 2005, against about 1,400 whites. Almost another four hundred between fourteen and seventeen.

It's just about the death toll for the World Trade Center attacks. *Every year.*

The killing is overwhelmingly concentrated in America's Over-the-Rhines: poor, desperate, black neighborhoods in big, medium, small cities. These are communities crafting new folkways for violent death, where shops sell "his picture here" memorial T-shirts—bring in a photograph, they'll print them up for you—where dead men's street names— RIP G-MONEY, KILLA—are spray-painted on walls, where shrines to the murdered—teddy bears, liquor bottles, photographs, plastic guns, "never forget" cards—dot the streets, where young men tattoo the names of their dead on forearms and fingers. There are no boundaries any longer, no sacred ground. At funeral services, young men surge in and out of church, seething, while women beg them to forgo retaliation. Security services redirect processions based on intelligence about victims' rivals. It doesn't always work. Clarence Glover, House of Glover Funeral Services, a little north of Over-the-Rhine—on the edge of Avondale, another hot neighborhood—has dodged bullets at burials.

Joanne Jaffe is a friend and colleague. She runs the NYPD housing police and she's working with young offenders who live in public housing in Brooklyn. Not long ago she showed me a portfolio of Facebook pages, RIP Facebook pages, RIP Facebook pages dated 2011 as I write this a few days into the new year. Yeah, I said, I know. I've been seeing it for years, families and friends honoring their dead. No, she said, you don't get it. These kids are *alive*. They're composing them *themselves*. They don't expect to live out the year. They're getting their affairs in order.

Young black men, every one.

The facts on the ground, the facts in the hot neighborhoods, are staggering. Our normal analysis, our normal discourse, is about the nation, about cities. We're in a long crime decline nationally; New York City, after more than fifteen years of falling homicide, had a small increase in 2010. That frame, those facts, those numbers, are real. They miss the point entirely. "Nobody lives in the nation," my colleague John Klofas at the Rochester Institute of Technology says. "They live in neighborhoods." David Cay Johnston is a Pulitzer Prize–winning former *New York Times* reporter, renowned for his work on economic inequality in America. Late in 2010, he wrote a piece about how he'd been getting his hair cut and the guy in the chair next to him started going on about how crime was out of control. It's not, Johnston said. It's all just lurid, cheap reporting. The country is way, way safer than it used to be. "Crime isn't running wild," Johnston wrote. Klofas wrote him a letter. I know your work, and really admire it, he said. "I oversimplify, but the

plight of the middle class, the gap between rich and poor and the delu-
sions of economic democracy in this country are enormously trouble-
some to me. But I must admit I am surprised that you argue such issues
so eloquently regarding the economy but you don't seem to appreciate
that the same general argument applies to crime. The rich have gotten
richer and safer but neither can be said for the nation's urban poor." He
showed Johnston his research: that the homicide rate for young black
men in the high-crime area of Rochester, New York, a crescent of Over-
the-Rhine-style neighborhoods, was 520 per 100,000. The math means
that more than one in two hundred are murdered every year.

That small increase in New York City's homicides in 2010? Driven
entirely by black dead, mostly young black men. White deaths were
down 27 percent, black deaths up 31 percent. Young black men fifteen
to twenty-nine were 3 percent of the city, a full third of the murdered.

Nickerson Gardens made this my world.

Ten years after I stood there in Watts, I grew deeply, desperately
frustrated: tired of sitting on the sidelines watching, tired of researching
and writing, tired of saying what other people should do. I went into
the field. Not, this time, as an observer. I wanted to *do* something. I
wanted to help, though I had no real idea how. I found, from the very
beginning, a gifted, dedicated, and still-growing band of partners.
We've been at it now for nearly twenty years, in cities all across America.
And we've gotten somewhere.

It has not been linear, clear, direct. It has been opaque, confusing,
deeply painful. I have seen pieces of a puzzle, thought I saw a whole,
found out I was wrong, doubled back, looked elsewhere, found new
pieces. I have found myself navigating a landscape littered with precon-
ception, prejudice, myth, misunderstanding: my own not least of all. I
have gone from feeling, at least from time to time, pretty damned smart,
to feeling deeply, profoundly humble and not infrequently ashamed.
Looking back from where I stand now, I can see that nearly everything
important was there to be seen, clearly visible, from the beginning, had
I the wit to see it. I didn't. Looking back from where I stand now, I can
see how essentially simple the answers are, how basic. I couldn't see it.
But I, we, saw some things, we did some things, we kept pushing, we

saw other things that led to still other things. And we have arrived at a place where we know something important.

We know what we need to know, now, to fix it.

We're not done; there's more to do, understand, figure out. Much more. It's all a work in progress. But we know enough to act, *now*. We do not have to live with the death, and the hatred, and the gunshot survivors who walk the streets with their canes and colostomy bags, and the young men who say matter-of-factly that they expect to be dead before they see twenty-five, and the warrior-priest cops who go through door after door after door and it never changes, and whole communities of black men going to prison, and whole communities that are unable to get anywhere on anything of substance because people are afraid to go outside, and poisoned relations between those who need each other the most. We do not have to go on like this. We once locked crazy people in stone buildings and chained them to walls; we look back at that now and say, What were they thinking? They did that? We can get there. We can make our way to a place where we look back at 2.2 million Americans in prison and say, What were they thinking? They did that?

The core of the problem, the key to the way out, lies in community, in communities. We have found our way, my partners and I, to strategies, operations. We have approaches to particular crime problems, we can teach them to you if you want to learn them, we have implementation guides and best-practice handbooks and research methods to support them and evaluations that gauge their impact. The real problem, though, is not in our currently ineffective strategies, and the answer to the problem is not just to substitute new strategies for the old ones. The real—the deep—problem is what happens between communities, and how that generates the appalling situation on the ground: the communities that look at each other and say, This is *your* fault; the communities that see each other as toxic and malevolent; the communities that cannot imagine working together for a common purpose; the communities that do not understand how profoundly they want the same things; the communities that do not see how they are backing each other, and themselves, into corners none chose, none wants. To see what's really going on, we have to see this. To truly change things, these communities must change the way they see each other, treat each other, act with and upon each other.

They can. Given the right opportunity, they will. We know that now.

We have three communities, at core, here.

First community.

Law enforcement.

The kind of relentless law enforcement that tagged Timothy Thomas with twenty-one violations and fourteen warrants is intended to save lives, to protect neighborhoods, to bring order to the streets. I have spent my adult life with the men and women who do the work, and I know this to be true. I've no time for the easy armchair cant that says this is all about profiling and racism and bias in the criminal justice system. It simply is not so. Nobody who has ever actually been on these streets could believe it for a moment. There is disparate treatment in law enforcement, no question, but that is not what is driving the problem. We cannot wish this away. Ask any defense attorney, who will tell you that all her clients are guilty. Police and prosecutors and probation and parole and all the rest focus on these neighborhoods because this is where the killing and dying is happening, and because the people living in Over-the-Rhine have the same right to peace and tranquility as those living nearby in safe and prosperous Mt. Adams. The smug notion that there is no problem here, or that this is all a moral panic, or that the problem with high-crime communities is the institutional racism of the criminal justice system, is a crock. The idea that the problem of America's Over-the-Rhines is institutional racism *is* institutional racism. Tell it to the mothers and fathers and loved ones of all the young black men who will die in Cincinnati if we don't do something real about all this. They are not being killed by the cops. They are being killed by each other. Black Americans are about a seventh of America. They do about half America's killing and half America's violent dying—young men, most of both—and it is the Over-the-Rhines that overwhelmingly produce the killers and the killed. After nearly fifty years of American progress on civil rights, with an American black middle class growing and flourishing, with a black man in the White House, poor black neighborhoods all across America burn white-hot.

If police were not focusing on these neighborhoods, they'd deserve to be hung from lampposts. The problem is that our response to the crime has become part of what is sustaining it. We are operating with the best of intentions, at least at the level where law enforcement actually takes place. I have worked alongside these police officers and prosecutors and probation and parole officers and federal agents for twenty-five years now; I am proud to call many of them my closest friends. They care deeply about the communities they are trying to protect, and I will tell you that they are doing their best.

Which does not change that we are destroying the village in order to save it. America has become a place where one in three black men will serve a felony prison sentence. One in nine between ages twenty and thirty-four is in prison *right now*. In Baltimore, where they've done the math, and many other places where they haven't, *half* of all young adult black men are in prison, in jail, on parole, or on probation. Most of those arrested, prosecuted, jailed, imprisoned, on probation, and on parole come from and return to the poor, hot-spot neighborhoods where the drugs, crime, and violence are also worst. In these places, most of the men can have criminal records. Felons, even those committed to turning their lives around, are deeply, permanently damaged. Nearly none will ever get a good job; permanently hobbled from advancement, they have little reason to invest in education and training; they are less likely to marry; they are less able to take care of their loved ones; many of them go to prison with children and families they leave behind and then return to, often to leave behind again, each step of which is profoundly disruptive; they have less to offer their communities; their communities mean less to them. Short of actual arrest and imprisonment, there is the grinding, intrusive policing endured by many poor black communities, the kind of policing that saddled Timothy Thomas with his twenty-one violations, the kind of policing that makes citizens in these neighborhoods think, at best, that the police are not on their side, and at worst that they are a race enemy. We are systematically injuring one of America's peoples. And we need to own that this is a *choice* that we are making. Law enforcement is not the tide or the weather. It does not just happen. We are doing this because we have *decided* to.

And we need to own an even harder truth: We have so decided, in considerable part, because law enforcement has in general written these communities off. There is a powerful conventional wisdom in the law enforcement circles I live in: that these communities are at heart uncaring, complicit, corrupt, destroyed. Nobody cares about the crime, the law enforcement narrative goes, or they'd raise their kids right, get them to finish school, have them work entry-level jobs—like I did, like my kids do—instead of working the corners. They don't care about the violence; nobody will even tell us who the shooters are. (Robert Tate, seventeen, was shot not long ago on the west side of Chicago. A police officer asked him if he knew who did it. "Yes," said Tate, "but I ain't telling you shit," and died.) Nobody cares about the drugs because everybody's living off drug money. That doesn't mean we don't do everything we can to keep people alive, to keep their streets safe, to protect, especially, the kids and the elders. But all we can do is occupy them, stop everybody, arrest everybody we can.

As long as this is how law enforcement sees the neighborhoods, they will continue to occupy them, stop everybody, arrest everybody, send all the men to prison.

There's a lot to say about this, but the most important thing is simple. It's wrong.

The second important community is the community in even the poorest, hardest-hit black neighborhoods. It's vital, caring, resourceful; it wants what any community wants: to be safe, to prosper, for its sons and daughters to prosper. It's not happening. It's not safe, and they're not prospering. The community looks around itself, at the poverty, the violence, the drugs, and asks, why? And it has an answer. Many in the black community believe that this is *all* happening because we—the outsiders, the cops, the white folks, the powerful—*want* it to happen. All of it: the drugs, the killing, the destruction, all of it. The day after I stood shocked in Nickerson Gardens, I called on a seasoned, weary, Watts community organizer. A former Black Panther, he had devoted his life to bootstrapping black neighborhoods out of squalor and despair. And we were finally getting somewhere, he said. We had businesses going, single mothers in their own homes, paying off their mortgages. We were making it. And the government couldn't stand it, so they brought this crack in, and now all those mothers are on the street chasing the pipe.

It has taken me most of my life to really hear what he said that day. That day, and long after, my mind simply shut it out: crazy talk. I'm white. This is part of the problem here: White folks hear this all the time, but they do not really hear it. I heard it, eventually. I watched with fascination the white response during the 2008 presidential campaign to the Rev. Jeremiah Wright's now-famous "God damn America" screed. *This is what he was talking about.* The larger excerpt from his 2003 sermon is

> The government gives them the drugs, builds bigger prisons, passes a three-strike law, and then wants us to sing "God Bless America." No, no, no, God damn America, that's in the Bible for killing innocent people.

This is just conventional wisdom in the neighborhoods I work in: The government brings the drugs in so they can put our kids in jail so the cops will have work and the cracker prison guards upstate can make union wages. My parents, who are smart, empathetic, informed people, and I got into it about Wright. They thought he was nuts. Wright's talk was endlessly reported and discussed; I saw no reference whatsoever, in any of it, to what I know to be true: *Many* black Americans believe what Rev. Wright believes. In some communities, *most* black Americans believe what Rev. Wright believes. Part of this book is about an entirely different way of dealing with drugs and drug markets, *designed* to keep people out of prison. We have worked these ideas in Providence, Rhode Island, and in many other communities. When I first raised them with Dennis Langley, black head of the Providence chapter of the National Urban League, he dismissed the idea immediately. The police will never go along with it, he said. Are you telling me the government couldn't keep the drugs out of the country if it wanted to? The *point* of the drugs is to put our kids in prison.

If you believe that, then that makes the police, and the larger community they represent, a race enemy. If the police are a race enemy, you can't work with them. Can't go to them when you need help. Can't make common cause on the most dire of neighborhood problems. You're about to die, can't tell them who shot you. As long as the community sees the police, the government, as a race enemy, there will be no rightful place for law. There can be no working together, no partnership, no common purpose.

There's a lot to say about this, but the most important thing is simple. It's wrong.

Third community.

The community of the streets.

Nearly all of the worst violence and crime in America's most troubled neighborhoods is driven by a small, superheated world of gangs and drug crews and drug markets. It is a world with its own rules, its own standards, its own understandings. It *is* a community, make no mistake; it is a community where men will kill for their brothers, die for their brothers, where being a thug is a good and honorable thing, where *thug love* means having your brothers' backs, no matter what the cost. It is a world in which young men stand against a powerful, malevolent world and say to themselves and to each other, Prison's no big thing; I'm going to be dead by the time I'm twenty-five, so nothing really matters; if a man is disrespected, he has to return violence or he's not a man; the enemy of my friend is my enemy; I'm a victim, so I'm justified in what I do.

It is a world that believes that it acts with righteousness. It is a world that believes that the community around it does not care, or is complicit, or is supportive. It is a world that believes that the police hate it and are motivated by racism and personal animosity.

If you believe that, then you're going to shoot other young men just like you for disrespecting you. That's going to go right sometimes, you're going to kill them, and the pain of their mothers and fathers and sisters and brothers is going to burn like fire. That's going to go wrong sometimes, you're going to kill wonderful young schoolgirls sitting on their porches or doing their homework in their bedrooms, and the pain is going to be even worse. You have a problem, you're not going to go to the police, your friends aren't going to let you go to the police, you're going to handle it yourself. You're going to take community silence about what you're doing as approval. You're going to do crime and go to prison over and over and over again. You're going to leave behind your friends, family, loved ones, grieving your death, grieving your absence. You're going to be part of making killing, dying, prison, *normal*. You're going to justify the worst notions of the outside: that you're remorseless, an animal, a sociopath.

As long as the community of the streets sees itself as righteous and justified, the killing will continue. As long as the community of the streets sees its own neighborhoods as approving, it will continue. As long as the streets see the police as racist and hateful, it will continue.

There's a lot to say about this, but the most important thing is simple. It's wrong.

It's *all* wrong. *This* is all wrong.

The government is not conspiring to destroy the community, the police are not uncaring, oppressive, racist. The community does not like the drugs and violence. Gang members and drug dealers don't want to die, don't want to go to prison, don't want—nearly any of them—to shoot people. It's *not true.*

To the contrary. Spend time, real time, with cops. Spend time, real time, with angry communities. Spend time, real time, with gang members and drug dealers. They are, none of them, what they seem to be from the outside. They are, none of them, their stereotypes. They are, all of them, in their own ways, strong and aspirational and resilient. They are, all of them, dealing as best they can with a world they did not make. They are all doing profoundly destructive things without fully understanding what they do. There is, on all sides, malice, craziness, and evil. But not much, it turns out, not much at all. There is, on all sides, a deep reservoir of core human decency. (Yes, for those of you shaking your heads and about to put this book down, because you cannot believe this is true of the cops, or the neighborhoods, or the gangbangers: truly. Bear with me. You'll see.)

This is what is at the heart of America's shame of violent death and mass incarceration and unspeakable community fear and chaos. These understandings and misunderstandings and the awful stereotypes they foster and reinforce, and the awful places into which they push ourselves and each other. The awful truth is that they are *understandable,* each and every one; they make perfect sense, each from their own perspective. One of the truest learnings of my nearly thirty years with cops and thugs and desperate black neighborhoods has been the slow—far, far too slow—dawning, the appalled gradual realization, of just how perfectly sensible they are, how reasonable they are. Come to understand each world, even the thug world, and they're not crazy at all, they make sense, they're *rational.* But they're wrong, these beliefs. They're wrong, and they're terrible, and they make each community look and act badly, and the gulf widens.

Deal with them, however, and something nearly magical happens. Humanity emerges, common ground appears, common interests manifest, common sense can finally prevail.

We can deal with them. It sounds too good to be true, but it's not. We *are* dealing with them, all over the country. This is *real*. It is *happening*. It is within our grasp. It works. We can *do* this.

And we can deal with the way in which all of this is *saturated* in race. Our real racial history, that has brought us where we are. The understandings, and especially the misunderstandings, that shape law enforcement's view of dangerous black neighborhoods. The understandings, and especially the misunderstandings, that shape those neighborhoods' view of the police. The understandings, and especially the misunderstandings, that shape law enforcement's and neighborhoods' views of the streets. The understandings, and especially the misunderstandings, that shape the streets' views of law enforcement. The dreadful behavior, by all parties, that follows. The ways in which we are all fanning the flames. The ways in which our very real, our dreadfully hard-won, our honorable progress on race in America has left untouched a national disgrace of violence, fear, alienation, and imprisonment. The ways in which that national disgrace is not open to the old remedies of racial justice, in which the old remedies of racial justice can in fact make the new problem harder to see. The ways in which different remedies are immediately before us, in our grasp. We can see it, we can face it, and we can move through it and beyond.

It doesn't change, fix, everything. We still have huge work to do on the other side. I'm a born and bred root causer, came up believing in fixing the economy, fixing education, supporting families, eradicating racism: Heal the community and the crime will take care of itself. That notion didn't survive the first five minutes in Nickerson Gardens. We can't do economic development when people are afraid to go outside, can't fix education when the corner boys get all the girls and face the other boys on their way to school, can't support families whose fathers are all locked up, can't eradicate racism when the neighborhoods and world outside are both fulfilling each other's worst prejudices. Deal with those things, and we have a chance to do the more important, deeper work.

Other way around, forget it.

The Rev. Wright was wrong. America need not be, should not be, damned. We can redeem ourselves. We just can't do it the way we've been trying to do it. We have to do something different.

I got the call from Cincinnati in the fall of 2006. The city had crumbled in the wake of the riot Timothy Thomas's killing had triggered. The Cincinnati Police Department knew it couldn't continue as before; it wasn't sure what else to do. In Over-the-Rhine and other hot neighborhoods, the police drew back. Gunfire picked up. Drug dealing became hotter and even more brazen. On the next to last day of 2001, the year of the riot, the *Cincinnati Enquirer* published a map of gunshot victims in the city. There had been sixty-one homicides in the city—up from forty the year before. There had been 107 shootings since April 13, after the riot quieted. The single largest number, twenty-two, was in Over-the-Rhine. It was nearly double that of the next most active neighborhood.

The body count continued to climb.

2002, sixty-six.

2003, seventy-five.

2004, sixty-eight.

2005, seventy-nine. And over *1,600* gunshot woundings.

The city had had enough. In April of 2006, under newly elected mayor Mark Mallory, the police department returned to what was, in effect, pre-riot operations. It included a crackdown in Over-the-Rhine that generated over a thousand arrests in a month. More than seven hundred were for Timothy Thomas–style misdemeanor offenses. The citywide sweep eventually totaled some 2,600 arrests.

It didn't work. 2006 would end with eighty-nine homicides, more than double than before the riot, and a historic peak for the city.

Shootings of *children* went up 300 percent.

Desperately watching was Dr. Victor Garcia, a black pediatric trauma surgeon at Cincinnati's Children's Hospital. I'd never met him; he'd shown up in my inbox several years earlier, and we'd written and spoken from time to time. I knew his extraordinary fervor only long-distance. Many of Cincinnati's surging number of gunshot kids came across his operating table. He'd been hounding the city, the state. I'm a doctor, a scientist, I've done my homework, he told anybody who would listen. Evidence matters here. There's something out there that works. We *must* do this. The crisis in the city finally got him his hearing. In late 2006, I found myself speaking to Mayor Mallory from my New York office at John Jay College of Criminal Justice.

Mallory said to me, is this true? This thing that I've been hearing about, it will really bring the killing down?

Yes, I said. And keep people out of prison, and heal the wounds between your police and your community.

We know how to do this.

Boston: Street Knowledge, Street Sense

The first piece of the puzzle came in Boston. Like the pieces that would follow, it came as a revelation, the first in a series of revelations. I don't mean it in the biblical sense, though I work with people, people of faith, who are quite sure that Providence is at work. It's that big, that powerful. But I mean it in the more mundane, the more literal sense. I mean that the pieces have been revealed, disclosed, unveiled. Looking back, it's clear. *This* piece went with *that* piece, then those went with *this* piece. Sometimes it was hard to see the pieces, sometimes hard to see how they fit together. But the pieces are there, they fit, and when you see how they fit it all makes perfect sense.

The first piece was *gangs*.

Or, as we would come to see, *not* gangs, not exactly. But close enough.

It came one day in January 1995, in a battered muster room at the Boston Police Department's special-operation headquarters on Warren Street in Roxbury, from Paul Joyce.

I was on the ground in Boston because America's streets were burning.

Boston, just across the river from my Cambridge office, was one of the many city stories that together added up to the national homicide epidemic. It was far from the worst, but it was bad enough and ran appallingly to type. Crack hit Boston hard in 1988. In 1987, there were around twenty killed, age twenty-four and under; in 1990, there were over seventy. It came down from there, but not enough. It wasn't

just the sheer volume of violence, it was the center-is-not-holding craziness of it all. In August of 1988, Tiffany Moore, a twelve-year-old black
girl, was shot three times while sitting on a mailbox on Humboldt Avenue in Boston's largely black Roxbury neighborhood. A mistake, but
she was dead anyway. The city hired outreach workers to try to pull the
kids off the corners. In 1992, gang members with knives and guns in-
vaded the Morning Star Baptist Church and attacked mourners at a
memorial service for a slain rival. Black ministers started walking the
streets at night. None of it worked. In 1994, kids fleeing a shooting at a
popular skating rink left so many guns behind the police had trouble
figuring out which might be implicated in the shooting. It was chaos.
Bernie Fitzgerald, chief probation officer in Boston's Dorchester neighborhood, was sitting in his office one morning, looking out the window,
and saw two kids on opposite sides of Washington Street shooting at
each other. A judge called for the National Guard to be deployed against
the gang problem *in the courthouses*. "I think there was a real question
in people's minds about whether Boston would remain a viable city,"
said BPD commissioner Paul Evans. The same story was being played
out all across the country.

Boston sergeant detective Paul Joyce: strong, silent, shaved head,
marathon runner, to this day I think probably the best street cop I've
ever met. In another life Paul would have been the sheriff who rides
alone into the mountains while the bankers and farmers cower and brings
back the entire band of outlaws that has been terrorizing the town, or a
Shaolin monk, meditating all day save for bursts of acrobatic, devastating, morally impeccable violence. In this life, he was the de facto and
spiritual leader of the Boston Police Department's Youth Violence Strike
Force: a gang unit, by any other name. We sat there that day in 1995, he
with his people and I with mine, and he said, We know what's going on
out there, we know what's getting them killed, and told us a story we'd
never heard before. The rest of the world saw chaos, pathology, irrationality, sociopathy. Paul Joyce saw gangs.

Our team from the Kennedy School had set up in Boston to try to do
something about the killing. We'd ended up with Paul Joyce on Warren
Street against our better judgment; we didn't think a gang unit was the

right place to start. We were wrong. Paul Joyce knew what was going on on the streets. He knew, in ways we had never heard before, who was doing the killing and who the dying. He knew what was *behind* the killing and the dying. He understood the unwritten rules, the community, of the streets. He knew what didn't work with that community. He had brought together around him a network from law enforcement, the neighborhoods, the streets, that collectively knew even more. He, and they, even knew—and told us that first day—what worked to *stop* the killing. It was a story dramatically unlike all the other public and political and academic stories about what was going on, and even more dramatically unlike all the stories about what to do about it. We didn't understand it, any of it, at first, and wouldn't for some time to come.

But we would come to understand it. And it would change everything.

We'd gone to Boston, to the Boston Police Department, had ended up with Paul Joyce, to try to map the new policing ideas onto the youth violence epidemic. When I had started to think, several years earlier, about leaving my spectator's seat and trying to do some real work, it was the killing I had fastened on. It was the biggest crime issue in the country; nothing else even came close. Nothing anybody was doing was working. From my vantage at the Kennedy School, my work with the Executive Session, getting to know the nation's best police chiefs, plugged into the policy conversations, on the ground in the hot neighborhoods all across the country, I'd had a very good view of the policy conversation in law enforcement, government, scholarly circles. I'd read the journal articles, followed the debates, watched the Washington action, saw what police departments and prosecutors and cities were doing, spent more time in the cities, at Justice. It was all nonsense. If you'd seen the streets up close, the debate, the plans, the actions were transparently ridiculous. Mandatory minimums. The federal death penalty for drug kingpins. Buy-busts. Just say no. Source-country interdiction. The Brady Bill. Reform the juvenile justice system. Waive juvenile killers to adult court. You've got to be *kidding*. None of it was making any difference on the ground, none of it was *going* to make any difference. *Man with an Uzi.* I wasn't trained—not a cop, not an academic, not anything—but I didn't have to be. See somebody step in front of a freight train and hold up their hand *Stop* you don't have to be a physicist or a doctor to know what's coming.

I had started to think. What might work, for real, on the streets, in the neighborhoods?

Looking at the carnage, I had been seized by one idea in particular. The kids were killing each other with guns, overwhelmingly handguns. Kids were not legally permitted to buy guns; they seemed to be having little problem doing so; all of this was illegal already; could anything be done about this illicit market? Would cutting off their access stop the killing? There was parallel work and thinking to draw on. A lot of the policing research I'd been doing for the last ten years had been on a portfolio of innovative, clever, and very effective efforts to shut down illicit *drug* markets. J. W. Collins, a powerful, plainspoken career Houston cop, had closed the Link Valley drug market literally overnight. Years of arrests hadn't made a dent, so Collins, armed with George Kelling's "broken windows" ideas, organized a big neighborhood coalition to clean the place up. As part of it, they published a notice in the paper that streets would be sealed off and checkpoints set up. They'd planned a huge law enforcement sweep, but the dealers read the paper; when the sweep rolled in there was nobody there. (It would take years to see how simple and central, how profound, that was.) Collins and his partners cleaned up, building managers reasserted themselves, problem gone; it didn't seem to reappear anywhere else. In Tampa, working with "market disruption" ideas developed by drug policy expert Mark Kleiman, police chief Bob Smith essentially ended street drug dealing, not by eliminating supply and demand but by driving the message home that selling on corners would simply not be tolerated. Police cultivated neighborhood informants who peered out their windows and phoned in details of the street action, like where stashes were hidden; officers would roll up, saunter to a tree, and dramatically ask, Does this bag of crack *belong* to anyone? No? Guess I'll keep it . . . Officers couldn't arrest a recalcitrant group of dealers who had the brass to set up lawn chairs and coolers on their spot; the cops showed up one day, pulled their own lawn chairs out of the trunk, and sat down with them until they just gave up. Six months of this and the streets returned to normal.

I wondered whether any of this could be mapped onto stopping kids from getting guns and dove into the research on illegal gun markets. It turned out to be amazingly sparse, but tantalizing. There was evidence, for example, that drugs and guns were sold side by side on the streets. The money was clearly in the drugs—there were lots of repeat-customer drug addicts, but not many gun addicts—so could police use undercover officers and confidential informants to find the gun sellers, arrest them on stiff federal drug charges, and get the word out that selling guns was a pretty poor business decision? Could parents be offered a deal so that if they told police that their kid had a gun, the police could just take it without charging the kid? Could police officers pose as kids, as they sometimes did to investigate drug dealing in schools, and make their way to street gun dealers?

The idea that something like this might be worth trying was arguably supported by new literature on kids and guns that suggested very strongly that it was fear, rather than core criminality, that was driving a lot of the current craziness. Carnegie Mellon's Alfred Blumstein, perhaps America's most prominent criminologist, did research suggesting that while guns and gun violence had begun with new, young drug dealers in the new crack markets, it had "diffused" from there into broader youth culture: Kids *not* involved in the drug trade were getting, carrying, and using guns because their world had become so objectively dangerous. Research by Joseph Sheley and James Wright seemed to tell a similar story: Nearly a quarter of the inner-city kids they surveyed carried a gun at least some of the time, and gave self-protection as the most powerful reason why. It made sense to think that the chaos on the streets was feeding on itself—had become "decoupled" from crack and crack markets—and that steps to sap that energy in various ways also made sense. If guns were harder to get, scared kids would be less likely to have, carry, and use them; if there were fewer kids getting, carrying, and using guns, kids would be less scared.

Maybe. A year and a half before our team met the Boston cops on Warren Street, I wrote a paper called "Guns and Youth: Disrupting the Market," laying out the case that it might be true, and ways we might go about it. (My paper actually had a section on gangs that reviewed the many reasons gangs probably weren't driving the problem and read, in part, "since violence by any affiliated group tends to brand it as a gang, it's unclear that 'gang violence' is in any case much more than a tautology." Stay tuned on that one.)

I'd gotten to know Bill Bratton through the Harvard Executive

Session. Bill was already a prominent, and would become a legendary, figure in policing. He'd begun his career as a street cop in Boston; taken over the New York City Transit Police, where with close advisor and my new friend George Kelling he'd reclaimed the city's subways; and come back to Boston, from whence he would shortly depart to launch the re-invention of the New York City Police Department and New York City's near-miraculous crime decline. In 1993, he was commissioner in Boston, where he was one of several police executives nationally taking a way-out-front role in support of the Brady Bill, the first serious gun-control measure to have a fighting chance politically in a generation. I went to see him in his office and gave him my paper. Brady is designed to keep adults with criminal records from buying guns at licensed gun stores, I told him. You know it won't help at all with what you're dealing with here in Boston, right? These kids aren't buying their guns at gun stores, they can't anyway. It's all illegal now. Brady won't touch it. Bratton stared at me from across his desk. He circulated my paper to a number of his command staff and kids-and-guns people. The distribution list included Superintendent-in-Chief Paul Evans, Superintendent James Claiborne, Lieutenant Kevin Foley, detectives Frederick Waggett and Robert Merner, and James Jordan. Jim Jordan I knew: He was the department's top civilian policy director. The rest I didn't know. Call Kennedy, Bratton said, this is worth thinking about. Nobody called.

Those names would return.

In November 1993, I presented my paper at my first American Society of Criminology conference, in Phoenix. After my panel was done, a tiny, whiskey-voiced, burnished walnut of a woman came up from the back of the room. "I've never thought of applying problem-oriented policing to guns," she said. "Who's supporting this work?" Nobody, I said, I just did this on my own time. (I had in fact written my paper while set up at home nursing a dying cat.) The woman was Lois Mock, whom I would come to know as a bulldog behind-the-scenes prime mover in American thinking on crime control. She went back to her post at the National Institute of Justice (NIJ), the Department of Justice's research arm, and worked language into the next year's research program soliciting submissions to do problem-oriented policing on the youth homicide epidemic.

It would get us to Boston. In 1994, Anne Piehl, a Kennedy School economist focused on criminal justice issues, and I wrote a proposal to use problem-oriented policing to address juvenile gun violence. We'd actually planned to field the project in New Haven, Connecticut, which had a terrible reputation for youth violence, but hard numbers we got just a couple of days before the proposal was due showed a problem small enough that even a very successful intervention would have trouble showing impact statistically. In a panic, we reached out to Jim Jordan in the Boston Police Department, who carried the idea to Commissioner Paul Evans, who'd taken over from Bratton. Names, both of them, on Bratton's memo. Evans blessed it, we global-replaced "New Haven" with "Boston" in the document, folded in some numbers for the city, and sent it off to the Justice Department.

The problem-oriented policing script we were following was an odd one. It said, basically, pick a problem, research it, find partners, and figure out a way to fix it. Our problem, we thought, was "juvenile gun violence." We didn't think we knew all that much about the problem; researching it and understanding it would be one of our core tasks as scholars. Our key partner, at least at the outset, would be the Boston Police Department; we expected to add others, in law enforcement, the community, and elsewhere. We absolutely didn't know what the operational response should be. We came to call what we were proposing the Boston Gun Project, but in fact we weren't sure that was really right. This idea about addressing gun markets might be right, or it might not; the research and our partners might suggest very different directions.

Academic research proposals are expected to be carefully specified: to say precisely what is to be studied, using what data, and what methods; to have any treatments or interventions precisely determined; to have very particular and high-quality evaluations attached to those interventions. The idea is to get as close as possible to a pharmaceutical drug trial: this exact disease, this particular medication, this many patients, this many doses for this long, a control group not getting the new medication, the statistics to tease out outcomes. *Our* proposal said, Kids killing kids is a big problem in Boston. We're going to follow the new policing playbook. Nobody knows exactly what's going on, so we're going to gather a variety of data—crime and victim and offender data from the police department and juvenile corrections; death and injury data from hospitals; gun data from the Bureau of Alcohol, Tobacco, and Firearms. We're going to survey at-risk kids, do ethnography in the city's hot neighborhoods, immerse ourselves in the street culture. We're going to find and interview police officers and others who are dealing with this. We'll try to come up with a new description and diagnosis of what's happening. We'll try to design an effective intervention, based on the diagnosis, but we don't know what that's going to look like; this idea of disrupting illicit gun markets might make sense, but we're not sure. We'll try to get our new partners to implement the intervention. And if they do, we'll certainly attempt to evaluate it rigorously, but since we don't know the intervention design, we don't know how the evaluation will be structured.

NIJ proposals go through a careful peer-review process; it's supposed to be confidential, but it's a small world and it can be pretty porous. Our proposal went to the NIJ director, Jeremy Travis, with a "no" vote. He, for reasons known only to him, approved it anyway. Anne and I were in business. One of the first things we did was hire Anthony Braga, a brilliant young criminologist, to work on the project. He came out of a very rigorous and traditional Ph.D. program at Rutgers. When I showed him the proposal NIJ had funded, his first reaction was, "They're actually going to let you do this?"

Late in 1994, with the NIJ grant in hand, Anne and I went to talk to Boston police commissioner Paul Evans. Evans told us to meet with Superintendent James Claiborne, commander of the department's Field Services division. Claiborne was a big, silent, sphinxlike man. We need, we said to him, to work with your people who know about juvenile violence: guns, crack, shootings, homicide. He heard us out and said, You need to go talk to the gang unit. Well, no, I said, we think the problem's different from that, bigger, gangs aren't at the center of this.

You need to go talk to the gang unit, Claiborne said.

Yes sir, we said.

Thank *God*.

The gang unit was the Youth Violence Strike Force—about a dozen detectives and forty uniformed officers. The Youth Violence Strike Force was, for all intents and purposes, Paul Joyce. It was thinking about guns and gun markets that got us to Paul Joyce, but the problem-oriented policing script said, *Keep an open mind; listen; learn.* Paul Joyce knew gangs. We didn't think they mattered. They did. I didn't know *anything* about gangs; when I started to do my homework, after Paul got us pointed, I'd discover that for all the gang experts in the world, and there are many, none of them knew what to *do* about gangs. Paul did, in at least one crucial respect. He'd show us that, too. Everything since, in a very real way, has come from walking through the door he opened.

In January of 1995, we started meeting regularly with Joyce and his people in the department's Special Operations headquarters on Warren Street in Roxbury. We'd drive in from Cambridge on Massachusetts Avenue, past the Boston Symphony, along the beautiful old Victorian row houses of Back Bay and the South End, turn right just before Boston City Hospital—the Boston Medical Center now—where, I would shortly discover, almost all of Boston's gunshot victims went, and head a couple of miles south into the heart of Roxbury, Boston's most dangerous neighborhood. We'd park on Warren Street or on the maze of side streets around Special Ops—one thing you can always count on around a police unit, there's never enough parking: cops drop their cars wherever they please, civilians be damned—and head up two flights of poured-concrete steps to a heavy locked door. (I would be inordinately pleased when the duty officers, after a while, came to recognize us and buzz us in unescorted.) Inside, just to the left, was a beat-up muster room, maybe fifteen feet by forty; a big, cheap, cast-off conference table; windows on one long side and a blackboard on the other; as often as not, a raid entry diagram was chalked up when we had our sessions. It became the working home of the Boston Gun Project.

That first day, Anne and I laid out our ideas, such as they were, about illicit gun markets and decoupling and all the rest. That makes sense, Paul said.

And told us about Operation Scrap Iron.

In 1994, there was an extraordinary spike in shootings in the Upham's Corner neighborhood in the northern part of Dorchester. Joyce and his people would later plot the killings, shootings, and gun recoveries: It looked like someone had thrown handfuls of gravel at the map. Starting with a tip from a probationer and working closely with the Boston office of the Bureau of Alcohol, Tobacco, and Firearms, their attention came to focus on an Upham's Corner resident named Jose Andrade, who was going to college in Mississippi. ATF traces of guns used in crimes in Boston led to gun stores in Mississippi and to their purchasers of record. Two of them, Christopher Todd and Terrance Smith, Mississippi residents, told federal investigators that Andrade had them ride the circuit of local gun shops and gun shows, buying guns they turned over to him and that he then got back up to Boston. Those were the guns Joyce's team was finding, used in homicides and shootings and seized on the street, all over Dorchester. The Boston and federal team put the case together, flipped Todd and Smith, and sent Andrade to federal prison. The operation—Scrap Iron— became a jewel in the crown of the Boston Police Department. Shootings plummeted.

There was something else we couldn't quite follow that the strike force had done, something that involved working with the gangs in the area, principally a crew on Wendover Street: Scrap Iron had ended with gang members literally dropping off shopping bags of guns at Special Operations headquarters. We'd never heard of anything like it. You did that how, exactly? "It's all about the way you talk to them," Joyce said in what I would come to recognize as a typical and maddeningly Zen-cop Joyce koan. *Let's come back to that*, I said to myself. But the idea of going after gun traffickers was crystal clear and resonated instantly with them.

That was good—a relief. Not unexpected, necessarily, but good.

In the coming couple of years we'd make progress on guns. Our research would uncover a massive trafficking problem; guns were so easy to get, and there was so little enforcement pressure on illegal sales, that a lot of it felt like kids standing in a liquor-store parking lot asking random adults to buy them beer. (The Boston ATF agents busted one dealer after getting a call from a local gun store that they were seeing a lot of a guy they didn't like the looks of. The store was in Cambridge on Massachusetts Avenue—I walked by it on my way to and from work— with a parking garage across the street and convenient for surveillance. ATF set up there and waited for the guy to show up, which he shortly did, with a young black kid he left standing on the sidewalk. He went in, came back out, and the two of them took the subway back to Roxbury. They split up coming off the train. One set of agents followed the older guy and arrested him; the others followed the kid back to his house. They knocked on the door, talked to his mom, and went up to the kid's bedroom, where he was filing the serial number off his new pistol. When the agents interviewed the dealer, it turned out he liked that gun store because it was close to a Red Line stop on the subway, and he didn't have a car.) We'd find out what guns the street kids liked, ways to identify trafficking, work with the police and ATF to shut it down. By mid-1996, those insights would go national, as the Clinton administration launched a program called the Youth Crime Gun Interdiction Initiative that brought the antitrafficking work to, over the next several years, more than fifty cities. Evaluation work by Anthony and his fellow researchers would later show that the operational work that flowed from our research did, in fact, have an impact on the guns most favored by Boston's gangs. It would lead to a major shift in how law enforcement approached firearms.

Next to what Paul Joyce was about to show us, it would turn out to be a sideshow.

The next thing Paul and his team said, that day in January, was entirely unexpected, would send our research and thinking off in an entirely new direction, would turn out to hold the key to an entirely new way of understanding the violence and what to do about it.

We know what's going on out there, they told us. And then they told us what they'd learned, what they knew, day by day, shooting by shooting, killing by killing.

Every time a kid gets killed, we know them, from the streets, they said. We almost always know who did it—we may not be able to prove it, to take it to a prosecutor, but we know—and we know them, too, from the streets. They're gang members. They're all drug dealers, but almost none of the violence is about money: It's beefs, disrespect, boy-girl stuff. They're really, really active offenders, that's why we know them; they're out there all the time, doing stuff, and we're out there too, and we get to know them. And there aren't that many of them, and they mostly hurt each other.

I, at least, didn't think they could be right. Everything I'd learned about the diffusion of guns, decoupling, gangs, drug markets, fear, said otherwise.

I was, it would turn out, exactly wrong.

Paul Joyce turned out to be our entrée into a gifted, passionate, and extraordinarily knowledgeable and street-savvy circle he had assembled, over years, to take on the killing in Boston. We didn't know it then—it took us a while to figure it out—but he looked at Anne, Anthony, and me in the same spirit he'd looked at the rest of the crew we began to meet that January: If you can help, whoever you are, you're in. They made us welcome, something I have never entirely understood, and for which I am eternally, unspeakably grateful.

Paul himself had been in the Boston Police Department's elite City-Wide Anti-Crime Unit, which as violence surged in 1989 had been deployed in Roxbury, Dorchester, and Mattapan: the hottest Boston neighborhoods. The city officially denied, but those involved were pretty frank about acknowledging, that they had stopped everybody on the street they thought needed stopping and shaken them down for weapons. It's a familiar moment in policing: The gloves are *off*. Get it *done*. It might even have worked; public and judicial backlash led to the unit's elimination in 1990, which is when Boston's violence peaked. Regardless, Joyce had learned a core lesson that he repeated incessantly. "We'd been out there trying to do this on our own, the only way we knew how, and it just hadn't worked," Joyce said. "It taught us that we couldn't do it alone and we couldn't do it without support from the community and other agencies. And that it couldn't be just policing, or just enforcement; there had to be prevention, too." Joyce had amazing gravitational pull; he drew into his orbit a stunning cast of characters. I'd never seen anything like it. To this day I don't think there *was* anything like it, anywhere else in the country.

There were probation officers Richie Skinner and Billy Stewart, who had seen the carnage in their waiting rooms as their supervisees—a word used advisedly, as both men were quick to acknowledge they hadn't been supervising much of anything—came in bloodied and gunshot. "It was like a MASH unit in there," Stewart said. (Richie, gone now, had what may still be my single favorite stupid-crook story. He got a call one day from police in Brockton, south of Boston, about one of his charges they thought had knocked over a 7-Eleven. He called the kid in and said, The Brockton cops think you knocked over a 7-Eleven. Not me, the kid said, I was wearing a mask.) Skinner and Stewart started seeing Bobby Merner and Bobby Fratalia, two of Joyce's gang detectives, around the courtroom all the time. "We were dealing with the same kids," Stewart said. The four of them began riding together in the evening, checking probationers at home and patrolling the streets. As simple an idea as it was, it was a breakthrough for probation, which rarely sees its charges except across a desk. The first night they were out, they responded to a shooting. In the crowd on the street, Stewart saw one of his kids, in flagrant violation of his curfew. "What are *you*

doing here?" the outraged kid said. "No, what are *you* doing here?"
Stewart said. Probationers began to learn that they'd best stay in at
night, and that their bedrooms were no longer safe places to store drugs
and guns. (The tip that started Operation Scrap Iron came to Richie
from a probationer who owed him a favor—someone's selling mad guns
in the neighborhood, the kid told him—Richie reached out to the YVSF,
and the rest all followed.)

There was Tracy Litthcut, head of the city's gang-outreach group,
the Streetworkers. Many Boston cops thought they were basically gang
members themselves; many of Tracy's people had no time for the cops.
Tracy and Paul got along fine, which meant that if a kid told Tracy
something was about to go critical on the street—which they did a lot,
Drive-by tonight—Paul could flood the area with officers, nobody gets
hurt, nobody goes to jail, nobody has to know who called it in. There was
the fiery Rev. Eugene Rivers, who had helped form the Ten Point Coalition of activist black clergy in the wake of the assault on the Morning
Star Baptist Church. He had no love for what was going on on the streets,
but none for the police either. He finally pressed hard enough on a local
drug dealer that the guy shot up his house. Joyce and his detectives sorted
it out, arrested the dealer, actually got an apology to Rivers out of him.
From there on, Joyce, Rivers, and Ten Point were good.

And more: local and federal prosecutors, state of Massachusetts
juvenile corrections officers, Boston school police, lawyers from the
state attorney general's office, gun agents from the Bureau of Alcohol,
Tobacco, and Firearms. Joyce had prosecutors, famous for never leaving
their offices, riding the streets with his guys, something I've to this day
never seen anywhere else.

What became the Boston Gun Project Working Group began with
Joyce's core team: Joyce, Merner, Fratalia, a detective named Freddie
Waggett, Tracy Litthcut, Billy Stewart, and Richie Skinner. Jim Jordan
from headquarters and Billy Johnston, a legendary Boston cop who'd
run the department's Community Disorders Unit during the Boston
antibusing riots and now commanded Special Operations, often joined
in. Anne and I made the rounds of the key law enforcement agencies—
probation, parole, the Suffolk County District Attorney's Office, the
U.S. Attorney's Office, the Department of Youth Services, the Bureau of
Alcohol, Tobacco, and Firearms—explained what we were up to, and
asked them to designate somebody they trusted and give us access to

what information they could. We're going to try to figure this out, we said; if we think we've gotten anywhere, we'll come back and brief you and we'll take it from there. Everybody said yes. In most instances Paul and his people knew whom to ask for to join the group; they'd found their kindred spirits already: Tim Feeley from U.S. attorney Don Stern's office, Hugh Curran from district attorney Ralph Martin's office, Phil Tortorella and Lennie Ladd from ATF, some others. We started meeting, same time same place, every two weeks.

Anne, Anthony, and I pretty much moved in to Warren Street, hung out, rode with the detectives, went out for coffee, asked questions, listened, watched, absorbed. And over the next couple of months, we discovered that Paul and his people *did* know what was going on. They knew *exactly* what was going on.

Early on, Richie Skinner and Billy Stewart put me in the back of their car and gave me the tour. They showed me which gangs had which turf, which corner marked the end of one territory and the beginning of another, the single apartment building in the middle of a block that was the entirety of one crew's holdings. Street corners triggered stories of homicides three, four, five years old, what had led up to them, what had followed, where the beef was now. Franklin Field, a park in Dorchester, was not just Franklin Field. It was where eight boys had gang-raped, beaten, and stabbed twenty-six-year-old Kimberly Rae Harbor 132 times on Halloween night in 1990. They took me to one of the city's most recent shootings, at the Academy Homes housing project, where a kid had run from his apartment building to one across the street, held a pistol up over a wooden fence, and emptied it into the yard. Why? I asked. The two of them looked at each other, looked at me, like I was missing the point. Which I was. "That's what they do," they said. "Been going on forever."

The Youth Violence Strike Force's granular insight into Boston's street scene was extraordinary. The X-Men used to be the city's worst crew—they liked to fight with police, Hector Morales pulled a shotgun on two officers, fired on them, they killed him—and they're still out there, but they're quiet now, nothing to worry about. The Cape Verdean kids are hot, we quieted down the worst of it a little while ago, but it's going to pick up again. Every gang used to wear its own sports gear, everybody would have on the same team's clothes, they were easy to identify, but they're smarter than that now. We're not worried about the

L.A. gangs, Boston kids don't like them; somebody tries to take over, they send them packing. The bushes around the courthouse are a good place to find weapons, they get ditched on the way in before the metal detectors. These guys are toast when they go to prison, they think they're tough, but all they know how to do is pull a trigger, they don't have any idea how to fight, on the inside the old-school guys eat them for breakfast. The Vamp Hill Kings are quiet right now, but the main guy's locked up, we think his mom's holding a gun for him, she wants him to avenge his brother who got killed, when he comes out it's going to be trouble. Some of the gangs won't *let* their members be violent, the smarter guys just want to make money, the shooting brings attention, the cops come, it shuts business down. Somebody stole a case of .40-caliber pistols from Logan Airport, they're on the streets, somebody just shot at a cop with one, we've got to get them back *fast*. (They did, but not soon enough to prevent one being used to blow out the windows of the Codman Square Library, where the local crew was pissed that the staff had been interfering with their dealing right outside; they went in and eyefucked the librarian the next day, just to make sure everybody knew what was what. I still have a hardcover copy of *Dune* I took from the stacks with a furrow where a round creased the spine.)

They couldn't predict exactly what was going to happen, not all the time, but they had an amazing sense of the streets, their ebbs and flows. The dark joke at Warren Street was that if they could take out life insurance on some of the kids, everybody in the unit could retire early.

To us, outsiders, it was a revelation. And it was completely, *utterly* different from what all the other outsiders thought. The youth violence epidemic was the biggest crime problem in the country, was getting an enormous amount of attention, was generating lots of action and opinion and research. On the conservative side, John DiIulio had coined the new word "superpredator"; he, William Bennett, and John Walters would shortly publish *Body Count*, warning about "the youngest, biggest and baddest generation any society has ever known." Their diagnosis: a wave of "radically impulsive, brutally remorseless youngsters," unleashed by a "moral poverty," to whom "nothing else matters" but "sex, drugs, money." Their argument was completely circular and almost entirely without evidence: Crime was caused by bad character, crime was horribly worse, therefore black kids' characters must be horribly worse, therefore black kids' bad character explained the crime. It stuck, though. Fueled by a similar straight-line prediction by Northeastern University criminologist James Alan Fox, who took the new violent-crime rates among young people, multiplied them by coming demographic increases in the relevant age groups, and came up with Armageddon, the "superpredator" idea found tremendous traction nationally, leading to wholesale changes in state juvenile justice systems and laws about charging and trying juveniles as adults for violent crimes. On the liberal side, the favorite diagnosis was "the increased availability of handguns," leading to calls for new gun control. There was no evidence for this either. It was simply reasoning backward from the killing to an assumption that there were more guns out there. Our research was showing that access had always been so easy that there didn't have to be increased availability, just the new demand. An emerging "public health" approach, championed by Harvard School of Public Health assistant dean Deborah Prothrow-Stith, found roots in, in addition to guns, violent popular culture, economic deprivation, the violent example of adults, and peer pressure. And there were the Blumstein "diffusion" and other theories that said that gun carrying and gun use had become widely common among young, urban black men: "the preferred method of dispute resolution," in the near-standard catchphrase.

What all these ideas had in common, along with virtually all the rest of the public, policy, and political attention to the homicide epidemic, was the core conviction that the problem was huge, amorphous, and deeply rooted, and that it perforce needed a similarly huge response. The units of analysis were all *massive*: guns, drugs and drug markets, youth, popular culture, the economy, the quality of inner-city life, the black family. The forces at work were tectonic. Points of purchase ranged from obscure—what did Bill Bennett suggest we *do* about "moral poverty" or Dr. Prothrow-Stith about peer pressure—through unencouraging—gun control advocates had been at it a long time, without getting very far—to nonexistent, as with the various demographic predictions. The microdynamics of the violence were unintelligible—when it came to any particular shooting, it was practically obligatory to tack on "senseless," "inexplicable," "irrational."

Nobody, anywhere, was saying what Paul Joyce and his people were:

This is about a small number of very exceptional kids whose names we know doing things we understand pretty damned clearly.

Anne, Anthony, and I had gone very little distance with our formal plans to gather and analyze data on juvenile violence in Boston when we realized that our new partners and friends already know everything we wanted to know the most. Let's ask *them*. So we did. Starting in the summer of 1995, six months into the project, in a series of research meetings in our Kennedy School building, we convened Paul's team and some of the other streetwise, frontline folks we'd met through them. It scared the natives: One of my Kennedy School colleagues took me aside during one meeting and said, David, there are all these people with *guns* here. We did two basic things.

We put them around a Boston city map and said, Tell us where the gangs are. They drew each piece of turf with a Magic Marker, we gave it a number, they told us how many people were in each crew, who it was allied with, who it was beefing with, whether the beef was shooting-hot at the moment, whatever else came to mind. I stood at a flip chart with a set of markers and drew circles with numbers, to match, and colored lines to connect other circles and signify beefs, shooting beefs, and alliances; the page filled with circles and a spaghetti of vectors. That page of flip-chart paper hangs today, framed, on my office wall.

And we made up a list of all of Boston's dead, aged twenty-one and under, killed with a gun or a knife, going back to 1991—155 in all, with 125 associated known or suspected killers. For each victim we said, Do you here today know what happened? Was the victim gang involved? Was the killer gang involved? And what happened, around this homicide? What was it about? Mostly they knew; their understanding of those incidents, what led up to them, what they led to, was dazzling. We went in with the standard criminologists' categories: robbery homicide, drug business, domestic, gang involved, individual dispute. We had to add a couple as the process played out. *Can't get good help*: When you're doing a drive-by and your boy in the rear passenger seat with the gun tracks his target badly, blows away your other boy sitting in the front passenger seat. *Bad girlfriend*: You loved him last year so you forgave him for beating you up, but he's with that other bitch now, so you drop a dime with the guy you know he stole the coke from back then, and he ends up burned to a crisp in the trunk of a car.

Cops, emergency-room doctors, EMTs, they laugh at this stuff. You have to, have to let it go somehow, or the darkness takes over. I knew I'd crossed a line when I started laughing along with everybody else.

The answers: sixty-one crews, with between 1,100 and 1,300 members, in Roxbury, Dorchester, Mattapan, Hyde Park, the South End, and Jamaica Plain: 3 percent of the right age group in those neighborhoods; 1 percent of the right age group citywide. Nearly 60 percent of the homicides were known to be gang-related; more were, to a moral certainty, but when it wasn't known for sure, we said not. The killing was overwhelmingly not about money, drugs, markets, or anything economic. Over and over and over, it was about "beefs"—standing vendettas between the groups. And to get at those, we now had, from the first exercise, a network diagram of the crews, who was beefing with who, which crews were allied. It cemented the realization that our old "juvenile gun homicide" framing had been entirely wrong: Very few of Boston's dead or Boston's killers, or the members of gangs, were legal juveniles—most of them were young adults, some a good deal older—and lethal violence was lethal violence, whether committed with a Glock or a knife or a car. We were dealing with these groups and what they were doing.

Richie lost a probationer around this time in what we were coming to see as classic fashion. The probationer was a seasoned gang member beefing with his best friend's sister's boyfriend. His friend had been beefing with his sister, who called in her boyfriend for support; that meant the best friend and the boyfriend were beefing; the enemy-of-my-friend-is-my-enemy principle meant that Richie's probationer and the boyfriend were beefing. They'd been trading shots off and on for a while when the probationer was wounded. He told Richie he was going to kill the boyfriend; Richie got him to give it up if the police would investigate the gun assault. He was found shot to death in his bed not long after. It was ruled a suicide; Richie was sure he'd been killed. I knew him and thought so, too.

Later, Anthony would run Massachusetts criminal histories on the dead and the known killers. The results were astounding. Of the 155 victims, 117—75 percent—had criminal records, 29 had been locked up, 65 had been on probation, 22 were on probation when they were killed. Those with records had, collectively, been charged with

an average of 9.5 offenses apiece: 173 drug offenses, 291 property offenses, 225 armed violent offenses, 132 unarmed violent offenses, 78
firearms offenses, 20 offenses involving other weapons, 196 disorder
offenses, and two homicides. Of the 125 known killers, 96—77
percent—had criminal records at the time they committed their homicides; 33 had been locked up, 68 had been on probation, and 33—over
a quarter—were on probation when they did their killing. Those with
records had, collectively, been charged before committing their homicides with an average of 9.7 offenses apiece: 141 drug offenses, 248
property offenses, 160 armed violent offenses, 151 unarmed violent
offenses, 71 firearms offenses, eight offenses involving other weapons,
146 disorder offenses, and three prior homicides. More than 30 percent on both sides had been arrested ten times or more. All the gang
turf put together was less than 4 percent of the city; it generated
nearly a quarter of Boston's serious crime.

So, for all practical purposes, this *was* Boston's youth violence problem: a few score groups, already well known, made up of shockingly active offenders, many of *them* already well known, hurting each other
along already very well-known vectors of group vendetta. It wasn't even
all of the gang *members*; the Strike Force officers, the Streetworkers, and
the rest of our operational team made a distinction between what they
called "impact players"—gang members who were really into it, made
things happen, shooters—and everybody else. There weren't a lot of impact players, they thought. Out of a crew of twenty, it's maybe two real
players, Tracy said, making money, pulling triggers. Otherwise it's fol-
lowers, they're scared, wannabes.

Not an entire generation, not everybody in the hot neighborhoods,
not all the young black men. Not everybody exposed to violent video
games or rap. Not everybody from a single-parent family. Not everybody
who could get a gun if they wanted one. Not everybody who was afraid.
Not everybody who'd been disrespected. Hardly anyone, in fact. Definitely not, contra to what I had been convinced, "diffused" into even
other local black kids in any apparent way. Even among this superheated
population, most gang members never killed anyone. Most years, most
gangs never killed anyone. Some gangs never killed anyone, *ever*. Father-
lessness, godlessness, and the rest, not so sure what to do about it.

First revelation.

This, maybe, we could handle.

Operation Ceasefire

As a research enterprise, the Boston Gun Project had struck gold. Anne, Anthony, and I would look at one another from time to time, while we were putting this picture together, and realize that we were completely rewriting the scholarly landscape on youth violence. Intellectually, it was exhilarating. But the data, the new analysis, were supposed to be the means to an end. The Gun Project was about *doing something* about the killing. We were fascinated and amazed by this new perspective on the homicide and the streets. As yet we had given our practitioner partners next to nothing. They'd been living it all along, that's why they knew it, how they'd been able to show us. All of our research had done nothing more than put particular values on what they already knew—this many gangs, this network of beefs and alliances, this distribution of criminal records. They'd been acting, and acting at a very refined level, on what they already knew, and for a long time. It hadn't been working nearly well enough, which was why we were doing what we were doing together. The Harvard team had added nothing practical at all.

For the first time, I began to feel a practitioner's sense of responsibility. This was no kind of abstract academic exercise. I'd been writing about people doing important things for fifteen years. I'd been part of a fantastically refined Harvard community, saying, Here's how people doing important things should think, act, for those fifteen years. Ever since Nickerson Gardens, I'd been thinking, urgently, *somebody should do something.* Now *I* should be doing something. I had no idea what it could be.

Anne, Anthony, and I had shadings of different responsibilities—
she focused somewhat more on evaluation issues, Anthony was doing
most of the quantitative work and spending a lot of time in the field
with Strike Force cops, I was chairing the Working Group—but the lines
blurred: We were all sorting out what we needed to know next, designing the research, feeding the results back to the Working Group, out on
the streets, absorbing information and perspective and context from
our new friends, thinking it all through. Final responsibility for the operational answer, though, that was mine, we all understood that.

While we studied and thought, people were dying. A lot. Boston
was going through a hot period as 1995 drew on. We lost seven kids in
August alone. The first thing I did every morning was turn to the inside
pages of the second section of the *Boston Globe*, where dead black kids
rated a paragraph, to see who had been killed. It was awful. I had made
this my problem. I've always been insomniac, ever since I was small.
Now I lay awake for hours: *What are we going to do?*

I continued to gnaw away at the question of the second part of
Scrap Iron: What made the Wendover kids give their guns up? I continued to get nowhere. I collected more details: The Strike Force had moved
one juvenile they thought was driving the gun violence into a DYS facility out in western Massachusetts; they'd brought the Streetworkers and
some of the Ten Point ministers into the area; they'd talked to gang
kids' parents; they'd done a bunch of drug enforcement, served outstanding warrants, taken away unregistered cars. I got nothing that explained to me why gang members would travel across Dorchester and
Roxbury to deliver their guns to gang officers. Paul Joyce continued to
be of no help. "We told them the truth," he'd say, and wander away. I
decided to write a case study of the operation in the hope that I'd come
to understand it and began interviewing detectives: particularly, as it
would turn out, Freddie Waggett, who seemed tolerantly amused by the
whole thing and agreed to give me some time.

Two clear themes, meanwhile, were emerging in the Working Group
discussions. One was the ignorance gang members had about the legal
risks they faced. The other was how *scared* they were.

Tim Feeley, the assistant U.S. attorney sitting with the group, had
brought up the risk issue early on and kept returning to it. The U.S. attorney is taking these cases, he said. Guns are a priority for Don Stern.
But a little difference in your criminal history makes a huge difference

under federal law, and these kids have no idea. If they did, I think they'd behave differently. In July, the Strike Force arrested, and Don Stern made an example of, one Freddie Cardoza. It made exactly Feeley's point. We prosecuted Freddie Cardoza, he said; that's fine, he deserved it. But the point of that kind of thing is to deter *other* gang members. Do they know what we did and why we did it? he asked the gang officers. If they don't know, what's the point? It won't change their behavior. No, said the gang officers, and Tracy Litthcut, who knew the same from his Streetworker experience. They don't know.

Freddie Cardoza, a Humboldt Raider gang member, had been singled out by Boston street law enforcement as pretty much the city's worst badass. He robbed people, assaulted police officers, did drive-bys, sold guns. He got a twenty-year state sentence for armed robbery and got out in two; a ten-year state sentence for assault and battery with a dangerous weapon, out in one. On July 14, 1995, he bought a gun and nine rounds of ammunition on the street for sixteen-year-old Myron Ragsdale. At two A.M. on the morning of the fifteenth, Strike Force officers saw the two walking along Humboldt Avenue in Roxbury. Ragsdale had the gun, loaded with eight 9mm rounds, tucked into his pants. Cardoza had the ninth round in his hand. In Massachusetts, a state firearms identification card is required to possess ammunition. Cardoza didn't have one. Strike Force officers arrested but couldn't even hold him—the ammunition violation was only a misdemeanor. But when he appeared in court on the misdemeanor, he was taken into custody by federal agents. In a flurry of coordination between the Strike Force, the Suffolk County district attorney's office, the Bureau of Alcohol, Tobacco, and Firearms, and the U.S. attorney's office, his case had been adopted by the feds. Under federal law, a felon cannot possess a firearm; under federal law, ammunition counts as a firearm; under federal law, the right three predicate felonies qualify one for prosecution as an Armed Career Criminal. Those three felonies Cardoza *did* have. ACC carries with it a mandatory minimum sentence of *fifteen years*. Federal law requires that at least 85 percent of a sentence be served. Federal authorities can send prisoners anywhere in the federal system—you don't stay close to home, locked up with your friends and with easy access by your family. Cardoza's misdemeanor pop—he would almost certainly have gotten probation, if that—turned into a nineteen-year, seven-month sentence in Otisville federal prison in upstate New York: fifteen years for the bullet and four years, seven months for giving Ragsdale, a juvenile, the gun.

He never saw it coming.

Would better information change gang members' behavior? Belief in the rational sensibilities of young street thugs was not excessive in the Working Group, but the general feeling was yes. Federal authorities, driven by both the awful reality of and the political attention to gun violence, were increasingly getting involved, with dramatic results for some crimes. State judges were responding to the public outcry around the street violence and toughening their stances. Massachusetts was about to put through a wholesale change in its juvenile justice laws, which would automatically lead to adult charges against accused murderers over age thirteen and give prosecutorial discretion to charge a range of other serious crimes, including gun crimes, as adult offenses and to hold convicted juveniles until they were twenty-one. Probation authorities were becoming more enforcement oriented and more willing to violate supervisees and send them back to lockup. The game was changing, and those who didn't understand were going to get themselves in trouble. Could something be done? Could we, for example, identify those most likely to be the next Freddie Cardozas and tell them, so they could step back? Could we make briefings on the juvenile justice changes part of being on DYS supervision? It made, at least, a certain amount of sense.

The second big Working Group theme, fear, was fascinating—a kind of distillation of the "decoupling" idea that the guns and the violence had first come with crack markets, but that ordinary kids were now getting so scared *they* were getting guns. Never mind the ordinary kids, the Working Group said. Even the *gang* kids are scared to death. They get shot at, they get shot, their friends have been killed, their friends have been shot, they've got real enemies out there. "I've been to crime scenes where ten-year-olds knew what guns were shot by the sounds they make," Freddie Waggett told us. Billy Stewart had a target hung on the wall in his office with three bullet holes in it, a .22, a .25, a .38; many of his probationers could eyeball it and tell him what the calibers were. The fear, the group said, makes them join gangs, it makes them get guns, it makes them carry guns, it makes them use violence to show they shouldn't be messed with. The fear, the group said, had become an independent force. It was both an outcome of and an input into the street craziness, a positive feedback loop.

Seen up close, it was clear that on the streets guns were *far* from the "preferred method of dispute resolution." As bad as it was, if the gang kids shot everybody they had an issue with, there'd be nobody left standing. Given the weight of what was pressing on them, I couldn't understand why there wasn't *more* violence. I was interviewing gang members in Dorchester—Billy and Richie were making introductions— and it was clear that even they thought a lot of this was ridiculous. "Killing's wrong," one told me. "But if you're going to do it, do it for a reason. Don't do it because he called you a bitch." And that they hated it. "It's like a video game," another said. "Every time you think you've mastered a level they move the level up. I don't know how much more of it I can take."

They were right to be scared. We'd run the numbers: Now we knew the size of the gang population, now we knew the number of gang kill- ings, and we did the math. The national homicide rate had hit about 10 per 100,000. The homicide rate for Boston gang kids was 1,539 per 100,000. If you were in one of the sixty-one crews, chances were one in seven that you'd die, almost entirely by gunshot, over a nine-year pe- riod. There were enough nonfatal woundings for every death that, on average, almost *every* gang member would get shot. It didn't work ex- actly like that—not everybody stayed in for nine years, and even within the gangs, risk was not evenly distributed; some were in much more danger than others—but the picture was clear, and bad, enough. This was a horrifically dangerous way to live. They were soaked in trauma and PTSD; they set themselves up to be killed sometimes, the Street- workers said. One of the gang members I was talking to told me he'd been shot at a lot, never hit, stabbed twice. "Everybody I know been shot," he said. "I guess I've been lucky." A couple of months later he was dead, shot.

One of my standard questions to gang members was, Have you ever been shot at? They wanted to know, Did I mean them personally? What if they'd just been with their friends when *they* got shot at? Did that count?

The way they saw the world was both through the looking glass and, once glimpsed, weirdly coherent. What could be done to stop this? I asked. Nothing, the gang members said. There's nothing anybody can do. It's always been like this. It hadn't always been like this—not even close—but I realized that *they didn't know that.* It just about broke my heart. If you were eighteen in 1995, then you'd have been eleven in 1988, when the Boston streets went critical. Your world from before adolescence had been a free-fire zone. It was all they'd ever known. Other neighborhoods aren't like this, I said. White kids don't have to live like this. Sure they do, they said. The guns are everywhere. Look at the bullet holes in the stop signs out in Brookline, they've got guns. The white folks just cover it up. Cover it up, I said, you can't cover up homicide. Sure you can, they said. Look at all those white kids on the milk cartons. What do you think really happened to them?

But they were crystal clear, particularly in private, that they didn't like it. "You see you shot this nigger, that doesn't do you any good," one gang member told me. "That's just more niggers you got to watch your back for." You have to wonder if you're going to die every time you go around the corner, he said. "Going to the bus stop is like survival camp." "I don't have any friends," another said. "It's too dangerous to have friends. They drag you into things. I mostly stay by myself at home, or I have one cousin I'll visit." ·

They were, emphatically, not lost to it all. They had standards, they had pride. Anne and I almost caused a riot at a program run by Jimmie McGillivray—"Jimmie Mac"—a crazy Irish street outreach worker Tracy Litthcut had brought into the Working Group. He had a unique ability to leap racial, class, and professional boundaries like they didn't even exist. When we got to know him he was running a strict probation supervision program for gang members in Roxbury called Project Turnaround. Anne and I had been trying to work up some surveys to get into the Boston public schools—it never worked out—and Jimmie had set us up to talk with his kids and test the surveys. (On one visit he let the kids out at the end of the day while we stayed to talk with him for a bit. When we went downstairs to leave, the probationers were smoking weed in the entryway—they politely offered us some—which tells you everything you'll ever need to know about probation.) We'd borrowed a lot of the survey questions from others that had been used in the literature; one was something like, "What do you like to do in your spare time?" and one of the multiple-choice answers was "Drive around in cars shooting at people"—some middle-class researcher's cartoon idea of what a drive-by was. We'd gotten along fine with Jimmie's kids, but when they got to that point in the survey, spread out over a couple of rooms at Jimmie's program, things got ozone-in-the-air, bad-things-about-to-happen tense. "*Drive around in cars shooting at people?*" one said. "What the *fuck*? Who do you think we are?" They were *affronted*. We were scared, apologized, the moment passed.

Jimmie Mac was particularly focused, and eloquent, about the danger and the fear and what it was doing to the kids. In a May 1995 session of the Working Group, he gave a riveting disquisition to cops and federal agents on Hobbes, political philosophy, and its application to Boston gang life. It worked, he made it stick. It's a state of nature, an absence of civil society, he said. It's unbelievably dangerous out there, and we, the adults, are not protecting them. (Some time after this, I was sitting with two gang detectives in their office at Warren Street when there were shots a block or so away. None of us so much as moved. That then seemed to warrant discussion—*Huh, we're not even doing anything*—so we discussed it, but we still didn't do anything.) They think they need to protect themselves because nobody else is doing it. Then you have a lot of kids with guns, and shit happens. They're scared, they want out, but they don't want to lose face. We have to look at the social contract, we honestly do.

This drew a sharp rebuke from ATF's Phil Tortorella—does that mean we think it's okay for them to carry guns? "No," McGillivray said, "but it does mean that if we neglect the real pressures on the kids, we're missing something important."

There were interesting suggestions that this was true in practice. Richie Skinner had run into a kid he knew on the street who was hurrying home to find a gun. He'd just had his chain stolen on a bus, he knew who did it, and he was seething. Hold up, Richie said. I can get the police on this. Would that be okay? Well, yeah, the kid said. It simply hadn't occurred to him that the police would help. I asked my gang sources what drove the shooting. "They do it because they don't believe in the law," one told me. "The law don't work, never will, in my neighborhood." Joyce and his Strike Force officers reported that the Wendover crew had begged them *not* to leave the area when Scrap Iron wound down. "They felt safe," Joyce said.

Scrap Iron again. Freddie Waggett is a huge guy. There's a culture of bodybuilding among many street cops, particularly those in special units, and Fred has a slab of power-lifter torso that dominates my memory of him; in my mind he's always leaning over, a head taller, with that chest like Kansas. I don't know if that aura of raw power facilitates his usual genial nature—I once saw him deal with a kid he'd taken a MAC-10 machine pistol away from with a mesmerizing mix of fatherliness and don't fuck with me—but it's a serviceable combination. He gave me a bunch of his time, and finally, one day, sitting, the two of us, in the Warren Street room we used for Working Group meetings, he finally got me to see what had happened with Scrap Iron. It tied everything together, fused what had been the Working Group's two separate tracks of information and fear, gave us a clear operational direction. It was the end of our studies and the beginning of everything else.

Okay, I said. I still don't get it. You'd taken down the gun dealer. You had the Wendover Street crew, which still had a lot of guns. You had this kid in DYS holding, out in western Mass, and you were going out to visit with him pretty regularly. You had the Streetworkers and Ten Point involved. You did a lot of enforcement up there—drug sales, warrants, public drinking, unregistered cars, driving without a license. I get that. How does that end up with gang members handing over their guns?

We told them what it would take to make us go away, he said.

This little detail had not come up before. Working cops do not live in a culture of exposition in the same way that, say, academics do. They are trained to write reports and give testimony, subtle arts guided by the formal and mannered needs of the law and of criminal justice agencies and procedures. They are trained in, and give a lot of attention and respect to, and can be very articulate about, tactics: use of force, how to run an investigation, how to set up an entry team. Much of what seems like extraordinary knowledge and insight to outsiders they don't understand as knowledge at all. It's what they know and do every day; everybody they work with knows and does it, too, it's simply the air they breathe. (And if you deal with death and degradation every day, pretty soon you only spend time with those who also do; the rest of the world is living a pretty fantasy you can no longer inhabit.) What had happened in Upham's Corner, what Scrap Iron was, was not a stand-alone investigation, like the Jose Andrade gunrunning case had been; it wasn't *illegal*, but it wasn't simply the straight application of standard law enforcement either. It wasn't just tactics, which they'd explained, I now realized, quite well. It was what was behind the tactics that they hadn't been able to get across, what I hadn't seen in the background. The second part of Scrap Iron was a *strategy*. Which Freddie Waggett proceeded to explain to me.

They had told the Wendover Street crew, at every contact, that the pressure they were under was *because of the shooting*, and that if they wanted things to go back to normal, the shooting had to stop. I learned, much later, that there had actually been a meeting between the Strike Force and gang members, in a parking lot, in which the message had been delivered: zero tolerance for *everything* until the gunplay stops. They reinforced that message ceaselessly. It was surgically focused on the gang members, not on everybody in the area. They made street drug buys and arrested the dealers. They put the area under twenty-four-hour surveillance, pulled over gang members' cars, checked licenses and registrations; nearly all the cars were unregistered, the gang members had no licenses, the Strike Force seized their cars, arrested the drivers. They arrested gang members for public drinking, for smoking joints. They ran gang members for outstanding warrants, formed up warrant squads, went and arrested them. They had their partners at probation and parole do compliance checks, search bedrooms, apply additional drug tests, enforce curfews, enforce area and association restrictions. They had DYS pick up the juvenile ringleader and take him across the state. They had their partners in the prosecutors' offices pay special attention to these cases, take them to the wall rather than just moving them through. The visits out west to DYS turned out to include a standard question to the kid: If you're willing to tell your gang to calm down, we'll bring you back. For a long time he wasn't: then he was. They talked to gang members' parents, made sure they knew what their sons were up to. They brought the Streetworkers in to try to calm things down. The handing over of the guns turned out to be the last act in the drama. "We knew by then who had what: makes, models, calibers," Waggett said. "And we pointed fingers and made them turn them over."

Let me see if I get this, I said. You knew the gang was driving things. You knew who was in the gang. They're committing all kinds of crimes all the time, so you could focus on all those crimes. You told them the special attention was because of the shooting and that if the shooting stopped, things would go back to status quo. Is that right?

Yeah, he said. We do that sometimes.

You've done this *before*?
Yeah, a couple of times.
What happened then?
It always works, he said.
Shit, I said. You can *do* that?
Yes, he said.

Second revelation.

For us outsiders, as it sank in and we started to see its simple, radical, transformative logic, this was astounding. There wasn't anything like it, in the literature or in our knowledge of field work, in either theory or practice. (We thought. That turned out to be wrong, too.)

This was deterrence, no question—they were telling gangs bad things would happen to them if they continued shooting, and the gangs were stopping. That alone was remarkable. Nearly everybody had given up on deterrence in this setting: These shooters were, almost by definition, young, impulsive, often stoned, often drunk, irrational if not literally sociopathic. Their massive criminal records spoke for themselves: These were overwhelmingly people who had firsthand experience with the criminal justice system, and it had demonstrably not deterred them. This did. It went against everything almost everybody thought. This was a new kind of deterrence: "coerced demand reduction," as the Kennedy School team christened it.

It was deterrence aimed at the *group*, the gang. Criminal justice is almost entirely about individuals. A drug crew can get some besotted juvenile to kill someone; when he does, he, not the drug crew, gets arrested. Short of exotic RICO and conspiracy prosecutions, which are in practice exceedingly rare, groups get no formal legal attention at all. But gangs were driving things, the Strike Force knew it, and they were acting accordingly.

It used heavy enforcement *announced ahead of time*. Law enforcement operates in secret until it's time to swoop in and make the grab. Tell them what's coming? Give yourself away? What?

This was face-to-face, retail. Normal criminal justice is distant, wholesale. There is no more shopworn phrase in the business than "sending a signal." Freddie Cardoza goes to federal prison for twenty years to send a signal that the federal government is against youth violence. Those sending and those supposed to hear are miles apart; the "signal" is thin, attenuated, notional, implicit; it is one-time; it may not be heard and understood at all. This signal was direct, concrete, literal, repeated, explicit: If you do *this*, we will do *that*.

It was built from existing tools and powers put together in a radically new way. Nobody had done anything they couldn't already do; there was no new law, no new authority, no new funding, no new resources. They had taken their existing capacity, exercised their existing discretion, and crafted something wholly distinct.

Law enforcement, criminal justice, is a massive, one-size-fits-all architecture: It's the same for everybody, everywhere, all the time. This was focused, customized, particular, highly specific.

It was narrow—*don't shoot*. The normal frame said, don't be in gangs, don't commit crimes, don't sell drugs, don't carry weapons, don't violate your probation, don't drink and drug. Turn your life around. Go back to school, get a job. Go forth and sin no more. This cut to the chase: Don't hurt people. Say any more—don't carry guns, don't sell drugs, don't recruit kids into your gang—you couldn't back it up. There was just too much of it, and too little of us. Draw those lines in the sand, they would cross them, and it would be obvious that the cops had lied. They were used to being lied to, lying to them was *normal*: The next time you drop a hot urine I'm going to violate you, don't let me see you back in my court, young man. Our side lied *all the time*. It was like we were training them to ignore us. This was focused, limited. We started to call it "focused deterrence": focused on one problem, focused on the core offenders.

It was close, intimate, but principled. There was no negotiation, no deal, no get-out-of-jail-free card. It was not Put your guns down and you can deal drugs. It was Keep shooting your guns and we will make your life miserable. Put them down and we go back to the same game as before: Sometimes you win, sometimes we win. Gunplay? We win, you lose.

It turned gang and street dynamics on their head, and made virtues out of what were ordinarily causes for despair. There was a kind of aikido brilliance about it, the centered and perfect touch that turns your opponent's momentum against him. Gangs are Roman candles of criminality, gang members flagrant, profligate recidivists. This said, *Excellent*. You're giving us everything we need to punish you for the guns.

Thank you for selling drugs, driving unregistered cars, dropping hot urines. We will now take full advantage. If you don't want us to, next time you see one of your boys picking up a gun, tell him to put it down. If the gangs weren't such profligate sinners, it wouldn't work, but they were, and it did.

Gangs are groups and driven by group dynamics. One guy could set a quiet drug group on fire, throwing his weight around, egging everybody on, starting fights with other crews, launching vendettas. This said, You want to be a leader? This said, *Excellent*. You're accountable. Control the violence or we pay special attention to you.

Gang rules and understandings sustain that sinning: I've got my boy's back, the enemy of my friend is my enemy. This said, *Excellent*. You guys want to be beholden to each other? Great, you're beholden. Anybody shoots, you all pay.

It was embedded with help and moral standards. The Streetworkers had been in there, too, saying the community needs the shooting to stop, we'll help you go back to school, help you get work. Ordinarily those who believe in law and accountability and those who believe in help and social responsibility don't work with each other, don't respect each other, don't even like each other. The cops think social workers are naïve, the social workers think cops are thugs. Everybody here was on one page: We'll help you if you let us, we'll stop you if you make us.

And it fit beautifully with the conversation that had been evolving in the Working Group. Boston's gun violence problem, we had come to understand, was groups of standout offenders. Our frontline partners knew very well, day to day, moment to moment, what was going on. Most groups didn't kill anybody on any given day, month, year; those who were hot stood out very clearly. Those groups and those offenders did terrible things, but it wasn't entirely true that they were terrible people; they were under horrific pressures and at enormous risk. It was the relationships with the groups and between the groups that carried a lot of the voltage that drove these dynamics. A lot of the offenders didn't like this very much; they particularly didn't like the violence, but they didn't see any way out, and the rest of their world was not protecting them or giving them a way out. And they had huge exposure to criminal justice sanctions that they often didn't understand. So maybe it wasn't such a stretch to think that something that focused on groups that were violent *right now*, singled out their most violent behavior, respected group dynamics, treated individuals as rational rather than sociopathic, spelled out the new sanctioned environment that had been created for them, protected them, and gave those who would take it a way out, made some sense.

And we were wrong: It wasn't unprecedented. Once Anne, Anthony, and I understood what the Strike Force had done with the Wendover Street crew, and could sketch it as a strategy, it turned out that it wasn't in fact all that unusual. Working cops do this kind of thing. They usually don't articulate it explicitly: It's street stuff, good craft work. But talk to them about it and they tend to have their own stories. Billy Johnston, the Special Operations commander, heard our version and said, That's what the Community Disorders Unit really did during the race troubles. When black families were moving into the white neighborhoods, and things were moving toward riots, the white guys driving things weren't ordinary citizens. They were all the worst local jerks. We knew who they were. So we'd have a talk with them, and say, You want to drink beer on your porch? *Back off.* That's really how we survived that time.

We started to see, this is actually part of core law enforcement practice on some issues. This is why the streets *don't shoot cops.* Not because the streets are full of good people who respect cops. Because the streets *know,* you shoot a cop, not only are you going down, everybody you're running with is going down. You're part of a drug crew, have a bad day, cap a cop? Too bad for your crew. You're done, count on it. But it won't stop there. Everybody you're running with is done, too. Patrol, narcotics, the gang guys, FBI, DEA, ATF, they're all going to make your crew a special project. And since everybody knows it, nobody crosses the line, and nobody has to keep that promise. It takes care of itself.

I struggled to explain it to my friends and colleagues. Yes, I said, they do monstrous things. So. Imagine you know a nice, white stockbroker, convicted for insider trading. The judge makes an example of him, he goes to a real prison, not a white-collar country club. Nine months after he goes in he's going to have a shaved head, Aryan Brotherhood tats, and he's going to shank whoever takes his dessert at dinner. Not because he's somehow become a racist sociopath. Not because he cares about his dessert. But because he needs someone to have his back, and the black and Hispanic guys don't care that he's not a racist and hates the Brotherhood, and if he doesn't shank the guy, everybody else will take everything he's got, or worse. It's not about *him*. He doesn't even *like* it. Doesn't matter. You want to change his behavior? He doesn't need anger-management classes. He's not angry, he's terrified. He needs *prison* to change. And he can't do it alone. These guys can't either. And nothing we've been doing is changing the reality of their world, the rules of their world. That's what we need to do.

In the new light of the long Working Group conversation, and with the outsiders' perspective Anne and Anthony and I could bring to bear, Scrap Iron was suddenly visible not as one occasional street option among many, but as the key to an entirely new way of operating. It was a fantastic moment, the intellectual tumblers falling into place, the lock opening, a whole new world of possibility springing free. We ran with it. The Working Group turned into a hothouse design team, all of us thinking it through, playing out implications and potentials, crafting a new architecture. Huddled at Warren Street, on the phone, still awake at three A.M. but this time fitting the pieces together. It completed the process of fusing the Working Group: We were all equals now, the street folks got the old/new logic cold, Anne and Anthony and I were now steeped in the street scene and operational stuff, all of us driving forward to something new. By the fall of 1995, as the violence in Boston continued to surge—in October, eleven kids were killed, the highest monthly total in our data set going back to 1991—we'd figured out something that seemed like it might work. Working title Scrap Iron II, or Wendover Plus, what would eventually come to be called Operation Ceasefire.

Scrap Iron was the touchstone, and we started there. The Working Group demonstrably had the capacity to "calm" one gang at a time. Once quieted down, the experience was that they stayed quiet for a while, often a long time; you didn't have to ride constant herd on them. The street dynamic was the reverse of what we usually experience in law enforcement. The normal worry is *displacement*: stomp on something here, it will splash out *there*. Here, the calming made the target gang *vulnerable*, drew its enemies in: That was why the Wendover Street crew, disarmed and chastened, had pleaded with the Strike Force to stick around, not to leave it open to its rivals.

We knew those rivalries now: We had literally charted them. Anthony had taken the page of gangs, vendettas, and alliances and digitized it into a formal network sociogram. So if we calmed a given gang, we knew who was on the other end of their vendettas; we knew who to go talk to and say: Okay, leave these guys alone, they've just gotten a whole lot of very unpleasant attention because they were shooting. Hands off. They get any trouble from you, we move to *you*. And we knew that we could tell the first gang, We've gone and talked to those other guys. You're going to be okay; you're safe. Any trouble, here's a number to call: We'll take care of it.

That meant we had to be able to keep those promises. Could we? Could the Working Group and the agencies they represented—the Boston Police Department, prosecutors, probation, parole, DYS, the rest of the official world—field more than one such operation at a time? *Yes*, was the consensus, if the agencies gave their backing—not massive numbers of operations, but three, four at a time, something like that, yes.

That might not be enough to enforce a "no killing" rule everywhere in the city, all the time: A wave of homicides, like the eleven that came in October, would be more than we could handle. If we couldn't keep our promise, we'd be back where we started. This was crucial. Law enforcement loves to feign omniscience and promise omnipotence: *We know everything you're doing, you carry a gun or sell drugs in my city and we'll hunt you down like dogs.* It's all bluster—*woofing*, George Kelling calls it—and the streets let it roll off like water. (We came to realize it was worse that that. The streets got away with almost everything they did, which meant that if they took the woofing seriously, the natural conclusion was that the cops were *letting* them get away with it, which was exactly what a lot of them did think.) Our promises had to be true. It became a central tenet of the new thinking: *Never write a check you can't cash.*

So the idea became to move out gradually. Begin with the hottest gang in the city. Calm them and make it stick. Then move out to gangs beefing with the first group. We had the network map, we knew where to go. Stick with them long enough to make sure they got it and would stay quiet. Move out to the gangs *they* were beefing with. And so on. The streets—the killings and shooting, or lack thereof—would tell us how quickly we could spider out along the web of vendettas; nobody thought it would go fast, but it seemed—possibly—workable. A year, two, to calm the whole city down? Nobody knew. But for the first time, as we chewed through it, there seemed to be something the Working Group could actu-ally do that could work. That would, if it worked, make a big difference. The internal consensus was that it was worth trying.

By late 1995 we had the outlines sketched. We'd come up with the idea of "forums"—formal meetings with gang members. This was, I thought, my big solo contribution to the strategy, a way of communi-cating with the gangs in a systematic way. We know who the gangs are; almost all the gangs have somebody on probation and parole at any given time; can we get probation and parole to bring them in for a meet-ing so we can talk to them? They can carry the message back to their crew. This was before I knew about the parking-lot meeting that had been part of the operation with the Wendover Street crew: There was a precedent even for this. But probation and parole gave us a way to sys-tematize things; we got permission from the probation and parole de-partments to try it. We'd pull in selected gang members, tell them that shooting was off-limits, that their whole gang would get attention if anybody put a body on the ground, offer them help and social services, come down hard if we had to. Make sure they got it and move on. It seemed almost simple once we got it framed. *Lather, rinse, repeat*, I re-member thinking.

We gained a couple of key new members. Gary French, a lieutenant, big, friendly, relaxed, a Rhode Island native, accent so thick he laughed at it himself, took over the Strike Force. We were terrified that he'd scut-tle the whole thing, but when we walked him through it, he got it imme-diately. He'd come to Special Operations from an assignment in one of the districts; tired of waiting for specialist headquarters units to move on the crack houses in his area, he took to going to the houses, banging on the door until someone cracked it, and saying, "I'm Gary French. If you don't close shop here, I'm coming back with a warrant and a batter-ing ram." Almost everybody left, which made him think our plan might make sense. Ted Heinrich, a young assistant U.S. attorney who had helped take down the entire Latin Kings gang network in Connecticut and had recently moved to the Boston office, joined the Working Group. He sank his teeth into the sketch and, in the first months of 1996, produced a de-tailed operational plan.

Anne, Anthony, and I went back to the leadership in the participat-ing agencies and briefed them: This is what we've come up with, this is how it's supposed to work, what do you think, will you support it? U.S.

attorney Don Stern brought what felt like half his office into a conference room to see the show. This was in the day of overhead projectors; we put up the slide of Anthony's gang network and Ralph Boyd, Stern's main guns-and-gangs prosecutor, leapt to his feet, ran over, kneeled down in front of the screen, and started tracing vectors. "That's it," he said. "That's what's going on out there." Commissioner Paul Evans brought his whole command staff in for a full-dress presentation at police headquarters. I was nearly sick to my stomach; this was the whole thing. The officers we'd been working with warned us about one senior guy in particular. He hates everything from the outside, they told us. He'll kill it on principle. I spoke for the group, laid it out. Kill-it-on-principle guy thrust his hand up for Evans's attention. I couldn't breathe. "That'll work," he said. "They'll stop. They'll have to."

All the agencies said yes. We were in.

And we lost Paul Joyce.

To this day, I don't really know what happened. My best understanding is that he and Gary French crossed swords. Paul had a nominal supervisor before Gary came in, but it was obvious to everybody that Paul wrote his own script and did exactly as he wished. Chain of command was a consensual fiction. Gary wasn't having that, Paul wouldn't give, wouldn't, word was, even tell Gary what he was up to. This time Gary won. Paul transferred from the Youth Violence Strike Force to the homicide squad—a promotion on paper, but it was clear he didn't think so. We stayed in touch but he wasn't in the thick of our things any longer. In his wake, we started hearing tales about problems that hadn't reached our ears previously: tensions between Joyce and his inner circle and other detectives, how the uniformed members of the Strike Force had been left out of his operations. Gary French moved to bring the whole unit in, involve it in the new strategy. I missed Paul personally, felt his absence from the project profoundly. And still had no idea, wouldn't for years, of the gravity of what had just happened.

We had to start somewhere; we had to pick a gang. In early 1996 the worst violence in Boston was coming out of the Vamp Hill Kings in Dorchester. The Kings were one of the city's most perennially, grindingly violent crews; it was they who'd gone after the mourners in Morning Star Baptist Church in 1992 with guns and knives. Their turf along Bowdoin Street in north Dorchester, near Geneva Avenue, was a smoldering hot spot, one of the first places the gang guys had taken me when they showed me around. It didn't look bad at all, neat streets lined with the three-story clapboard houses that are the mainstay of traditional ethnic working-class Boston; it didn't have the rep that, say, Blue Hill Avenue did. But the Kings were trouble. They were in the air at Warren Street constantly, shooting-hot or about to be. As we got close to going operational, they went critical over what the gang guys knew to be some sort of internal beef, the two factions conversing by firing shots up and down the block. It was all but automatic: They'd be our first target. Late in March, after fifteen months of learning, thinking, and planning, we launched.

Gary French saddled up, got the Strike Force into the field, mobilized his partners. Police officers served warrants and did street drug enforcement, swarmed the area to shut the drug market down, make the Kings broke. Probation and parole officers paid home visits, searched Kings' rooms for drugs and guns; they came back in the evening for curfew checks; called supervisees in for drug tests. DYS had four juvenile Kings under community supervision; they went out, picked them up, locked them up. One King was a resident alien with the wrong kind of criminal record; INS deported him. ATF officers worked the streets with Strike Force cops, showing the federal flag. Billy Stewart tracked down probationers' parents and told them the heat was on and why; we later found out that he'd enthusiastically tracked down *non-probationers'* parents and told them the heat was on and why, just because it seemed like a good idea. Ralph Martin's assistant DAs fast-tracked cases, raised bail requests, shopped cases to the U.S. attorney, looked for old, "cold" cases they hadn't been able to prove against Kings: Maybe they could reopen them. Don Stern's office took cases it would normally have kicked back, adopted them for federal prosecution. Gary even brought in the MSPCA and had the Kings' pit bulls taken away. Sometimes BPD literally parked officers in front of the main players' houses.

The Kings didn't get it for a while. Bernard Wilder was killed on April 10; a week later Dana Wright was shot off his bicycle. Hours later Dillon Herbert was killed in retaliation. An officer stopped a King on the street one night with a gun, gloves, and face mask: assassination kit.

He drew on the officer, then thought better of it. That would be one of the cases Don Stern took federal. Warren Street turned into a war room: What's going on, who's out there, what are we going to do? We all lived it pretty much hour by hour, and a lot of the time it was awful. On one horrible day, April 23, Gary, Billy, and ATF agents visited the mother of a King named Dwayne Banks and told her face-to-face her son was being gunned for and to get him out of the area. As soon as they left he was killed on his porch, shot off a milk crate.

We knew who was driving things, one guy in particular, and for the first time I felt the evil temptation I suddenly realized my law enforcement partners had to live with *all the time*: the guy was a scumbag, he was getting people killed, he was standing in the way of everything, we could just drag him into an alley and beat the shit out of him. It was no more than a passing thought, but it was real. To its enormous credit, the Strike Force team never once showed any sign of having any similar impulse.

It took six weeks or so, but by May, the Kings had gotten it. The heat was too much; it wasn't worth it. Things were calm.

It was time for the first forum.

May 15, 1996. The Dorchester District Courthouse, big sprawling brick building, obligatory huge columns, massive glass entryway facing the stretch of Washington Street where years earlier Bernie Fitzgerald had looked out his probation-office window and seen kids shooting at each other. Bernie, still on the job, had given us the go-ahead to use probation to stage the forum. We'd thought a lot about where to hold the forum and had settled on a courtroom: Offenders were used to behaving themselves there, there were metal detectors on the entrances, offenders were used to shedding their weapons before coming in, it would be relatively easy to maintain security inside. Bernie had set that up, too, with the administrative judge. Gary had people all over the area outside—we wanted no trouble as the Kings came and went.

Anne and Anthony and I drove in from Cambridge with a carful of easels; we had posters we wanted to display, so we stole them from the Kennedy School classrooms. Late in the afternoon, our team gathered on the judge's side of the courtroom we'd been given, set up the easels and the posters so they faced the empty rows of dark wooden benches on the other side of the bar, and reviewed our lines. Police, probation, parole, the DA's office, the U.S. attorney's office, the Streetworkers. We were all vibrating, even the coolest of the cops: Nobody had ever done anything like this before. The logic of what we were trying to do said, It works here or it doesn't. There had been lots of crackdowns before, but it was this weird next piece that was new and different: *Put your guns down.* Opening night at the improv, gang-member audience.

We didn't even know if anybody would show up. Probationers and parolees ignore their terms and conditions all the time and hardly anything ever happens to them. Even new crimes aren't necessarily enough to get them revoked. It's why working cops, especially, think probation is a bad joke. Nobody would have been shocked if the Kings just ignored us.

They didn't. Kings started walking into the courtroom. Billy Stewart and other Dorchester probation officers brought in some of their charges. (We later found out that they'd brought in some other gang members, not on probation, just by convincing them to come. It would take us fifteen years to see how significant that was.) The Streetworkers brought in a dozen more. They sat down on the other side of the bar, facing us. DYS brought in some Kings who'd been locked up; they sat off to one side in orange jumpsuits and manacles. The Kings looked like gang members look: hoodies, sport franchise jackets and sweatshirts, puffy down parkas, baggy jeans, running shoes and Timberlands, the street-gang shoe of choice, dreads and braids and bad haircuts, baseball caps angled off to the side, chains and big rings. Bad attitude they somehow train their pores to exude: Look at the floor, look at the ceiling, look at nothing, slump back, spread your legs. A couple were wasted. Not kids, mostly, young men, some not so young. One, I was amazed to see, was a hard-road mid-fifties, at least.

We'd scripted and blocked the forum like a play. Billy Stewart played emcee, kicked things off, moved it along from speaker to speaker.

"Thanks for coming," he told the audience. "This isn't a sting, everybody's going to be home for dinner, we just wanted you to know a few things. And this is nothing personal, either; this is how we're going to be dealing with violence in the future, and you just happened to be first. So go home and tell your friends about what you hear today." All of us, up here, we're all working together for the first time, he said. We share information—anything any of us know, we all know. The violence got so bad, it made us get together. *You* made us get together. We looked for the most violent gang in Boston, and it was you. *We* are the ones who brought you the storm you've just been through. We did it because of the shooting. If the shooting starts again, we'll be back. He was flanked by a poster Anthony and I had cobbled up on his computer back at the Kennedy School, spelling out what had just happened on Bowdoin Street—all the agencies involved, how many arrests, warrants served, drug enforcement, probation and parole enforcement, priority state and federal prosecution, review of cold cases for new opportunities, "Shut down drug market: When there is violence, no one profits," all the rest. Representatives from the other law enforcement agencies backed him up, committed themselves, said what they'd do if they had to.

The Kings smiled, looked bored, looked hard.

Not when Ted Heinrich spoke his piece. He got their full attention. "This kind of street crime used to be a local matter," he said. "Not anymore. Attorney General Janet Reno cares more about youth violence than almost anything else. My boss works for Janet Reno, so that's what he cares about more than anything else. Right now, the youth violence in Boston is happening in your neighborhood, which means that the U.S. Department of Justice cares about *you*. We can bring in the DEA, we can bring in the FBI, we can bring in the ATF; we can prosecute you federally, which means you go to Lompoc, not stateside, and there's no parole in the federal system anymore: You serve your time. We don't want to do that, and we won't if we don't have to, but it's violence that will get that kind of attention."

The room went frigid when the conversation turned to Freddie Cardoza. Anthony and I had made another poster:

FREDDIE CARDOZA
PROBLEM: VIOLENT GANG MEMBER
"Given his extensive criminal record,
if there was a Federal law against
jaywalking we'd indict him for that."
—Don Stern, US Attorney

SOLUTION: ARMED CAREER
CRIMINAL CONVICTION
Arrested with one bullet
Sentence: 19 years, 7 months
No possibility of parole

ADDRESS:
OTISVILLE FEDERAL
CORRECTIONAL INSTITUTE
Maximum Security Facility, New York

"One bullet," said Gary French. "We are *not* putting up with this stuff anymore."

Here's how it's going to be in Boston from now on, the group said. When a gang kills someone, or shoots guns, or terrorizes the neighborhood, this group steps in. We'll focus on everyone in the gang. We'll arrest drug dealers and shut the markets down. We'll serve warrants. We'll call in probation and parole. Nobody's going to smoke a joint or drink in public, nobody's going to have any fun. We'll talk to the judges and make sure they know what's going on. We'll talk to your parents. It's up to you whether you get this attention. This group, no violence, no harm no foul. It's not a deal, it's a promise. Somebody else might come get you for dealing drugs, you take that chance. *We* go where the violence is.

Most of the attitude was gone, they were leaning forward, focused, paying attention, taking it in. Even those who were still fronting *Don't care*, they were listening, you could tell.

Then we turned it around. Tracy Litthcut, by design, sat in the audience: *not a cop*. "We know you're all caught up in something you can't control," he said. "We know it's dangerous out there. And we'll help, any way we can. If you need protection from your enemies, if you want a job, if your mom needs treatment, if you want back into school, tell us—here's my phone number." But he had starch, too. We're tired of black kids dying, black kids killing each other, he said. It makes us sick. We know you're hurting. But nobody has a right to pick up a gun and shoot somebody else, terrorize the neighborhood where they live. We'll help you any way we can. But the violence has to stop. "If you don't hear what's being said to you today," he told the Kings, "it's on your heads. Take what we're offering. I've been to over one hundred funerals, and I'm not going to any more. The violence stops *now*."

Even the law enforcement team turned it around, using a trope we'd worked out carefully ahead of time. You know what happens when someone kills a cop, they said. We don't stop with the shooter; we go after everybody involved, we never back off, we never stop. That's what we're going to do if you guys hurt somebody. That's what we're going to do if somebody hurts *you*. Hurting you is like hurting a cop. It's all off-limits now. It's over, today.

We gave them copies of the posters, we gave them the Streetworkers' phone numbers, and we sent them home.

And Boston went quiet.

The Streetworkers and the gang officers reported over the next days that the streets were buzzing about the meeting all over the city. Freddie Cardoza's name was everywhere. The Vamp Hill King I'd pegged as in his fifties—he turned out to be barely thirty—visited Billy Stewart to check his record against Cardoza's; Stewart just showed him the two thick criminal histories matched side by side. Girls dragged their boyfriends in and made them check with *their* probation officers. Bowdoin Street stayed calm; the Streetworkers moved in with a summer-job program. Gangs elsewhere started to heat up; as intelligence reached the Working Group, we sent messengers—Streetworkers or cops who knew the crews involved—out to tell them, they're watching you, we're watching you, it goes no further, *stop*. Our team went and talked to the gang in Codman Square, no more trouble. Went and talked to the gang on Stanwood Street, no more trouble. Tracy reported back amazed after one such warning. "They believe," he said. "There's nothing happening."

Revelation. The gangs were *rational*. They listened, they learned, they responded. They *changed*.

Except on Intervale Street.

The Intervale Posse was the Freddie Cardoza of gangs, the worst crack crew in Boston. They owned their street in Roxbury: threw pregnant women out of their apartments and used them for stash houses, robbed kids who strayed in and threw their shoes into a huge "Adidas tree" on a vacant lot, ran extension cords and set up an area with couches, a barbecue, and a TV to deal from, had a target range back in the woods, were implicated in a long string of homicides. Gary French went repeatedly to Intervale's alpha, Sam "Sam Goody" Patrick, and warned him to stand down. He didn't.

Before he left, Paul Joyce had been running several slow-moving,

Wendover-style gang operations in the neighborhood. Gary drew them together, focused them solely on the Intervale Posse, reached out to the DEA, which had a long-running but stagnant operation going against the Posse—once behind the veil with law enforcement, one soon learns that "we have an open investigation" is often federalese for "the check is in the mail"—and woke it up. A team of BPD officers and DEA agents worked up a volume of drug buys. Commissioner Evans, furious at the Posse, wanted an example made of them before school started. On August 29, an interagency task force swept onto Intervale Street and took fifteen of the Posse federal and another eight stateside. "State or federal?" Sam Patrick asked when the task force took him. Federal; he hung his head. A bunch of them were in a holding cell at the federal courthouse and learned that it was a bad idea to attack the jail staff the day of their bail hearing; federal marshals discussed the matter with fire hoses, the way we heard it, and the judge kept them inside. Gary got the Massachusetts National Guard to roll in combat earthmoving equipment and level the Adidas tree.

Over the next couple of months, the Working Group said, in forums all over Boston, *We did this*: what we started to call "Operation Ceasefire." We did this *because of the shooting*. Intervale was warned, they didn't listen, and this is what happened. It was a drug operation, yes, that's what the papers say, and that's right, they went down on federal drug charges, and some of them are probably never coming back out. But *we* made this happen, and it was *because of the shooting*. The shooting is *going to stop*. The shooting is *over*.

In one crucial respect these forums were different from the first one with the Vamp Hill Kings. These involved multiple gangs. The Strike Force and the Streetworkers identified gangs they knew were hot, we worked with probation and parole to figure out who was under supervision, and we brought them all in together. We were, we hoped, systematically getting the word where it most needed to be heard. You're here as a messenger back to your group, they were told. When you leave here, we're going after the first gang that kills someone after this meeting. Don't be part of that first gang. You see one of your boys picking up a gun, *tell him to put it down*.

Schools arranged assemblies and we talked to students en masse. We went to the one secure DYS lockup in Boston and had four forums back-to-back in one day, forty kids in each one. I talked to a counselor at the DYS facility the night of the day we did the forums there. What's going on? I've never seen anything like it, he said. They talked about it in group, they talked about it at dinner, they talked about it until lights-out. What are they saying? I asked. "They're saying," he said, " 'those guys aren't playing anymore.' "

The Ceasefire forums could be magical, church, distilled truth telling, Quaker meetings with body armor. It never ceased to amaze me, hasn't yet. Every time, we'd wait with our hearts in our mouths, *Is anybody going to show up*, but every single time they did, gang members filing into a room, allies, rivals, it didn't matter, there was never any trouble, to sit face-to-face with the cops and the feds. In one, a woman came in, said, These young men asked me to come with them, they're afraid, I work with them in the community, I said I'd come and make sure everything is okay. She heard us out, *Don't shoot*. Got up, turned to the gang members, said, You *listen* to them. They're telling the truth. It's not okay, what's been going on. You do what they say, take this chance you've been given. We started to get gang members showing up who hadn't even been directed to appear by probation and parole. I heard about this, they'd say, can I sit in?

The forums were scripted and blocked, but as we got our feet under us, or by dumb luck exactly the right people were there, they became jazz, and when the spirit was right, it was transcendent. Zina Jacque, a wonderful preacher from Cambridge who joined with us for a while at the DYS forums, second week of September. "We blew it, big-time, ten years ago," she said to the locked-down kids. "We're guilty, you're pissed. You're afraid to go home without a gun. But it's a new day. We're going to reinstitute the social contract. We're going to make the streets safe again. We're here to say two things. One is, we're sorry. But sorry is never enough. The second thing is, we're going to fix it." Tito Whittington, one of the Strike Force detectives, thin, dapper, always beautifully dressed, in a huge middle school assembly at the end of September, sixth, seventh, eighth graders. Who knows somebody who's been shot? Most of the students raise their hands. Who knows someone who's been stabbed? Most hands go up. Who's heard gunshots at night? Most hands go up. *We're stopping this*, Tito said. *It's over*. Eugene Rivers, who by now was putting in appearances at some of the forums, talking to a courtroom full of gangsters: You're not getting rich. You're living at home. You've got no bank account. You're driving hoopties. Don't you get it? The noise brings heat. All this noise is *bad for business*. You think real gangsters behave like this? If you're going to be gangsters, at least be *good* gangsters. They laughed, but they clearly got it.

At one forum at the Dorchester courthouse, one of the gang members pushed back. Our side had told them to put their guns down and he didn't like it. He came back with the textbook street narrative. This isn't my fault, he said. The CIA invented crack, not us, they're bringing it into the neighborhood. We don't make the guns. We don't bring them in. George Bush is a bigger hustler than any of us will ever be. Why are you picking on us? One of the black ministers heard him out, said, *That's interesting. Killed any CIA agents lately?*

You could *feel* the room change. The street line was bullshit. Bullshit had been called. Even if the CIA was driving the crack trade, it didn't justify black men killing black men. The truth vs. the thug party line, and the truth won, and the thugs clearly knew it.

We started calling it *the moral voice of the community*.

Moral engagement with thugs. The very last thing anybody thought you could do.

Revelation.

The streets were spooky calm. Gary French, in one Working Group meeting, said that he was used to getting beeped every time there was a homicide or a shooting and that he'd thought for a while that his beeper was broken; it just wasn't going off anymore. Tracy burst into another meeting practically dancing. "I just saw a fistfight!" he said, delighted. "I haven't seen a fistfight in *years*!" We were flying fast and low, making it all up as we went along. In the fall, the crew at the Villa Victoria housing project started to act up; word was that an old beef was getting hot, guns were being stockpiled. The Working Group sat with the streetworker who worked the area. Can we get word to them that we're watching, that they should calm down? "You know what we should do?" he said, suddenly smiling broadly. "Walk Marcy Jackson through. That'll do it." Marcy was a prosecutor with the state attorney general who'd been seconded to a project in the city; a few years back she'd prosecuted a bunch of the Villa Victoria gangsters. She was young, thin, pretty, and an absolute bulldog in court; she'd won most of her cases, lost some, but did it in a way that left her with respect in the eyes of the street. Guys she'd gone after would talk to her when they crossed paths; she treasured the street name they'd given her: Robobitch. They see Robobitch again, the streetworker said, they'll head for the basement. I don't think we did it, we just sent word the now more standard way; Villa Victoria calmed down.

Gary and I came to Warren Street one morning having had the same epiphany over the weekend: what it was we were doing with the "we'll go to the next body" line in the forums. It's like all the old westerns, we'd figured out. The sheriff is up in the mountains looking for the outlaws' hideout; he comes around the corner and there they all are, and he's one guy facing them down. Everybody knows what the next line is: *The first sonofabitch that moves, I'm going to drop him.* Get it right and nobody moves, nobody gets shot. An uneasy but stable equilibrium. And, for the first time, it felt like we were on the right side of that equilibrium, the spiral of decline had reversed. "I remember saying to you, six, seven months ago, we're responding all the time, we may not be able to stay in one area for long," Gary told me in December of 1996. "But now that we're not just putting out fires all the time, the guys really want something to do, we can do it right."

Not everybody was happy. A lot of Tracy's streetworkers were deeply suspicious of the police and prosecutors; they thought Tracy might be passing on information he shouldn't, putting them at risk on the street, thought the cops wanted to and would jack up all the kids they were trying to save. They'd been close to the Kings and Intervale, were close to gang members still on the street they were convinced could be saved. They were especially concerned about the draconian federal sanctions that had brought down Freddie Cardoza and Intervale. I put together a meeting at Warren Street between the Working Group, the Streetworkers, and U.S. attorney Don Stern. Tracy's not snitching for us, the law enforcement team said bluntly. We have our own sources; we'd be embarrassed if we had to go to him. There are things he doesn't tell us, and things we don't tell him. It's okay, it has to be that way. One of the older streetworkers came directly at Don Stern. I can't be sure *my son* won't go to the corner one day, he said. I hope not, I'll do everything in my power to see that he doesn't, but it's hard. If he does, if he goes and sells a couple of rocks, is he going to go away federal for the rest of his life? No, said Don. No. We're saving that for the worst of the worst. This is about violence. My office wouldn't come anywhere near your son.

And he turned it around. What do you need to keep this going? he asked. We've got their attention, it's quiet, but how do we keep it? Jobs, the streetworkers said. We need jobs. The kids want out, and we don't have anything to give them. Not just summer jobs, real jobs. Okay, Don said. We have credibility, me, Commissioner Evans, DA Martin. Nobody's going to say we're soft on crime after what we've just done. We'll go to Washington and try to get some job grants that you can administer. I'll take the lead on it. (Which he did: His office made a major effort, and succeeded.)

All right, then, said the streetworker who'd been worried about his son. I believe you. So I want to tell you that the gang I work with asked me to tell you something. They knew I was going to be talking to you today, and they asked me to deliver a message. They asked me to tell you, "We get it. We've gotten the message. Leave us alone; we're not doing anything."

So now the gangs were communicating, too. *Stop it*, we'd said. *Understood*, the streets were saying, *we've stopped it. No need to prove the point any further.* It was extraordinary; nobody had ever imagined anything like this. But it started to dawn on us that the gangs were *better off* than they had been. Operation Ceasefire left them pretty much as they were before: minus the violence. It didn't stop drug dealing or any of their other hustles. It didn't stop them from being in a gang. It didn't make them go to school or stop them from hanging out with their friends. It didn't even stop them from carrying weapons if they wanted to. But it surgically excised the violence from the mix. More than anybody else, it protected *them*; they were the ones doing most of the dying and getting shot. Why shouldn't they like it? They could, as Anne said in her economist's way, unionize, fight back. But they didn't. Why would they? Why would they want to go back?

And, we thought, it gave them a way to do what Jimmie Mac had said they wanted to do all along, a way to step back without losing face, what we started to think of as an "honorable exit." Lots of gang members didn't like the violence, we knew that. They couldn't, in any realistic way, say to their friends, I've been thinking about this, and I believe shooting each other is a bad idea, and that we should reconsider our

patterns of behavior. Even if they did, they could hardly have that conversation with their *enemies*. The *Baltimore Sun* sent a reporter to Boston at the end of 1996.

> "The police is very definite about what the rules is," says Rashad, a
> gang member who spoke on the condition that his last name not
> be used. "It helps because we say to each other now, 'Don't shoot
> that boy because we're going to have problems with the police.'"

Honorable exit.

For some, it went further. In the summer of 1997, almost unbelievably,
gang members came to the Working Group through DYS to complain
about a new gang that had sprung up in Codman Square. Young and
wild, the new Buckshot Crew was throwing its weight around, advertising its guns in graffiti, shooting the place up. "They're going to ruin it
for everybody; you have to do something," the other gang told our
team. We had a quick forum with the Buckshot Crew, which they ignored, so Gary sicced undercover officers on them and took the whole
crew off on drug buys and stateside prosecutions. The gang members
that had come to us rode surveillance with the Youth Violence Strike
Force to finger the Buckshot Crew.

It was knife-edge, but it was powerful—you could feel the primal
forces at work, wheeling together, converging, focusing, reaching straight
into the heart of what everybody had seen as an impossible situation and
just . . . changing it. Law. Police, prosecutors, the DEA, the Justice Department. Tracy's people, out on the streets. Probation and parole, out
on the streets. Faith communities. Communities themselves. The gangs
themselves. Truth, the power of the word. What had been separate was
synced, had found a groove and a rhythm, had an almost palpable pulse.
It was amazing. I remembered an interview I'd read in college with Frank
Zappa. Zappa, for all his electric flamboyance, was something of a
chamber musician; he charted his music very carefully, often stood at the
front of his band with his back to the audience, conducting. Don't you
lose something playing arenas? he was asked. Some kind of intimacy?
No, he said. He liked all the amplification and power and sound that

came with those spaces, hit your note and send all that energy out, shake the rafters. You got *big air*.

We were getting big air.

And people were changing. We had cops acting like social workers and trying to get gang members jobs, outreach workers acting like cops and bringing law enforcement to bear, street ministers acting like prosecutors and fingering impact players, prosecutors organizing job programs, gang members turning in other gang members, neighborhood people reinforcing the law enforcement messages. There were no divisions, no differences of opinion, or at least none that seemed to really matter. It was remarkable; we all talked about it. I started to write about it: "collapse of category," I called it, in awkward academese. The racial code talk is gone, I told George Kelling. If this group says black kids are killing each other and it has to stop, it doesn't really mean that it thinks the black family is collapsing, or that black kids are sociopaths, or that the community is hollow and corrupt. It means that black kids are killing each other and it has to stop. If it says the kids need jobs, it doesn't really mean that the killing is a racist plot by outsiders, or that the criminal justice system is oppressive, or that the government doesn't care about the community. It means that the kids need jobs. I saw it, we all saw it. But we missed it. If we'd seen what it really meant it would have changed everything.

The Buckshot Crew operation was the first since Intervale that rose to the level of a concentrated gang crackdown. Despite all the strategizing that had gone into designing Ceasefire, it had turned out not to be necessary to move out meticulously along the gang vectors and slowly, gradually turn the tide. The streets had just flipped. Violence was way down. Gary and I actually started scheming to expand Ceasefire. Basically we'd taken the violence out of the drug crews; the rest of what they were up to seemed a bit diminished, but was far from gone. The street drug scene was the clear next biggest problem, volatile, chaotic, dangerous. I started thinking about this again, now in the light of the new lessons. The gangs, the drug crews, the individual offenders, they were a lot more rational than they got credit for. You could talk to them, they'd listen. You could tell, looking at them, they weren't making much money, weren't getting rich. Maybe they didn't actually think standing on the corner, getting arrested and robbed, was all that great. You could let them know the community hated what they were doing, they'd listen. The Streetworkers could try to get them jobs. Could we come up with something they'd listen to, shut the street markets down?

We thought, maybe. Gary used to knock on doors and tell the dealers to leave, and that had worked. Could we do what Tampa had done without six months of arresting everybody in sight? Could we post signs in the ten worst drug zones in the city saying, Don't be here on Monday, BPD and DEA are coming? See which ones listened and closed shop, go to the busiest market that hadn't, deliver the promised drug enforcement, go to the next busiest, say, We said it, we meant it, shut down or you're next? Work our way through the list until everybody had gotten the message? Match it up with help from the Streetworkers, a *We don't want this* message from the community? Talk to dealers' parents, say, Your son's about to go to prison, get him off the corner? It wasn't a plan, not close, but Operation Ceasefire hadn't started as a plan. Could it be worked out, figured out? We actually took the idea of trying to Commissioner Evans, and he passed it on to his narcotics people. Nobody took it seriously; we never heard back.

I'd come back to the drug question. Dealing with it would become one of the most important parts of my own education.

The quiet on the streets held. We were keeping track of homicide victims aged twenty-four and under as a rude way of gauging Ceasefire's impact. Our month-by-month chart went back to January 1991, when crack had been fully established and the killing had stabilized. The line plummeted after the Vamp Hill King forum. In 1995, there had been forty-six such dead; in 1996, with Ceasefire kicking off in May, there were twenty-six; in 1997, Ceasefire's first full calendar year, fifteen. In November of 1996, for the first time in our data set, no young person was killed in the city. It happened regularly after that. Our formal evaluation was spearheaded by Anne and Anthony. It couldn't use the medical-model design beloved of methodologists, since we'd gone after the whole city and all the gangs, the whole problem, at once, so couldn't wall off controls from the intervention, but it used a quasi-experimental design with other cities as comparisons, was peer-reviewed, published. It looked at the data through the end of 1998. When all the statistical adjustments were made, it said that there had been a 63 percent reduction in homicide victimization among those aged twenty-four and under, and a 50 percent reduction in homicide among all age groups citywide. We went into police records in Roxbury and pulled out assault-with-a-gun incident reports for the city's most active precinct so we could look at twenty-four-and-under victims. There had been a 44 percent reduction in youth gun assaults. No other comparable city in the country had seen as sharp and large a reduction. And it kept on getting better. After Boston's horrible year in 1990, when it had 152 homicides, the city averaged about one hundred a year. Operation Ceasefire kicked off in 1996. By 1999, it was down to thirty-one. The city was safer than *before* crack came to town—a lot safer.

And the streets had changed. Ted Heinrich and his people debriefed an informant they'd flipped; they were after information on a weight crack dealer, wanted to know whether he had, carried, a gun. The informant finally said, "Look, he always said, 'Guns and drugs don't mix. That's when the feds come.'"

Guns and drugs don't mix. Perfect.

We don't *do* that here.

They called it the Boston Miracle.

We took it on the road.

Building Out I

The Boston Miracle—I always hated that name, it wasn't a miracle, it was hard damned work—went off like a bomb. On July 8, 1996, the *New York Times* published a front-page story by Fox Butterfield on the White House event announcing the Clinton administration's launch of the Youth Crime Gun Interdiction Initiative and its roots in the Boston Gun Project. It said, in the kind of magical thinking that would characterize much of the press coverage of what was behind the "miracle," that antitrafficking work in Boston had meant that no juveniles had been killed in the city all that year. It was absurd; there was hardly any trafficking enforcement going on yet, and whatever was being done, it couldn't possibly have touched the vast number of guns already on the street. No matter. The world descended. For the next couple of years, Boston was swamped by reporters and law enforcement; local, state, and federal government officials; community activists and the odd academic. It was, for a while, the biggest story in crime, one of the biggest stories in urban issues, one of the biggest stories in public policy. Our team went from obscurity to being minor celebrities: in the news, on television, testifying before Congress, getting called to the White House.

It was gratifying, but almost overnight we were also dealing not just with the chaos of the streets but the chaos of national-level politics, media, and ideology. What had happened in Boston was important, for good and for ill, to a lot of different people, for a lot of different reasons. They wanted, some of them very, very badly, to name and to own it. Our core group, still doing the work on the ground every day, instantly lost control of the discourse. Normally, in academia, one gets to specify the intervention—the journal article says, Here's what we did—and there then ensues a long, painstaking, and highly technical open debate about impact: Did anything happen, and if so, what? With Operation Ceasefire, the world decided immediately that something had happened—the Miracle. The knife fight was about what the *intervention* had been, and who, and whose ideas, would benefit from it or be harmed by it.

President Clinton came to Boston in 1997 to use the Miracle as a backdrop for a major policy speech on his juvenile-crime platform. There was a large, open event at the University of Massachusetts, and a smaller power players' session held at the John F. Kennedy Library. The latter was considerably above my pay grade, but Don Stern, the U.S. attorney, was a gentleman and made sure I was invited. It was my first contact with really top-level politics. The main event was a panel discussion with the president and key Boston and Massachusetts politicians and local figures. It was to include Dr. Ray Hammond, the leader of Boston's Ten Point Coalition of activist black clergy, who at the last minute couldn't make it; rumors of an auto accident were circulating. I stood in front of the stage, just before it was to begin, while Eugene Rivers told me with great satisfaction that he had taken the president's advance men aside and told them that if he was not up on that platform with Clinton when the panel began, he would have black protesters at every stop the president made for the rest of his visit. It got him up there, a key moment in what became his push to say that the black ministers stopped the killing.

Dr. Deborah Prothrow-Stith and some of her colleagues at the Harvard School of Public Health wrote a series of *Boston Globe* op-ed pieces, articles, and ultimately a book saying, We did it. Their argument was simple: They did a bunch of things in Boston to address juvenile violence, going back to the early 1980s—high school antiviolence curricula, gun buybacks, and the like—and juvenile violence went down, so those things were responsible. This kind of *post hoc ergo propter hoc*—"after this, therefore because of this"—argument is a formal logical fallacy first-year graduate students are taught to avoid like the plague. (I clapped my hands, then the sun came up, so I caused the sun to come up.)

It didn't add up. Evaluations of the high school programs didn't show any impact on serious violence, and there was a large scholarly literature showing that gun buybacks don't work. For most of the time they were at work with their program, Boston violence was going *up*, often catastrophically, only to fall precipitously when Ceasefire was implemented. By far the largest part of Boston's homicide decline was adult, not juvenile. Dr. Prothrow-Stith's 2003 book, *Murder Is No Accident: Understanding and Preventing Youth Violence in America*, written with Howard R. Spivak, which draws heavily on Boston, barely mentions the Boston Gun Project or Operation Ceasefire, and makes no mention at all of the extensive scholarly literature on what did, or did not, drive down violence in Boston.

The national narrative galloped away like a startled horse; we were utterly helpless to rein it in. It was, for those of us who'd been at the core of what had happened in Boston, a through-the-looking-glass experience in which people who'd had little or nothing to do with it stuck their hands up and said, Here's what happened. The Boston Police Department put together an all-day conference when the press of outsiders finally became so severe they could no longer be scheduled; Commissioner Paul Evans introduced a stage full of people who had been central to the operation, half of whom I'd never seen or even heard of. The press coverage, for the most part, fueled the confusion rather than clarifying it. Fox Butterfield's second *New York Times* story, in November 1996, focused on the gang-meeting element of Operation Ceasefire but conflated it with the city's field-probation program, Nightlight, that dated back to 1992. I would field calls for the next ten years about "that probation program that stopped the killing in Boston."

This kind of piece-of-the-elephant approach almost defined the reporting. It seemed impossible to get across—I spent truly vast amounts of time trying—that Operation Ceasefire was a *strategy*, with a core logic and a lot of moving parts. The coverage mostly grabbed a single moving part and skipped the logic entirely. Elements that together had been central to what *did* happen were made to carry a weight they never had, and never could. Going after the guns had stopped the killing. Taking every gunslinger federal had stopped the killing. The black ministers had stopped the killing. The Streetworkers had stopped the killing. Wraparound services for at-risk kids kept them out of gangs and stopped the killing.

We hoped that what we were doing on the gun front was mattering; we were absolutely sure that the other pieces were part of the new whole that had flipped the streets. On their own, alone, it was clear that they hadn't. We knew the gun-trafficking work hadn't gotten all the guns off the streets: the streets just weren't using the guns they still had nearly as much. (But the line that the Boston Gun Project had gotten all the guns off the street was picked up by the gun-control movement, which made the project a target for the gun-rights movement, which meant I started getting hate mail from gun enthusiasts convinced I was part of a national push to take their guns away.) There were hardly any federal prosecutions, and what Don Stern's office had done—take a few extreme offenders—was nothing new. The Streetworkers had been hard at work since 1990, Ten Point and Nightlight since 1992, and the killing had continued. Nothing at all had happened with services for "at-risk kids." Our core insight, that we could put all this together and fuse it in an entirely new way, disappeared. People saw what they thought they were going to see, what they wanted to see. Ceasefire told gang kids to stop doing crime, I started reading in papers from all over the country, and if they didn't, put them in federal prison for as long is it possibly could. *No*, I said. *No, no, no.* It was hopeless.

It was nice, in a way—it seemed like every key piece of the Boston partnership got its own *Time* or *Newsweek* cover at one point or other—but it made the real story impossible to understand. Some of the reporting was surreal. "Boston demands that police and district attorneys act, at times, like worried parents. Working with teachers, they search out youngsters who skip school or whose grades have nose-dived. They provide them with counseling, mentoring, after-school jobs or send social workers to their homes," wrote the *Washington Post*. "Periodically, scores of police invade gang-troubled neighborhoods to question any teenager who so much as looks furtive."

The academic literature and debate, while far less visible, tended for quite some while toward the conclusion that *nothing* had happened, or if it had, it wasn't Ceasefire that had made it happen. To the uninitiated it may seem strange that when a massively criminal population had largely stopped shooting and killing at exactly the time an intervention to make them stop had gone into effect; when no similar decline had happened anywhere else; and when alternative explanations for the decline didn't really make sense, the most plausible conclusion is obviously "nothing happened." Among scholars it wasn't a stretch at all.

The academic reaction fell into camps. One held that in the absence of a formal experiment with control groups—the cancer patients who *don't* get the experimental drug—it was impossible to say anything at all, end of discussion. Our explanation that Ceasefire had had to intervene with all gangs and all gang members at once, because that was the logic required by the diagnosis of the violence—we were engaging with the gang *community*, not with individual neighborhoods or gangs or gang members—got nowhere with this group. One camp said the violence reduction just happened by itself. Jeffrey Fagan, who had been one of Anthony Braga's professors at Rutgers, wrote an article saying that violence in Massachusetts had been declining before Ceasefire. *I controlled for those trends statistically in the evaluation,* Anthony wrote him—*you taught me how to do that.* One camp said no answer is possible. Richard Rosenfeld from the University of Missouri–St. Louis published an article basically saying, This is interesting, but the volume of Boston homicides is too low to get real statistical certainty. Not everybody felt this way. Carnegie Mellon's Al Blumstein took a look at the graph of homicide in Boston and said, What else do you need to know? All that fancy evaluation is for the subtle stuff; this is a slam dunk. This discussion proceeded with the blazing speed and crystal clarity needed by real people in the real world facing real life-and-death decisions. In 2004, going on ten years after Ceasefire kicked in in Boston, a blue-ribbon panel of the National Academies of Science looked at the evidence and concluded, promising, but . . . more research is needed.

I wrote a paper trying to capture the new deterrence logic behind the Boston operation. Lots of crime problems are driven by small groups of high-rate offenders, it said. We can communicate with them; we can lay out clear rules that certain things they do will be taxed by attention to all the *other* things they do; we can deter groups, like gangs and drug crews, not just individuals; we can control whole populations of groups by saying, The first to do this proscribed thing gets all of our attention. We could use that basic approach to take one problem at a time out of the streets, salami-style: first no killing, then no shooting, then no street drug dealing, then no selling drugs to juveniles. "We ought to be able to play these guys like pianos," I'd been telling the policing class at the

Kennedy School I was coteaching with George Kelling. My paper got a hearing at what's called an "author meets critics" panel at an American Society of Criminology conference. One of my heroes, Franklin Zimring, the dean of American gun scholarship and of modern criminological thinking on deterrence, opened the discussion by saying, Let's face it, Boston is a small city without much gun density—we shouldn't pretend that anything that happened there has any general meaning. *Take that, upstart.*

The political, media, and academic action was cork-in-big-surf stuff to experience firsthand. Fun, a lot of it; educational, all of it. But damaging, a lot of it. The interpretations, and misinterpretations, mattered. They were, in toto, massively misleading and confusing. And they were simple, appealing stories, far more appealing than the truth. Soon people would be standing up to correct me when I gave conference presentations: *That's* not what happened in Boston—you've got it all wrong. Soon cities all across the country were working to organize their black churches, which had never happened in Boston, and to get those churches out on the street to stop the killing, which of course also didn't work. Soon cities all across the country would be launching Nightlight replications to stop the killing, which, of course, they did not do. Ceasefire was a Rorschach test for people interested in crime, I came to see. They looked at it and saw what they wanted to see. Different people, different kinds of people, wanted to believe the churches could stop the killing, that social services could stop the killing, that federal prison could stop the killing, that running programs in high school could stop the killing, that taking the guns away could stop the killing, that you could, and had to, save every kid to stop the killing, that you could stop the killing without the cops. Some wanted to believe that nothing had happened, that you had to do far more work in and for the community than we had been able to do. It played on their deepest convictions, whatever those might be. I'd end up on NPR, years later, while a woman called in from somewhere in America and told me that the kids wouldn't stop shooting each other until the nation renounced its militaristic ways: We're teaching them to shoot each other, she said, look at what George Bush is doing in Iraq. Actually no, I told her, you can pretty much tell them to stop and they do. She was apoplectic. "That's . . . that's . . . *idiotic*," she spluttered. When the National Academies released its report—we need to know more—a *Boston Globe* reporter called. What's your comment, she said, on the National Academies' conclusion that Ceasefire didn't work?

And none of it did anything whatsoever to answer our burning question: Are we really on to anything here? Those of us involved in the work in Boston, and those of us who took the evaluation issues seriously and were involved in that process, had no real doubt that what seemed to have happened there was real. That didn't necessarily mean it would travel. We didn't know if the situation we'd found on the ground was the same elsewhere. Was there the same kind of gang presentation? Was it driving the violence? Were there the same kind of fear and self-defense and I-hate-this-but-there's-no-way-out dynamics? If there were, could they be addressed in similar ways? Would local actors want to put the same kind of operation together? Could they, if they wanted to? And would the streets react in the same way?

If it wouldn't travel, what we had in Boston might as well be a miracle. Did we have a fundamental new tool to save lives?

My most trusted guidance still came from practitioners, and the early returns were not encouraging. I was talking with police departments and others in law enforcement all over the country—at conferences, when they came to Boston to scope out Ceasefire, on the phone when they called to ask about that probation program that stopped the killing in Boston, in site visits—and experiencing a solid wall of, a torrent of, Oh, come *on*.

You've got to be *kidding*.

And then would begin a litany I would hear, over and over and over, for the next ten years. It got to the point that I knew almost exactly what was coming, could recite it in my head along with them.

We don't have gangs. We do have gangs but they'd never put their guns down (those *Boston* gangs are *pussies*). Our bad guys are so bug-fuck crazy they'd never listen to anybody—they don't care if they live or die, they don't care about anything. Our probationers and parolees would never come to a meeting, they do anything they want and they never get violated, they'd just never show up. Our community would never stand with us. Our judges are so liberal they'd never impose any consequences. Our DA is so skittish he'd never take these cases. Our media is so hateful they'd never let us get away with this. Our mayor would never back us. Our law enforcement agencies would never sit at the same table. Our families are more broken. Our streets are more out of control. I came to think of it as the "race to the bottom"—no matter how bad it is anywhere else, you wouldn't believe how bad it is *here*. The devil's Lake Wobegon, where all the children are below average.

It was very, very hard to answer. We'd learned something big, fundamental: The guys on the street are not crazy, they don't like what's going on, they're rational, they're a community, too. They're doing awful things, but they're trapped and they want out. It sounded impossibly naïve when it was just said straight out. We'd figured it out slowly, had had time to sit with it and absorb it. Go at it straight on, it sounded like lunacy. *They'll just stop? Right.* When we tried to build to it step by step, tried to explain how it worked, the whole structure got too rickety, you had to believe too many strange things and see how each strange thing tied in with each other strange thing. It's the group, not the individuals, I'd say, this isn't about the individuals. There aren't that many groups, not that many guys. They're at terrible risk, they're not being protected, they're scared. They do terrible things to protect themselves, they have terrible norms and values pressed upon them, they may act accordingly but it doesn't mean they like it. They're actually looking for a way out. I'd go through it and feel myself losing the room. It just didn't work. I remembered my *Alice in Wonderland*: To believe what we believed, you had to believe six impossible things before breakfast.

The other big thing we'd learned—we can create a rational structure, on *our* side, that the streets will respect and respond to, but we're not doing it, so they don't—well, that didn't go over so well either. We're not protecting them, so they're protecting themselves. We're not creating consequences for the violence, so they're violent. We lie to them all the time—*next time, young man, there's going to be trouble*—so they learn not to listen to us. They're not irrational, *we're* irrational, we're not surrounding them with something that makes sense, so they don't respond. *So this is our fault? I don't think so.* It was part of why the wave-a-magic-wand explanations—get the black ministers out on the corners, visit probationers at home—had such appeal. It was never clear at all how they were supposed to work, what the ministers were supposed to *do*, why making a few bed checks on juveniles would stop the adults from shooting each other, but they were easier to swallow than the alternative. *We've completely misrepresented the streets? This is partly our doing?*

There was the fact of Boston, but it didn't really carry much weight. We got, over and over, the simple, forthright shorthand: *This isn't Boston.* That might have worked in Boston, but we're not Boston: we're bigger; we're smaller; we're more northern, western, southern; poorer, blacker, whiter, more Hispanic, more Asian, meaner, more lost. It won't work here.

Maybe they were right. We would get the chance to find out. The call from Minneapolis came in early 1997.

Quiet, sane, respectable Minneapolis, full of Nordic blonds and blue eyes, where "Minnesota nice" is both a point of pride and a wry epithet about personal and social repression. (Minnesota is called "the land of a thousand lakes"; the local joke, we found, is that it's "the land of a thousand treatment centers.") It's friendly, easygoing, has a deep, long tradition of good government and civic virtue: One of the big scandals when we got there was a group of public employees who had been caught filling up their cars at the full-service pumps. It's so clean it made me nervous.

Which made it completely unprepared to be known nationally as "Murderapolis," courtesy of a *New York Times* front-page story in June of 1996. Minneapolis had traditionally been a very safe city; with a population of about 370,000, in 1983 it had fewer than twenty killings. Things had been slowly getting worse through the eighties and nineties, but something had gone badly wrong recently: Homicides had jumped from around sixty in 1994 to nearly one hundred in 1995. Minneapolis was more dangerous, by the numbers, than New York City. Minneapolis's Tiffany Moore—there always seems to be a Tiffany Moore—was Byron Phillips Jr., an eleven-year-old black boy killed on his porch in June of 1996 by an errant round in a gang beef. The worst violence was concentrated in several northern Minneapolis neighborhoods and in Phillips, a neighborhood just south of downtown. The city had in fact disbanded its gang unit: The police department launched Operation Safe Street in the summer of 1996 and made 2,200 street stops, from which *one* felony arrest was sent to the district attorney. This failed to convince Minneapolis's violent offenders.

Honeywell, one of the city's biggest corporate concerns, had its headquarters in Phillips; there had been some bad incidents involving Honeywell employees, and Honeywell CEO Michael Bonsignore had gone to the governor and to city leaders and let it be known that things had to change; he let it be known that Honeywell had other cities vying for its headquarters. It set off a near panic. It's a common pattern: Dead black kids, we can live with that; skittish powerful white folks, not so much. Honeywell, some other corporate and foundation partners, and the state and city launched Minneapolis Hope, Education, Law, and Safety: Minneapolis HEALS. Minneapolis HEALS reached out to the Police Executive Research Forum, a Washington, D.C., group, and PERF brought in Anthony and me. By January 1997 we were boots on the ground, in regularly from Boston.

Even before we got there, it was looking very familiar. In December, the *Minneapolis Star-Tribune* had published a superb investigative piece charting the killing. It could have been Boston with the names changed: gangs, small groups of drug dealers and street friends, linked networks, cascades of shootings and retribution shootings and more retribution shootings, an involuted, superheated street scene, cops close enough to the action that they could sometimes warn particular people that they were about to get killed (it didn't work for them either), hard-core offenders who were terrified themselves. The *Star-Tribune* story began with one killing—Neilyn Wright, in March 1996—and traced through some ten more that either led up to it or stemmed from it, all among acquaintances (except for the dead mistakes). There was an overlay of outside influence—Bloods and Crips, Chicago gangs—but mostly it seemed like the same script. It was, in a weird way, encouraging: This was something we were hopeful we knew how to deal with.

Our Minneapolis partners said otherwise. We set up with the Minneapolis Police Department—Inspector Sharon Lubinski, a clear rising star, had been given the job of managing the project—and started talking to the gang and drug guys. They had a palpable outrage that this was happening on their doorstep. Minneapolis has a very particular civic culture; it takes enormous pride in being civilized, sensible, contained. Our new law enforcement partners saw the Minneapolis violence both as a personal affront and as an alien virus. When we asked what was going on, the repeated response was, "Detroit, Chicago, and Gary": the three cities the police saw as exporting their thugs to Minneapolis.

There was a very coherent narrative. Those cities had long-established drug markets and gang scenes; it was easier and more profitable to operate in Minneapolis; it was being colonized by franchise operations from outside. They were particularly concerned with the Chicago gangs and what they called the Detroit Boys. There was a second, complementary narrative—that higher Minnesota welfare payments were drawing people in from other states and that single mothers were bringing their sons and their sons' gang culture with them. Their most fundamental conviction was, *Not invented here*, with the implicit corollary that fixing it was outside Minneapolis's reach.

We did two things. Unlike what we had found already orbiting around Paul Joyce in Boston, there was no existing interagency group focusing on the violence: The police, prosecutors, probation, parole, and the rest had literally never all been in the same room at the same time. They were perfectly willing; it was simply that nobody had ever made it happen. So we convened a Minneapolis version of the Boston working group and started meeting twice a month. Everybody was game: Sharon Lubinski, the MPD gang and drug cops, line probation and parole officers, line prosecutors. We met in another featureless muster room, the Minneapolis equivalent of Warren Street, at MPD headquarters. One day one of the probation officers came in laughing; he'd done a home visit on a supervisee, opened a door, and found a pit bull flying through the air at his face. He hit the dog in the head, one punch, knocked it cold in midair, couldn't believe he'd gotten away with it. They were great. It was familiar, comfortable.

Just as we'd found in Boston, the street guys knew exactly what was going on on the streets: the hot crews, the beefs, the fine details. We did ride-alongs, got to know people, saw the hot neighborhoods. Phillips was nice, the same kind of Midwestern frame houses I'd grown up with in Michigan, healthy businesses, nice restaurants. Below the surface there was trouble. We've got Hmong gangs, the cops said, hill people from Laos; they came here out of the resettlement camps after Vietnam, got picked on, their kids formed up to protect themselves, now they beef mostly with each other. We've got some Native American crews, we can't handle them at all, anything happens here in the city they bolt north for the reservations, we've got no jurisdiction there, there's not a thing we can do about it. We listened, absorbed, had coffee, made friends, just as we had in Boston.

And we repeated the two basic research exercises. We sat down with the frontline guys and mapped out the gangs, groups, beefs, and alliances, and we went through a whole bunch of killings and said, What happened? It wasn't different from Boston. It was *exactly* the same.

Or almost exactly. There were differences; they just weren't differences that mattered. The Minneapolis Police Department had a gang database that included thirty-two gangs, with 2,650 members. This was an exaggeration, everybody knew, because it hadn't, for a long time, been cleared—"purged," in law enforcement lexicon—of those locked up, aged out, reformed, moved away, or dead. But even that count represented only about 3.5 percent of the young men in the city. They were unquestionably serious: There was a huge Vice Lords set, there were Gangster Disciples, P-Stone Rangers, Latin Kings, classic hard-core Chicago gangs. There were Rolling 60s Crips and other Crip and Blood sets, classic hard-core Los Angeles gangs. There were the Hmong gangs, some Lao gangs, the Native American sets. (Plus the Rough Tough Somalis. I savor the gang names. Favorite ever: the Grumpy Winos, out of the San Fernando Valley in Los Angeles.)

Anthony dove into homicide files and reviewed the 264 killings in the city between January 1, 1994, and an arbitrary cutoff of May 24, 1997; he matched victims and offenders against the gang database, and went through the killings with the frontline officers. (As Anthony worked through the files at MPD headquarters, one of the recent killings felt weird. What's up with this one, he asked a nearby cop. Oh, that's our gay serial killer, the cop said. Sure, Anthony said. No, really, the cop said. It was—it was Andrew Cunanan's first victim, his lover Jeffrey Trail. Cunanan stole Trail's .40-caliber pistol and left a string of bodies across the country before killing designer Gianni Versace, and then himself, in Florida.) It was, again, just like Boston. Forty-five percent of homicide offenders and suspects were gang members; a quarter of all victims were. Three quarters of offenders and suspects had criminal records; they averaged almost eight priors apiece. (These were *underestimates*; Minnesota had no statewide criminal history system, so we were limited to checking for Minneapolis arrests, which missed arrests elsewhere in, or arrests outside, Minnesota.) We were looking, this time, at all homicides, not just the "youth" homicides we'd examined in Boston; when we reran the data looking at just young victims and their killers, the similarity to Boston was even stronger.

The gang scene looked the same, too. Despite the Chicago and Los Angeles flavors, the dynamics were almost identical: mostly small and disorganized groups, clearly identifiable beefs and vendettas, mostly beefs and "respect" issues and the like driving the violence. There was hardly any discernable outside influence; the dead, those who killed them, and the gang members themselves were almost entirely local, and the issues that drove the violence were local. Nobody was calling shots from Chicago or Los Angeles. The one "Detroit" set we could find didn't even have any beefs; it sat in a lonely corner of the network diagram, along with the Hell's Angels, who weren't bothering anybody either. If it had ever been Detroit, Chicago, and Gary that were driving things, it wasn't any longer. This was Minneapolis's problem.

So should we try the Boston intervention? The working group thought yes. Anthony and I were in constant touch with Sharon Lubinski, either on the ground in Minneapolis or on the phone from Cambridge, days, evenings, weekends. She was working like a woman possessed. *I'm in trouble at home*, she told me on one visit, *my partner's getting pretty mad, I'm never around.* We were meeting with Minneapolis police chief Bob Olson, meeting with the mayor, the U.S. attorney, getting to know some key partners like Jan Smaby, a tall blonde amazon of a woman who ran Hennepin County probation. We'd need her support if we were going to make a local version of Ceasefire work; she loved the idea, was a delight to work with. Everybody said yes.

The corporate sponsors behind Minneapolis HEALS wanted an open community process, to take the research findings and the plan to the public and get their response and, they hoped, approval. Sharon, Anthony, one of the guys from PERF, and I held an open-door session in the spring. There were probably a hundred people there, about half black. Here's what we've found, we said, and presented all the numbers and the gang network. Here's the intervention that worked in Boston; it looks like it should work here as well. We're ready to go. If it works like it did in Boston, we'll see big results quickly. It failed, almost completely, to connect with the people in the room; they hardly even wanted to discuss it. For two hours, instead, people threw up their favorite ideas. The kids need parks and programs, there's nothing to do in the neighborhoods. We need job development. The schools need fixing. *The guys doing this aren't in school,* we said, *and they're not kids.* Nobody was interested; what we were talking about was simply too distant from the normal discourse. Finally, one older black man said, Look, what's the point of this anyway, we're all just going to go on vacation and forget all about it. Sharon and Anthony and I looked at each other. *We're not.*

The working group process continued in parallel to the high-level agency and public conversation. We needed a demonstration crackdown to begin with—Minneapolis's Intervale—to show the streets things were different and we meant business. If you could get rid of one gang, I asked the group, which would it be? The Bogus Boyz, everybody in the room said immediately, the MPD gang officers with particular vehemence. We'd heard of the Bogus Boyz before—they were in the gang network, with a singular number of active beefs—but we proceeded to hear a lot more. The Bogus Boyz, word was, was made up of guys *thrown out of other gangs* for being out of control. Law enforcement was convinced that they had shot Byron Phillips, in a gun battle with another crew called Shorties Taking Over. They'd been the target of a shooting that killed Davisha Brantley-Gillum, a four-year-old girl sitting beside her pregnant mother in the back seat of a car parked at a gas station; her mother was shot, too, but survived. One of them had stolen a car, driven it the wrong way down Interstate 94, killed a limousine driver. The room *hated* the Bogus Boyz.

In my work with law enforcement, I'd learned to be the one who asked the big, dumb, obvious question. What's going on to get these guys now? I asked. Everybody looked at each other. Nothing, was the answer. This happens *all the time*—justice is frequently not only blind, but also deaf, dumb, and stupid. Without some center of gravity between agencies, some overall direction, the most obvious stuff never happens. "I've been working a recreational case up on them," one of the gang officers said. A recreational case? I was confused—what's that? On my own time, the guy said. Just hoping something will happen. Should we make this our first action? I asked. Yes, the room said. The working group formed up a task force. This is normally the beginning of a long, careful, unpredictable investigative process: gathering intelligence, mounting surveillance, sliding in undercovers, flipping confidential informants, reviewing old cases, maybe assembling the legal predicate to apply for judicial permission for a state or federal wiretap. Before we could even really get started, the Bogus Boyz gifted themselves to us—in

May, they got into a running public firefight, fled the scene, got pulled over with firearms and Molotov cocktails. It was the law enforcement equivalent of finding a big gold nugget lying on the ground. The feds took a core group of the cases: done.

Excellent.

According to the Boston script, this is when we would begin the forums. Our working group wanted nothing to do with that idea. Our defense bar will *never* let us get away with that, they said. It's perfectly legal, we said; there's no problem there. We get that, they said. This is Minneapolis. Our defense bar will *never* let us get away with it. It's not a fight we want to take on. Instead they hatched a plan to take the forums to the streets. Probation and parole officers would tell gang-involved supervisees to be at home at a certain time; they and MPD officers would visit them there and deliver the message: The violence is over, the Bogus Boyz were our first target, we'll be following the bodies, tell your crew to stand down. That sounded good, so we kicked it off in mid-June, cops and probation and parole officers making the home visits and delivering the message.

On June 17, the mayor, police chief, and some of the key partners held a press conference, another device to get the word out: This is what happened to the Bogus Boyz, and why, and this will be what we do from now on. The working group added a twist of its own, visiting gunshot gang survivors at the hospital, saying, This is terrible what's happened to you, we're taking it very seriously, but we're going to handle it— often with the victim's boys all around—*no retaliation* or we'll be coming your way. They posted explanations of the new strategy at the jail.

And Minneapolis went quiet.

In the first half of 1997, there were twenty-eight homicides in Minneapolis. In the summer months the year before, June, July, August in 1996, there had been *forty-one*. June, July, August 1997, there were *eight*: an 80 percent reduction, the lowest in twelve years. I'd been *here* before, I had the same day-to-day, minute-by-minute, heart-in-mouth feeling I'd had after the Vamp Hill King forum. Is this real? Will it hold? I was on the phone from Boston pretty much daily with Sharon Lubinski. I have the vivid memory of standing at my kitchen table in my apartment in North

Cambridge, looking out the window, getting the update. "It's spooky," she said. "It's quiet. Nothing's happening." That's what it felt like here, I told her. It seemed impossible, too good to be true, but it wasn't. Even the doctors noticed. "I think there's been a general feeling down here that this summer has been remarkably less violent than the recent past, certainly than last summer and maybe the last couple of summers," Dr. Steve Sterner, assistant chief of emergency medicine at Hennepin County Medical Center, told the *Star-Tribune*.

Midwest, check. Chicago gangs, Los Angeles gangs, Asian gangs, Native American gangs, check.

Pretty much stopped. Check.

Okay.

Looks like it *will* travel.

Looks like it *will* work here.

The third city was Stockton.

This was the doing of Stewart Wakeling, a Kennedy School colleague of Anne's, Anthony's, and mine. He hadn't been involved in the Boston work, but he'd kept an eye on it. He was a California kid and wanted to move his family back there. In 1997, he took a job in Stockton as the San Joaquin county administrator's criminal justice coordinator. Stockton is the seat of San Joaquin County and one of the biggest cities in California's Central Valley, about 300,000 people, making a rough triangle with San Francisco to the west and Sacramento to the north. It's an agricultural hub, about a third Hispanic, with a large migrant-farm-worker and undocumented population on top of that. A quarter of the city was below the poverty line, and it was regularly in the top handful of most violent cities in the state; homicide ran in the high forties annually. Stewart's job had been created because several young women had been shot in gang disputes—mistakes—and the city was reeling.

He brought us out to brief the local team he was assembling. Stockton was not Boston, not Minneapolis. Stucco and western frame buildings, perfect California sunshine, miles of crops, arrow-straight state highways. Different ways of doing things. Anthony, Gary French, and I parked for a meeting downtown, started across the street, and got yelled at: We were jaywalking, crossing in the middle of the block. The citizenry was irate.

We don't *do* that here.

The locals filled us in. They knew what was going on; we were seeing what would turn out to be true, the locals *always* know what's going on. Stockton had scores of gangs—black, Asian, Hispanic. It was the first time I heard of the Tiny Rascals, a very serious Asian crew, violent, mobile. I'd run into them again in years to come in Portland, Maine, and elsewhere. It was my first contact with Norteños and Sureños, the core California Hispanic gang families, big, traditional, intergenerational, with Mexican roots. Sureños, "Southerners," are strong in southern California, have strong prison-gang connections, tied to La Eme, the Mexican Mafia; Norteños, "Northerners," are strong in northern California, strong prison-gang connections, tied to Nuestra Familia, Our Family. The story goes that a La Eme guy in Soledad prison stole a pair of shoes off a Nuestra Familia guy in the late 1960s. They'd been killing each other ever since. They were killing each other in Stockton. They were killing *themselves* in Stockton, one of the worst beefs internal to the Sureños, South Side Stocktone vs. East Side Stocktone, they killed each other but still got together sometimes to fight the Norteños. We laid out how Ceasefire worked, Gary hugely effective, cop to cop, poking fun at his broad New England accent, everybody laughing. They went for it.

There was no time for the niceties. Stewart and Anthony did a rough, fast-track gang audit and homicide review. The Stockton Police Department, under a lieutenant named Wayne Hose, formed up a gang-enforcement team and started hitting the most violent gangs Wendover style. Surfer-blond Stewart, soft-spoken, relaxed, turned out to have a gift for stitching together the partnerships needed to get all this done, drew in the U.S. attorney, the district attorney, social-service providers, churches, hired away Boston's second-in-command streetworker to launch an outreach program. Stewart and Anthony bonded—they'd plot homicide prevention strategy, then head up to the mountains to go snowboarding—and Anthony did almost all the outside support work. They followed the basic Boston and Minneapolis script. Stewart would call me from time to time wanting to know, What more should I be doing? He thought it was too simple. You're doing it, I'd tell him, you're doing everything we've done before. The timeline for Stockton homicides Anthony later put together begins in 1990 with twenty-seven dead. Thirty-nine the next year. Thirty-four, thirty-six, thirty-seven, thirty-three, thirty-seven, thirty-seven again in 1997. The first forums were held in the fall of 1997.

And Stockton went quiet.

There were eighteen gang homicides in 1997. In 1998, there was one. The timeline looked just like Boston's, plummeted down. The overall homicide count went to nineteen in 1998. Then twenty-one, seventeen, eighteen. Anthony caught the problem analysis up with the rolling intervention: forty-four gangs, 2,100 members—2 percent of the city between ages twelve and thirty-four—61 percent of homicide offenders and 53 percent of victims gang members, beefs and vendettas driving the violence. Just like Boston.

Anthony's later evaluation—quasi-experimental, peer-reviewed, published—found a 42 percent reduction in gun homicide. There were no statistically significant reductions in the comparison cities of Anaheim, Bakersfield, Fresno, Riverside, or Sacramento. None of the differences mattered, any more than they had in Minneapolis.

West Coast, check. Rural, check. Intergenerational Hispanic gangs, check. Prison-gang connections, check. Pretty much stopped. Check.

Looks like it *will* travel.

Looks like it *will* work here.

It was so obvious, once you saw it. Our team paid a visit to Chicago, where a public-health doctor named Gary Slutkin was thinking about implementing Ceasefire. While we were there, a girl was shot off her porch—mistake. The newspaper story quoted a Chicago police officer: There's a gang feud in the area, it'll take a while to die down, we're monitoring it. *Monitoring* it? Gary French and I looked at each other across breakfast. We knew what to do. Go out there, find one guy from each side, say, One more shot fired and DEA comes calling. *Monitoring* it? Made you want to go shake somebody. (Slutkin would ultimately adopt only the street-outreach component of the larger Boston architecture but cribbed the Ceasefire name for his "Chicago Ceasefire" program; it would confuse things irredeemably in the years to come, two very different approaches wearing the same label.)

Things were building. The Department of Justice was watching. Lois Mock, back at NIJ, was working with researchers in several cities to help them get operations going; DOJ had me talk at the annual conferences of the U.S. attorneys, and my phone would start ringing afterward. Cities in trouble were looking at the new ideas: not many, still, but some. The next move was a big one: We went to Indianapolis, New Haven, Winston-Salem, Portland, Oregon, and Baltimore. All at once.

The first four cities were the Strategic Approaches to Community Safety Initiative, or SACSI—it turned out to be a bad acronym once you said it fast a couple of times. This was the big time; this was Attorney General Janet Reno. She'd paid careful attention to the Boston Gun Project, had gotten regular briefings from the National Institute of Justice's Jeremy Travis, knew and liked Boston U.S. attorney Don Stern, had paid a site visit to Boston, was extremely concerned about kids and youth violence. The word went down to her people in 1998: I want more of Boston. Suddenly the work was a Department of Justice priority. One of her top people, counselor to Attorney General Kent Markus, took the lead. DOJ staff flew up to Boston to get briefed on the structure of the Gun Project and how it had proceeded, how it could be replicated elsewhere. Jeremy Travis from NIJ called: Can you come down to Washington for the weekend, have dinner at Kent Markus's house, we want to work this through. Well, yes, I think I can make time for that. I got on a plane.

DOJ reached out to U.S. attorneys it thought were sharp, interested, in cities with high violent-crime rates, and pitched the idea. Two of the ultimately five cities were in fact in motion already. Walter Holton, the U.S. attorney for the Middle District of North Carolina, had heard me talk at a DOJ conference and called me at my office at Harvard. Holton is slow, Southern, silky, one of the most seamlessly seductive human beings I've ever met; I don't remember ever saying yes to him, but the next thing I knew I was on a plane with Gary down to High Point, North Carolina—a smallish furniture-manufacturing city next to Greensboro, then experiencing one of the highest homicide rates in the state. We laid it all out in a gorgeous High Point University conference room overlooking the athletic field, Gary again hugely effective, cop to cop, still playing on his New England accent. They went for it. I've been involved there ever since. The High Point work was bringing what they call the Triad cities, Winston-Salem and Greensboro, along in its wake; Winston-Salem became one of the five formal SACSI sites and High Point became a shadow sixth.

Lois Mock had chosen Indianapolis for one of the NIJ replications; Edmund McGarrell, then at Indiana University Bloomington and director of the Crime Control Policy Program at the Hudson Institute, took the lead as project coordinator and researcher. Ed and I knew each other a little bit and had been talking strategy and implementation long-distance, me pacing around my living room. DOJ added Memphis, New Haven, and Portland to the mix as additional SACSI sites.

We worked out a basic architecture for moving the project along. There'd be big, formal site meetings, all the DOJ and site teams in the same place at the same time, hosted in rotation by the SACSI cities and moderated by the Kennedy School's Frank Hartmann. In between, we'd have smaller working meetings for the core research and operational people, which I'd chair, held at either the Kennedy School or in Washington. I'd make site visits and hold conference calls with the site teams; NIJ and other advisors would do the same.

We saddled up and got to it. More meetings, more planes. In one of the first big SACSI meetings, with Kent Markus, the top DOJ people, Jeremy, the site teams, all the rest, Don Stern said, Part of what makes this stuff work is that you pick off a bite-size piece, something you can handle. You don't try to do everything at once. That's why we started with just homicide. I started laughing; I couldn't help it, everybody else heard it and started laughing, too. Stopping gang killing citywide had turned into a bite-size piece. How things had changed. *Didn't feel like it at the time*, I said.

Baltimore came by way of a community nonprofit, the Safe and Sound Campaign. Safe and Sound—really its executive director, Hathaway Ferebee—has been the relentless leading voice on children's issues in Baltimore for years. Hathaway is tiny, pixieish, burns with energy, her diamond basic goodness luminously self-evident. In Baltimore, she rolled her rocks uphill. Baltimore did not then figure in the public mind as one of America's high-crime cities; that conversation ran to Chicago, L.A., Detroit, East St. Louis, sometimes the two Richmonds—Virginia and California—Newark. *The Wire* has changed that somewhat, as it should. Baltimore is consistently one of the most dangerous places in the country. It was one of the original, late-1960s heroin-epidemic cities; for some reason, it's the only one where the epidemic didn't burn itself out. Heroin is still going strong in Baltimore—*her-ron*, as it goes locally—and the city has the highest rate of injection drug use in the country. It was hit hard by the decline of the shipping industry that made it a thriving port city, by the decline of its manufacturing base, by both white and black flight, by the crack epidemic that stacked itself on top of the heroin epidemic. (In 1986, its goodwill flagship, the schooner *Pride of Baltimore*, went down at sea, which said about all that needed to be said.)

Baltimore's Tiffany Moore was six-year-old, braided Tiffany Smith, shot in the head in 1991. A mistake, a shootout between drug-dealer rivals. She got the street corner where she was shot dead named after her: Tiffany Square. Four more people would be killed on the same corner over the next several years; it was a thriving heroin market when I hit town. Mayor Kurt Schmoke had started a branding campaign: "Baltimore: The City That Reads." In 1993, with a population of around 730,000, the city had 353 homicides, six times New York City's rate. What everybody said: "Baltimore: The City That Bleeds." There were boiling open-air drug markets a skip and a jump from the trendy inner harbor. In its worst quarters, it's Beirut.

When Hathaway came calling, I took it personally. My two sisters live in and just outside the city; my younger sister is a critical-care nurse at Johns Hopkins, which sits in one of the hottest parts of Baltimore. I would get calls when they heard about particularly awful things on the news. Why'd they do that? my youngest nephew said. Can't you make them stop? I'll try, I said.

Anthony, research assistant Gillian Thomson, and I hit Baltimore in early 1998. By then I'd spent more than ten years in the worst corners of the worst cities in the country. Baltimore shocked even me. On my first ride with a Baltimore police officer, we turned a corner and a block and a half up, in broad daylight, was a heroin dealer standing in full view on the sidewalk holding what looked like a gallon freezer bag full of vials, their orange caps blazing in the sun. Drug dealers respond and adapt to law enforcement, an intricate pas de deux; they slide off when the heat shows, take pains to separate their main stash from what they're selling right that moment, separate the drugs and the money, use legally invulnerable juveniles to do the dirty work. This guy stood there watching us as we rolled up, by, past, never moved, never hid his dope. There must have been forty people in the twin lines standing in front of him waiting to get served, and they never moved either. Everything was amped up in Baltimore, the streets worse, the offenders more lost and pathetic, the law enforcement response particularly relentless and particularly pointless. Some time later I'd be out at night with a drug cop, turn down an alley, crawl through as a crowd of dealers fishbowled us from all sides. "Who's winning?" the cop said cheerfully through his open window. One, heroically intoxicated, thought about it for a while. "We are," he decided. He was right.

But Baltimore was what we, what I, wanted. It was the next step, what gunsmiths call the proof test: Fire a hot shot and if the gun survives the extreme heat and pressure, you know it won't blow up in your face. If we could handle Baltimore, we could handle anything. Boston itself was still quiet, the streets looked great, there was hardly anything for the Ceasefire working group to do. It was still too early for the formal evaluations—Anne and Anthony wanted data through the end of 1998—but the calm was holding. The homicide rate was still falling. Over in the Boston Police Department homicide squad, they were focusing on old, cold cases; there weren't enough new ones to keep them busy. The Streetworkers were exultant. Things still happen, one of them told us, but they don't spread like they used to, don't turn into the beefs and the crazy vendettas, they just die out. "They never used to let us outside and stuff, because they was scared we were going to get shot or something," a Boston kid told the Jim Lehrer *NewsHour*. "But now we can go outside and do anything we want most of the time 'cause there's not other people here to do all the bad things." Anne and Anthony and I were speculating about what we called "the firebreak hypothesis": that if things were quiet enough, long enough, maybe the cycle of fear and violence and guns could be broken. Maybe quiet would beget quiet, just as violence had begotten violence. Maybe it would really be *over*. It did not seem out of reach.

We were getting enough traction that there was a competition brewing between Boston and New York, the two big national success stories on crime reduction. What was going on in New York was, by any measure, extraordinary. Bill Bratton had taken over; whipped the dormant, creaky NYPD into shape; armed it with a state-of-the-art crime-reporting system; infused it with a new culture of responsibility for outcomes on the street; and launched what would become by far the country's largest and most sustained decline in serious crime. From a peak of more than 2,200 in 1990, homicide in New York would fall by over 70 percent by 1998, and would eventually dip below five hundred. For a while the plummeting killing in New York drove most of the big national crime decline *by itself*.

The debate was over strategy. The new NYPD was heavily invested in aggressive street policing, what would come to be called "zero-tolerance" policing. Boston, the line became, was smart, collaborative, and subtle; New York was simpleminded, confrontational, and crude. The charge was that New York was getting results, but at the cost of relentless policing, angry communities, and awful incidents like the station-house plunger-handle sodomy of Haitian immigrant Abner Louima. ("It's Giuliani time!" one of the NYPD officers was said to have said; it wasn't true, but the phrase captured everything thought to be wrong with the New York mind-set.) Boston has become a national model, the *New York Times* would write in a typical story early in 2000: We had, I was fascinated to learn, launched Ceasefire by "consulting black ministers to win their cooperation in going after the ringleaders" on the street, while "in the eyes of many police chiefs and criminologists" looking at New York, "there is a sense of sadness that a great opportunity has been squandered."

My own take on this was complicated. I wasn't fond of the more aggressive street work, especially the department's gun strategy, which relied on very large numbers of street stops in minority neighborhoods, but at the same time knew that "zero tolerance" was a bumper sticker, not a strategy. New York police officers still exercised a great deal of discretion; no department could arrest everybody for every crime they were committing, or it would grind to a halt within an hour of hitting the street. I was enormously impressed by the managerial seriousness Bratton and his team, and their successors, had brought to the NYPD.

They were *running* the place, saying, every day, We are going to have an impact, we are going to do better today than we did yesterday, we are going to get results, and if you're not up for that, there's the door, and they were making it work. I spent time in NYPD and saw the voltage they'd developed: The department was focused on results, trying new things, keeping the good stuff and tossing the rest; good people who wanted to do work were being raised up and backed up. There was a real excitement in the air. The energy and vitality, the emerging culture of performance and improvement, was palpable. My dream was that that seriousness and energy could be matched with the strategic ideas we were working with, but the head-to-head matchup made it impossible. The Boston-vs.-New York narrative sparked an animosity in the NYPD and in New York City government that would play out in some extremely nasty ways over the next few years.

And it wasn't just Boston anymore. People were paying attention to Minneapolis, to Stockton, to how what was beginning to be called "the Boston model" was traveling. We were surfing a huge wave, we had the attorney general of the United States believing, the big D.C. gears turning, the U.S. attorneys engaged. If you were close enough, paying enough attention, there was more. We'd dealt with moderate, steady levels of killing in Boston; an epidemic spike in Minneapolis; stable high levels in Stockton. We'd dealt with East Coast gangs, Chicago-style gangs, Asian gangs, West Coast Hispanic gangs. We'd worked with a law enforcement team that was amazingly integrated from the outset in Boston, with teams that had to be put together from scratch in the other cities. Everybody had been able to do the work with what they had at hand; the grants had started pouring into Boston once the publicity started, but the city hadn't needed them to turn the corner. Minneapolis and Stockton did fine with what they had. It was beginning to feel like this was something that you really could *do*.

It *did* work, it *would* travel.

Which raised the stakes enormously, as far as I was concerned. If we knew how to do this, and it worked, then we had a very real responsibility to get it where it was needed. We'd come a long, long way, but that wasn't the point. The point was, there was so massively much to *do*. Could we do it? Boston, Minneapolis, Stockton, SACSI were good, they were proving the point, moving things around. But they weren't Baltimore. They weren't Detroit, Philadelphia, East St. Louis, the two Richmonds, Los Angeles. They weren't Chicago. I heard it all the time, in most places the skepticism was barely dented, not at all dented—I heard it over and over and over: *Boston isn't Chicago.* And that was exactly correct. It was an empirical question. Would it travel to those places, could we make it work, where it was needed the most? No matter what happened with SACSI, in Portland, in Indianapolis, they weren't Chicago. Baltimore was as bad as it got. Baltimore would tell.

Baltimore: Politics, Resistance, Obstruction

The next couple of years were a blur. I traveled so much I began not to know where I was. The meeting rooms all looked the same, the hotels were all the same, the death and the drugs were all the same, the crushing work of trying to *move it along* was the same. I'd find myself literally not knowing what city I was in, developed a trick of thinking back to the last airport I'd flown out of, what plane I'd gotten on to leave *there*, and where *it* had been going: somehow that worked for me. It seemed normal, which should have been a sign. In one memorable three-day stretch, I found myself chairing my working group in Baltimore, going up to New York the next day to do an MTV special on kids and guns—in the green room with Left-Eye Lopes from TLC, John Popper from Blues Traveler, and a guy from 98 Degrees I later figured out was Nick Lachey—and in Washington testifying before the House Judiciary Committee the third day. MTV put me up at a Euro-chic hotel in Times Square; I went in, saw all these handsome guys head to toe in black and thought, I'm not cool enough for this, and then realized they were the bellboys. I sat in the hearing room on Capitol Hill waiting my turn to testify and thought, Which of these experiences is weirder, and what are the decision criteria?

The work went hard. We'd been extraordinarily lucky in Boston, Minneapolis, Stockton, we were learning. As much work as it was, they'd been *game*. The new Justice Department sites—New Haven, Winston-Salem, Indianapolis, the rest—not so clear. Baltimore, not at all. The streets, I was about to discover, were nothing compared to the offices, the gang rivalries nothing compared to the political ones.

There was a lot at work with SACSI. Our first projects had been police-centric—there were lots of partners and lots of moving parts, but the police were first among equals. Moving the project through DOJ and the U.S. attorneys' offices shifted the center of gravity to the lawyers. Lawyers are like gang members: I like them fine individually, but they're terrifying in groups. Prosecutors are the worst. They don't think, discuss; they . . . prosecute. Our lawyers in SACSI went to it with a will.

Kent Markus, Janet Reno's counselor, blazingly smart and presiding over SACSI, was determined to have the sites select the problems they were going to work on through some kind of "data-driven" process. We went round and round on it at the big SACSI conferences. New Haven, for example, wanted to work on shootings. *Prove to me shootings are your biggest problem*, Kent challenged Steve Robinson, the Connecticut U.S. attorney. *I want data*. Problem was, it's not the kind of thing you can prove. There's no analytic process that can say, This is objectively the most important issue. That's inherently a value judgment. No matter how much you know about shootings and their costs, you can't *prove* that they're more important than domestic violence, or driving under the influence. You can't put a price on Tiffany Moore. The academics, those of us who were supposed to know about data and what you could and couldn't do with it, all said that. Ultimately you simply have to decide where you want to focus. It didn't seem to matter. Kent and Steve went at it hammer and tongs, meeting after meeting.

The DOJ folks and the U.S. attorneys themselves were all, at least, committed to the process. The cities' assistant U.S. attorneys, the line federal prosecutors, were not at all convinced. SACSI said, this is different. This will work better than what you've been doing. It took a while to see it, but that was very easy to hear as *What you've been doing is wrong*. This did not go down well. They wanted proof, too. Prove that this will work better. Prove that we shouldn't just arrest everybody. Prove that if we went for more, tougher prosecutions, that won't work. Prove that it's better to work on problems than on cases. Prove that our mayor, our DA, our police, our community, will sign up. (They were federal prosecutors, so they had the additional, and very real, concern that they might in fact end up prosecuting their mayors, which would complicate things.) There were the kinds of real problems that lawyers love to settle in with: How do we go to our business community and ask for help without making it look like a shakedown? If we do that and don't get what we want, and then have independent knowledge of crimes, will we be compromised in subsequent investigations?

Round and round and round.

The academics were trouble, too. I'd told my Justice partners that this part would be easy: naïvely, as it turned out. The research methods we'd used to unpack the violence problem in Boston were simple. There was no elaborate data gathering, no intricate econometric modeling; Mark Moore, back at Harvard, said once that there was nothing in the Boston Gun Project more advanced than long division. He was right. Anybody could do it. That turned out to be the *problem* for a number of the sites' new research partners. It was déclassé. Asking cops what they knew and taking it seriously was beneath them. The Winston-Salem site researchers, from Wake Forest University, simply wouldn't do any work. We finally got them to do a focus group with young offenders—Winston-Salem had decided to work on juvenile gun violence—and at the next meeting one of them came back all excited. You're right, he enthused, that was great. *Breakthrough.* What did you learn? I asked. It confirmed my previous research that this is a group that shows early onset of marijuana use, he said. Thank God for experts. Walter Holton started muttering privately about prosecuting them for fraud. Sylvia Oberle, the Winston-Salem project coordinator, a former corporate-communications specialist Walter had hired, finally said, This research stuff doesn't look so hard to me, cut them loose, and did it herself, did a great job. For some of the other academics, the demands of the work were just overwhelming. They didn't have time to, or didn't want to, move in with the cops, do ride-alongs, soak things up by osmosis; they didn't want to put on bulletproof vests and go through doors.

Some of it, it turned out, we brought on ourselves. All the sites but Memphis decided to focus on gun violence; Memphis had the highest reported rape rate in the country and decided to work on that. For the other sites, the focus on gun violence brought the Ceasefire work into play, and that brought gangs into play. *We don't have gangs*, the law enforcement site teams said, over and over and over. We got rid of ours, took out the Latin Kings statewide, said Steve Robinson's people—the prosecution Ted Heinrich had worked on before coming to Boston. There are no gangs left. That's not really what we meant, we said. Boston's gangs were just drug crews, disorganized, no structure, no hierarchy. The New Haven team went and talked to the New Haven Police Department: What's driving the shooting? *Little neighborhood groups.* Ed McGarrell did his own homicide incident review in Indianapolis. Official Indianapolis Police Department data said the city had no gang problem: one killing in 1998. Ed debriefed frontline folks, seventy-five representatives from ten agencies, on a year's worth of homicides, 157 killings. Sixty percent showed group involvement.

It was a definitional question, but a particularly vexing one. "Gang" means something pretty particular to people—structure, purpose, cohesion, leadership. It's a myth, almost always. Most street groups don't have much of any of that. Therefore, in the eyes of most people, especially in law enforcement, they're not gangs. But none of us—law enforcement, academia, government, media—has a placeholder for what's really out there. We all work with a received ascending hierarchy: solo gunslingers, gangs, organized crime. It simply turns out, as a matter of empirical fact, that almost all the action takes place in the no-man's-land between "solo gunslingers" and "gangs." We'd picked up the "gang" usage in Boston: It was how the cops and probation officers and prosecutors talked about Boston's drug crews. Now we were hearing police officers and prosecutors say, That won't work here, we don't have gangs, we've just got drug crews. I made a site visit to Indianapolis, sat with Ed McGarrell's working group while an IPD officer ran down a particularly awful murder he'd just worked on. A guy had pushed a woman out of a moving car, killed her in traffic. I did my usual stupid-question thing: *Was he group involved?* "I don't think he's a member of any group," the officer said. "He's just a lieutenant in a drug organization." He heard what he'd said and started to laugh, we all started to laugh. The core reality—*it's all about the groups*—was terribly hard for law enforcement to take in. We learned our lesson, stopped talking about gangs entirely. Groups, groups, *groups.* It helped, but not that much.

Still, we made progress. Sylvia's research on Winston-Salem's serious juvenile offenders showed a tiny hard-core population. It also showed that they were being heavily influenced by older, group-involved offenders, who were using them as drug runners, dealers, shooters. *Groups and networks.* You couldn't look at juveniles in isolation. You *could* think about adding to a Ceasefire-style message—don't kill people, and don't involve juveniles in your groups—which is what Winston-

Salem decided to do. All of the SACSI sites except for Memphis decided to replicate some form of the Boston strategy; their research was finding the same patterns on the ground, and nothing else made more sense.

High Point was ahead of the curve and operational already. They'd put together what was becoming the standard law enforcement partnership—the High Point Police Department, the DA's office, the U.S. attorney's office, probation, parole, ATF, a community group called High Point Community Against Violence. They called it the Violent Crime Task Force, had identified their Freddie Cardoza, Brian Keith Cash, a thin little guy called "Ultraman." Ultraman was a stickup boy in the White Oak Posse, did home invasions, shot people, had all kinds of beefs going. Walter Holton's office took him on a cocaine-distribution prosecution and sent him to federal prison. In their forums, what they called "notifications," the Violent Crime Task Force put the streets on notice: Don't put the next body on the ground.

Excellent.

Me, I was starting to crumble at the edges.

Some of it was the constant *on-ness* of it all. I was, for better or for worse, the person who understood all this the best, and I was constantly in the air, on the road, fielding questions, planning agendas, answering the phone, in a drug market one day and talking to DOJ the next. (Rule of thumb: When you find yourself in a random airport and know precisely where the closest men's room, the best book store, and the least awful restaurant are, you're traveling too much.) Part of it was the accumulating weight of the streets. I know what I am and what I'm not—I'm not a cop, not a black grandmother—but I'd been mainlining degradation for a long time and it was beginning to catch up. I was plugged into cities all across the country, getting constant updates. High Point had gone really quiet

Looks like it *will* travel

Looks like it *will* work here

but when something *did* happen in High Point, I answered my phone and got an earful about the homeless guy who had beaten another homeless guy to death over a woman. It had been a long time since I could sit with my back to a door. Anthony and I were walking near City Hall in Baltimore one day when a black kid on a corner locked on hard, eyefucking me down the street and out of sight. Did you see that? Anthony asked. Oh, yeah, I'd seen it. He knew who I was.

I'd learned how to carry myself on the streets: how to move, shoulders back, hands free, head up, a little faster than the other foot traffic, the small head movements that let you watch everything, the whole thing assembling to say, *Don't try it, not worth it, not bait.* I learned for myself the nod my guardian cop in Nickerson Gardens had used with the drug boys: meet the eyes, the small nod *I see you* don't slide the gaze away, don't challenge, don't retreat, not too long, not too short. It's a whole conversation. What to do when that didn't work, the body language that said, *no.* Gary French had taken me aside and said, You need to start carrying a gun. That wasn't going to happen (though I'd done some research and discovered that a lot of the earliest police scholars *had*), but I *had* found a teacher of a particularly ruthless Filipino martial art, and I carried a blade everywhere it was legal. The SACSI team was in New Haven for a site meeting, one of the Justice staff had gone to Yale and wanted to visit his favorite old pizza place for dinner. We went down to the hotel desk for directions and they said, *You don't want to go over there.* We went, were in the elevator down to the street, one of the out-of-town cops said, I wish I had my gun. One of the women from Justice said, A gun won't protect you. The cops and I looked at her: *Yes it will.* I'd crossed over. I just wasn't sure to where.

Part of it was the relentless grinding of law enforcement. I didn't have any moral problems with what I was part of—we weren't doing anything wrong—and I didn't have any moral problems with my part of it. That was real, something I had to take seriously. I wasn't arresting or prosecuting anybody, but I was close enough to the action that I might as well have been. I was calling down the thunder, people were going to prison who wouldn't have if I hadn't been involved. I could live with that, but I didn't have to like it, and increasingly I didn't like it. I looked at the guys on the street, watched their faces in the forums, talked to them in private, got both intellectually and viscerally the losing game they were caught up in. They hadn't chosen this, hadn't voted for it. Zina Jacque was *right*: We'd let them down. Jimmie Mac was *right*: We weren't keeping our end of the social contract. And while they hustled and scuffled and died, we stopped them on the street and kicked their doors in and sent them to federal prison for decades. *One bullet.* I thought back to when I was starting to see the shape of the new deterrence, how *excellent* it was that the street guys gave us so many ways to get at them, how we should be able to play them like pianos, and felt ill. Except tactically, there was nothing excellent about it.

Who's winning?

We are.

No, you're not. You're losing, badly. The enforcement we were doing, at least, was surgical and effective. Most of the rest of it, which was almost all of it, I *knew* didn't work, *knew* caused endless pain.

I went to Don Stern in Boston, didn't have the backbone to say what I was really thinking. I said, not-quite-asking-the-gorgeous-girl-out style, wouldn't it be cool to bring Freddie Cardoza back? Boston's safe, it's over, it's changed. We could bring him back, get him set up, it could work. It would make a statement. I don't think that's going to happen, he said.

A lot of it was Baltimore.

Baltimore was *hell*. The worst of it was on the streets, but the rest of it was pretty bad, too.

We'd been welcomed to Baltimore with open arms: Mayor Kurt Schmoke's backing, U.S. attorney Lynne Battaglia's backing, State's Attorney Pat Jessamy's backing, Police Commissioner Tom Frazier's backing, Hathaway Ferebee's backing. It had gotten us a nice January 1998 story in the *Baltimore Sun*, describing the Boston Miracle and laying out solid support from Frazier, Jessamy, top police officers, and others. There were public launch meetings in the same spirit of togetherness. Everything seemed and felt good. Then the cameras went away.

Baltimore had the worst law enforcement politics I've ever seen. The three main players, the police department, the state's attorney's office, and the U.S. attorney's office, saw crime control as a zero-sum game: anybody gets any credit for anything, the others lose. I've been involved there off and on now for going on fifteen years, and it hasn't changed. One agency is always playing spoiler. The agency changes but the dynamic doesn't; it's like balance-of-power politics in nineteenth-century Europe, you line up with allies of the moment to make sure nobody else can succeed. I'd walked into the goddamn Hapsburg court. If we'd done our standard gang mapping on official Baltimore, it would have been easy: Everybody was beefing with everybody.

As best I could figure out, the alignment of the moment was U.S.

attorney Lynne Battaglia against State's Attorney Pat Jessamy, with Police Commissioner Frazier seemingly ranging around but mostly weighing in on Lynne's side when called for. Pat detailed a simply extraordinary assistant district attorney, Kim Morton, to be the on-site project manager, and gave us space in her offices. It sealed our doom, I think, though I had no clue at the time; it meant the project was Pat's, the credit would be Pat's, and *that* couldn't be allowed to happen. We formed up a working group of the by-now usual suspects and set to work in the spring of 1998. What had taken a year and a half to *invent* and implement in Boston, six months in Minneapolis, a couple of months in Stockton, would take almost *two years* in Baltimore: all of it grindingly fractious and painful.

What was ordinarily the easy part, the research, was bad enough. The street scene was incredible. Everywhere else we'd been, we could gather frontline folks together, huddle around a map, sort out the city's groups and turf. Baltimore was so insanely active that Anthony and Gillian had to go precinct by precinct and do each one separately. Setting it up and doing it took months. The result made your blood run cold: gangs and drug markets and homicides *everywhere*. When we looked at a year's worth of homicides, it was 303 victims and 210 suspects; we filled an auditorium with frontline officers and debriefed them for days. It cemented our schooling about "gangs": We mentioned gangs the first time and they all rose up. Baltimore didn't have gangs, they thought; department management had been pushing gangs on them, they thought; they didn't like it, and so we were management stooges, they thought. We don't care, tell us what you see, we said. *They're not gangs.* Okay, we get it. What are they? What we see elsewhere is sort of neighborhood networks. What are they here? *Neighborhood networks.* Okay, neighborhood networks it is.

Some 325 of them, with between three and four thousand key players, connected to half of all Baltimore killings. Three quarters of victims and almost 90 percent of offenders had criminal records, the highest we'd ever seen, averaging 8.5 and 9.6 priors respectively. Nearly 60 percent of all killings happened in or near a street drug market. Despite the superheated street drug scene, only about 20 percent of killings had to do with drug business; the usual beefs, vendettas, and respect killings were the order of the day. There were some new twists. There were the "stickup boys," first time we'd run across this. These were guys who made their living ripping off street dealers and stash houses; we'd come to know them as a feature of really advanced chaotic drug markets, a poor career choice, you die early and often. There were a bunch of jitney killings, unlicensed taxi drivers who transported drug dealers and got killed, or got killed by drug dealers for their cars.

(There was the old guy who walked into the emergency room with a hatchet in his head. When they X-rayed him he had not only the hatchet but two small metal objects in his skull. They lost him. Turned out the small metal objects were two old .22 slugs; he'd been shot twice decades ago, lived, the doctors had left the bullets in. He'd been hatcheted by his roommate, another old guy, over who would turn out the light. Same guy who'd shot him the first time around.)

Okay. This was to a different scale and at a higher pitch than we were used to, but we'd known that going in, this was what we needed to figure out how to deal with. *This isn't Boston*, we'd been hearing in cities all over the country. *That will never work here.* Well, this *wasn't* Boston, that's why we were there. We stepped back to something like the original Boston idea. We'd calm down the groups in the worst drug market in the city, make sure we could hold it, move on to the next one. Take back the city piece by piece, with any luck gathering credibility and momentum as we went.

We took the findings and the basic strategy to the agency heads, to Safe and Sound. There was another big formal meeting, everybody in the same place at the same time, everybody smiling. They all blessed it. Maybe they even meant it, in the moment; maybe it was more of the same public pretense. Whatever it was, it wouldn't last.

Things weren't much better in the core line-level working group we put together to handle implementing the operation. Vicious undertows were everywhere; for the first time in my work I was acutely conscious that a lot of the people in the room were armed. *Somebody's going to get shot.* The police thought that probation and parole were literally letting their guys get away with murder. The police thought the state's attorney was tanking on their cases and just letting everybody off; the state's attorney's people thought the police couldn't do police work and were bringing them garbage cases they couldn't prosecute. The worst tension, nasty thick, was between the police and U.S. attorney Lynne Battaglia's guy, and especially between the Bureau of Alcohol, Tobacco, and Firearms gun agents and Battaglia's guy. Lynne Battaglia had set up a program in her office called Project Disarm to prosecute certain gun-possession cases, cases that would normally be pursued locally, in federal court, where they would bring far higher penalties than in state court. It was a sort of institutionalization of the Freddie Cardoza idea. Unlike local prosecutors, U.S. attorneys take—"adopt," in the parlance—only those cases they want; they're free to kick them back if they wish. The police and ATF had one main beef: *The U.S. attorney won't take any cases.* Her guidelines—not legal guidelines, office guidelines—limited the gun cases she would accept to offenders with the most extreme criminal records, which in Baltimore was saying something. Not even all of those would be picked up. It was a way of cutting down on workload, but the way it was implemented made the more street-oriented players viciously angry. They thought her office kicked everything back. ATF circulated a story that her office had declined a case in which somebody had drawn down on a cop. This was not abstract; in one of our working group meetings one of our regular BPD officers was badly shaken up—somebody had just emptied a machine pistol at him in an alley.

We needed federal support, something we'd readily gotten in all our other projects, to make the Baltimore operation work. The U.S. attorney's office didn't have to do much, didn't have to take a lot of cases, but needed to be flexible, to adapt to circumstances, to make the right statement at the right time: the Freddie Cardoza case in Boston, the Bogus Boyz case in Minneapolis, putting a marker down, *We will not put up with this, you're dealing with us now.* It was clear that even in Baltimore, as bad as it was, real consequences still mattered. One of the drug guys took me to a street where he'd helped run a federal operation a couple of years earlier. *It's still quiet,* he told me, *it's like there's an electric fence around it, nobody will go near it.*

I went round and round and round with Lynne's people, and finally with Lynne herself. Things would get so bad within the working group that I went home from one meeting and set up a conference call with Lynne and her guy. This is going to fall apart, I said. Okay, she said. Under certain circumstances, when the strategy demands it and this office approves, I will allow my office to go outside the guidelines. *Great.* I went back to the next working group meeting and told everybody that the U.S. attorney's office had graciously agreed to be flexible and would depart from the guidelines when appropriate. No we won't, her guy said. I don't have any authorization to do that. I went to her and said, this has got to stop. It's going to kill the whole thing. Replace him. She did, and came to the next working group session to introduce her new guy, said, Here is my new groomsman.

It wasn't just the prosecutors. The Baltimore Police Department had overwhelmingly given itself over to low-level street drug enforcement; you could go anywhere, pretty much anytime, and scoop dealers and buyers off the street. It had deeply damaged the agency operationally. The prosecutors complained that police officers didn't even bother to show up for court, they made their arrests and vanished, the prosecutors had to cut everybody loose. Our operation needed high-quality, focused drug investigations—two or three months' worth of work that could take a drug crew off the street. If we were going to make the plan work, we needed to be able to do those in some small volume across the city. BPD couldn't do it. There turned out to be only one guy, a detective named Ed Bochniak, at least in the right place in the department, who remembered how to do that kind of police work. The department had simply forgotten how to run undercover operations, manage informants, do wiretaps.

Ed set up on some of the groups we'd identified and went to work, allied with one of Pat's people, an indefatigable prosecutor named Jill Myers. Looking forward, that clearly wasn't going to be enough; they couldn't do it by themselves. A tough-looking FBI agent was around for a while, promising a big federal wiretap—we were kind of counting on that case coming through—but he disappeared and nothing ever came of it. *The check is in the mail.* We found ourselves talking with the department about setting up training for their own officers in drug investigations, having Ed and Jill teach them how to do it again. Commissioner Frazier had made Colonel John E. Gavrilis, chief of investigations, our point man within the department; Kim and I would go to meet with him and he'd say, Don't worry, I can give you more of these operations, I can give you times five, times seven, times twelve. Ed's work wasn't itself going all that fast; one day I finally looked at Gavrilis and said, Could your people start with times one?

We weren't going to get any help from the rest of the department. There was some sort of fight going on between Gavrilis and his opposite number at patrol, Colonel Bert Shirey. Shirey was civil when we met face to face, but my new friends in the police department took delight in reporting back the obscene things he said about me when I wasn't around. (We'd made good friends with the cops by now—you know you've made it when they start giving you shit. Anthony has long hair, is a power lifter, broad and strong; I have long hair, am none of those other things. You know what they call you, Kim said. "Jesus and Fabio.")

Early in 1999 I stopped sleeping.

My insomnia had been getting steadily worse, but now something snapped. It was one of the working-level SACSI meetings in Cambridge. We had conference space in a Radcliffe building facing Cambridge Common. I ran the first day of the meeting, had dinner with the group, the DOJ folks wanted to work on something and we went back to it, I finally left at around eleven o'clock. I got home, went to bed, nothing. I ran the meeting the next day, got in my car, drove home, and arrived in my driveway not knowing how I'd gotten there. Next night, same thing. When I get sleep-deprived enough I start seeing gorgeous deeply colored geometric solids floating in the air, rich greens and cobalts and reds, glowing from deep inside. They're beautiful, I can watch them all night, while away the hours. I'd been seeing a sleep specialist at the Lahey Clinic in Burlington, went to him, said, Enough. He put me on sleeping pills. I'm not stupid about drugs, I told him, I see enough. I don't want to get in trouble. You won't be taking much, he said, and only at night. It's not a problem. They helped. I started functioning again.

It wasn't all bad. On the national front, SACSI had settled down. The early issues had been resolved, the research was getting done, the site teams were pulling together, the operations were under way. In April of 1999, the Indianapolis team brought down the Brightwood Gang, their Intervale. Thirty-three search warrants, sixteen arrests, seventy-eight guns, twelve kilos of powder cocaine, five hundred grams of crack, over $150,000 in cash. There were forums before and after. I flew out to Indianapolis and went to one. The DA's representative lost it; he'd been dealing with a horrible murder, and he laid into the offenders, you could see them shut down. The U.S. attorney's representative followed. She was respectful, businesslike. *There are things you need to understand,* she said quietly. She took ten minutes and said, These are the federal statutes, the mandatory minimums, the sentencing guidelines, this is what you get for felon in possession of a firearm, for armed career criminal, for possession of a firearm in the presence of drugs, for brandishing the firearm, for firing the firearm, for postal and wire fraud, here's how federal conspiracy works, we never have to put you with guns or drugs, you serve at least 85 percent of your time, you can be sent anywhere in the country. The probationers and parolees *applauded* her. Killings in Indianapolis dropped abruptly in April. It got so quiet the SACSI team thought about moving on to domestic violence.

(Columbine happened in April, too, chickenshit Dylan Klebold and Eric Harris playing dress-up and shooting thirty-three people because *they were mean.* Public reaction: black kids kill people, godless superpredators; white kids kill people, video games, subtle problems at home, big high schools, bad medication. I gave an interview to NPR saying that in all the years of the youth-violence epidemic there were exactly *no* incidents of inner-city black kids shooting up a school for no reason, which meant that inner-city black kids used guns more responsibly than suburban white kids. I don't believe they ran it. The Departments of Justice and Education threw together a hasty meeting of youth-violence and school experts at the JW Marriott Hotel in Washington, D.C. The attorney general herself sat in in the afternoon. The JW Marriott is built around a tall central atrium, the conference rooms on the bottom floor overlooked by terraces of balconies. I was standing just outside the doorway to our conference room after the meeting broke, talking to two of the other academics, when a red dot of laser light started playing across the three of us. *Gun sight,* my hindbrain said, and I rolled back through the door, around the corner, and onto the floor before I knew I was moving. The other two stood there amused. *Laser pointer,* they said. You'd better hope you're right, I thought. It upset me enough that I called one of my ATF friends: Did I overreact? *I would have gotten there first—you would have been lying on top of me,* he said.)

The published, peer-reviewed, quasi-experimental evaluations of the Indianapolis intervention showed a 34 percent reduction in total homicide, a 38 percent reduction in gang homicide. Gun assaults in the city's most active neighborhood went down 53 percent. Gun homicide in High Point dropped from fourteen in 1998 to two in 1999. In Portland, murder went down 36 percent citywide; victims under age twenty-five went down 82 percent. In Winston-Salem, gun violence was down substantially in SACSI's project neighborhoods. In New Haven, a 32 percent decrease in violent gun crimes and 45 percent decrease in "shots fired" calls citywide. (The Memphis team, using other means entirely, cut rape in half in Memphis, a vote of confidence for the original problem-solving idea.)

Looks like it *will* travel.

Looks like it *will* work here.

By the summer of 1999, more than a year after we started, even Baltimore seemed like it was finally coming together. Kim and Hathaway and Jill Myers worked ceaselessly: getting the core law enforcement work organized, rubbing balm on injured egos, lining up support in the business community and in Annapolis, drawing in community partners, organizing social-service providers, managing the media. We were tight, had our own inside jokes: "Kim's favorite restaurant" was the hot dog stand out in front of the state's attorney's office. We had designed what the partners had decided to call "Operation Safe Neighborhoods." Jill and the law enforcement team had a set of cases ready to go in east Baltimore, the Big Boyz and Starz groups. All the agencies were lined up. Kim and I had traveled to Annapolis and gotten Lieutenant Governor Kathleen Townsend enlisted; she was on board. We were preparing for the first call-in.

Then, in June, I got panicked word from my law enforcement partners that Lynne Battaglia was about to have police officers start handing out fifty thousand business-size cards all over Baltimore advertising her gun prosecution program, Project Disarm, and the federal gun laws: "Carry a gun. Go to jail." The cards were modeled on something called Project Exile in Richmond, Virginia, where the U.S. attorney had hugely increased his intake of gun prosecutions and advertised it with the cards, television spots, and billboards. Exile looked to have brought homicide down and was enjoying a real vogue in Congress. (The reductions, it would later appear, were spurious; Exile probably hadn't worked in Richmond, and didn't seem to work in the other places it was implemented.) Lynne's Disarm had taken 220 cases over about the last five years; police took *thousands* of guns off Baltimore's streets every year. The cards were a lie. *Never write a check you can't cash.* I tracked Battaglia down by phone. You can't do this, I said. *Everybody's looking at the violence in Baltimore*, she said. *I have to be seen to be doing something.* I was seething. You won't take the cases. You won't even take the cases that ATF and BPD are trying to give you now. The cards say if you get caught with a gun you'll go federal, and it's not true. Just at the time we're trying to get these core messages out that *are* true, that we've gone to all this trouble to *make* true, you're going to make us look like idiots. *I don't have any problem with it*, Battaglia said. *I've made it clear to Congress how the program will run.* I'm sure Baltimore's thugs will get that clarification from the *Federal Record*, I said. *Don't talk to me like that*, she said. I finally got her to agree to restrict the cards to the police district where we were planning to launch.

I might as well not have bothered. We'd orchestrated a formal public announcement of the launch of Operation Safe Neighborhoods: the mayor, the police department, the state's attorney's office, the U.S. attorney's office, probation, parole, ATF, the lieutenant governor, fourteen city, state, and federal agencies in all. It was scheduled for mid-July. We were finally going operational. Just before, preparing to go down, I got word: the U.S. attorney had reached out and told all the federal agencies not to attend. The *Baltimore Sun* had just run yet another series of pieces on troubles in Pat Jessamy's office and between her office and the police department. Lynne yanked her own office and all the other feds out of the Safe Neighborhoods launch. "I'm not going to go to a news conference to announce a program until I'm clear that it has a chance of working," Battaglia told the *Sun* afterward. "All of us have to give the public assurances that what we are doing is totally collaborative and that we can make a difference. This is a massive undertaking. None of us want to be part of a potential failure." It was as raw as anything I've ever seen, before or since. The *Baltimore Sun* was blistering. Operation Safe Neighborhoods "was supposed to show that deaths and violence could be reduced if everyone pulled together, united by a common mission. Instead, the effort is now in danger of becoming a monument to the jurisdictional disputes, turf fights and bickering that have demoralized and paralyzed effective law enforcement in Baltimore for far too long." It would be six months before we were ready to go operational, time spent rebuilding relationships and working out formal interagency understandings that had been handled through common sense and consensus everywhere else. Anthony Braga backed way off from the project;

we'd been at it in Baltimore for a year and a half now, we were pushing harder and harder, and we were hardly getting anywhere: Everybody hated everybody else. He had better things to do.

I was beyond crumbled around the edges. By now there were some pretty large chunks breaking off. I was exhausted and couldn't sleep again. I could work and do what I absolutely had to do but there wasn't anything at all left over. I was going to more doctors, something wasn't right, but we couldn't figure it out. Emotionally, I was played out. Clark Abt is a famous Cambridge scientist and entrepreneur, founded Abt Associates, a respected consulting firm. He'd sold his firm, was spending a lot of time working with troubled kids in Boston, and I'd gotten to know him slightly. He came to see me at the Kennedy School. *I'm teaching these wonderful kids,* he said. *They're in terrible shape.* I know, I told him. *They're in terrible danger, they get hurt all the time, they're worried about being shot.* I know, I told him. *What do I do?* I don't know, I told him. I don't really think there's very much you can do at the individual level—that's why I do what I do, try to change these bigger dynamics, reset the context. *But they're so bleak, so hopeless, they need something in their lives,* he said. Clark, I said, you're doing wonderful work, I admire you for it, but I really can't do this. I can't do anything about it, I can't offer you anything, and I don't have the resources to take this in. *But their mothers are all on drugs, they don't have anybody to take care of them,* he said. I know. Stop it. Please. *I had them write raps, the raps are so revealing, let me read you some of their raps,* he said. I got up and left, got in my car and went home, found myself parked at a light with tears streaming down my face.

I was still giving Baltimore everything I had. By now I could hardly stand to be in the city; I'd come down, push through the day, collapse in my hotel room, nothing else—the meetings were all I could handle. But once again we seemed to be getting somewhere. By the end of 1999, we were ready to move, this time in Park Heights in northwest Baltimore. In early December, I came in for a working group meeting. My people were shocky, silent. A home-invasion crew had wiped out five women in a row house in northeast Baltimore. Three of them were three generations of one family. Mary Helen Collien, fifty-six. Her daughter, Mary McNeil Matthews, thirty-nine. Her granddaughter, Makisha Jenkins, eighteen.

The others were two family friends, Linda Spearman and Trennell Alston. The newspapers said the massacre was intended to make a point about who was to deal where; rumors inside law enforcement said the killers had gone in for a shipment that turned out not to be there. Whatever. I sat there in our conference room, frozen, and thought, *We should have stopped this. We know how to stop it. We should not have let this happen. This is on us.*

They were buried in Whitesville, North Carolina, where Mary Alice McNeil, Mary Helen Collien's mother, had raised her. She'd lost another great-grandson, Tavaris McNeil, found shot to death in Baltimore the day after the women were killed. "We live in a nation so proud, so full of opportunities, so strong with mighty armies, navies, and all matters of technology," said the Rev. Isaac B. Horton, pastor of Friendship Baptist Church, at their service. "How could we produce such a day as this?"

I can answer that, Rev. Horton.

It was around then that I began to think, I know we can control the bad guys. The bad guys are not the problem.

I don't know how to control the good guys.

Right before Christmas, I got a call from Hathaway at home. Martin O'Malley's just said on live TV that you won't talk to him.

Martin O'Malley was Baltimore's mayor-elect.

O'Malley had been a dark-horse candidate, a city councilman, for Kurt Schmoke's empty mayoral seat. The two leading candidates had self-destructed, each in his own way, and O'Malley won the election. He had run on a crime-control platform and had been studying the New York City strategy and cultivating two of its architects, Jack Maple and John Linder. I knew both of them through Bill Bratton, and liked and respected them. My Baltimore team started working to fill O'Malley in on what we were doing and to get me a meeting with him. The day I went down for it I got word that Maple and Linder would be there as well. I'd gotten dispensation from my law enforcement partners to speak frankly to the mayor-elect about their plans and activities; I was not empowered to do so in front of outsiders. I reached out, got advice, and was urged to stand down. I called O'Malley's office and pleaded sickness. We had tried, over and over since, to get back on his calendar. Now this.

Hathaway reached out to him; he wanted me in Baltimore on December 26. I went. Hathaway, Kim, Jill, a couple of others from my team. Jack Maple joined us in the waiting room. I hadn't seen him for a while, we caught up, talked about mutual friends. He'd been working in New Orleans, and we talked about that. We went into O'Malley's office, shook hands with the mayor-elect, met some of his transition staff, sat down, and Maple ripped me limb from limb. *When's your team going to be operational?* It's not really a team, it's a strategy group that *How many drug investigations can your team do?* It's not really an investigative group, it's putting together *How big an impact do you expect?* Well, what we've seen in other places *We did better than Boston in New York. When do you expect to see impact?* We hope to be operational inside of six weeks, and we usually see impact *I'll have the city under control by the end of January.* It went on for an hour. O'Malley smiled and read his mail. When Maple was done, everybody got up and pretended that what had just happened, hadn't. I walked around that table and shook O'Malley's hand. It's an honor to meet you, sir, I said. If I can ever answer any questions you have about how this is supposed to work, please let me know.

We left, stunned. I think what you did at the end will make a big difference, one of my group said. I think that's what he needed to hear. Over the next couple of weeks his office sent signals—don't stop, don't give up. One of his top people took me out to lunch. Hard to get your point across when you can't finish a sentence, he said. He's figuring out what he wants to do. Hang in there. Word came that Eddie Norris was coming in as the new commissioner; that was encouraging, too. Norris had been deputy chief for operations at the NYPD; I knew him, liked him, had friends who respected him a great deal. He'd been part of a process to implement Ceasefire in New York that had been sponsored by the U.S. attorney's office and made it all the way to the commissioner before being sidelined. Hopeful.

We held the Park Heights call-in in February 2000. After more than two years, Operation Safe Neighborhoods was finally live. Probation and parole and BPD had hit the streets to deliver the call-in notices hand to hand. Most of the "supervisees" weren't at their addresses of record; lots of the addresses of record didn't even *exist*. The streets started to buzz; guys were calling their POs and saying, Just thought I should check in, let you know where I am. We went through the same heart-in-mouth unease as always: *Will anybody show up?* A lot of the BPD guys were absolutely convinced nobody would. "They always do," I said, but I knew it didn't mean they would here, this time. I was miserable. They did, though. They always do. On the day, almost thirty probationers and parolees walked into the Wabash District Court near Park Heights. One of my BPD friends came over. I can't believe my eyes, he said. Maybe this *will* work. They were, if anything, even more beat-up looking, rawer, than I was used to. Jill Myers was there. She was not happy. "Talk about us versus them," she remembers. "This was a room full of shooters and killers; I was the one who'd put half of them away." They sat, parkas and puffy down jackets, stared their see-nothing, care-nothing stares.

They heard law enforcement say, We will protect you like one of our own; somebody hurts you, it's like somebody killed a cop. They heard about a recent crackdown where a key guy had gone federal for a single heroin sale. They were handed flyers with the stop-it message on one side and where to get a wide range of help—drug treatment, remedial education, more, on the other. City officials told them where to go to get started on job placement.

They heard from Bishop Douglas Miles, a leader in Baltimore's Interdenominational Ministerial Alliance and one of the most prominent civil-rights leaders in the city. I believe in you, he said. I believe in what we're doing here today. Things are desperate, we need jobs, this city needs so much. But *we have to stop killing each other*. I'm not working for the police, he said. But I would rather see you locked up than see you kill someone, or see you be killed.

Rev. Eleanor Bryant, pastor at Agape Miracle Church in Park Heights, walked to the front, small, frail, stood with a cane. And stood. And stood. And stood. The room was silent.

And then she began to sing a hymn. I didn't know it. The thugs knew it. They rose to their feet and sang with her. Beautifully.

We *do* do that here.

"For a moment there was honesty in the room," Hathaway Ferebee says. She mingled with the men we'd called in when it was over. "They were saying, 'The party's over.'" There was a palpable change in the neighborhood after the call-in. "People noticed it," Hathaway says. "'Oh my God, what is going on?'"

But it was all downhill from there. Operation Safe Neighborhoods was dead, it just didn't know it yet. O'Malley didn't want it, didn't like it, wanted New York–style zero tolerance in Baltimore. He got it. The Baltimore Police Department started arresting everybody in sight. When the courts expressed uncertainty about how they were going to process everybody, O'Malley sent Maryland's Chief Judge of the Court of Appeals Robert M. Bell hand-drawn cartoons of a stick-figure bad guy arrested by a stick-figure police officer, taken before a stick-figure prosecutor, and then to a line-drawing courtroom.

O'Malley did bring Eddie Norris down from New York. I believed that he'd come to play. Lots of police executives leave big departments and go to smaller ones as a sort of working retirement; that wasn't Eddie. But I also thought that he didn't know what he was getting into. Police in New York tend to think that they've seen the biggest elephant there is, that no place else can rise to that level. They're wrong. Pound for pound, there are worse places than New York: worse on the ground, worse politically, worse racially. Baltimore's one of them. After he'd been around a little while, I'd go into his office and he'd close the door and we'd say to each other, I don't *believe* this place.

Operation Safe Neighborhoods hung on life support for a bit. There was both enforcement and community follow-up work to the original call-in in Park Heights, and call-ins—the partnership started to call them "sit-downs"—in the Cherry Hill and Oliver neighborhoods. Maybe it would have worked. Anthony found a 74 percent reduction in shootings and a 22 percent reduction in homicide in the five months after the Park Heights call-in, relative to the year before. But it got no real backing from the mayor or the police department, the working group fell apart, the tenuous interagency relationships fell apart. The politics got even nastier, O'Malley in open public warfare with Pat Jessamy and a new U.S. attorney. Kim and Hathaway struggled to keep something together, but there wasn't much they could do. In my field notes for Baltimore is a page, late March or early April 2000, on what was going on with the project. Halfway down the page, it reads

- Interagency/personal rivalries
  - There is no "criminal justice system"
  - Interagency sabotage
  - Intra-agency sabotage

O'Malley's strategy didn't work. By 2006, Baltimore's homicide rate was behind only Detroit's for major cities. Norris was gone by then, having pleaded guilty to federal charges that he'd used a discretionary fund in the commissioner's office for cases of liquor, lingerie for multiple mistresses, and luxury hotels on dirty trips to New York. Turns out he *had* come to play. Eddie had better things to do while Baltimore bled than run the police department. The federal case turned on flipping his chief of staff, whose apartment Norris used for nooners. His wife accompanied him on his first visit to federal court, but not on his last one, when the government was going to introduce the lingerie into evidence. He's now a talk-show host in Baltimore, where he holds forth on . . . criminal justice policy. Any time a black ex-con who can't get a job because of his criminal record complains to you, tell him Eddie Norris made it and he can, too.

More than six hundred people had been murdered in Baltimore since we started two years earlier. Martin O'Malley went on to be elected governor. Lynne Battaglia got a judgeship. Tom Frazier got a senior Justice Department post.

I wasn't around to see Safe Neighborhoods die. In May of 2000, I fell apart. I gave a lecture before the board of my center at the Kennedy School—later everybody there said I was perfectly coherent—went home, and that was it. I didn't have anything left: couldn't think, couldn't work, couldn't figure out how to take care of myself. I called Anthony and asked him to take over my classes, called my parents in Maine and asked them to come get me. The next day I was on my way north.

It was the work, mostly, and some bad things going on privately, somewhat. It also turned out to be the sleeping medication. I figured it out doing research on my mom's computer. Thank God for the Internet, or I'd still be sitting on the Maine coast. Long-term use of the lorazepam

I'd been prescribed is very much contraindicated: Some people get very, very sick. It was all there: the slow-building long-term exhaustion, the emotional volatility, the sleeplessness, which it turns out is eventually *caused* by the meds. (Ironically, one of the medical articles that tipped me off was about how the entire family of medications had been withdrawn from use in prisons, because it was clearly linked to increases in violence.) I read all this on a Sunday, ran it down for the on-call physician at the Lahey Clinic. "No, I don't think so," she said. "These medications don't do that." I called my sister at Johns Hopkins. Give me a minute, she said. She called back in a couple of hours. "I've talked to some of my pharmacist friends who know detox," she said. "They say you're in big trouble." I was. I had what is bloodlessly called an iatrogenic condition: *caused by treatment*. (I was in interesting company; the same thing, on the same meds, happened to Stevie Nicks.) You can't just stop taking the stuff; you can have seizures and die. You have to taper off gradually, which brings its own suite of horrific symptoms. I wasn't able to go home until August, and I wasn't really right for a year.

It gave me plenty of time to think about the work.

Some of that was about my own orientation. I had let myself be seduced by the narrative that I could make things happen, anywhere, against all odds. Baltimore exposed that as the hubris that it was. Time to let that go. I had felt a sense of responsibility for the problems on the ground, and what I could see could be done about them, and that had now clearly just about killed me. I'd have to work on that.

Some of it was what was going on with the projects in the various cities.

They were all falling apart.

Not literally all of them. Some were healthy, even thriving. But in some of our best cities, the work was dead or dying. Minneapolis was done. Anthony and I had turned things over to PERF and the city, and within a couple of years it was as if it had never happened. Ed McGarrell was no longer giving Indianapolis his undivided attention and things were unraveling there; it too would essentially go away altogether. Stockton would soon follow; Operation Peacekeeper was healthy, and effective, until a new gang commander discontinued the call-ins and the interagency meetings. The SACSI interventions dissolved in New Haven and Portland. In all of them, the killing went back up.

Worst of all, Ceasefire was dead in Boston. Paul Joyce had, deservedly, been promoted to deputy superintendent. One of his first actions was to remove Gary French from the Youth Violence Strike Force in January of 2000. *Score settled.* There were no more Ceasefire operations, no more forums. There was more to what happened than that one move: The streets had been so quiet that the Ceasefire Working Group had lost some of its focus; the celebrity and the unequal attention and the unequal *response* to the attention had caused rifts; people had been promoted and replaced and otherwise moved on. But Joyce finished the job. Homicide immediately began to creep back up. In 1998, there were fifteen youth homicides in Boston; in 1999, there were fifteen. In 2000, there were twenty-six. Overall homicide had continued to fall under Ceasefire, down to thirty-one in 1999; it went to forty in 2000, more than doubled to sixty-eight in 2001. Joyce took it in stride. "Most likely, we've seen our best days," he told *Governing* magazine. "Crime will move up. It's how you monitor that and how you deal with that as crime trends start to move up again." The killing would soon be at almost pre-Ceasefire levels.

It wasn't a miracle. If the work doesn't get done, it won't work. If the operations don't exist, the work won't get done. I sat at home, emerging from my daze, and remembered something I'd read long ago, a comment from an engineer in the nuclear power industry. "Our power plants are perfect," he'd said, or something to that effect. "People just can't operate them."

I don't know how to control the good guys.

Maybe it *doesn't* work.
Maybe it *won't* travel.

Across the Race Divide

My people at the Kennedy School, Anthony, Mark Moore, Frank Hart-mann, huddled up, formed a defensive line, and kept the world at bay, gave me space to put myself back together. I took leave; Frank had talked the National Institute of Justice into giving me a small grant to write up the new crime-control theory and do the scholarly thinking that the flat-out fieldwork had left no time for. I set up at home, massive stacks of books and journal articles, read a lot, thought a lot.

I thought I was studying deterrence, finding the junctions and the disjunctions between the old ways of doing deterrence and the new ways we'd figured out: *Tell them to stop.* It was fascinating. Powerful old ideas took on new shapes, dusty notions seemingly fit only for corners of the ivory tower turned out to have huge voltage on the street, the things we'd seen on the street were illuminated, clear and sharp-edged, by brilliant but near-forgotten scholarship. Pieces clicked into place, footnotes led to new books and new articles and new pieces. As they found their places, something big and new started to take shape. There *was* a whole new way of doing crime control, the ideas behind Ceasefire *did* make bigger, broader sense, there *was* real power and potential here. The little NIJ essay would turn into a full-blown book on the new deterrence.

Which turned out not at all to be the point. The research, the reflection—all the deterrence cleverness aside—led straight to another piece of the puzzle, another revelation, this one also hiding in plain sight. It would be about community, communities, the community of law enforcement, the community of the most dangerous black neighborhoods; about how they saw each other, influenced each other, drove each other. It would go straight back to the twisted awfulness of Nickerson Gardens and all the other Nickerson Gardenses across the country, show that to be even more awful than it appeared. It would be about drugs and the drug war: how we were fighting it, how we couldn't win it, and what that meant for all of us. It would suggest the next step beyond Ceasefire: how to deal with drugs, how to truly make the streets safe in America's Nickerson Gardens. But it was more than that. It went to the damage we were doing to each other in those places and how we could stop doing that damage, something as far beyond Ceasefire as Ceasefire had been beyond mopping up after gang killings.

And it would lead to the place in all this of race. It would say, If you want to get beyond *stop it*, if you want real, lasting change, if you want the cops and the neighborhoods and the streets to really see each other, hear each other, trust each other, you have to face how where we are now is infused with racial history, racial understandings, racial misunderstandings.

And it would lead to a way to face that, and move beyond.

It started slowly, and in the same way all the other work, the field work, had started. *We know what's going on out there.* It was true in the scholarship, too; the pieces were all there, they just needed to be assembled in different ways. The most basic element of Ceasefire—*Tell them to stop*—was a core element of classic deterrence theory. Frank Zimring and Gordon Hawkins, *Deterrence: The Legal Threat in Crime Control*, 1973: "the deterrent threat may perhaps best be viewed as a form of advertising." Let offenders know what the law is, what's coming, they may respond; if they don't know what's coming, they can't possibly respond. It was just that in practice, everybody promptly forgot this. Tommy Farmer was amazed, in 1995, when he became the first to be prosecuted and sentenced under the new federal three-strikes law: He had no idea it even *existed*, he told the *New York Times*. "I ain't never heard anything about the law until they applied it on me. I never thought anything like this would happen to me, man." He was not, he said, alone. "It is going to make a few guys think," he told the *Times*, "but some other guys don't even watch TV or care; they don't know nothing about the law." As I write this he's sitting, serving life, in a federal prison in Terre Haute, Indiana. Would a letter from the feds—*we've changed the law, thought you should know*—have both stopped his offending and kept him out of prison? The literature said quite possibly yes: It was full of examples in which direct notice had produced compliance. The literature was even full of examples of what it called "anticipatory benefits," announcements that had produced compliance *before* laws or enforcement practice changed: The publicity alone was enough to get results.

So, *Tell them to stop*—not as absurd as it sounded.

Tell them to stop because shooting people is *wrong*, because your excuses for shooting people are wrong? Not so absurd, either. There was an overwhelming consensus in the literature that what social scientists called "informal social control"—shame, conscience, guilt, what your friends think, what your mom thinks, what your community thinks—meant far more than "formal social control": cops, courts, probation. Most people do what they think is right, most of the time. They don't have to be bullied into it by the police. Most of the time, when they're on the fence, it's not the police that sway them, it's that their friends and family and girlfriends will disapprove. People and communities, even rough ones, mostly control themselves. Good norms are pretty often there, even in very rough people—*Killing's wrong*, my Boston gang member had told me—so having people they respect reinforce them, and take away their excuses for violating them, can matter.

(Try to get the cops to see this. You can go through the logic, go through the research, connect the dots, it doesn't matter, they are not having it. When I was back on the road I finally came up with something that works. Room full of cops. *Show of hands, please, everybody who was really afraid of the cops growing up, please raise your hand*. Room of a hundred cops, three, four, five will. *Show of hands, please, everybody who was really afraid of your mother, please raise your hand*. Every hand goes up. My hand goes up, the AV guy's hand goes up, the people replacing the coffee raise their hands. "I'm *still* afraid of my mother," somebody will say. *There you go*, I say. *Everything you need to know about informal social control*. Communities have tools law enforcement can but dream of. Years later, as I put the deterrence manuscript in final form, I came across the story of the women of Pereira, Colombia, who announced to their *narcotrafficante* husbands and boyfriends that they were going on "crossed-legs strike": Turn in your guns, or you're cut off. Some of the men did. "We need our women, and you'll change for your women," one told *CBS News*.)

Offenders have their *own* standards, their own norms against bad behavior, that they enforce on each other? An abundant literature said, absolutely. A study of the huge crime decline in New York, led by drug-market ethnographer Bruce Johnson, found that one driving force was young crack dealers' *own* rules against violence and smoking crack. They'd deal, but they wanted things quiet. They had seen what violence and addiction had done to the previous generation, and they didn't like it. They didn't want to act that way themselves, and they'd refuse to work with people who were violent, used crack, or drugged and drank too much. There's similar evidence of older Chicago gang members shopping crazy young gunslingers to the cops: They bring heat, it's bad for business.

Gang members come forward to shut down the Buckshot Crew: *They're going to ruin it for everybody.*

Not such a stretch.

So. Communities have standards, offenders have standards, sensible people want to be safe and quiet. Terrific, everything should be okay. But it's most definitely not: We've got Nickerson Gardens and Tiffany Moore and one in two hundred young black men dying every year in Rochester's hot neighborhoods. What's going on?

One answer was *groups*. Vast amounts of theory and research from all kinds of different fields converged on the same core idea: Groups are important, groups are at the heart of a lot of crime problems; groups behave in very special ways, often in self-destructive ways. I made my way to a brilliant book by David Matza, once standard reading in criminology, now nearly forgotten. A slim little volume, 1964, *Delinquency and Drift*. Tells you everything you'll ever need to know about gangs, just about literally.

One of Matza's big ideas: *drift*. People don't sit down and decide to become gang members. They don't think it through, add up the pluses and minuses, and make a calculation to sign up. They ease into it, do some things, meet some people, ease back out, ease back in again, do some more things, find themselves on one side of a divide they can't easily cross again, and there they are, fully involved. Like drifting into being a high school dropout: It's not a conscious decision to work crap jobs for the rest of your life. Or drifting into law school: You're out of college, no idea what to do, take the LSAT, and forty years later you've spent your life doing probate. One day you're hanging with your boys, seems cool, got thug love, next day they've done a drive-by and *that* crew is after *your* crew, which means *you*, and there's not a thing in this life you can do about it. It happens, it's very real, it's consequential, but it doesn't necessarily imply careful calculation or, crucially, wholehearted commitment.

Matza's next big idea: *pluralistic ignorance*, one of the oldest concepts in social psychology. Here is a notion that will change your life, let me tell you, help you make sense of the world. August, big formal meeting, everybody's wearing business clothes, the men in suits and ties, every single one miserable. Nobody's going to come to the next meeting in short sleeves. If somebody does, everybody else around the table's going to punish him for doing something *they'd* all like to do. Pluralistic ignorance is the condition of *everybody in a group believing everybody else in the group believes something nobody in the group believes*. It happens all the time and explains a great deal of manifest stupidity in all walks of life. Gang members don't have written codes of conduct, Matza said. They figure things out from each other. Somebody shoots a little girl off a porch, mistake, everybody's afraid to say anything, *That's fucked up*, they don't want to be the only one. Nobody says anything. Everybody in the gang sees nobody in the gang saying anything. Everybody continues to act like it's okay to kill little girls in stupid respect beefs. Everybody's belief that everybody else thinks it's okay gets reinforced. Every single gang member may be thinking to himself, *I hate this*, nobody says anything, nobody knows. Nothing changes. Get them alone

Killing's wrong

and you hear what they really think. They never hear it from each other. If they do hear it from somebody brave enough, the group will shut him down, the *group* still thinks he's the only one, the mistake is reinforced still more.

Matza: *Groups are different; behavior doesn't imply commitment.*

It works *across* groups, too. Another old, basic idea: *fundamental attribution error*. We see somebody do something and we're inclined to say, He *chose* that, wanted it, it's an expression of who he is, his character. We're *not* inclined to say, Huh, maybe he didn't want to, got forced into it, had no other choice. We infer, attribute, intent and disposition on the basis of behavior. It can be deeply, terribly wrong. Cops see that little girl shot, they think, *These kids are monsters, no respect for human life.* They don't see that there was somebody shooting at *them*, they were terrified, the kid who pulled the trigger wanted nothing to do with it, he had his friends pushing on him, he puts the gun down *everybody's* going to turn on him. The gangs see the cops putting their friends face-down on the street, they think, *The police don't like black people*, they don't see how hard they're trying to protect the community, how scared they are, somebody shot at them last week but they held their fire, they're still shaking, they know what they're doing isn't working but they can't think of anything else.

It was the central error of *Body Count*, of the whole toxic super-predator idea. They're doing terrible things, so they're terrible people; these communities are doing terrible things, so they're terrible communities. Wrong. First part, terrible things, yes. Conclusion, terrible people, terrible communities, no. Wrong. Not that simple.

Now we're almost there.

It can happen *between communities*.

We tend to think high-crime neighborhoods don't care about, are more tolerant of crime. It's not true. Fundamental attribution error. They're *less* tolerant. In 1998, Rob Sampson and Dawn Bartusch published a paper in *Law and Society Review*, Rob's the chair of the sociology department at Harvard now. We've been inferring attitudes from behavior, they said. We see violent neighborhoods, we think there's a subculture of violence, normlessness, anomie. We think the people there support what's going on, approve of it, at least don't disapprove. That's wrong, they said. Looking at a massive, detailed data set of interviews with Chicago residents across various neighborhoods, they found that blacks were far *more* disapproving of crime and violence than whites (Latinos were even more disapproving), that people in poor, troubled neighborhoods were far *more* disapproving than people in affluent neighborhoods. It stands to reason, we shouldn't be surprised: They're the people suffering the most, of *course* they don't like it. The notion that the hot neighborhoods don't mind the death and destruction is pretty close to a blood libel.

It wasn't what Sampson and Bartusch called "tolerance of deviance" that characterized high-crime neighborhoods. They didn't think what was going on was okay. It was what Sampson and Bartusch called "legal cynicism." It was that they *didn't like the police.* Didn't trust them, didn't think they'd help. Where legal cynicism was high, violence was high. There turns out to be a direct link between that alienation and crime. When the face of the law is ugly, the law's ugly. When the law's ugly, the things law stands for are undercut. When the cops, the agents of the law saying, *Don't shoot, don't deal,* are offensive, the community won't say those things with them. When the law's ugly, people don't go to the law when they need help. People handle things on their own.

They do it because they don't believe in the law. The law don't work, never will, in my neighborhood.

And, finally, the other, perfectly symmetrical attribution error: the neighborhoods looking at the cops and the larger outside world. Like everything else along this road, it was hiding in plain sight. I'd been hearing it literally my whole time in this world. The community organizer, the day after I walked Nickerson Gardens. *The government is doing this to us. This isn't just happening. This is a conspiracy. Because black single mothers are succeeding, and the government of the United States can't stand that.* I had not been able to take it in. I had heard it, in the years to come, over and over and over: on the street, in community meetings, in living rooms, in the offices of elected officials. John Klofas interviewed drug dealers in Rochester; *they* thought the only way they could be operating was because the police were choosing not to stop them. It took me the better part of twenty years to really hear it, to take it seriously, instead of having my brain go, *tilt.* Most white folks don't really hear it. If we did, and gave the blacks saying it the respect of at least taking them seriously, we would say, The government would never do something like that. To which many blacks would reply, But the government has done things *just* like that, and not so goddamned long ago, either. And they would be *right*—we'll get to that in a minute—which might not advance the conversation very far but would at least give us white folks pause. But we do not hear it.

To hear it, it helps to be close to the neighborhoods, but you don't have to be. In 1990, the National Urban League issued a report on the state of black America. On drugs and the black community: "genocide." In a 2007 *New York Times* article on a Harlem activist group of mothers of murdered children, Timothy Williams wrote matter-of-factly of one mother's church-basement discussion of "conspiracies to flood poor neighborhoods with guns and drugs." The Rev. Wright, *God damn America*.

This is just the conventional wisdom in the hottest neighborhoods. The drugs and the guns don't come from here. Somebody's bringing them in. The government could keep them out if it wanted. The dealers are standing out in plain sight, for heaven's sake, and nobody's doing anything about it. We see the police cars drive right by. We call 911 on the crack house next door, nobody ever does anything. Somebody else is making all the money; our kids certainly aren't getting rich. The white folks drive in and buy the dope, but they're not getting arrested and their doors aren't getting kicked in. There's more dope in the suburbs than there is here, but the police and the government don't care about that. The CIA invented crack, everybody knows that, Ollie North needed money to fund the contras. And look at him—our kids try to put food on the table and they go to federal prison; he pisses all over the Constitution and he's got a talk show. (And since I'm going to say in a moment that they're wrong, I'd like to note that on the commit-a-major-crime-and-get-a-talk-show point, they're right. And add Eddie Norris to the list. And Buddy Cianci in Providence.)

This isn't the only thing that people think; there are other narratives, important ones, but in the hottest neighborhoods this is the dominant *public* narrative: The government brings the drugs in so they can put our kids in jail so the cops will have work and the private prisons can make their dividends. And it's not just the hot neighborhoods where people believe this. As I write this, civil-rights lawyer Michelle Alexander's book *The New Jim Crow* is getting a lot of well-deserved attention. America had slavery and we got rid of that, she says, and America came up with Jim Crow. We got rid of Jim Crow, and America came up with the drug war and mass incarceration. "Like Jim Crow (and slavery), mass incarceration is a tightly networked system of laws, policy, customs, and institutions that operate collectively to ensure the subordinate status of a group defined largely by race."

Sitting there in Boston, I finally saw how Ceasefire had papered this over. Everybody—cops, communities, gangs—was so desperate about the killing that they'd come together despite all this. Working together to stop the killing even did something to bridge the gulf. It changed the narratives by letting each party see that the other wasn't what had been thought. The cops weren't trying to lock everybody up, the community hated the killing, the gangs hated the killing. But it only went so far. It didn't reset everything. It needed constant propping up, it was still mostly the outside reaching in and trying to keep the lid on. Lose that and it all went away.

And I saw, even more clearly, what had been happening as I tried to get the drug work under way.

I'd never stopped trying to figure out the drug strategy, the notion I'd had early in the Boston Ceasefire days that we could somehow map it onto drugs. Ceasefire, it was now pretty clear, *worked*, all other issues with it aside: It hugely reduced the violence. But even in the worst neighborhoods, the killings were, relatively, rare. The drug markets were *all the time*. I didn't see anybody shot in Nickerson Gardens. Its time-lapse implosion was drug stuff. Young men with guns owned the place, and white folks treated it like some landfill where they could wander in, drop the larger weight of the misery they spawned, and wander back out unburdened. It was bad enough on its own; it was also one of the main drivers that would bring the violence back if Ceasefire lost its focus. When Anthony mapped gang turf in Boston, this was basically what he'd been keying out: Boston's gangs *were* drug crews, the turf pretty much *was* their drug zones. Less than 4 percent of the city drove about a quarter of the city's serious crime. *Reported* crime. In real life, way, way more.

When you get behind closed doors in law enforcement, you learn: Nobody thinks they can win the drug war. Nobody. They may believe in it; may believe that they're doing God's work taking sociopathic scumbags off the street; may believe that they're holding back the tide of something even worse; may believe, every day and every year, every life spent on the job, that they're doing an important job well.

May not. We'll get to that.

I've never spoken to anybody, federal, state, local, who thinks they can win.

Not anybody. They didn't pick this fight. The politicians did. Richard Nixon didn't go to the police in Baltimore and say, I'm about to declare war on drugs, what do you think? What strategy, what assets, what order of battle will it take to win? He just did it. The cops, the prosecutors, the parole officers with their cups of warm piss: They're draftees. Behind closed doors, they've got the same attitude toward brass as draftees ever have. Behind closed doors, it's a given, been a given as long as I've been around.

Law enforcement looks at drugs and sees absolutely nothing they can do. They can't keep drugs from being produced, in Peru or Mexico or a grow house in Arcata. They can't keep the stuff out of the country, muled in or driven through tunnels or shipped by sea in the new cartel submarines. They can't keep it from being distributed. They can't stop it from moving to the streets, to the gangs and the drug crews. Can't keep it from being sold, can't stop young men from wanting cool easy money, or get them jobs, or fix their schools. They can't help people with their addictions or stop them from just wanting to get high. They see no point of entry to making any of it work, no way to bring the chaos under control, no alternative except surrender, which they simply will not do. At the local level, a lot of departments are brutally frank behind closed doors: Drug enforcement is all public relations. They need to show activity. Somebody calls their city councillor, the city councillor calls the chief, the cops have to do something. Nobody expects it to make any difference at all.

Who's winning? Not us.

I thought we could do better.

Ceasefire basically disciplined the drug crews, made them put their guns down. It didn't do much about the rest. From the time Gary French and I speculated about whether the Ceasefire ideas might be mapped onto the drug markets, I'd been thinking about it. I'd come up with the sketch of an approach to shutting the drug markets down. Like Ceasefire, it was really pretty simple.

First step: It's not about the drugs, it's about the drug *market*. Drug *use* doesn't cause much violence, much public chaos. It can be very bad, for individuals, their kids, their families. Some people will get addicted, neglect their kids, ruin their health, beat their wives. Not good. But a community can handle that. It's the street scene that tears the community apart. A community *can't* handle drug crews shooting the place up, seducing their sons into the trade, floods of buyers from outside the neighborhood trolling for dope, floods of hookers chasing the buyers and the dope, stricken homeowners and businesses collapsing or decamping. Angry black communities say that there's as much dope in the white suburbs as here, but you're only kicking in our doors, only arresting our sons. They're close to right. What the suburbs *don't* have is dealers with guns standing on street corners and outside buyers flocking into the neighborhood to find them.

I delighted in setting up my graduate students at the Kennedy School. When it came time to teach about drug markets, I'd give them a week's readings about the worst urban craziness: street markets, drive-bys, gangs, have them read chapters out of *The Corner*, David Simon's and Edward Burns's brilliant, heartbreaking ethnography of a West Baltimore drug neighborhood. Then I'd come in, close the door, and say, Show of hands—who can buy drugs in this building? There'd be shocked silence, then, year after year, two thirds of my students would raise their hands. So the Kennedy School is a drug market, right? This was not what they thought they were going to talk about. Universities, high schools, hotels, they're *all* drug markets: want weed or oxy, have a discreet word with a bellboy. Brokerage houses: Somebody's going to have blow, or know where to find it. I have a graduate student at John Jay who worked at one of Manhattan's poshest hotels as a cocktail waitress: The management sent the undocumented kitchen workers out to score coke for the drinkers, they did lines in the bathroom. She'd come to see me, incensed: *I know where white people go to do crime.* But they're *quiet.* When I was at Swarthmore it was awash in drugs—weed, hash, acid, mushrooms, some speed, it was too early for coke. Nobody even thought about the police. In my four and a half years there, I knew one person who got arrested, and that was off campus over break. It was like lightning striking, exotic, everybody was whispering. Didn't slow anybody down, wasn't going to happen to *them.*

I didn't have a clue what to do about drugs as such, nobody does. But to give America's most troubled communities their fundamental domestic tranquility back, you don't have to. You just have to get rid of the street sales, the crack houses, the drive-through buyers—what I started calling the *overt market*. Make it quiet.

Give them what the white folks already have.

Second step. The overt market is about the white assholes from outside the neighborhood. The only reason to stand on a corner and hawk crack, or run a house where a stranger can knock on the door and cop, is to serve outsiders. If you live there, you'll know somebody to buy from, or be able to find them, quietly and privately. Like my students did. When the market is rolling in public, sure, local people will use it. But if it went underground and out of sight, they'd follow it, no problem. White lawyers won't, can't. They're not going to get out of their BMWs and stroll around a black neighborhood at night stopping strangers and asking where to buy drugs. They're going to be cut off. They might find a quiet new connection in their own neighborhood, might start drinking heavily, not my problem. But they're going to stop coming around and tearing the guts out of *this* neighborhood.

Third step. Massive enforcement pressure sustained over time can shut down the overt market. That's what Tampa did. The NYPD had closed the old Alphabet City market on New York City's Lower East Side with something called Operation Pressure Point in the mid-1980s; there had been a similar operation in Lynn, Massachusetts. Doing it that way took a long time, massive numbers of cops and huge numbers of arrests, clogged the prosecutors' offices and the courts, overburdened the public defender and the jail and probation, but it could be made to work. But maybe it could be done cheaply instead. *Tell them to stop.* That was the lesson, finally evident, more than ten years too late, of Houston's Link Valley operation: They *announced* it, and when they moved in there was nobody there. Maybe that could be made to work routinely.

So. Pick a market to shut down. Working out Operation Ceasefire had taught us an enormous amount about how to get offenders' attention and shape their behavior. You could make federal cases against a few midlevel dealers and get the word out through the jails that other midlevels supplying that market had best back away, or DEA would come calling. You could identify the low-level dealers on the corners and in the houses and review them for outstanding warrants, probation and parole violations, cold cases, unpaid child support. You could go talk to them on the corner, knock on their doors Gary French–style, and let them know that as of Monday next the heat was on: There would be CIs and undercovers all over the place, there'd be no plea bargains for any arrests, the DA would take those cases to the wall. You could visit their mothers, tell them their son was a step away from having his life ruined and we'd like her to help us keep him out of prison. You could bring community people along, let the dealers and the mothers know the community absolutely needed it to stop. You could take license-plate numbers on the drive-through buyers, send letters to their DMV addresses telling them that the area was off-limits: The cops will be posing as dealers, arresting buyers and taking their cars. You could just park officers at the corners and in front of the houses, Tampa lawn-chair style, so nobody would make any money. You could shut it down.

Once the area was quiet you could get the word out that the first dealer to try to set up again was going to get maximum attention from everybody in law enforcement, you don't want to be that guy. When somebody *did* set up, do what you said you were going to do, reach out to all the other dealers and say, Good for you, you're behaving yourself, but he didn't, you should know what happened to him. You could work with landlords and residents to clean the area up.

Make it work, hold it, stabilize it, move on to the next market. Shut them all down. The markets would reset themselves, somehow; the dope was going to go *somewhere*. A given. Beepers, bicycle delivery, the backs of bars, quiet business among friends. Of course, bound to. But could we get rid of the violence, the chaos, the guys firing their guns, the drive-through buyers? I thought maybe so. I thought we should try to work it out.

One of the first things I did once I got back on my feet was give a paper at the RAND Corporation in Santa Monica, in March of 2001: "Closed Until Further Notice: Focused Deterrence and the Regulation of Illegal Drug Markets." It was back-to-back with a big public meeting that San Francisco mayor Willie Brown held, a city summit on violence. Brown brought me out. It was bad in San Francisco, gangs killing witnesses, killing witnesses' family. There were shootings between public housing projects where the cops found rifle brass side by side with heaps of pistol brass: somebody, probably with military training, sniping the opposition while his or her second laid down suppressing cover fire. I spoke at the summit, laid Ceasefire out. Brown liked it. District Attorney Terence Hallinan liked it. "This isn't rocket science," he said. "There's no reason why those of us in law enforcement can't get together on this."

People, more people anyway, were becoming more receptive to the Ceasefire ideas. In May of 2001, the Justice Department would make it a central plank in the new Bush administration's urban crime agenda. All this had been invented on the Clinton administration's watch, so we worried. We needn't have. The Bush Department of Justice launched Project Safe Neighborhoods—PSN—explicitly "built upon the foundations of previously-existing gun crime reduction efforts such as the Clinton-era Strategic Approaches to Community Safety Initiative (SACSI), Richmond's Project Exile, and the Boston Ceasefire program." It operated through U.S. attorneys' offices, SACSI-style—but all ninety-three of them this time—and made the Ceasefire playbook one of its main thrusts. Word in my circle was that it was going to be one of the administration's top priorities, that Attorney General John Ashcroft was taking a strong personal interest. I got a call: Would you come to Washington, D.C., to meet with the attorney general? I would. The meeting was set, my flights purchased: for September 12, 2001. After September 11, 2001, domestic gun crime stopped being anything like the administration's, or the attorney general's, top priority. Some very interesting things, regardless, would come of PSN in the next little while.

I had lots of very good friends in policing. They thought I had something to offer, trusted me, had come to believe that as odd as the new strategies might seem—*You're going to sit the worst guys down and tell them ahead of time what you're going to do?*—they were worth a hearing. My drug-market ideas weren't a plan. I don't work that way. I wanted a willing police department to work with, to take the sketch and work out the plan together, as we'd done with Ceasefire. I laid out the sketch over and over. I could *not* get anybody to listen.

I got laughed out of police departments all across the country. I thought I finally had a foothold in Winston-Salem. Linda Davis, the police chief who'd implemented SACSI there, gave me enough of a hearing that she put together a meeting of her command staff and let me make my pitch. I had my hopes hanging on Captain Pat Norris, who'd done a lot of the hands-on SACSI work; she got the gun-violence stuff thoroughly, liked it, had really thrown herself into it. Now I laid out the new logic of the drug-market strategy. Pat was sitting in the front of the room, off to my left; I was watching her. Nope. They heard me out, we talked about it, Pat shook her head. "That'll never work," she said. I thought I had a foothold in Rochester, New York. Late in 2002, Chief Bob Duffy reached out to me. Rochester was horrifically violent, way worse than New York City on a per capita basis. The old, upstate industrial city has a string of neighborhoods, an arc around the downtown area, called the Crescent. It has Baltimore-level street drug markets, stickup boys, pretty much the worst I've ever seen outside a big city. Duffy wanted to know, did I have anything that would work against drug markets? Well, maybe, yes.

We started in early 2003 and immediately were hit with a string of killings. One was Craig Brown, a nineteen-year-old construction worker who was being hounded by a drug crew called Thurston Zoo. They finally shot him, he ran, died in front of me on the gas station asphalt where he'd finally collapsed, clothes cut away, EMTs working feverishly. You could tell they didn't think they could hold on to him. They were right. A witness identified the shooter right away. Antonio Williams. He got locked up. Jail phones all have signs next to them—CONVERSATIONS MAY BE RECORDED—he talked to his mother, she said, Did you kill that boy, he said, Yes. That was that, twenty years to life. So the drug-market plan went on hold as we geared up Ceasefire, took down the Zoo, started the call-ins, took down a gang called Dipset. The call-ins began in the fall of 2003. Rochester went quiet. By April of 2003, there had already been ten black men aged fifteen to thirty killed in Rochester. By April of 2004, there were . . . none. Seeing Ceasefire work made no difference at all on the drug front. Duffy may have liked my ideas, but his command staff wanted no part of it. We went round and round and round, got nowhere.

I got nowhere with *anybody*.

It turned out to be the most enormous favor.

I was sure that what I was proposing wasn't ridiculous. I wasn't at all sure that we could actually shut the markets down. That would take working something out, trying it; that was an empirical question. But I was sure that I was basically making sense. The fact that everybody thought it *was* ridiculous made me dive deeper into why I *did* think it made sense, why they *didn't* think it made sense. It clarified things. Enormously.

Some of it was technical. There was the issue of focusing on the overt market, rather than on "drugs." People didn't think like that, it was a hard move to hold on to, you'd set the frame around closing just that particular kind of market and five minutes later the conversation was back to "you can't do anything about drugs": can't do anything about supply, can't do anything about demand, can't do anything about the dealers who have to put food on the table. There was displacement: the absolute conviction that no matter what you do, "they'll just go somewhere else." Law enforcement believes in displacement with religious fervor. Research says otherwise. Research says that displacement is rarely absolute, often minimal, often *reversed*, that things get better around the area of an intervention, what criminologists call "diffusion of benefits." Doesn't matter. The conviction is total: *They'll just move.*

Okay. New ideas, unfamiliar, complicated; we can work on that.

It wasn't the real issue.

If Ceasefire papered over the differences between the police and the community, got people to stand together, got them to suspend their disbelief, drugs brought those differences to the fore, emphasized gulf and division, focused both sides on their anger and suspicion.

I started to see it more and more clearly. I'd been seeing it firsthand for more than fifteen years. But I'd never really seen it, had never put a name to it.

The real issue was, the police thought the community was completely corrupt, from top to bottom.

The real issue was, the community thought the police were predators deliberately doing them horrendous harm.

The real issue was the way the relationship between the police and community was being poisoned by toxic racial narratives.

Here, things get ugly.

I learned to say, over the next couple of years, when I began this part of the conversation, Please bear with me. This stuff is hard. I'm going to insult everybody in the room. If you feel like getting up and leaving, hang in there, because it comes round to a good place. But I don't know any way of getting there without going through some really bad terrain.

So.

Please bear with me.

* * *

You can come at this from either direction; it turns out to be almost perfectly symmetrical, a mirror-image catastrophe. It's maybe a little easier if you start with the community.

Let's start with the fact that the idea, common currency in these neighborhoods, that the government is running a carefully organized racial conspiracy against black America is not as crazy as it sounds. Up until the late 1960s, when the civil-rights movement finally won out, *America* was a carefully organized racial conspiracy against black America. Written into the Constitution: blacks are three fifths of a person, free states will regard fugitive slaves as property. The Supreme Court of the United States, *Dred Scott*, 1856: "The Black man has no rights which the White man is bound to respect." Slavery's *still* in the Constitution. Thirteenth Amendment, Section 1: *Neither slavery nor involuntary servitude, except as a punishment for crime whereof the party shall have been duly convicted, shall exist within the United States, or any place subject to their jurisdiction.* There's no slavery in the United States. Unless you're in jail or prison. To this *day.* If you're in prison, your labor can be forced. As Douglas A. Blackmon documented in a sickening 2001 *Wall Street Journal* article, and then in his devastating book *Slavery by Another Name: The Re-Enslavement of Black Americans from the Civil War to WWII,* leasing slaves was one of the state of Alabama's chief sources of revenue after emancipation. Death rates for black prisoners at some companies hit 25 percent; hundreds of mostly unmarked graves lie in what locals call "the U.S. Steel cemetery" in Birmingham, where the company relied on convict labor to work coal mines. Challenged about the astronomical convict death rate at another mining company, its president wrote officials that "the negro dies faster."

It went on in Alabama until *1928.*

The long, miserable history of the Black Codes, Reconstruction, Jim Crow, separate but equal, we all know it. All that was *legal.* From much more, the law did not protect. It was illegal to kill a black man, but no jury would convict. It was illegal to lynch, but lynching was common. The Ku Klux Klan was one with many Southern law enforcement agencies. Police governed what blacks could do, who they could associate with, where they could live and travel. Long time ago, right? Not so much. The FBI infiltrated the civil-rights movement; its COINTELPRO operation schemed to disrupt the Southern Christian Leadership Congress and the NAACP; it wiretapped and tried to blackmail Martin

Luther King Jr. Police set dogs and fire hoses against peaceful civil-rights marchers. My friend and colleague George Kelling, who grew up in Milwaukee, teaches that Milwaukee police used to turn blacks back across the bridge that separated—and still does—black Milwaukee from the white downtown. I brought this up a few years ago at a small dinner in Milwaukee. I was being taken out before a mayoral town hall on violence the next day. Several whites took grave exception. Maybe a long time ago, they said. Maybe back in the 1960s. A white police officer took me aside afterward. I did that, he said. My training officer showed me, and told me to shut up when I protested.

The black man has no rights.

This was America, our America. Whites tend barely to know it, or to diminish it, or to set it aside as *then* against wherever it is that *now* begins, like hoop skirts and the Lone Ranger on the radio; interesting, in a quaint kind of way, but of no real significance. Over, long ago. It is living memory for many in the black community, and a collective memory for many, many more. Bloody Sunday, the march on Selma, was 1965, little more than forty years ago. As we set up Operation Ceasefire in San Francisco, Gregg Lowder, Mayor Willie Brown's criminal justice coordinator, and I briefed a black minister's group about our plans. One of the ministers took violent exception. You mean, he said, that just because you think somebody is a gang member you're going to go into his house and drag him out, take him away? I tried to talk to him, got nowhere against a raw wave of mistrust, anger, and pain. Gregg gracefully ended the meeting and talked to him privately afterward. As a boy the minister had been in his grandfather's house when the Klan had taken the man out and lynched him.

When I first began spending time in black communities I was struck by how many older residents were terrified of dogs. Somebody finally taught me that dogs meant overseers and sheriffs and chain gangs; they meant very bad things. One version of the etymology of "hush puppy" is that the little fried treats were made to be thrown to, and quiet, the dogs of overseers and slave catchers. Long time ago, right? Not so much. In the early 1990s, I ate lunch with a Tampa K-9 officer in his car, his German shepherd in the back seat. The dog suddenly went berserk, barking and scrabbling against the window behind me. He does that when a black walks by, his handler told me. Too many black suspects.

Our American history is not nearly as far behind us as we would like to think. But it's different now, no question. It's better, no question. We've gotten beyond slavery and poll taxes, beyond back-of-the-bus. The civil-rights movement won out, an epic struggle and glorious victory. But in many black communities across America, the new freedom brought neither prosperity nor tranquility. It's as if history truly has conspired. Black America had slavery, got emancipation, had its new freedom taken away by the slave codes and Jim Crow. It won its civil rights, won freedom again, and the world turned on it again. The decades after the civil-rights victories should have been a celebration. Racial segregation declined; the black middle class grew dramatically. But both the absolute number of blacks living in poverty and their concentration in poor neighborhoods increased. For these neighborhoods, those decades were a spiral of decline. The heroin epidemic of the late 1960s and 1970s, the first national wave of drug addiction and homicide, was concentrated in inner-city black neighborhoods. White flight in the face of desegregation weakened the core cities. Black flight, enabled by desegregation, took many of the better-off residents with it. School desegregation, busing, and more white withdrawal weakened school systems and eroded tax bases. The decline of manufacturing and the growth of outsourcing took away living-wage jobs. The increasing education requirements of jobs in the new economy left the marginally schooled further and further behind. When I delivered the *Detroit News* in the early 1970s, only about 11 percent of Detroit blacks lived in high-poverty neighborhoods. By 1990, 54 percent did.

There was nothing inevitable about the crack epidemic that took these neighborhoods down. But it was inevitable that when it hit, it would hit here hardest. It was, especially, where young men whose present and future both offered next to nothing were most likely to think that standing on a corner and selling it was a good and reasonable choice, and where the reeling community around them would be least able to keep them in check. Crack and crack markets and already desperate community conditions and our law enforcement response fed on one another, a positive feedback loop of destruction that turned the spiral of decline into an endless free fall.

In these neighborhoods, the historical experience of abuse under color of law continues. It is a kind of arithmetic truth that the worst of this is in the most desperate neighborhoods, that the worst law enforcement, and the worst of law enforcement's unintended consequences, gets focused on the already most damaged, most alienated, most suspicious communities.

Where the police break the law all the time. *All* the time.

There are cities where "clearing corners" is an accepted and administratively supported practice: Officers routinely roll up on groups of blacks in public and order everybody to leave. They invariably do, which means that they know that there will be consequences if they don't. It is blatantly, flagrantly, *unbelievably* illegal, and when I first saw it I could scarcely believe it. I've seen it many times now. In one city, I asked a senior officer who happened to have come recently from another agency what was going on and, in evident distress, he closed his office door to tell me that he had had the same reaction. He'd asked his new colleagues about it and gotten a puzzled response that told him they had no idea that what they were doing was wrong. He was basically waiting for someone to file a class action suit and for the federal consent decree that would inevitably follow. The Detroit Police Department ended up under federal control in 2003 because somebody at the Justice Department noticed that a standard investigative technique was to arrest everybody at a murder scene as a material witness, hold them, and sweat them. The Justice Department told it to stop, but it didn't. Next stop, federal master.

Street stops. Search-and-seizure law is very clear: Officer safety allows a pat-down. Stop somebody on the street, you can run your hands over them, check them for weapons. It's also very clear: Going further requires probable cause. Forget that. Lots of cities, certain neighborhoods, officers feel totally comfortable tossing anybody they feel like. Jam the unit to a stop, boil out the doors, form up on whoever's on the corner, on the sidewalk, turn them inside out. Go though their clothes, turn out their pockets, look in their socks, shine your flashlight into their mouths, some cities, drop your pants. Routine. Officers forget it's even crossing a line. I was in a hotel room once, turned the TV on, *COPS* was showing. I never watch stuff like that, but the episode was set in Boston, so I kept an eye on it. Street officer was looking for somebody who'd stolen some lawn furniture, ran across a kid he knew, stopped him, went through all his pockets. Totally illegal. *On TV.*

Routine.

I was on the street with drug cops not long ago. Where isn't the point, they're not the point—they're good guys, I liked them—the point is *this is what goes on.* They stopped a group of young black men, held them, got ID, called in to dispatch to check wants and warrants. The young black men had been through this before, knew their part, waited. One was respectful, contained, and very, very angry. After half an hour or so the radio check came back—nothing. The unit's supervising officer told them that they could move on. There was no explanation or apology or word of thanks. There almost never is. The angry one—still civil and respectful, but furious—said, *I live here. My house is on the next block. All I was doing was going home.* Then stay in front of your house, the officer said. This is a drug area. You know what's going to happen.

I was on the street, elsewhere, with other drug guys. A couple of cars moving in tandem, a clutch of black people on the street, one car vectors in, the group scatters, the car I'm in tears for the next street over, slews around the corner, there's a black man coming through the yard between, we all bail out, stop him. He's maybe sixty. The cops go through his pockets, drop everything they find on the ground, get his driver's license, give him shit for not living at the address on his license, give him shit for running, give him shit for being slow to answer their questions. He's clean, got nothing, got nothing going on. We all pile back into the car. I'm the last one in, standing by a rear door, I look at him, standing there, his dignity, his manhood, in tatters, his stuff at his feet, and he looks at me. Looks me full in the eye. I can't move, I'm frozen, excruciatingly ashamed.

He says, "For *nothing.*"

This happens all the time. Again, recently, on the phone, a very senior police executive in another city, where, who, again, doesn't matter. There'd been a killing, we were talking about the police response to the killing. We went into that neighborhood, we cleared corners, the police executive said. Said it right out loud, was proud of it, it's how they do things. I wanted to crawl down the phone line. You think anybody on those corners did the killing?

You think *everybody* on those corners did the killing?

Warrants. Lots, most, are letter of the law. Some aren't. In 1988, a Boston police officer, Sherman Griffiths, was serving a warrant on Albert Lewin. It would have been just another drug raid, but Lewin fired through the door and killed him. In the investigation that followed, it turned out that Griffiths's partner, Carlos Luna, had falsified the affidavit that got the warrant. "John," the informant who made the undercover buys Luna attested to, didn't exist. "John" was implicated in dozens of other warrants. If Griffiths hadn't been killed, nobody would ever have known. Nobody official, at any rate. The streets know, a lot of the time. Lots of departments have this go on. Most go to great lengths to keep it from happening; mostly they succeed. But it happens. The streets: *They all lie.*

What happens on the other side of the door when the drug guys go in: Everybody there is shouted down, manhandled, put on the floor, handcuffed. Every door opened, every room entered. Shoot the dogs, sometimes. Cereal, flour, milk poured into the sink, onto the kitchen floor. The baby's toys and videos broken open. Drawers pulled out, dumped, everything pawed through, on the floor. Beds upended, mattresses slit, furniture upended, cushions slit. The guys in armor are relieved that they haven't been shot, haven't had to shoot anybody; they're laughing, stomping around, tearing the place apart. Neighbors gather outside, watch through the door and windows, hear things. Most places when it's over the team piles out and leaves, doesn't even secure the shattered door. Anybody not arrested gets cut loose, shocky, crying. It's *horrible.* If it weren't the cops who'd done it to you, you'd . . . call the cops.

The research is very, very clear that these things don't have to happen to you to make you feel their weight. You hear the stories, repeat the stories, they're part of the fabric of the neighborhood. You're angry, too; you're scared. It doesn't even have to be local. In the months after the Rodney King beating, I was with cops on streets three thousand miles away from L.A. and people were shouting at them about it. Edward Copeland is a black Baptist minister in Rockford, Illinois. I'm not a psychiatrist, he said to me, but there is a phenomenon of vicarious trauma. "If it happened to your cousin, your nephew, your classmate or your fellow choir member, it might as well have happened to you, and you might be next," he said. "When you add media coverage of incidents like Oscar Grant, Amadou Diallo, Sean Bell, and others, a communal anguish and anger occurs that is hard to define or express." It reinforces what everything else in the neighborhood—the lack of work, the useless schools, the decay, all of it—says every day: The outside world does not care, is dangerous, touches us only to do us harm.

Nothing says that more than sending the neighborhood to prison. "If you want to destroy a civilization, lock it up," I heard a black man say once. This is the biggest thing of all: what happens when everybody, all the men, in the neighborhood get arrested.

Our normal debate about right and wrong, due process, guilt and innocence, misses what's going on here completely. That's a debate about each incident, each arrestee, each disposition. Did it happen? Did he do it? Was the sentence justified? Let's skip that. Let's say that each crime is real, each arrest and prosecution well grounded, each sentence statutory. That doesn't make what's going on okay. It doesn't undo the damage that's being done. The point is that no community can survive many, most, of its men having criminal records, surging back and forth between prison and home, damaged for life no matter what they want and do. No community can survive its young men growing up and seeing this and thinking, *This is the way life is.*

America's orgy of imprisonment is fantastic. Al Blumstein from Carnegie Mellon tells a running joke on himself: In 1973, he and Jackie Cohen, also from Carnegie Mellon, published a paper in *The Journal of Criminal Law and Criminology*: "A Theory of the Stability of Punishment." Looking back to 1930, they pointed out, even as crime had gone up and down, the U.S. had imprisoned its citizens at a remarkably steady rate of about 110 per 100,000 in the population. There's something about a country, a culture, they theorized, that finds ways to keep a steady level of those it punishes. That level starts to go down, because crime is down, lesser issues start to be defined as criminal, and imprisonment will come back up. It starts to go up, because crime is up, some of those crimes will be shed, and imprisonment will come back down. Although, they pointed out, since 1961, when the prison population had peaked at about 220,000, it had declined steadily, to about 196,000 in 1970. U.S. prisons had cells sitting empty. "In fact," they wrote, "there has been an increasing tendency throughout most of the nation for shorter prison sentences, for more use of probation and for other forms of community supervision."

At which point the prison population started to soar and didn't stop for thirty-five years. More people who were arrested went to prison, sentencing guidelines and mandatory minimums and judges' decisions meant prison sentences got longer, parole release rates went down, changed attitudes toward probation and parole violations meant more people on community supervision ended up locked up, drug enforcement soared. There was no connection to crime rates. Crime went up, more people in prison. Crime went down, more people in prison. The sheer volume is staggering. Current prison population versus 1970 prison population: an increase of more than *1,100 percent*. More than one in a hundred American adults are locked up.

White men, over eighteen: one in 106.

Black men, over eighteen: one in fifteen.

Black men, twenty to thirty-four: one in *nine*.

One in nine.

It is the intersection of law enforcement and America's Over-the-Rhines, Nickerson Gardenses, Terrace and Bedells that drives imprisonment. They're the uncapped oil wells, the Deepwater Horizons, of jail. The concentration is *fantastic*. In New York State, not long ago, two thirds of all prison inmates came from New York City. Half of them, researchers found, came from three blazing hot spots: one in Harlem, one in the South Bronx, and one in Brooklyn. Those three hot spots represented 17 percent of the male population of New York City.

That means that those three hot zones generated a *third of all imprisonment* in New York State.

The growing academic literature on the effect of incarceration on the hardest-hit neighborhoods sums to one long scream of pain. Individuals, families, and communities are all savaged. The prison boom meant that by the end of the century, black men born in the late 1960s, by then in their mid-thirties, were nearly twice as likely to have prison records as to have graduated college, were more than twice as likely to have gone to prison as to have been in the military. If they were high school dropouts, 60 percent went to prison. Men who've been locked up work less when they get out, and earn less when they do work, than others just like them who avoided prison. They're less likely to marry or to live with the mothers of their children. In many states they can't vote: Estimates are that one in eight black men in the country has lost the franchise.

The imprisoned leave almost three million children behind; they too are of course concentrated in hard-hit black communities. One in nine black children has a parent in prison. It's not just their fathers, it's increasingly their mothers, too. Black female incarceration is also soaring; one in one hundred black women aged thirty-five to thirty-nine is locked up. And it's not just that their parents are locked up. The kids are in the house when the warrant squad blows in to get their mom or dad, they're in the house when their mom or dad goes out one morning and never comes home. Their lives are disrupted: They move, change schools, as their remaining parent can no longer afford where they were living, goes to live closer to the prison the other is in, leaves the neighborhood in shame and embarrassment. Federal law says that if anybody in a family, or even a visitor, catches a drug case, everybody can be evicted from public housing. It happens a lot. A son cops a plea and the whole family ends up on the street. Kids end up with relatives; the hot neighborhoods are *full* of grandmothers, aunts, uncles raising the imprisoned's kids. Almost a quarter of children whose fathers have been locked up get expelled from school; it's 4 percent, otherwise.

The men come home and their families struggle to get to know them again, to find money for the clothes and food and phone and gas they need to get started again, to fit him into what's become a different family. Many of them can't get honest work; some become the guys hanging around on the street, drinking and drugging and bringing rough friends home. Neighborhoods churn as men go away, come back, go away again, as families lose their houses and move and splinter apart, as neighborhood bonds fray, people don't know each other as much, don't trust each other as much, don't look out for each other as much. People who know someone who's been imprisoned tend to think that criminal justice authorities are racist, are less likely to call the police when they need help, are less likely to support community standards and actions against crime.

We have taken America's most vulnerable, most historically damaged, most economically deprived, most poorly educated, most stressed, most neglected, and most alienated neighborhoods and imposed on them an epidemic of imprisonment. We have given America's poor black communities an iatrogenic condition. They cannot stand against it. It has become an independent source of terrible damage, like racism or terrible schools or official neglect or vanishing jobs. It is the one thing that will prevent anything else from working, make meaningless all of our aspirations for better schools and economic development and community uplift. Nothing else will work until we fix this.

And we need to understand the way all this *looks* to the community. At best, law enforcement is not solving their problems. They are not safe, they are not secure, drug dealers own the streets, their kids are getting shot, they're getting shot. I heard no poor black grandmothers say, after 9/11, that their world had changed forever because now they knew the world was a dangerous place. Their world is not Westchester and Grosse Point and Georgetown and Palo Alto. Their world has been dangerous for a long time.

And they do not think, do not say to the police and to the outside, We know you're doing your best. We appreciate your efforts, it's not working out very well, but of course we believe in your good intentions. Given the truth of our American history, it is all too easy for angry black communities to believe that this is not just incapacity: that it is malign. Add the very real and awful history of the community with the law and with law enforcement. Add the present illegality, abuse, disrespect. Add the corrosive impact of years, generations now, of whole cohorts of men being arrested and imprisoned. Add the objective damage of arrest and incarceration on individuals, families, and communities. Add the larger context: the absent government, the shitty public services, the missing grocery stores, the useless social-service providers, the crumbling schools, the predatory lenders, the endless suspicion and contempt of the outsiders. Add the suspicion, or perhaps the conviction, not in fact all that wild-eyed, given history, that outsiders might be seeking to control and to oppress. It becomes not so hard to understand why conspiracy might seem a live option. Overseer, slave catcher, Ku Klux Klan, cop, DEA—all seamless.

It's wrong, of course. The CIA did not invent crack. There is—today—no government conspiracy to destroy the black community. The government is not bringing the drugs into the country and distributing them. There are no shadowy kingpins pulling the strings and making all the money. There's no easy way to stop the drugs that we're not pursuing in order to continue to imprison generation after generation of young black men. This isn't a conspiracy; it's a train wreck. I tell the angry blacks I work with that were the conspiracy idea to be true, it would mean that a fantastically complicated covert plan would have had to be meticulously developed and implemented for some forty years—the more elaborate version of the theory begins with the first national heroin epidemic, in the late 1960s, as a government device to contain the civil-rights movement—over multiple presidential administrations, God knows how many attorney generals and DEA administrators and FBI directors, and fifteen thousand state and local law enforcement jurisdictions, all dealing with some very capable and scary foreign bad guys: and that I don't know any white folks competent enough to pull that off.

I've had this conversation with black street dealers, elected officials, academics. What a lot of them say: *Prove it.*

Gives me pause. I can't. I can't prove that there's no shadow cabal scheming to destroy black America out of sheer racist malice, pulling the levers of law and government to make it happen. But I know, nobody planned this. There is no conspiracy. But if we were *trying to play to the idea that there is*, we could hardly do a better job. To a people that has suffered systematic abuse under color of law, that has not been accorded equal protection under the law, that has been deprived of economic opportunity, that has in cold fact been abused in long and terrible ways, it is no kind of stretch to imagine that bad outcomes today are the result of similar things done and left undone. Angry black neighborhoods have not been quiet about what they think is going on. We do not respect them enough even to listen and respond. It is hard, then, to fault them for continuing to believe what they believe.

Other side now.

What law enforcement thinks.

This part's pretty simple.

They think the community *likes* what's going on, or at least doesn't care enough to stop it. They think that everybody's living off drug money. They think that there's no moral backbone left, that nobody holds their kids accountable to finish school, go to work, raise *their* kids right. They see middle-class blacks thriving while these communities languish. (Lots of people in law enforcement, black and white, come from gritty backgrounds, and they take some of this pretty personally. I came from poverty, they'll say. My parents taught me right. I finished school, I started out bagging groceries, did the right thing, and here I am. I got to be the one, starting about now, with the happy task of saying, *Yes, but when you decided to finish school and start bagging groceries, did you have a felony jacket that made all that completely pointless?*) They think the dealers are sociopaths, crazy, irrational: They get arrested all the time and they don't stop, they kill people for no reason, they blow little girls off their front porches, they use little kids for runners, they sell poison to pregnant women. They don't care about prison, it's a cost of doing business. They don't care about dying, they'll tell you to your face.

Say to cops and prosecutors and the rest, we're going to work with the community to stop the killing, get rid of the drug markets, they say—I've heard it a thousand times, I can hear it coming, count it down in my head—*there's no community to work with.*

I understand it.

They're right that there's no consistent community voice against the violence, against the dealing, against getting arrested over and over, against going to prison. They're right that black men are killing each other but that nearly all the open community outrage is against the police. They're right that the kids are working the corners and dropping out of school and the community voice says: racism. The big open meetings—*The precinct commander will address crime in the neighborhood and discuss police/community relations*—are hopeless. The cops sit at the head table and take a hail of fury.

Residents want to know why their kids, good kids, get stopped all the time. Ministers want to know why they got pulled over and treated rudely, got treated like a drug dealer. People want to know why they're getting treated like this, the white folks in the suburbs aren't, and they're the ones driving in to buy dope. They want to know why the county is building a new jail when the ceilings in the school are falling in. They say the cops are selling dope to the corner boys. They want to know why their cousin got tuned up by the cops who arrested him. They want to know why nobody's talking about how the government is bringing the drugs in.

They want to know why the cops aren't doing their job.

I've taken my share of this over the years. I'll eat glass before I go to these meetings now. My breaking point came in a big open-door meeting in Park Heights, in Baltimore, before we went operational there. It went south fast. When I said, *Enough*, a black resident said to me, *You're white, this is no concern of yours, this will never come to your neighborhood, makes us think you're only in it for this*, holding up his hand and rubbing his fingers together in the universal sign for money. It was flawless, perfect. White people don't care about dead black people;

you're white; therefore you don't care; you're here; therefore you're a violence pimp. I completely understood. I also swore to myself I'd never go to another such big open-door meeting ever again. It is a promise I've been unable to keep, unfortunately.

The cops don't understand the anger, see only excuses and victimhood. They get tangled up in the specifics—Sir, here's our standard operating procedure for traffic stops; Sir, I'll look into your cousin's case and get back to you; Sir, have you made a complaint against that officer, I can't act without a complaint, I'd be happy to direct you to our complaints process—and miss the raging subtext: *Why do you treat us like this?* The community tells them what it thinks *all the time*, right out loud—this is a racist plot, the government's bringing the drugs in—but law enforcement can't hear it. It hits them and bounces off and falls with a thud to the ground. They know it's not true, they know who they are, why they do what they do, can't get the distance to understand and find a way to respond. They never actually engage. They don't say, Here's why we drive by the guys on the corner. Of *course* we know they're dealing. Here's what it takes to make a case, we can't just grab him. The DA doesn't want to see it, the judge doesn't want to see it, he's going to end up on probation anyway, there's no point. They don't say, We know we can't keep the drugs out. We're doing our best, it's just not working. They don't say, We're as frustrated as you are. But we're *not* bringing the drugs in. If the drugs went away, we'd have plenty of work to do; we don't keep it going to protect our jobs. They don't say, We don't get up in the morning to put black men in prison. That's not why I signed up. We don't hate your sons. We're doing the only thing we know how.

And they don't dare say what they're really thinking: They're *your* sons, what are *you* doing about it?

They don't say it, they can't hear the conspiracy theories, they just roll their eyes in private later, and the rest of what they hear is anger, and the rest after that is . . . silence. Of all the ways that all of this is deeply, horribly, monstrously destructive, this may in the end be the worst: *It makes the community silent.* When standing against guns and drugs and violence means standing with a race enemy, not many will stand. When doing something means putting your own sons and grandsons and neighbors in prison, not many will do something. So law enforcement, and the rest of us on the outside, don't hear the fathers and

mothers and grandparents, in despair over the loss of whole generations. Spend time with them and it will sear your soul. Loretta Scott,
black grandmother, Rochester's commissioner of parks and recreation
whom I got to know while working there, tells a story about her young
granddaughter. Hearing that Loretta was attending the funeral of a
neighborhood elder, the little girl asked, "Who killed him?" "Not 'What
did he die of?'" Loretta says, full of pain and anger. "'Who killed him?'"
The outside doesn't hear the desperation and the terror of those they
write off as thugs, carrying guns because their friends want them to and
their enemies don't care if they don't and nobody is making their world
safe and they see no other way. The outside doesn't register the fear and
frustration of the mothers who are doing everything they can and still
losing their kids to the streets. The mother in, again, Rochester who came
to pick up her son caught dealing crack on the street—the cops gave him
a bench-appearance ticket but didn't hold him—and stood there panicked, distraught, while he nonchalantly got out of the back of the unit,
gathered up his things and, completely ignoring her, stood on the sidewalk and checked his messages.

Law enforcement hears the silence, and they read complicity, profi-
teering, corruption, disinterest. And the community never says, clearly,
crisply, *We hate this, too*. We hate the violence, we can't leave our houses,
we're terrified for our kids, we know prison's no place for a man to spend
his years. Of *course* we know it's wrong. We're doing our best, too. We
don't want to put all of our own in prison, so of course we don't volunteer much. But we *hate* what's going on. We don't know what to do.

There are public voices in the most dangerous communities that say,
This is wrong, we have to act, *this is not okay*. There are public voices
that think it's a decent trade, what the police are offering, more enforcement for a chance at relief. I talked to a member of Mad Dads, a black
anticrime activist group, during a site visit to Jacksonville. *I tell people,
you're going to get stopped*, he said to me. *That's how the police do
what they do. It's going to happen*. The public voices are almost always
lost in the anger and the silence.

There are *many* more private voices, saying, This is wrong, it's got
to stop. I've seen ministers tell drug dealers, You have to stop this, you
have to stop going to prison, the church is full of fine young women,
they have nobody to marry, you're all dead or locked up. I've seen young
women implore roiling groups of young men not to go shoot the ones

who just killed their friend: Stop it, please, this has to stop, please, end it now. But they're private. The outside doesn't hear them.

Here is the perfect, awful, searing symmetry of it. Both sides look at the other and say, You *want* this. You are corrupt and hollow and beyond hope.

They're both wrong. It's infinitely complicated, but it's also at its heart very, very simple. Both these core ideas are *wrong*. Law enforcement is not indifferent, is not deliberately implementing a genocidal conspiracy. Troubled black communities are not all living off drug money, do not support violence, are not filled with sociopaths.

Not *true*.

This isn't about racism, at least not very much. There's racism in law enforcement, no question, some conscious, more unconscious. I've never spoken to a black man about this who hasn't been stopped, pulled over, who doesn't feel that he's been profiled. Common sense, the research, it all says that they're right. There's disproportionate treatment of blacks all the way through the system. It's evil and wrong. Fixing it, if we could, would not fix this. This isn't being driven by racism. The cops have not, in their minds, turned on black people, written off black people. They've written off the *neighborhoods*, the communities. I've never heard a racist word spoken in all my years with cops—never. I cannot tell you how many times I've heard, *Everybody in the community is living off drug money, nobody cares, there's no community left.* Part of why it's so hard to name and face the terrible things that are going on is that the most usual explanation *is* racism—that's where everybody goes—and the cops know they're *not* racist, and they are profoundly, deeply offended. It's the end of the conversation, every single time. It's why what many hoped would change these dynamics, having more black cops, hasn't. Black cops don't hate black people. This isn't about black and white. It's about the community of the cops and the community of the neighborhoods. The first has given up on the second.

But it's all *soaked* in race, simmering every day in our real, toxic history of racism, in the racism that remains. Similar things go on in other neighborhoods, especially Hispanic neighborhoods, and a lot of the dynamics are nearly the same. But the racist history, the long trauma of black America, makes relations between cops and black neighborhoods especially jagged, especially hurtful, especially explosive. It shapes them, gives them different meaning. Rod Brunson, now at Rutgers, interviewed young black men from poor neighborhoods in St. Louis. He heard a litany of abuse. The men had been stopped for no reason, been put on the ground, beaten, had their money taken, been driven into rivals' territory and dropped there, made to take their clothes off, searched illegally, choked, maced while handcuffed. Brunson used a direct quote from one of them as the title of his article. It's called "Police Don't Like Black People."

This is what I was really dealing with. This is why Ceasefire wouldn't hold if we took our hands off the wheel. This is why nobody thought anything could be done about the drugs. Not some complicated concerns about economics and addiction and displacement and market dynamics. This. This is what we were going to have to fix if we were going to get anywhere.

We'd get that chance.

In the fall of 2003, Rob Lang called from North Carolina and said, You've got to help me, you've got to come down here, there's a new chief in High Point and he's going to shut everything down. On October 17, I was there on the ground, meeting Jim Fealy.

High Point: Truthtelling and Reconciliation

Jim Fealy came up through the ranks in Austin, Texas, and made it all the way to assistant chief. About a year before I got my call from Rob Lang, Jim had flown in to High Point to interview to be chief of police. Then he'd gotten in his rental car and taken a drive around the city. And came back and said to his wife, There are drug dealers *everywhere*.

He was right. High Point is an old, established city, growing, then about ninety thousand souls, adjacent to much larger Greensboro. It's got serious old money, was a famous furniture-manufacturing town, an industrial hub. It has rolling estates and manicured horse farms, beautiful antebellum buildings downtown. It's still at the heart of international furniture commerce; Furniture Week, held twice a year, spring and fall, brings in so many people that flights sell out, rental companies run out of cars, and you can't get a hotel room. People move in with their in-laws, rent their homes, and make enough to pay their mortgage for a third of the year. It's a huge deal: Las Vegas has been trying to steal Furniture Week for years. High Point sweats bullets, but so far they're holding on to it. But it's mostly sales now—the manufacturing has all gone overseas. High Point neighborhoods, where people could once find pretty good living-wage jobs, have fallen on very hard times.

Jim Summey can tell you. Jim's a Baptist preacher, born in nearby Davidson County, got his seminary degree at Wake Forest in Winston-Salem, studied at Union Theological Seminary in New York before finishing his doctorate at Columbia Theological Seminary in Atlanta. I'd get to know Jim well. He is simply one of the world's good people. If you need help, Jim Summey will help you. He will sit at your bedside, mow your lawn, drive you to the market, take care of your kids, pay your rent. If he can do it, he will do it. He goes where the need is greatest, which means that he is devoted to urban ministry. In his time in New York, in the early 1990s, he worked in Harlem during the worst of its gun and crack days.

He'd never seen anything like High Point's West End.

In 1992, Jim took over the English Road Baptist Church in the West End. The West End neighborhood is tight, just five or six square blocks, racially mixed but heavily black, detached wood-frame housing, mixed rental and owner occupied. It's literally the wrong side of the tracks; the railroad runs through just to the southeast. It *swarmed* with drug dealers, junkies, prostitutes. Parents wouldn't let their kids out to play. Hookers turned tricks in full view in the park. There were traffic jams of drive-through buyers during morning and evening commutes. Sunday mornings, there were so many johns curb-crawling that Jim's parishioners couldn't make the turn into the church parking lot for services. Robberies, burglaries, shootings, gunshots, car breaks, home invasions. There were four or five really bad drug zones in High Point, but in 2003, when the police department mapped the city for drug-related crime, the West End shone bright red, the hottest spot in the city. The department didn't need maps to know it was bad. They'd been working it for years, sweeps, buy-busts, warrants, doors. The usual. Made no difference. The usual. Jim joined his church with a couple of others to form West End Ministries, try to make a difference. Made no difference.

In his own way, Jim Summey is hard-core, hews to the drive-the-moneylenders-from-the-temple branch of Christianity. "I'm godly," he told me once. "I never said I was saintly." He's barrel-chested, strong, physical. A drunk came into the church during a wedding and went after the bride, Jim wasn't having it, the guy went after Jim, Jim decked him. He confronted the johns outside the church, tried to work with the hookers, talked to the dealers. He had one girl almost off the streets, lost her again, she died of an overdose. Jim took a picture of her lying in her casket and confronted her dealer in his house, shouted, "Look what you did." The streets shouted back. They shot fifty-eight windows out of Jim's church, threw a brick through a window of his house, slashed his tires over and over, put rounds through his car. Jim started carrying a gun.

Jim Fealy got the job and took over as chief in January 2003. He made rounds. One stop was in the West End. Residents, including Summey and some of his fellow pastors, gave him an earful. We'll get to work on it, the new chief said. "I know the police are working hard," Summey said. "I see that. I just don't believe anymore that you can do anything." Don't give up on us, Fealy said. I'll think of something. *I just don't know what that might be,* he said to himself.

That's the word that had made it back to Rob Lang. Rob was the assistant U.S. attorney who handled the Department of Justice's Project Safe Neighborhoods initiative for his office, the Middle District of North Carolina. Rob had seen what High Point was doing with the Violent Crime Task Force and what Winston-Salem was doing with SACSI and had a burning-bush moment—had become a balding, tireless, multitasking, urgent, omnipresent, law enforcement Saul. It *works*, he'd tell anybody who'd listen, and quite a few who wouldn't. This is the *future*. It drives crime down, gets the agencies on the same page when we never have been before. It gets the worst of the worst off the street. It gets the attention of the other street guys, they're not crazy, irrational, you can reach them. It builds new relationships with the community, helps them find their voice, gets them calling the police again, makes them your friend when they sit on juries. He was making progress, the work was solid in High Point, pretty solid in Winston-Salem, was moving into Greensboro, Durham, elsewhere, seemed to be working on the ground: A University of North Carolina Greensboro evaluation showed that violent offending dropped 75 percent for the guys who went through the Durham notifications. But like all the rest of us, he lived in fear that every new day would bring collapse. A new chief, for example, sweeping in from the outside, not liking what he saw, needing to put his own stamp on things and send the department off in a new direction: years of work gone in the time it takes to write a memo. That's what he thought he was hearing from, about, Fealy. Fealy was going to shut the VCTF down, do something else. Boston, Stockton, Minneapolis, all over again. That's why I got the call: *Get down here.* Fealy now says, No. I liked what I saw, he says, liked it a lot, I wasn't going to be the one that ended it. But it wasn't reaching the drug stuff. I wanted something that would work *there.*

By the time I hit High Point again in October of 2003, things had settled a bit. The new chief wants to do something about drugs, I was hearing from Rob. Got anything in mind?

Well, yes, actually.

Rob hosted a meeting in Winston-Salem in a small conference room downtown. Fealy came in from High Point with three officers I knew: Major Marty Sumner, Major Randy Tysinger, Lieutenant Larry Casterline. They'd all been part of the Violent Crime Task Force work, really got it, really liked it. It was the first time I'd met Fealy. First impression: *Texas.* Big, slow Texas drawl, the cop's cop backbone you learn to see a block away. "Give me half an hour before you decide I'm crazy," I said to him.

What if you could shut down your drug markets for good, no extra resources, hardly any arrests, and win back your community at the same time?

I went through the drug-market ideas I had been pushing, fruitlessly, for years. That it was the market, not drugs, that we had to go after. I'd learned how hard it was to get that idea across, so I'd come up with an analogy. "Let's not talk about drugs," I said to Fealy and the others. "Let's talk about sex." Neighborhoods went crazy if they had streetwalkers strolling the block; they never called 911 about the escort services that advertised in their yellow pages. It was the same crime, everybody knew that, but it brought little of the rest of the chaos that came with street markets. It's the *market* that matters. They laughed, they got it.

I said that there was every reason to think that overt markets were a tipping phenomenon. Neighborhoods had two natural states, as far as this was concerned: completely out of control, and completely quiet. Once completely out of control, they were almost impossible to deal with using ordinary methods. But when they were quiet, they tended to stay quiet. Drug dealers didn't want to stand out like sore thumbs on corners by themselves, buyers didn't cruise through ordinary neighborhoods looking for drugs, residents in quiet neighborhoods policed themselves and called the cops when they needed help. An active drug market that was effectively shut down might turn into a self-sustaining quiet neighborhood after a little while. All you'd have to do to keep it that way would be to watch like a hawk for the first guy to try to set up again and stop him. You keep doing that and it would never come back—and people would stop trying.

There aren't that many dealers in most drug markets. The research we'd done on violent groups had been almost the same thing as looking at dealers; the guys in those groups *were* the dealers in their areas. And it said that very small numbers of people—seven guys, twelve guys, twenty guys—drove things in particular markets. There may be lots of people, over time, that deal, and lots of people out on the street. But in any given market, at any given time, there weren't that many active dealers. "What if we really did our homework," I asked, "really pinned them down, figured out how to reach them?"

They're a lot more rational than we think. They say they don't care about prison—after they've been arrested. But they never know when they're going to be arrested until it's too late. And in fact what they're doing isn't all that irrational. Peter Reuter and David Boyum, drug researchers, calculated the prison risk for selling cocaine: how much cocaine gets sold, how many transactions, how many prison sentences. It's *one in fifteen thousand*. They almost always get away with it.

We could create absolutely sure and certain consequences, I said. There was no conceivable way to do so with ordinary law enforcement, no way to crack the one-in-fifteen-thousand problem. But it could be done another way: get a drug case ready to go, and then *don't arrest the dealer*. Tell him that if he starts selling again the case would be activated and he'd be picked up, without any new investigation or a single bit of new evidence. Next time he goes to the corner, he knows his chance just went to about one in one. What we were learning about even drug dealers' rationality suggested it might work. (This idea—what I was calling "banking" a case—had been the major addition to my old back-of-the-envelope sketch about how to do this. It was so simple, once glimpsed.) If they're as rational as we're beginning to think they are, they might really respond.

And not arresting them could get the neighborhoods back on your side. It thinks terrible things about what's going on now. This would play against type. It would show, in a very, very powerful way, that the police are not what the neighborhoods think they are. It could free them to speak up. And if we get that, we'll win.

It won't go perfectly. Not everybody will stop, not everybody in the community will step forward, not every mother will say, Stop. But we don't need that. We need to shock the market closed, keep it from coming back. If we can close the market for a spell, get the community saying, We don't do that here, if we can come up with an enforcement strategy that shuts that first guy down when we have to, we can keep it.

We make it our beachhead. We take it, never give it back, make sure we can hold it, move on to the next one. Keep going until there aren't any overt markets left. Right now the dealers are used to winning. If you do this, show you can win, make a statement, you'll have a *lot* more credibility. It could go easier and easier.

It wasn't anything I hadn't said before. I was used to getting a wall of silence and rejection from cops when I talked about this. You could feel it, see it in their body language. I wasn't getting that this time. Rob Lang loved this kind of thing, I'd thought it might make sense to him. Marty Sumner, Tysinger, Casterline, I'd known them a long time, they'd been working VCTF for six years or so, I'd thought they might give it a chance. None of that mattered. Police departments are not democracies. Nobody in the room mattered except Jim Fealy.

Jim Fealy said, That doesn't sound crazy. I think that might work. I think maybe we could do that.

Finally. I didn't know why he was going for it, didn't get it, just . . . finally. I'd find out, not too long to come.

We talked, they had questions, we worked through some initial stuff. I was in shock, don't even remember the details. They left, got in the car, went back to High Point. It's only about half an hour; I later learned that by the time they got there, Fealy had said, We're going to do this.

Make it so.

They did some work internally, started talking it through with the rest of the command staff, the narcotics guys, patrol. Everybody would have a part to play. Marty Sumner took the lead on the command staff; Casterline worked to bring his skeptical narcotics officers along. This has worked for us with violent crime, he said. Let's think this through, give it a chance. They wanted everything they did from there on out to be as scrupulously objective as they could make it, didn't want to look like they were picking on some neighborhood for no reason, didn't want to let political pressure push them to some neighborhood that didn't really need this kind of attention. The High Point Police Department has a brilliant Ph.D. data guy, Lee Hunt, degrees in geography and anthropology, had worked in the private sector, got bored, wanted to do something grittier. He started mapping out drug markets: drug arrests, drug calls for service, officer contacts with drug dealers, major violent crimes, weapons offenses, sex and prostitution offenses. Hot zones: the West End; Daniel Brooks, a public housing project to the north of downtown, and the adjoining Washington Drive neighborhood; Southside, a neighborhood across the tracks from the West End.

It would be the West End. It was the worst area. And they'd just had a homicide there, three kids who'd gone from breaking into cars to doing a home invasion and killing the guy inside over the course of a few months. And they had Jim Summey and West End Ministries to work with.

They got to the point that they wanted me to come back to lay it all out for the rest of the department. I got on another plane in mid-November and went off, for the very first time, a sick feeling in the pit of my stomach, to talk to cops about the place, in this awful mess, of race.

They set it up in an off-site place they used for training, a big room in a light-industrial complex. A long row of police cars assembling out front, most of the room filled already, Fealy and Sumner and Tysinger coming in. It felt like you were walking into a warehouse, through a short entryway and then into a big, open space nearly filled with cops: There must have been fifty or sixty of them, about an even mix of uniforms and plainclothes. The entire command staff, all the narcotics guys, others they thought needed to hear it. It was the first time I'd seen Fealy with the rest of the department. Chiefs are chiefs, they always get respect; it goes with the job, no matter who they are or what their people really think of them. Sometimes it's barely skin-deep, though, you can tell. This didn't feel like that; they really seemed to like him. He was easy with them, relaxed: in command but not needing to prove it.

I had a lot of friends in the High Point Police Department. Normally I would have been delighted to see them. I said hello, shook hands, and felt ill. I'm not a cop groupie, I never have been, but it had meant a lot for me, for a long time, to be welcome in their world. I'd taken pleasure in it, maybe a little more than I should have: *the long-haired guy the cops like.* I wasn't sure they'd still like me in an hour or so. I was terrified; it was the scaredest I'd been since Nickerson Gardens. *I did not want to say these things to them.*

I laid it out. The idea that this was about drug markets, not drugs. The technical pieces: the tipping idea, the idea about banking cases, the fact that there weren't all that many dealers. The notion that it could be kept from coming back, that if we did a good job on the "stop the first dealer" front, we could hold it forever. Nothing that was going to threaten anybody. I'd been giving talks like this, more or less, for years. *That's the nice thing about Ceasefire*, I thought. *It doesn't threaten anybody. That's why it's not good enough.*

And into the nasty stuff.

The way the drug neighborhoods get policed. "This is a good police department," I said. You can tell the bad ones, they reek of it, and this is a good one. But these neighborhoods do not get treated like other ones do. Bad stuff goes on. There's the cop who tunes people up, the cop who keeps the drugs and the money, the cop who uses the hookers. The community sees it, it doesn't like it, and we all wear it. The community says, White neighborhoods don't get treated like this. And they're right.

The unintended harms we do. How a lot of what we blame the community for, especially the men, we're actually contributing to, by arresting people, ruining their lives, tearing families apart.

How we're not creating anything rational around the street guys. How we see them getting arrested all the time and we see craziness and self-destruction. How they see one in fifteen thousand. How they can't see us coming, can't get out of the way.

How what we're doing plays into real racial history, still vivid in the community's mind. How they tell us *all the time* what they're thinking. "You've all heard it, you know what I'm going to say," I said. " 'The CIA invented crack.' " It's *not true*, I said. I *know* it's not true. But we have to take it seriously. We have to deal with it. We're not running a racist conspiracy. But if we were trying to look like we were, we could hardly be doing a better job.

How we cannot get the community to say *Not here*, and to work with us, until that changes.

Basic rule of talking to a room full of cops: Nobody moves a muscle until they know what the senior officer present thinks. Never in my life has that been more true than that day in High Point. I was getting nothing back from the room, nothing at all, a solid wall of blankness. Everybody in the room was staring at Fealy: Marty Sumner, Larry Casterline,

Tysinger, all of his officers, me. He was sitting just off to my right. My memory of it is etched with the tunneled, silent focus you get in the moment before the car you're crashing hits the wall.

I watched him get up, look over at me, look at his people looking at him. I watched him take a deep breath.

He said, "David's right."

Jim Fealy is what Jim Fealy looks like. He's Texas, all right. His hero is John Wayne; he has Duke memorabilia all over his house, a John Wayne memorial-edition Winchester lever-action rifle hung on the wall. He spent his Austin career in SWAT and narcotics, was on Governor George Bush's security detail. He chews tobacco. He was so lonely for brisket barbecue in High Point—barbecue in the Carolinas is pork, he wants nothing to do with it—that he got one of the local places to start making it, put it on the menu. He told me once that he had failed miserably as an undercover narcotics guy: He couldn't pass with the drug dealers. "You have to pretend to like them," he said. "I couldn't do it." He shoots expert. He *likes* to go through doors. What you see, with Jim, is what you get.

You get some things you don't see, as well. His second hero is Winston Churchill; he's an amateur scholar. His *third* hero is George Harrison; he's rarely far from his iPod of Harrison music. He's more complicated than he looks.

And for all his love of cuffing and stuffing, he stood there, that day, and told his people about Rock Crusher. And Scottie Ivory.

Central East Austin. The old heart of proud black Austin, once a thriving black commercial and cultural center, Austin's Little Harlem: shops, beautiful homes, clubs where Nat King Cole, Ike and Tina Turner, Jimmy Reed, and B. B. King played. Hurt by the civil-rights movement and desegregation, which let blacks move out and do business elsewhere. Hurt by misbegotten "urban renewal," which tore big chunks down but passed on the rebuilding part. Hurt by a changing economy. Turned into . . . you know what it turned into. Crack hit in the late 1980s. December 27, 1992: Tamika Ross, a sixteen-year-old black girl in the parking lot of the Grant Chapel A.M.E. Church. A late-model Ford Tempo jams to a stop, two guys jump out with shotguns, shoot her in the back, kill her, wound five others. Austin police say she was the target, had helped set up a drug deal that went bad; her family says absolutely not. It was the fifth homicide in and around East Twelfth Street that year. The city proposed a curfew for juveniles for the area. Won't work, says Louis White, a retired Austin cop who once worked the area. "Kids are not just shot on Twelfth Street. They get shot at home on their front porches and in their yards. And what about the shootings that happen before ten or twelve o'clock?" The community demanded action: This is the cops' fault. "There have been many shootings along that street and we haven't seen a concerted effort to work that area," said Velma Roberts, vice president of the Black Citizens Task Force. "If this were another area of town, that activity would have been stopped long ago."

They got Operation Rock Crusher, a combined Austin Police Department, Travis County Sheriff, FBI, DEA, IRS, and ATF mission planned by, among others, one Lieutenant James Fealy. Four months on the ground, 133 officers and federal agents, 188 sealed indictments against 142 people, 109 of them picked up in a sweep in early December 1993. It was the biggest operation in local history. FBI agent Byron Sage saw a job well-done. "It was a tomb," he said the day of the sweep. "It was absolutely vacant."

It didn't last. "Basically, everybody kind of scattered for a while," David Zepeda, a bus driver, said two weeks later. "But look at it this way, they took a vacation for a few days and now they're back." And the police department was taking a hail of criticism: Virtually all the arrestees were black. Victor Aquino, president of Southeast Corner Alliance of Neighbors, was affronted. "The majority of the outcry from the community came from East Austin because it's more of a noticeable problem on the east side," he said. "But there are big-time dealers and suppliers on the other side of I-35. This is an insult." Outsiders weighed in with the inevitable, seamless conflation of drug *dealing* with drug *use*. "There's no question the war on drugs has had a severe disproportionate effect on African Americans," Marc Mauer, assistant director of The Sentencing Project, told the *Austin American-Statesman*. "In 1984, 30 percent of drug arrests were black, and in 1990 it was 41 percent. That's far out of line with the proportion of blacks who use drugs." The *Statesman* published a letter from one Bill Clark. "I know from personal experience that there is a large drug problem on the other side of Interstate 35. An entirely different class of people is involved: middle-class professionals, and above, who continue their habits in relative security. The APD is unwilling to risk a sweep of drugs other than crack, for fear of whom they will catch and of their political clout. For all the accolades that the drug sweep received, I for one believe it was intrinsically a cowardly operation. Target the prosperous and influential drug users in the Austin community—the very people who lend drugs an air of respectability among the poorer and more impressionable citizens—and you will have my respect. Clean up Austin for all classes of citizens and the APD will be doing their duty." Lt. Fealy had his full righteous on. "To those of you who insist that our police department targets only poor citizens with little political pull, please feel free to report any of these influential drug dealers to APD Narcotics," he wrote in return. "We provide the same service to all of Austin."

East Austin had his back. Scottie Ivory, an elderly black woman, a longtime resident, said it in no uncertain terms. Gave a television interview at her home on Twelfth Street; Fealy was there, some other police brass. We have the same right to be safe as the folks who live in the white neighborhoods, she said. Don't go after the police. They're doing what we wanted them to do. Fealy felt great.

And then, when the interview was over, the cameras turned off, she took him aside. "And you're just about as bad as the drug dealers," she told him.

It broke my heart, he said, that day in High Point.

I've been doing this my whole life, he said. It doesn't work. We move into these neighborhoods like an army. We occupy them. We stop everything that moves, turn them upside down, shake them, see if crack falls out of their pockets. If it does, we cuff them and take them away. If it doesn't, we send them along, be on your way. We never ask the community what it wants from us; we say, We're the police, we know how to do our job, get out of the way and let us do it. We scorch the earth and roll back on out and think we've done a good job. We say, Look at all the arrests we've made. Look at all the warrants we've served. We stand tall next to the tables full of coke and cash and guns. It doesn't work. It doesn't stop the drugs. It doesn't stop the violence. It all comes back as soon as we leave. And we go home and the people we're supposed to serve, the people who need our help the most, are no better off, and that much more alienated than before.

I loved Scottie Ivory, he said. I loved that woman. I wanted to protect her. I was doing it for her. And she thought I wasn't much better than the drug dealers. And you know what?

She was right.

I want to do this, he told his people. I think we can move from carpet bombing to smart bombing. I think we can work with laser precision. I want to get the neighborhood back on our side. I think we can do it. I think we can do something about the unintended consequences. I think David's right, this is about the market, not about drugs. I think we can affect the market. This is the next step for this department.

I sat there *astounded*.

It was done. We were in motion.

There were lots of questions, that day and over the next couple of months. But Jim Fealy had said, We're going to do this. He'd made it safe for his officers to say, Okay, it's not working, we all know that, now let's figure out something else. The questions weren't the depressed footdragging I'd gotten everywhere else. We had to go back, over and over again, over the basics: Why would the drug dealers listen? Why do we need to hold the case over their heads? Why won't the market just come back? It was like the early days after Boston—people had to sit with the new logic and get used to it, you couldn't just say it once and be done. It was fine. There were real issues, new ones, that needed to be figured out. Don't we have to proceed with a case, when we have the evidence, don't we have to make an arrest? *No, actually, the law's very clear on that, there is absolutely no legal obligation, your discretion is entire. Besides, we do it all the time—that's how we get CIs.* Will the DA go for it? Fealy and Sumner went and talked to Stuart Albright, Guilford County district attorney, saying, We want to try this, we'll bring you way fewer cases, we need you to take the ones we *do* bring really seriously, we won't do it unless we have the community's backing. Albright said, I'm in, makes sense to me.

Marty Sumner and Larry Casterline started figuring out who the drug dealers in the West End were. The High Point police had been doing sweeps there, month after month, for years; Marty Sumner and the narcotics guys knew there were hundreds of dealers. But as they'd promised, they hunkered down and did their homework. Patrol and narcotics officers reported who they thought were active. The police department reached out to probation and parole officers, asked them the same question. They pulled incident reports for West End violent and drug crimes, identified offenders, checked and cross-checked their associates in criminal-history databases. Who was running with who? Were *they* dealing? Marty Sumner assigned each apparent dealer to a narcotics investigator. You're going to be the expert on this person, he said. Figure it all out. Is he really dealing? How much? Inside or outside? How extensive is his record? Is he violent? Is he locked up, does he have any pending cases, is he about to be locked up? Who's he run with?

The answer was *not* what they expected. The answer was:

Sixteen dealers.

Not everybody in the neighborhood. Not all the young men. Not everybody on the street. Not everybody with a criminal record. Not everybody involved with drugs, using. There were sixteen active dealers in the West End. *Sixteen.* "That's when I thought, This is manageable," says Marty Sumner. "The small number of dealers in any given market became quite apparent to law enforcement when we researched identified markets," says Larry Casterline. "This exercise helped officers realize that they may have been directing enforcement action toward individuals who lived in and around the drug market but who were not actually involved in it."

Would the community play? Fealy had me talk to some of the key community people from the West End, some other High Point community figures he thought needed to be involved. Another big room, mostly black this time. I was, again, terrified. *How did I get to be the white guy standing in front of angry black people talking about racial anger?*

I hate drug markets, I told them. I've been doing this my whole adult life, and I hate them with a passion. The violence, the chaos, the fear, the idiot white guys driving in from outside and tearing the community apart. But I've come to hate drug enforcement almost as much. It's bad, what goes on, really bad. I know the cops, I know them really well, and I know they're trying to help, but it doesn't work. Some of it's illegal, a lot of it's really, really ugly, it doesn't fix things, it does your own people irreparable damage. A lot of what people blame the community for, blame the dealers for, is on us. We say, Why doesn't the community stand up for itself, call us, come forward, and we don't see that we're not offering anything the community wants. We don't get that what we do doesn't fix things—why should the community ask for more? We look at guys who keep on going back to the corner and say, He's crazy, corrupt, and we don't see that we've put him in a position where he's basically got no other option.

We especially don't see how what we do plays into our terrible racial history. I will tell you, white folks do *not* get it. It's taken me twenty years to finally start to get it.

I know that hardly anybody is really dealing, is really violent, that even of the young men, almost everybody doesn't act like this, stays clear. When white guys in suits say gangsta rap is the authentic voice of the black community, I want to throw them out an authentic window. I know that almost everybody hates what's going on. I've come to understand that even most of the guys on the street hate what's going on. They're not getting rich, they get robbed all the time, get hurt, everybody has friends who have been killed. They love their mothers, love their little sisters and brothers. They may want to hustle, I'm not stupid, not naïve, but they don't like the craziness.

I'm going to say you have a lot of reason to be angry. History, the present. A lot of really bad things have gone on, and are still going on. I think there's a way to go forward that can really change that. I think it's the key to being able to work on deeper community issues. But here's the thing. What the guys on the corner need to hear from you is a steady, simple community stand: *We don't want this.* Nobody can set standards for your community from the outside. If the only people saying, *Don't shoot, don't sell drugs,* are from the outside, in uniform, the streets won't listen. The cops have less than no standing. If the guys on the corner don't hear it from you, they think you don't care, think you're supporting them. I know you're not. I know you hate what's going on. But they *don't*. So the question is, Are you being as clear as you can be with your own about how you want the community to live?

And, again, held my breath.

No, they said. *We're not. Our parents, our grandparents, would never have put up with this. If I misbehaved when I was a kid, on the other side of town, I'd get whipped on every block on the way home, and when I got there my parents would be waiting to do it again. We're not saying, Here's right and here's wrong. That's on us.*

Just like Fealy. Just that quick.

It is, I've found, what the community *always* says. They know. They're ready. Somebody just needs to break the silence, say it out loud.

Early in December, Fealy went to the Rankin Memorial Church in the West End and said, in a broader community meeting, Here's what we'd like to do.

Actually, that came second. What he said first:

"I'm sorry."

I'm sorry, he said. I know we've let you down. We haven't protected you. What we've done hasn't worked. And we've done bad things. We did them with the best of intentions, we were trying to do the right thing, but we've done harm, and I'm sorry. But you've let us down, too. You stopped calling, you stopped holding us to a high standard. If you'll meet us in the middle, I give you my word we'll never leave you again. We will not abandon you. I believe there's a much, much better way that we can do this, and I want to share it with you, and I want to know what you think and whether you'll work with us.

He laid it out. The community said yes. "The first time I heard it, I thought, that'll work," Jim Summey said. "It'll work. It's fair. It's redemptive."

We had at it.

Narcotics investigators set up on the West End. This was off-the-shelf stuff, they knew how to do it, they knew how to make drug cases. Only the persistent focus was new. Nearly all the dealing was inside, in crack houses, so they sent in undercover officers and confidential informants: wired for sound and video, full surveillance. They were given instructions to buy from whomever was selling, not to target specific individuals; if people weren't selling, no problem. "We didn't want to turn anybody into a drug dealer," Marty Sumner says. The department had already gone public, had said the West End was a target, continued to hold community meetings in the area, so it went a little more slowly than it might have, but it went. They got buys from almost everybody they knew was dealing.

Fealy and Sumner got the community and social-service side roll-ing, enlisted High Point city manager Strib Boynton, city councillors Laura Wiley and John Linton, Gretta Bush from the parks and recre-ation department, Jim Summey and half a dozen other pastors, High Point Community Against Violence, High Point Community Develop-ment, Family Service of the Piedmont, Macedonia Family Resource Center, Caring Services drug and alcohol recovery, the federal Weed and Seed coordinator, the federal public defender, the Department of Com-munity Corrections. On the community side, there was another host of questions. A lot of them came from people's movie-and-TV mispercep-tions about the drug scene. The law enforcement people and I knew better, but the conversation had never been joined. Why would anybody give up making thousands of dollars a day to take an entry-level job? *They're not, they're hardly making anything, they all live with their mothers, the research says they barely make minimum wage.* Won't the gang leaders make them keep dealing? *There isn't that kind of struc-ture, it's basically just chaos at the street level.* They have to pay rent, have to eat, they'll have to keep dealing. *That's not where the money goes, it happens but not much, most of the money goes for beer and parties and clothes and rims.* Won't it just move somewhere else? *Actu-ally, no, it probably won't, it might actually get better in other places, that happens a lot.*

A lot were spot-on and very practical. What if they *are* paying the rent? *Right, we need to set up emergency assistance for families, if they need it.* What kind of support will they need, if they want to stop? *Edu-cation, remedial education, job training, job placement, maybe drug treatment, but these are likely to be people with drug-dealing problems rather than drug-addiction problems. The real basics: good clothes, counseling on how to do a résumé, how to do an interview, how to dress, transportation.* Who's going to do that? The city made commit-ments, federal Weed and Seed money was found to hire a resource pro-vider, High Point Communities Against Violence and West End Ministries and other churches would provide clothing, food, transportation, coun-seling, the service agencies said they'd put them at the head of the list and give them special attention.

One of my recent ideas was that we should find what I was calling "influentials": somebody in the life of each dealer who cared about him, was respected by him, and who would reinforce the community message in the call-in and, even more important, afterward. Who? How do we find them? I didn't know. The police and probation officers cracked it, said, We think we can do that. Most of these guys have been in the system before. We have records that tell us a lot—probation and parole reports, sentencing reports, who went bail for them, who showed up in court, who was on their visit logs and phone logs when they were locked up. We can tell who cares about them; if they've ever been on probation or parole, their supervising officers know their families, their situation. We think we can figure it out.

How do we get them into the call-in? We've been bringing people in, the traditional call-ins, who are on probation or parole. We can compel them. How do we get these guys in? Why would they show up? Let's just ask, we started to think. Tell them they're at a turning point, there's going to be a meeting, it's important, it's not a trick, not a sting, you should come. Let's go to their mother, their grandmother, their influential; tell them their son is at a turning point; tell them they could be arrested now but we're hoping to avoid that; tell them that they'll be offered help, bring them, come with them. Would it work? *Won't their mothers think it's a setup, they must be in denial or they'd have done something already, they're on the pipe themselves, they don't cooperate with us now.* I don't know, I said, nobody's ever tried this before. But there's a big difference between going to somebody and saying, Tell me about your kid so I can arrest him, and saying, I'm trying to keep your son out of prison, will you help? And there are a lot of mothers out there trying desperately to keep their kids off the street—and losing. They may *want* help.

It all came together. Jim Frabutt, the PSN research partner from the University of North Carolina Greensboro, and researchers from my old friend Sylvia Oberle's Center for Community Safety in Winston-Salem, affiliated with Winston-Salem State University, got involved, lent their ideas, documented the process. Jim created a formal logic model of how the whole thing was supposed to work.

By April of 2003, the drug investigation was done. Crucial question: Who should be asked to the call-in? Who would law enforcement and the community take the risk of not arresting? The consensus: history of violence, history of guns, they go. The police and the DA's office sat down and went through the sixteen dealers' criminal records, shared street intel, looked to see if there was an outstanding case or a parole violation or something that was going to take them off the street anyway. Four failed the cut. The team started working up the other twelve: Where do they live? Who's close to them, could be their influential? How do we reach them? How old are they, what do we know about them, what might they need?

In late April, the home-visit teams hit the streets. A police officer, a service provider, and a minister—Jim Summey did a lot of these himself—knocked on drug dealers' doors, on drug dealers' mothers' and grandmothers' doors, and delivered a letter signed by Jim Fealy. It said:

> As Chief of Police with the High Point Police Department, I am writing to let you know that your activities have come to my attention. Specifically, I know that you are involved in selling drugs on the street. You have been identified as a street level drug dealer after an extensive undercover campaign in the West End Area.
>
> I want to invite you to a meeting on May 18, 2004, at 6:00 PM at the Police Department. You will **not** be arrested. This is not a trick. You may bring someone with you who is important to you, like a friend or relative. I want you to see the evidence I have of your involvement in criminal activity, and I want to give you an option to stop before my officers are forced to take action. Let me say again, you will not be arrested at this meeting.
>
> If you choose not to attend this meeting, we will be in contact with you along with members of the community. Street level drug sales and violence have to stop in High Point. We are giving you one chance to hear our message before we are forced to take action against you.

There was surprise, there were questions, there was consternation; there was little of the denial or anger or accusations of racism and profiling we had feared. One mother, only, went critical, screaming at the visit team, screaming at her son not to trust the cops, not to go.

First two weeks of May. Warrant teams went out, full force, full theatrics, picked up the four who'd failed the cut.

May 17. Big, carefully staged rally against crime in the West End's Barber Bradshaw Park. Making the point, to be used in the call-in the next day: People *do* care, they *don't* like what's going on.

May 18, 2004, five o'clock in the afternoon. Marty Sumner and I huddled in a back room at police headquarters, so nervous we couldn't sit still. Marty said, *If just one walks in the door, I'm going to call it a success.* Police officers shuttled back and forth from the front of the station, where they could look out the windows and see the parking lot, to where we vibrated in back. Finally—*we got one, he just drove up with his grandmother.* And another. And another.

Nine of the twelve walked in the door, most of them with family members, mostly mothers and grandmothers. The kid whose mother told him to stay away walked in by himself.

They were escorted through the locked doors that separated the public part of the station from its secured areas. Back through corridors and more doors to a large muster room, held probably fifty people, standing room only. No law enforcement. It filled to the point that there was no place for one of the dealers to sit. "Jim, if you don't mind giving up your chair and let this gentleman have a seat," Chet Hodgin, chairman of High Point Community Against Violence said to one of his friends. He turned back to the dealer and said, "If you'd go over there, sit at the table, and take your hat off."

Chet stood on the left side of the room and said, "Ladies and gentlemen, I appreciate your coming in tonight."

And it began.

"My name is Chet Hodgin, and I'm with the High Point Community Against Violence. I'm an advocate for crime victims in this area. I can't emphasize enough that this could very well be the most important day of your life, to date. So listen and listen close, because we all mean exactly what we're saying. When we get through here we'll go down and hear what law enforcement has to say to you. But the reason we have brought you in tonight is that you have been selling dope in your neighborhood. And we're tired of it. And we're not going to put up with it anymore. You've all had your pictures taken, you've all had buys made from you, there's no question about what you're doing, so don't anybody say, It wasn't me. Yes, it *was* you. But what we're here for tonight is to get you to turn your life around. You need to find something else to do to make a living. And you think about what you need that we can offer you. Do you need a job?" One of the dealers was staring at the table in front of him, slumped, unmoving; when Hodgin said that, he sat up, came to life, twisted around, looked at Chet. "Yes," he said. There was a chorus of *yes* from the other dealers, from their mothers and grandmothers. *Yes.* "Well, you've come to the right place," Chet said. "We can help you find jobs. We work with a lot of companies that are willing to hire you. You won't start off as vice president, but you will have an *honest job*. When this is over, I want you to make appointments with our resource coordinator, Delilah Summers; she's the main one on this. You need a place to live? We'll try to convince our realtor friends to rent you an apartment, or a room, or a house."

"That's what I want," said one of the dealers. "Out of the neighborhood."

"That's what we need to know," Chet said. "But we are tired of our neighborhoods going downhill. And we're not going to stand it anymore.

"We're tired of people killing each other, and shooting each other, stealing from each other. And it's going to *stop*," Chet said. "The people you see in this room today, we're not law enforcement officers. We're the community. This is where we *live*. It's where we *work*. This is where a lot of us *grew up*. And we're going to make it safe again."

Chet finished, looked out over the room, and stepped aside for Jim Summey. Jim stepped forward, bowed his head, put his hands together, looked out at the room, spoke slowly. "Some of you know me, because you've seen me. I'm the pastor at English Road Baptist Church, right there on the English Road. I have seen some of you grow up, a little bit. Known you. You might have frequented the church a time or two, come by and picked up some food or something." He paused. "No judgments. I'm not acting like I'm up here and you're down here. That's not what this is about. The reality of this situation is that there's a lot of people's lives being *ruined* because of drug use. And you might be saying in your own defense, Well, yeah, but they choose to buy it. That's right, they do. They choose to buy it. That's right. But you're still selling an illegal substance. It's illegal. It's *wrong*.

"We are tired of this, we're sick of it, it can't go on anymore. I'm tired of the West End being an eyesore in the city of High Point. I'm tired of people saying, I'm afraid to go to that part of town. I'm tired of people saying, Well, West End's just *bad*. Because West End is full of people; people are precious," he said. "There's a word that you've heard, all of you have probably been to church, you've heard the preacher talk about *redemption*. Redemption is a word that means your life is worth something, and your life is worth something to God. And so we're saying, You're worth something, that's why you're here tonight. Otherwise all this wouldn't be done for you. And all the people in here are going to say, This is what I'll try to do for you. But you've got to do your part. I'm telling you, you've got to do your part. If you don't do your part, your life is not going to turn around, and your life is going to be ruined. Because you're ruining it right now. I've seen a lot of people come through West End. I've seen some people come into the West End doing pretty good, and I've seen people *die* in the West End because of drug abuse and drug use. I've seen girls come in on that street out there, get cracked up, come in actually looking like somebody, and leave in a *bag*, emaciated, because of that crap. We don't need that anymore. Their lives are worth something, too, but they can't turn it around now. They're *dead*. I'm asking you to stop it. I'm asking you to stop it for the community's sake. I can even ask you to stop it for Jesus's sake. But most of all, I'm asking you to stop it for your sake. And if there's something I can do to help you, I'll do it."

Next up was Louis Allen, federal public defender. "Most of the time we don't see y'all until the feds have already decided they're coming after you," he said. Yesterday, he said, I had to tell one of my clients in Winston-Salem that the federal judge he's about to appear before couldn't give him probation even if he wanted to—it's illegal. He's facing thirteen to thirty. I'd like to do something, but I can't. "They're trying something for the first time, and you guys, I promise you, the rest of the country is going to be looking at what happens here tonight," Allen said. "They don't know it yet, but if this helps turn things around, it's going to be the start of treating people better. Of talking to people first, and arresting as a last resort, instead of arresting first, treating them like dirt, no need to talk to them after that."

Becky Yates, from Caring Services, a drug and alcohol recovery agency. "We get your victims," she said. "You don't *tell* them, when you sell them that crack, that their teeth are going to rot out. You don't *tell* them that they might end up dead." One of the dealers laughed. "It's not *funny*," she said, carefully, quietly, furious. No, the guy said. "It's not funny at *all*," Becky said. "It's not funny when they come up in our door and they've been beaten half to death by some *pimp*. It's not funny when somebody knocks half their *teeth* out, they get in a fight. And you guys are responsible for that. It's not funny when somebody's *kids* get taken away from them, they go to social services. We see them. We see their pain. We feel their pain. And you guys need to stop *killing people*."

Bobby Davis, looking like Charles Atlas in his tight red shirt, introduced himself as a community volunteer. "I have never in my life heard tell of any law enforcement agency being aware of what you have done and calling you in to share what they have found you to be involved in, call you in and tell you, if you don't stop, what's going to happen. I've never heard of that before. So as was said at the outset, you have been given a golden opportunity, they have taken it upon themselves to call you in, to ask you to stop what you're doing," he said. "They are giving you an opportunity to turn your life around, and certainly if we can assist you in doing that, then that's what we are willing to do, whatever that is. But you have been targeted. And yes, we are tired of it. And yes, if I have to point my finger, I have no problem in doing that."

John Linton, city councillor, kept it short, direct. "Ladies and gentlemen, I just want to tell you, one way or the other, you're out of the drug business. Please take advantage of what's being offered to you. Because here in High Point, Winston-Salem, anywhere in this state, you're out of the drug business."

Delilah Summers, the resource coordinator. I'll work with you, she said. I want to, I hope you come forward. I'll meet you more than halfway. "The last call-in we had, I think we had twenty-seven," she said. "I found twenty of them jobs, they are now working. We had eight that needed houses, and they have houses now. So we can find you housing. But you have to be willing to do your part. I will do my part."

Stick around when we're done in the next room, with law enforcement, Chet Hodgin said. We'll talk to you, find out what you need, sign you up, get started right away.

And we moved to the next room.

The biggest room in the High Point Police Department, two or three times as big as the one we'd just been in. Seats reserved for the dealers, with space for their mothers, grandmothers, friends to stand behind.

Facing the seats, a big trestle table stacked with blue binders, each of them with a dealer's name prominent on the spine. U-shaped table set up along three sides of the room, open end facing the dealers and influentials, trestle table in the middle. Four empty chairs, each with a photograph of one of the four West End arrestees. On the walls, poster-size blow-up photographs of the West End crack houses. At the tables, along the walls, standing-room-only law enforcement: High Point police, Winston-Salem police, Greensboro police, DEA, ATF, FBI, sheriff, Guilford County prosecutors, federal prosecutors, probation, parole, North Carolina State Bureau of Investigation. The community folks piled in, everybody together.

Marty Sumner presided, introduced himself, welcomed the dealers. "You've been invited here to hear a very important message. Something's changed, something's new, in High Point. I think you're going to find your time beneficial, and I appreciate your coming in." He brought up a PowerPoint slide on a screen on the wall: a list of killings in the West End. "There's been ten homicides there in ten years," he said. "Most all of those is drug-related, in one way or another. If you're not a perpetrator, you're more than likely going to be a victim of violent crime if you're involved in street drug sales. And when I say street drug sales, I'm not only talking about what goes on on the street, it's dealing from a house—I'm talking about anybody who sells dope to somebody they don't know, indiscriminately, somebody who comes down the street. It's dangerous. You've got to carry a weapon, to protect yourself. You're going to be robbed; many dope dealers expect to get robbed. Some cities across the country, dope dealers are called ATMs, quick source of cash. It's the reality of the game."

He threw another slide up, three young black men, just boys. DATE, the slide said: 12/3/2003. LOCATION: 1311 Bradshaw Street. (Three tenths of a mile from Jim Summey's church.) TYPE OF INCIDENT: Murder. "Five months ago, these three gentlemen right here, they were out breaking into cars on the north side of High Point. Well, they graduate. They find themselves a place to sell drugs from in West End. Well, the next thing they decide to do is a home invasion at 1311 Bradshaw Street. It doesn't go so well. Shot and killed a man. They're all in prison now facing murder charges. This little guy right here on the end, sixteen, he didn't even have a record before this happened. Hanging with the wrong people, involved in street drug crime, led to violence.

"This case really brings into focus what we're talking about to you tonight. It happens. It already happened there. You've got to know that we and the community are tired of the shooting, murder, armed robberies, prostitution—all these things happen in front of the children. The people are afraid to set outside in their yards. They're afraid of drive-by shootings. They're afraid of what the kids find on the playground."

People do care, he said. Sometimes the guys we call in, they say, Nobody cares. Last night we had a rally in the West End, invited anybody who might want to come. There were seventy people there last night. They do care.

The West End's been bad for a long time, he said. Violence, prostitution, dope. How'd you get here? We've been concentrating on just that area. We did our homework, did our intelligence. We asked every police officer in this department, Who's slinging over there? We got a list of about twenty-nine people, looked harder, got it down to about twenty-one. We did an undercover investigation in that area. We started doing surveillance, put undercovers out there, paid people to watch you, paid people to talk to you.

He went to the trestle table, picked up one of the binders. "I assigned a detective for each one of you that were identified, and these cases here represent what these detectives have already done on your behalf," he told the dealers. "Now I'm going to go ahead and tell you this, this is what's a little different tonight. We've already bought drugs from most people we called in. Let that sink in. We've *already bought*. Most of you *could* be arrested tonight. But we already told you, we don't want to arrest you. That's not why you're here.

"We've tried to force you to make a choice. You've got to have a moment, in the morning, when you look in the mirror, say, I'm not going out there today."

And then, in a move carefully orchestrated ahead of time, a BATF agent stood up and delivered, almost ten years later, the Freddie Cardoza message: You don't want to mess with the federal gun laws. He reached into his right-hand coat pocket and pulled out a round of pistol ammunition. "That's all it takes, right there. One bullet."

Another carefully orchestrated move. We do federal drug conspiracies, a DEA agent said. You may think you're going to skate by on the street, he said. You're not moving weight. But we can connect you to tons in Mexico, if we work at it, he said. If I find out that you're dealing again, and I can connect you to a larger network, I will do so, and I will prosecute you. "That said, I really do hope that you take part, trying to better yourselves, with the program that they've got for you tonight."

A ponytailed agent with the North Carolina State Bureau of Investigation was calm: and chilling. We never, ever, ever stop, he said. I just went down to Alabama and arrested somebody who hired a murder done. "She said, 'I've been expecting you.' That means, she'd been looking over her shoulder for four and a half years. She's doing life." I started out in a gang, he said, and then I got smart and joined a *real* gang: the Marine Corps. "You can have a living, you can have a good life," he said. "If you don't, it's up to you."

And on. Strib Boynton, the city manager, said that he'd make sure High Point police got anything they needed to make this work. The HPPD narcotics captain said, Right now, you're the only people my unit and I care about. An intensive-supervision probation officer said, If you don't listen, and you get prosecuted and you end up with me, we can set up on your house, search you, search your bedroom, search your car. We have statewide jurisdiction, can go anywhere, we'll follow you wherever you go. Take the help you're offered, please.

"I'm not here to try to scare you. I don't need any more cases; I've got all I can say grace over right now," said Stuart Albright, Guilford County district attorney. "I can promise you, with the seven thousand felonies and over one hundred thousand misdemeanors we prosecute every year in Guilford County, I can't remember every single name. But I can remember y'all's name. I got every one of y'all on a list, all ten, eleven of y'all here. And every one of my assistants has your name. And if they don't prosecute you—if you show up in their courtroom, show back up in the system—and they don't prosecute you as aggressively as they can, I'll fire them."

They showed a video, guys who'd been in the VCTF call-in, some doing really well, working, at home with their families, raising kids. One caught with a gun, doing fifteen years fed time in West Virginia. "When they warn you, and let you know the punishment you could receive, they mean it," he said, sitting in prison. "I wish to God I'd listened."

And then they turned it over to Rob Lang.

They're not stupid. Nobody wants to talk after Rob talks. Rob is the biggest hammer in the toolbox, your dad, and a street preacher all rolled up together. When he talks about this stuff, he can't contain himself, can't sit down, can't stop. "We're winding down here," he said. And then wound it right back up.

"I work for the U.S. attorney, Anna Mills Wagoner," he said. "We're out of Greensboro. We prosecute crimes against the federal government, the Middle District of North Carolina. We represent about 2.3 million people in the district. And I'm more interested in you than any of them. For a couple of reasons. I want you to *succeed*. I want you to stop what's going on over in West End."

He couldn't contain himself, got up, pacing, gesturing, urgent. "What did the major tell you, and your family members? We have *made buys* from you. *Now.* You're *done*, if we choose so. Do you know how powerful that is, for the police department to hold a charge? Do you know how much they believe that there is redeemable value in each one of you? That they're willing to hold a charge on you, to spend their money, without any immediate return? To let your family come in and say, Look, you better quit, before they take you down? They don't have to. In fact there are some *legal issues*, about them *not* enforcing the law, in front of their *face*. But they chose to hold off on this, because the community wants to try this and see if it can work, to see if we can change what's going on out on the street.

"We're tired of people coming over to buy dope, getting ripped off and shot. We're tired of people coming over to rob *you*, because they know you're holding good money." He went almost sing-song. "We're tired of *you* going back to rob *them* because they *took* your money. We're tired. The community's tired.

"You've heard, all throughout this, there's a faith piece in this. The clergy over in there in the West End area, they're *ready*. They're waiting. They're ready to help you make the change. The community is *ready* to help you make the change. And I'm going to tell you, if you don't take that option"—his voice rising again, strong, urgent, Rob leaning forward over the table—"we are going to make the change for you, and you will find your faith *in prison*. We believe very strongly in *prison ministry*. And if you keep it up, you are going to get to do it, there. It's going to happen, at some point.

"I want to tell you, from the bottom of my heart, *Listen to what we're trying to say*. This community has proven, over the last seven years, it *will* scratch and find resources for you. This probation officer here, he's employed more people through this strategy than a lot of employment agencies. If you're clean, if you're acting right, if you listen to what he's saying, he will get you a job. He will *help* you. We will *help* you.

"You do the crime, you get the flash, but Mom's got to sit at home, right, and pay the price, right?" The mothers and grandmothers were getting into it, standing behind their sons and grandsons, *Mm-hmm.* "Momma's got to pay the price when you're the *target* of violence, and a *target* of turf wars, and a *target* of the drug game. She's got to pay the price when *her* window gets shot up, and she's got to get up at six o'clock and *go to work*, and *pay* for that window to get it fixed before the landlord puts her out. Is that the truth?" *Amen.* "Is that the truth?" *Amen.*

Rob finally ran down. Marty took it over again. "Here's what you need to know, in closing," he said. "The deadline's Friday, eight o'clock in the morning. There will be no more drugs sold in the West End."

Everybody started getting to their feet. Most of the dealers stuck around, talked to the community folks, talked to the cops, talked to Delilah, signed up for services. There were so many people in the room you could hardly move. Chet Hodgin was locked in conversation with one young man. There was only one note of protest. I didn't do it, Mom, they're picking on me, one of the dealers said. She took him by the ear and dragged him bodily out of the room; we could hear her screaming at him down the hall and out of the building and into the parking lot.

The West End call-in was on a Tuesday. The idea behind the Friday deadline was to give a little time for the word to get out, for the dealers to stand down. Didn't need it. Wednesday morning dawned and the West End was a ghost town. No dealers. No prostitutes. Delilah's phone rang, six o'clock in the morning, guy on the other end said, I'm a drug dealer, off to the edge of the West End, you missed me, can I sign up? The drug buyers and the johns drove in from the outside, nobody to do business with, drove back out.

Here's the only thing that really matters.

It never came back.

There's so much more that does matter. Did it go somewhere else? *No place you can see; the other open markets got quieter.* What happened to demand? *Don't know; don't, for these purposes, really care.* How'd the dealers do? *Not so well, in this case, we'll come back to that.* Didn't people try to set up again? *Yes, not much, though, easy to deal with if you go about it right.* All interesting, all important.

All irrelevant, next to what matters the most.

There hasn't been a homicide, a shooting, or a reported rape in the West End since May 18, 2004. It's been six and a half years, as I write this. The community has its streets back. People started going outside, using the parks, fixing up their houses. The *Greensboro News & Record* went in to talk to people six weeks after the call-in; Melissa Nichols said, "Now we can sit on the front porch, and it will be quiet. It's kind of spooky." Marty Sumner put two officers on foot patrol for a while, there was nothing for them to do, they were so bored he pulled them back out. Jim Summey ran a summer Bible school at English Road Baptist Church, got almost no kids from the neighborhood. The summer of 2004, he got dozens. He was in his office one day as class was letting out, heard one of the West End kids say to another, Are you getting a ride home? No, the kid said, Mama says it's safe to walk.

The homicide trial for the three kids who'd done the home-invasion killing was coming up. Police went to talk to the woman who'd called 911 at the time. On the day she had told the police, Something's going on over there, I didn't really see anything. Joyce Chavis. This time, Joyce said, I saw it all. I was scared, the neighborhood was terrible, I knew I was going to have to get out of here, I didn't want to talk. But everything's different now, I like it here, I'm going to stay, I'll testify. I know Joyce now, she's a sweetheart, terrified of public speaking, goes to other cities and stands in front of rooms full of people, trembling, and says, You have to do this, it will change your life. People started to call the police again. "They got their outrage back," Marty says. Any sign of action, they couldn't take care of it themselves, they called, the cops went out, knocked on doors, said, *Not happening,* that almost always did it. One guy moved in from a neighborhood next door, boasting about how he was going to take over, HPPD did a warrant, took him down, didn't have to do any more.

The overt market is *gone.* High Point police sent CIs and undercovers in a steady stream after May 18; they couldn't buy. High Point police still do; they still can't. Rob Lang's brother-in-law is a state judge. Rob got a call one day: *What are you guys doing over there in High*

Point? He'd had a hearing on a weight dealer who had flipped and had an obligation to, as the phrase goes, "provide substantial assistance" or go to prison. The ADA running him had gotten tired of him not producing, gone to the judge, said, Slam him. The judge talked to the dealer. I can't buy over there, the guy said. I've really been trying. All I've been able to get is one dime bag. The drug-market maps Lee Hunt had produced are public—HPPD had given them out in community meetings. Cops started finding them elsewhere in High Point, stuck to dealers' refrigerators, in their cars. Word on the street: *Stay out of the red zone.*

Years later, I would be having a late breakfast at an inn in downtown High Point. I was the only guest there. The woman who ran the restaurant was tidying up, setting tables, chatting, Southern courtesy, What brings you to High Point? "I'm here doing some work with the police department," I said. *All* I said. She put down her armful of place mats and silverware and said, We are so *proud* of our police department here. They are so *wonderful*. There's a neighborhood here in High Point? The West End? It's on my way to work, and it used to be so terrible, so dangerous, I'd drive all the way around it. It's completely different now, it's really *nice* now.

Marty Sumner says, "We thought we knew our community. We thought we had good relations with our community. We didn't know our community at all."

Jim Summey says, "This is the most amazing thing I've ever seen. This is truth, the Word, in action. This one thing did more good than all the good works in all the churches I've ever been in. I'm a Christian. The most important day of the year, to me, was December twenty-fifth. Now it's December twenty-fifth and May eighteenth."

Revelations.
Drug dealers are rational.
The cops can see the community in a new way.
The community can see the cops in a new way.
Both sides want the same things.
Looks like it *does* work.
We took it on the road.

Building Out II

Winston-Salem. Pat Norris, who'd told me I was crazy back when I'd tried to sell it to her, was chief of police there now and was beside herself. "We could have done this *first*," she told me. "I will never forgive myself." She went to her narcotics guys and pitched it. They hated the idea, called it "hug-a-thug." She brought me down for a command staff meeting and had me go over it. Reaction: tepid, at best. I finished and the narcotics guys took me into a smaller room where they had a crime map of the city set up. David Clayton, a tough, compact narc, spoke for the group. That might work in High Point, he said. Not here, it won't. We're bigger, it's been going on here longer, our street guys are tougher, our worst places are in public housing, not in a residential community like the West End. (Those High Point drug dealers are *pussies*.) We went round and round, they weren't convinced; they did start to think maybe I wasn't the liberal idiot they'd assumed I was. You kind of know what you're talking about, one of them finally said.

Pat stayed with it, threw them a barbecue at her house, went to roll calls to say, No, this isn't hug-a-thug. Said, I *really* want to do this. The worst drug area in Winston-Salem was the Cleveland Homes, an old public-housing area. Clayton and the narcotics guys got into it, started to feel competitive with High Point. I started getting phone calls about how much better they were going to do this. They set up on Cleveland, did their homework, found thirty-one dealers: eighteen they called "hard-core"—between them 708 police contacts, sixty-three felony convictions, and forty drug convictions—and thirteen they called "lower"—393 police contacts, thirty-four felony convictions, twenty-six drug convictions. Pat brought me back down to talk at the first community meeting, at the New Hope Baptist Church. Sylvia Oberle, the original SACSI coordinator, still at it, drove me over. We came over a little rise, and I said, Wait, I've been here before, didn't there use to be a little store up ahead on the right there? A drug hole? Yeah, she said, we could never keep it quiet, we finally just knocked it down.

The church was beautiful, quiet, filled with residents from Cleveland Homes just across the way, some prominent city figures, a city councillor. I spoke briefly. I laid out how the strategy was designed to work, and how well it had gone in High Point. There are only a couple of dozen dealers, I said, and we know their names. Shame on us if we can't control them. And the most important piece of that is that you make sure that they know what it is you want and don't want. No, the room immediately said, we're *not* setting standards the way we should. You know that Richard Pryor routine? Where the kid steps over the wino in the gutter, and the wino looks up and says, Boy, why aren't you in school? That's what we *should* be doing. We're not.

Mattie Young, old black woman, full of grace, lived in Cleveland Homes for decades, stood up and said, I have been praying to God for this, and my prayers have been answered. Steve Hairston, head of the Winston-Salem NAACP, stood in front of the room. "I never would have believed that the police would hold our young men in the palm of their hands, able to put them in prison, and not do it," he said. "If they can do that, we can do our part."

Word circulated in the meeting that there were drug dealers in the back of the church, listening, checking things out. The cops were starting to make their own way through the new logic. Cool, they said, they'll tell their friends, everything will head underground. The community partnership grew: the Center for Community Safety, the NAACP, the Housing Authority of Winston-Salem, the Northwest Piedmont Council of Governments, the Urban League, the Partnership for a Drug-Free North Carolina, the Cleveland Avenue Residents Council, New Hope Baptist Church, New Jerusalem Baptist Church, other local churches. The cops added a new twist to the process. Want to find out who a dealer's influential is? *Ask* him. They did, and got good answers. They took the eighteen hard-core off, went out, and invited the other thirteen and their influentials to the call-in.

The twenty-ninth of March, 2005, the call-in, at police headquarters: a year after the West End call-in. The dealers and their influentials walked into the police station. Clayton and his team had come up with another new twist. The cops had remarkably high-quality video of the undercover buys, which they'd been gleefully showing to me over the preceding months. They edited it down to a kind of greatest-hits reel, each of the notified dealers selling to an undercover. At the call-in they dimmed the lights, rolled tape, and the district attorney said, "Gentlemen, when you see yourself committing a felony, raise your hand." They did. "That was a thing of beauty," David Clayton would later tell the *Wall Street Journal*. "They knew we had 'em." The community said, We care about you, you need to stop this, we'll help you. Law enforcement said, You're done, don't make us come after you and finish the job.

Cleveland Homes went quiet. Ghost town, just like the West End. The Winston-Salem police added another refinement. They said, We're going to go out, do reverse stings, bust the white guys coming in to buy dope. Cleveland Homes loved it. They went and set up, pretending to be drug dealers, and people ran up to them, said, You've got to get out of here, the police are *everywhere*.

It was good for a couple of years, then it started to creep back. It never got as bad as before, not close, but when we reconstructed it later on, it turned out two things had happened. As the original police team moved on, the new one thought the work was about getting the dealers' jobs, not about closing the market, and they let their maintenance slip. The other was the high turnover in the Cleveland Homes, a feature of public housing. New people moved in, they didn't get the new rules, that would take maintenance, too. Sitting down with them, briefing them, here's the way things are here—that needed to be built in. We learned, and folded that into our portfolio for such places.

High Point closed a second market, in April 2005, Daniel Brooks, the public housing project north of downtown. Same deal, only more so. This time HPPD did its drug investigation before alerting the community: It went a lot faster that way. They found, again, sixteen dealers.

Same conversation with the community. It didn't go quite as easily. Daniel Brooks residents were pretty wary, but it came out the same way. This time, though, the market disappeared *before* the call-in: As soon as police started talking to the community, word got out and the market evaporated. Same magic in the call-in. Same community turnaround. Bobby Davis went over to have a look, see what things were like, and residents thought he was a drug buyer and chased him out. Marty Sumner opened a letter one day, it was a Hallmark card directed "To all the High Point Finest." "I would like to thank you all for the wonderful job you have been doing around the Daniel Brook area and beyond," the inscription read. "I am praying for you all." One day I got a worried phone call from Marty: The violent-crime numbers aren't down as much as they should be. Is the market gone? I asked him. Yeah, he said, it's quiet, we can't buy over there now either. That's the point, remember, I said to him. We know the crime numbers in these places are next to meaningless. Crime doesn't get reported when things are off the hook, reporting goes way up when things are quiet and your relationship with the community improves. So what's going on now? Marty took a look; it turned out the numbers were all being driven by domestic violence. They started working on that.

The annual Problem-Oriented Policing Conference was held in Charlotte, North Carolina, late in 2005. Marty Sumner and I gave a talk: "Getting to 'No': Closing Drug Markets in North Carolina." Our session was packed. I gave my police-and-angry-black-communities talk: This is nasty, please don't walk out, it ends up in a good place. Marty did the operation, had broken the whole thing down to PowerPoint level, twelve bullets on the "Elements of Implementation" slide, beginning with "Identification of target area through mapping" through "Mobilize community commitment" through "Call-in/notification" to "Enforcement," "Analysis," "Follow-up." This really works, he said. He showed city crime maps for 2003, before the West End call-in, and 2004, after— the drug-market hot spots visibly fading all across the city, almost no red left. There was intense discussion afterward; ours was the last session of the day, we went way over time. Rana Sampson, the conference organizer, an old friend, finally shut it down by saying, Marty and David will come down here tomorrow morning, eight thirty, for anybody who wants to keep this going. Okay, sure, we said. *Right*, we said to each other, *like anybody's going to show up*. There was a reception that evening. I was standing at the buffet when a big cop came up to me. I was at your talk, he said. I didn't like how you were talking about the police, I almost did get up and walk out, everybody from my department almost did. But I'm glad we stayed. That makes sense, what you said. We're talking about it, we might be able to do that back home.

The room was filled the next morning. A lot of people from the day before came back, a lot of people who'd heard about it wanted to hear more. One was Janet Zobel, with the National Urban League. She was in charge of a small grant NUL had gotten from the Justice Department's Office of Community Oriented Policing Services, the COPS Office, to do work in a couple of cities nationally. She'd had her own plan, but after hearing the High Point talk she tossed it, went to COPS, and said, This is what we should be doing. COPS blessed it. In January 2006, Janet hosted a meeting at a hotel outside O'Hare with me, Marty Sumner, and the NUL affiliate heads and police chiefs from Tucson; Fort Wayne, Indiana; Kansas City, Missouri; and Providence. Dean Esserman, the chief in Providence, couldn't come; he was represented by Deputy Chief Paul Kennedy. Janet had with her George Suttles, a young black man who worked with her at NUL. Marty and I laid things out. Janet went around the table, asked the people from each city to share what they were thinking.

I have a soft spot for Providence—my mother was born there, I spent a fair amount of time there growing up, my grandmother used to ride horses in Roger Williams Park. Providence is a tough, tough town; one of the poorest in the country, the seat of the New England mob. Historically it's rotten with corruption: Buddy Cianci, famously, was elected mayor, went to state prison, came back, was elected mayor, and went to federal prison. He's a talk-show host now. Dean Esserman was an old friend; Teny Gross, one of my best Boston friends from the Ceasefire days and the best streetworker I've ever met, had moved down to Providence to work on gang and violence issues. So I watched with particular care the exchange between Dennis Langley, the black head of the Providence Urban League, and white Paul Kennedy.

Langley was beside himself with disbelief. Come *on*, he said. You've got to be *kidding*. The police will never go for this. The *point* behind the drugs is to put our kids in prison. Everybody knows that. The government has satellites that can see bugs on a leaf from orbit. Are you telling me they can't keep the drugs out of the country? We're not idiots. If the drugs went away there'd be no work for the police to do, nothing for the prison guards to do, it's their rice bowl, they'd never let it go.

I was watching Paul Kennedy. He just about fell out of his chair.

Providence is a small town. At a certain level, everybody knows everybody else. Dennis knew Paul; Paul knew Dennis. They had worked on things together, moved in the same circles; the Providence Urban League is headquartered in Lockwood, one of the most dangerous neighborhoods in the city; they and their work and their worlds overlapped in all kinds of ways. They'd never talked about this. Paul Kennedy had *no idea* Dennis Langley felt like this.

Dennis Langley had no idea Paul Kennedy felt the way *he* did, which he proceeded to express, stumbling a little but then hitting his stride. We can't stop the drugs, he said. Nobody can. I've been doing this my whole life, and nobody in law enforcement thinks you can win the drug war. We're just throwing ourselves at the wall and bouncing off, over and over and over again. I'm not saying it's working, we know it's not, but it's nobody's *plan* to hurt the community. I'm not sure about this plan, I'd have to think about it, take it home, talk to people, but it's interesting. And would we be willing to try something that would work, put fewer people in prison, do less harm, work more closely with the community? Yes, we would. Of course we would. We wouldn't be out of work, believe me, there's more than enough to do.

I watched Dennis just about fall out of *his* chair.

We had at it for most of two days. Everybody was provoked, interested, moved into the details. What resources are required? How do you get the agencies on board? How do you approach the community? What *is* the community—do you go citywide, just to people in particular neighborhoods, where's the real leadership? What services are required, how do you make sure they're lined up? How do you approach the families? What if there isn't any family member who will step up, what then? Why will drug dealers listen, again? All good questions, all things that had been worked out, all things that were also works in progress, needed more thinking, development, refinement. The teams from the four cities all wanted to go back and try to move it forward.

Before we broke for good on the second day, Janet said, George Suttles would like to say something. I think this is important.

He had been there the entire two days, working logistics, making sure the tech stuff functioned, staffing Janet. He hadn't said much of anything.

Now he said:

When we were back in New York, talking about this, getting ready for this meeting, I told Janet, Don't even bother. This will never work. You'll never find police that will go for this.

I grew up in Harlem. I *hate* the police, for good reason. Everybody I know hates the police. We've had nothing but bad experiences with them. They stop us for no reason, they've been stopping me since I was a kid. We don't like them, don't trust them, they're violent, they lie, we're scared of them.

I cannot believe what I've seen these last two days. I cannot believe that there are chiefs of police who would think seriously about how to keep black people out of prison. I cannot believe that police are willing to say that what they're doing isn't working. I would never have believed it. I'm amazed, and I'm glad I've witnessed it, and I want to wish you luck.

Paul Kennedy went home and talked to his chief, Dean Esserman; Dean brought me up and I spent a day laying things out for his command staff and narcotics people. They weren't impressed. The usual: can't do anything about drugs, it'll just move somewhere else, the community won't step up, dealers are crazy, all the rest. I met with a group of community people Dean put together, some of them from Lockwood. Immediate interest: *Let's go.* I saw Teny again, always a very good thing, and sat with the street narcotics guys, talked it through some more, got a tour of Lockwood. Old New England neighborhood, frame houses, some public housing, gritty and beaten down. The city and state were literally *busing* junkies in to a cluster of treatment and social-service agencies. People came in from all over the place to get help, hung around on lawns and the streets, drifted off across the neighborhood to get served. It was right off I-95, which had been dropped onto the neighborhood in the 1960s, damaging it badly and cutting it off from downtown. Drive-through buyers just slid off the highway and slid back on out.

We reached out to High Point and the Urban League underwrote a site visit; a team of street guys from Providence went down there to talk to their peers. They still weren't buying it. Providence is urban New England, Dean's cops said, this is the South, it feels different. Dean and Paul kept at it with them, brought me back up a couple more times. "I don't want to lead a parade nobody will walk in," Dean kept saying to me. *What we're doing isn't working*, he and Paul kept saying to their guys. *It's not working.* It took almost a year, but finally they got there. Their guys still didn't believe in it, no question, but they'd give it a solid effort.

The drug investigation they launched in Lockwood grew into the biggest the state had ever seen: 104 dealers, in the end, from across and even outside Providence. Thirty-three were from Lockwood, all the dealers the police could find there. Everybody from outside Lockwood was arrested. Police and prosecutors went over the Lockwood cadre, dropped everybody with a record of violence or guns, came up with what came to be called "the Lucky Seven." Esserman wrote the come-to-a-meeting letter. Providence cops and members of the Urban League went out to deliver them. Amanda Milkovits, a reporter with the *Providence Journal*, would later write a splendid investigative article on the operation.

The police expected to find what they usually found on drug raids—houses strewn with trash and drug paraphernalia, and families who knew or condoned their children's drug dealing. Instead, the officers found parents working, a father who was a minister, a mother working two jobs.

"One officer said to me, 'My God, what are they doing different from us?'" Langley said.

One mother told the Urban League she'd given up on her son: Take him, I can't do anything with him. Another parent said in disbelief, I call the police all the time on those drug dealers—and he's one of them.

A hard-working mother in the neighborhood was stunned that her nearly 16-year-old son was selling drugs. Not my son! she insisted to the police in her well-kept apartment. I'm on him all the time. But the boy confessed. He wanted expensive sneakers and his family couldn't afford them. He hid the sneakers at a friend's house.

One dealer couldn't be found; the team talked to his mother and then his girlfriend. He finally agreed on a meet in public and took the letter. The call-in was the sixth of December, 2006, at police headquarters. All seven walked in with their families. One particularly skeptical mother sat outside in her car with her son, talking to the police on her cell phone, demanding further reassurance the whole thing wasn't a trick. She finally brought him in. They sat down with ministers, social workers, the Community Development Corporation, the Providence Housing Authority, the Urban League, the vice principal of Hope High School, where a lot of Lockwood kids go. They heard: We care about you, you're doing terrible harm, we need this to stop, we'll do everything we can to help you. They moved into a room with law enforcement: the police, the Rhode Island attorney general, the United States attorney's office, FBI, the Bureau of Alcohol, Tobacco, Firearms and Explosives, DEA. Photographs of the arrested dealers, pictures on empty chairs. Police rolled a video made from the undercover footage: one buy for each of the seven, everybody watched it. One of the older dealers started to laugh. Dean was furious, kept himself contained. The dealer later told him, I didn't think it was funny, I'd thought I was so slick and you had me on video, I was laughing because I'd been so stupid. Mothers watched their sons up on the screen and cried.

Stop it, law enforcement said. Stop it now. We don't want to arrest you, but we will. Listen to the community. Take the help.

All seven signed up with the Urban League for help.

I wasn't there. I called Dean the next day and asked him how it had gone. It was amazing, he said, I wouldn't have believed it. It was the experience of a lifetime. I couldn't sleep last night, I lay awake all night. "How could we have missed this?" he asked me. I went and walked Lockwood today, he said, talked to people. They're really angry. Not about what we've just done, they love it. But about everything else. They said to me, Why did this take so long? What about everybody else you didn't treat this way, has been getting arrested for years and years? I thought I knew my community, he told me.

I didn't know them at all.

Lockwood went quiet.

Same story as the West End, as Daniel Brooks, as the Cleveland Homes. Ghost town. People went outside again, kids started using the parks. Residents told Amanda Milkovits that they couldn't believe it was the same place, the dealers and the prostitutes and the junkies were gone, they went for walks at two in the morning. "The Providence Police Department has changed attitudes, changed race relations, and now we're getting the fruits of what we sow," Ken Cabral told Milkovits. "It could go either way, if we're not vigilant. That's on the part of the neighbors." It stuck. Two and a half years later, I'd attend a cookout the police threw for the neighborhood. Standing in line behind two black women, I said to them, How is it here? It's great, they said. It used to be horrible, but that's all over. "All the bad boys are gone," one said, smiling mischievously. "I'm not sure the young girls like it so much, but we like it fine." A twentysomething white kid came over, asked me what was going on. It's a celebration, I said, this used to be a really dangerous neighborhood. Huh, he said. I just rented a place here, seems fine to me. He was a graduate student at Brown University.

I don't trust the numbers to capture these shifts, we know they're wrong. You can track the gang intervention really well using formal data, we're good at counting bodies and shooting victims, but we know that formal data simply don't capture the drug stuff. When a drug market is rolling, most crime never gets reported: The bad guys don't call the cops, and most of the time the good guys don't either. When you shut it down, the good guys call a lot more, so both before and after are biased. But the numbers can be interesting. Lockwood, after a year: calls for police service down 58 percent, drug crime down 70 percent, drug calls down 81 percent.

The other parts of Providence? Where the other seventy-one dealers were arrested, in the original drug sweep? No change. It all came back. Dean would repeat the Lockwood operation in the Chad Brown public housing project, the next-worst drug area in Providence. It worked there, too.

Rockford, Illinois, hub of a metropolitan area of over three hundred thousand, not quite two hours northwest of Chicago. Chet Epperson, a new police chief, heard about the strategy and reached out. I went out to Rockford. Had the law enforcement talks: The line narcotics guys were really skeptical. Had the talks with some key community leaders Chet identified: They were ready to go immediately. Chet had one of his best narcotics people give me a tour of the local drug scene. It was mostly familiar, with some interesting little variations: lots of dealing from in front of gas stations, a bunch of little crews occupying the entryways of apartment buildings. He was a good guy, smart, open-minded. I liked him.

Chet said, We're going to do this. He went and talked to the community, laid it out, said, We think this will work, we want to work with you. We've been waiting a long time for something like this, the community said. Police analysts started the mapping work and picked an area for their first try.

Then Chet started hearing rumblings from inside his narcotics squad. He looked into it. They were right. Doing business the old way, some of his narcotics officers had been cutting corners with informants and lineups. One of them was the guy he'd had drive me around. Chet disciplined them, didn't fire them, but he disciplined them. It set the union against him and led to long bad trouble, went as far as a no-confidence vote. He survived everything, forged ahead, shut down first one market, then another. A formal evaluation in the first area, by Nicholas Corsaro, Rod Brunson, and Ed McGarrell, published in *Crime and Delinquency*, found statistically significant reductions in reported crime and very positive community perceptions.

For instance, Ted remarked, "Now the people who walk down the street aren't outsiders trafficking drugs. Now [when you see people outside] it's residents from this community. Outsiders don't come in and cause problems anymore, at least not as much as they did before." Similarly, James stated, "We used to have 'trash pickup' days every couple of months to make the neighborhood look good. We've had to cancel several of those because we just don't have the amount of trash in this neighborhood as we used to. And that's a good thing."

I still get regular e-mails from Chet, updates. All good, he says. Crime's down, the streets are calm, our relationship with the community entirely different, better.

Looks like it *will* travel.

Nothing proved the point better than Terrace and Bedell.

Terrace Avenue and Bedell Street, Hempstead Village, Long Island, New York. An intersection in the rough center of six square blocks, some six thousand souls, some 1,500 of them in the block-long apartment building called Jackson Terrace.

Terrace and Bedell.

Hell.

Crack hit Terrace and Bedell in the late 1980s, as it did much of the East Coast. Twenty years later it was still there, along with heroin, weed, powder cocaine, some prescription drugs, and occasional exotica like Ecstasy. It was the worst drug market in Nassau County; it was probably the worst drug market on Long Island. I knew Jackson Terrace before I ever actually saw it with a gang officer who was taking me on a greatest-hits tour of the county's worst turf. My old friend and colleague Jeremy Travis, from NIJ and SACSI, had taken over John Jay College of Criminal Justice in New York, and I left Boston and joined him there early in 2005. One of the first people I met was Ric Curtis, the chair of John Jay's anthropology department. Curtis works like a nineteenth-century botanist, bounding ashore to record in meticulous detail the native and fascinating flora and fauna. His Botany Bays are the shadow worlds of injection-drug users and drug gangs and the underage prostituted. He gave me his study of heroin addicts on Long Island, among whom he had found one common theme. They might buy in Manhattan or Brooklyn; they might buy in small drug markets locally (Long Island drug markets tend to cluster around train stations, as dealers take the LIRR to and from New York); they might have a discreet personal connection, or, if truly fortunate, a few in reserve. But when their source dried up, all across Long Island they knew they could cop at Terrace and Bedell. They came in droves.

Hempstead is gritty, not at all like much of tony Long Island, but the Terrace and Bedell neighborhood was raging. In many years it produced half of Hempstead's murders, and averaged around 150 dealing arrests a year; in one operation alone, in 1996, law enforcement charged 172 people. The market rolled on. *One block*, over five years, logged five homicides, fifty-five robberies, and eighty-eight assaults. In 2001, the Terrace and Bedell intersection alone produced six homicides. RIP graffiti chalk the sidewalk and walls. An ABC *Primetime* crew filmed a dealer on Terrace taking delivery of Chinese food; he ordered, paid off the driver, and had dinner right there on the corner.

That made Terrace and Bedell an obvious, immediate, and top priority for Kathleen Rice when she was elected Nassau County district attorney in November 2005. Which begat Operation Family Affair. A street buy at Terrace and Bedell grew into a classic, Swiss-watch, climb-the-ladder drug investigation involving Rice and her federal counterpart, the United States attorney for the Eastern District of Long Island, five assistant district attorneys, three assistant U.S. attorneys, supervising attorneys in the Justice Department in Washington, D.C., two investigators from the district attorney's office, thirty Nassau County police officers, ten Drug Enforcement Administration agents, and six civilian wiretap specialists. They followed the chain to Florida, Texas, and finally all the way to the cartel in Colombia. In January 2007 they took down eighteen people on state charges and twenty-nine, including the Colombians, on federal charges; they seized 250 kilos of cocaine and a million dollars in cash.

In 2006, there were 109 drug arrests around Terrace and Bedell. In 2007, after Family Affair, drug arrests *increased*. A week after the huge takedown, Rice had intelligence that a relative of the original Hempstead sources was the new supplier.

It doesn't work.

In early 2007, as the on-the-ground failure of her huge investigation became manifest, Kathleen Rice came calling. She reached out to John Jay, and Jeremy Travis and I went out to the DA's office in Mineola on Long Island. We talked through the drug-market intervention and had some additional conversations with Police Chief Joe Wing. I'd first met Wing, of mixed Chinese/Hispanic heritage—"try that for a clash of cultures," he says—about five years earlier, when as a Hempstead gang lieutenant he'd paid his own way and taken his own time to visit the gang-violence project in Rochester. We met with Hempstead's mayor, with a few established community figures. They all wanted to try it.

Rice, Joe Wing, and assistant district attorney Meg Reiss launched a meticulous undercover investigation of the community they usually focused on. They would find thirty-nine dealers working Terrace and Bedell. *Thirty-nine.* The worst drug market on Long Island, scores of homicides going back over the years, thousands of drug arrests, tens of thousands of lives damaged, incalculable pain and misery. Right now, today, thirty-nine people driving it.

They launched an investigation of the *other* community at Terrace and Bedell.

Family Affair had taken a year, a cast of hundreds, wiretaps, and millions of dollars to ferret out the drug tributaries that flowed to Hempstead, to arrest a couple of Colombian dealers. It took, in Meg Reiss's words, "a month of lunches" to meet privately with Terrace and Bedell residents, and some key actors from around Hempstead, and finally simply to recognize what had been hiding in plain sight. Terrace and Bedell feared, mistrusted, hated law enforcement. "People were thinking that the police and the DA were just waiting for their kids to reach a certain age so that they could lock them up," said Eddison Bramble, president of Hempstead's 100 Black Men, a grassroots black leadership group. "We're black folk. We see overseers. That's what we see." They found a Terrace and Bedell so locked in anger at the police that it had made a civic virtue of disengagement. "We said, if we clean things up you're going to have to call us if it comes back, and they said, No, that's your job, we don't snitch," Reiss said. They found a Terrace and Bedell so alienated, so detached, that it no longer knew, if it ever had, what the police could and couldn't do, in a way that fed directly back into the conviction that law enforcement was conspiring against them. "They thought we could just grab people off the corner," Reiss said. It was a perfect storm of misunderstanding. The cops are all-powerful, they do whatever they want. The drug dealers are standing there in plain sight ordering Chinese food, so the cops could just grab them, but the cops aren't just grabbing them. Therefore the cops want them there, therefore the cops are behind it. Hasn't it always been thus? "People were free to say, There's police, there's the mayor, there's prosecutors, we're oppressed," said Bramble. "That was the perception. You're dealing with a culture."

They found the alienation and anger and suspicion cloaking incredible pain. "I remember you couldn't go out without seeing people laying in doorways, just cracked out," said Danielle Lombardo. "The drugs, the violence, the gunshots, the crackheads, I've seen it my entire life." She is twenty-three; four of her friends have been killed at Terrace and Bedell. "They called me when I was on my way to the mall," she said. "They said, 'Hen-Rock just got shot and he's lying on the floor. We think he's dead.'" Hen-Rock's father was asleep and dreamt that his son had been killed; he awoke to find that he had been. The *drug dealers* didn't even like it. I'm supervising a graduate student at John Jay who's interviewing dealers who used to sell in the area for her master's thesis.

"Terrace is like the walk-through of Hell and Bedell is like the dead end . . . there was a lot of killings, a lot of shootings, a lot of drug dealing, a lot of people jumping other people for their goods. It was just corrupted," one told her. "I used to give my friend eighty dollars a day because he was on Terrace doing dumb shit," said another. "I found out he was robbing people . . . and we don't rob nobody you know or who are from around here. He was starting too much violence. You can't make good drug money with violence. It don't mix."

Amid the chaos, anger, and pain they found incredible strength. Inez Dingle is short, loving, beloved, the unofficial mayor of Jackson Terrace. She'd lived there for thirty years, knew everybody by name, patrolled the halls in the middle of the night, and *would not give up*. They found Reynaldo Brown, RoRo, out after a twenty-nine-year homicide bit, connected to Nicky Barnes, the legendary black Harlem heroin kingpin. He'd beaten a man to death for impugning their product; now he was with a street-outreach group called Council for Unity and taking advantage of his huge street cred to pull young black men out of the life.

And they found openness. It is the most amazing thing. Despite all the hatred, the pain, the damage, the failure, the demonization, the misunderstanding, the suspicion, the abuse, the violence, despite all the history, the community is always ready to come to the table.

I talked to the first more or less open meeting Rice put together in Hempstead, held in a Salvation Army conference room in October of 2007. She'd brought together forty or so of the community people she'd been meeting. Some of her staff were there, along with Joe Wing and some others. I walked them through what we were contemplating, if they wanted to do it. There were questions, there was debate, there were differences of opinion. There was nothing that could not be addressed and dealt with. There were no deal breakers. There was a willingness to work.

There always is. God only knows why, but there always is.

And so they went to work.

It took three months. After all the years Terrace and Bedell had been killing people, destroying people, feeding people into the mouth of the criminal justice monster, *three months*.

On January 8, 2008, 250 people filed into Hempstead's African-American Museum. The event was scheduled to begin at seven o'clock; people started showing up at two thirty to be sure of a seat. Rice and

Reiss were there. Chief Wing was there. Hempstead mayor Wayne Hall was there. Nassau County Executive Thomas Suozzi was there. Eddison Bramble was there. RoRo Brown was there. Inez Dingle was there. Ministers and social-service providers and Risco Lewis, an assistant district attorney Rice has committed to community organizing, and Karl Burnett, who runs the funeral parlor where most of Terrace and Bedell's dead were prepared, were there. Residents from Jackson Court and all over Terrace and Bedell were there.

Of the thirty-nine dealers, seventeen made the cut. Thirteen walked into the African-American History Museum. Rice and Reiss and Lewis had made home visits to deliver letters of free passage to the meeting: come, bring someone you care about, you won't be arrested, come. They stood in dank hallways shouting through closed doors. Risco Lewis has a mouth on her. Open the door, she said, at parade-ground volume. Take the letter. Most of them came with mothers and grandmothers and ministers and other loved ones. Seats in the center of what the Hempstead partners had chosen to call the Gathering were waiting for them. The thirteen dealers the Hempstead partners had chosen, after much thought, to call the Brothers and Sisters sat down, their families and friends around them. They said you wouldn't come, Inez Dingle told them. I knew you'd come. I know all of you, and I love you, and I knew you wouldn't turn down a chance like this.

"I'm at the funeral home late nights with sisters that could have been prom queens, looking like their grandmother's age because they're strung out," said Burnett. "You need to take advantage of the opportunity," said Brother Reginald Benjamin, executive director of Hempstead's Able Body of Believers Alliance. "I cannot face another year of seeing young men die on the streets like dogs because you guys are leading them down a bad path." RoRo Brown said, "We'll help you do what's right. We won't help you lie, or steal. We'll help you get on your feet and get right. And all we require is that you help somebody else."

The meeting broke up, everybody went home. Joe Wing was worried about the buyers all over Long Island who were used to coming to Terrace and Bedell, so he had officers in the area for a long time, letting people know that things had changed. (One pulled up next to me as I took a walk around, and I explained what I was doing; Meg Reiss called the next day and said, Are you okay? People are saying you got arrested on Terrace.) He'd been taking license-plate numbers with an automated reader during the undercover investigation; now he sent scores of letters out to their registration addresses saying, There's intense drug enforcement going on in this neighborhood and I thought you should know: Here's a number to call if you have any questions. Nobody called. Jim Fealy and I gave a talk about the High Point strategy in Atlanta at a meeting of the National Organization for Black Law Enforcement Executives. When we were done, an NYPD deputy inspector named Corey Pegues stood up. I live in Hempstead, he said, I know that area. Since I heard about what happened there I've been driving through. I don't know what you guys did, but it's a ghost town.

And the dealers listened. One was Everett Hairston, sixty-three years old, once a guitarist with the Platters before he fell down the crack hole; the man played with Smokey Robinson. He cleaned up. Two months later he was onstage for the celebration Kathleen Rice threw at Terrace and Bedell to celebrate the neighborhood's transformation. "I can see clearly now, the pain is gone," he sang, the Johnny Nash classic:

> I think I can make it now, the pain is gone
> All of the bad feelings have disappeared
> Here is the rainbow I've been prayin' for
> It's gonna be a bright, bright, bright sunshiny day.

The market at Terrace and Bedell is gone. It did not come back, it did not go somewhere else; drug arrests overall in Hempstead are down, and no other open-sore public market emerged to take Terrace and Bedell's place. In 2007, the year before the Gathering, there were 124 drug arrests around Terrace and Bedell. In 2008, after the Gathering in early January, there were sixteen. In 2009 there were two.

Two.

"For a while people were saying, Miz Dingle, we're scared to go outside, there's nobody outside," said Inez Dingle. The *New York Times* sent a reporter to the area. " 'Used to be nothing but young drug dealers out here, but now it's a place where little kids go outside,' said Irving Gilreath, 42, a chef who was pushing his 6-week-old son in a stroller last week." And the Brothers and Sisters? All thirteen signed up for services and entered programs and a weekly Council of Unity recovery group.

Some are working. Nine have shown no recidivism of any kind. One was violated on a pre-Gathering parole offense; he has returned from upstate and rejoined the Council group. Three have been arrested and prosecuted. The Gathering's Brothers and Sisters have been joined by more than a hundred volunteers who also want out. Kathleen Rice developed, among other things, an apprenticeship program to move them into the Long Island building trades.

And stop snitching is over; Terrace and Bedell likes its new face and is not about to give it up. Early in 2009 the first gun crime since the Gathering was two street robberies by the same small crew in the same day. The first happened to be captured on a store's security camera. Residents organized a viewing, recognized the thugs, and turned them over to the police.

We don't *do* that here.

High Point would shut down three more drug markets after Daniel Brooks, before there weren't any more to close. One was in the Southside neighborhood across the railroad tracks from the West End; one in East Central, and one in a neighborhood called Washington Drive. Sherman Mason was one of the community principals in Southside, pastoring at a Baptist church after hunting Scuds with the 82nd Airborne in Desert Storm. Southside dried up almost completely after the call-in. Sherman was outside his church one day when the cops were talking to somebody in the house across the street. The guy came out, started shouting at Sherman. He's the one who called the cops on me, he shouted. That fat pastor over there! Sherman looked left, neighbors were coming out. He looked right, neighbors were coming out. I'll call the cops on you myself, one shouted back. I'll come right over and tell you to your face. We won't stand for this stuff.

Washington Drive was one of High Point's oldest, most established, and most alienated black neighborhoods. Jim Fealy was afraid to try it there, the community was so suspicious and angry. In a series of meetings, he sat down with a growing number of residents and apologized for how they'd been treated and neglected. They made him welcome. When the call-in came, there were so many people who wanted to attend that it had to be moved to a bigger room. When Fealy told the drug dealers that dealing in Washington Drive was over, a whole section of the audience stood and cheered.

And more. Nashville, Tennessee. Commander Bob Nash heard about High Point, got himself there, went back and did it. He got this e-mail from a resident:

> Let me give you a bit of a picture of what this area was like a year ago. On Hancock St. between Dickerson Rd. and N 2nd (a two block strip), it was not unusual for there to be a dozen or more people milling the streets. This went on 24/7. No attempt was made to hide the drug deals or prostitution. A decent uninterrupted nights sleep was impossible due to people yelling up and down the streets all night long. Men and women alike used the alleyways and peoples yards for restrooms. I live on a corner, and there were times I would have to water down the side yard of my house just to cut through the stench of urine. There were *bags* of trash to be picked up daily from my yard. The litter consisted not only of fast food wrappers and beer cans and liquor bottles, but crack pipes, debit cards, condoms and other personal hygiene items of which I will spare you the details. Pretty disgusting. It was not unusual to find people hanging out in my yard. (Upon the advice of the officers patrolling the area, I posted a "No Trespassing" sign and was able to have a couple of them arrested.) It was not unusual to leave for work at 6 a.m. and be approached by a panhandler. When I would work in my yard, constant interruptions were the norm by people bumming money, a glass of iced tea, anything they thought they could get out of you, or just plain talking smack. Anything left outside was inviting theft. I had to have my trash can replaced three times last year due to theft. Now it is like a whole new neighborhood. The drug dealers and prostitutes are gone. There aren't people hanging out in the streets all of the time. The volume of litter is down. The nights are quiet. I see the residents coming out of their homes again, the children are beginning to play outside. I can work in my yard without having to fend off bums and without feeling like I have to "watch my back" constantly.

Nashville would be the second drug market operations scrutinized in a formal, published, statistically controlled evaluation. The numbers were good: an almost 56 percent reduction in drug crime, with spillover into an adjoining area, over 38 percent down there. The researchers talked to residents. One said, "I wouldn't have been standing outside [when the research team came up] if things were like they used to be. It was rough; just a rough place. There were drugs everywhere and shootings all the time. There were also a lot more empty houses then than there are today. Now people are out on the streets walking their dogs and nobody is afraid anymore."

Raleigh, North Carolina. February 8, 2007. I sat, along with 150 community members and the Raleigh Police Department and all the alphabet agencies and watched Burlee Kersey, seventy-one years old, while he sat with fifteen other drug dealers and, frozen, watched himself selling crack in the video unscrolling on the wall. But then members of the My Brother's Keeper social service and outreach team—put together for the purpose—stepped forward. Who amongst you here is eldest, they asked the dealers. Kursee looked around, raised his hand. The Keepers gave him a gift. We're a community that honors its elders, the Keepers said. The Rev. Dr. David Forbes, pastor at Christian Faith Baptist Church and chair of the Triangle Lost Generation Task Force, spoke. He stood before the dealers and said to them, gravely, passionately, that as black men and women they hailed from the cradle of civilization, that the blood of kings and mathematicians ran in their veins, and that the community needed them to live up to that and would help them to do so. Police officers watched approvingly, voiced encouragement. When the call-in was over, police officers served the dealers pizza; little groups of dealers, residents, law enforcement, and ministers hung around and talked. It was like a community picnic. Six months later, most of the dealers were in a recovery program and doing well, a number of them were working, and, just as in Hempstead, more than a hundred additional people from the neighborhood had come forward and joined them of their own volition.

Late in 2007, Burlee Kersey spoke publicly in North Carolina. "I am seventy-two years old and I have been on drugs for forty years," he said. "I was given a second chance when I was chosen to be in the CHOICE project. I was given hope when I thought there was no hope for me. I am forever thankful to the Raleigh Police Department for choosing me. The right name was given to the program. The police department called it CHOICE, because you have a choice to either turn your life around or go to jail. When God asked Cain, 'Where is thy brother?' and Cain replied, 'Am I my brother's keeper?' I believe God probably answered him back and said, 'Yes, you are your brother's keeper.' The CHOICE program showed all of us that they really are their brother's keeper.

"When I was first asked to be part of the project, I was asked, 'Do you want to be on drugs all of your life?' I made it up in my mind I didn't want to be, so I am struggling to stay clean every day, every minute. But today I have support. I know I have people who don't look down on me.

"I had been on drugs for so long until I had lost everybody that cared about me. I didn't think no one else cared so I got to the point where I didn't care. I was living on the streets. I sold everything I could get my hands on. My family and nobody else had trust in me. My daughter and I had not spoken in twenty years. Today all of that has changed. My family cares and looks out for me. I have a nice place to live and I'm not out on the streets. I am kicking my drug habit one day at a time. But I thank God today that I am clean."

The Justice Department picked it up. In September 2007, with backing from Ed McGarrell's team at Michigan State and me, the Bureau of Justice Assistance started walking nine cities around the country through the process, and nine more a year later. BJA is launching a third round as I write this late in 2010.

In 2007, the High Point Police Department won an Innovation in Government award from the Kennedy School of Government at Harvard.

A couple of months ago I was up in Providence working with Dean Esserman and his people. Dean interrupted the meeting and pulled me aside. There's somebody here who asked to see you, he said. Out in the hall was one of the Lucky Seven. The last time I'd seen him, early in 2007, he was in rough shape. It was a meeting at the Urban League's Lockwood office with this kid, in his early twenties I'd guess, and some of the other Lucky Seven. He was almost hysterical with anger, cursing at Dean, Dennis, Paul Kennedy, borderline violent. I was ready for him to come across the table. I'm not getting what I need here, he had said, I'm desperate. I need a job, I'm not getting anywhere, I've been paying my dad's rent, at least when I was on the corner I could take care of him, I know I was doing wrong, I can't go back, but he's about to lose his house, I've got a baby coming, I can't take care of my girlfriend. Dean let the obscenities roll off and said, I'll handle it. He got him a job at one of the Providence hospitals.

He stood in the hall at the Providence police headquarters, calm, sport coat and slacks, beautifully put together, and told me he wanted to thank me. What you brought here saved my life, he said. I'd probably be dead now, I'd certainly be locked up. I've been working at the hospital, taking care of my family, we have a nice place, we're doing really well. I'm about to go into a two-year program, I'm going to be a radiologist.

He looked at me, both of us standing there crying, and he said, My mother was so ashamed of me, she pretended I didn't exist. Now my mother's really *proud* of me. My mother talks about me *all the time* now.

I walked Terrace Avenue a year or so ago. People were sitting out on their porches and visiting on the streets. I spoke to a group of young mothers standing with their strollers in front of Jackson Terrace and asked them how the neighborhood was feeling. "It's wonderful," one said. "We never would have come outside before, but now we can bring the babies out." She pointed to the nearest corner, Terrace and Jackson, a block down from Bedell Street. "They used to stand there," she said, "and shoot their guns up and down the street."

Stopping It

What is going on in America, what has been going on for a long, long time, is *obscene*. All of it. All sides of it, not just one side. The 2.2 million people in prison, the dead cold in their graves, the children and husbands and wives and lovers and parents left broken behind, the lawless cops on the street, the hero cops blowing through doors to almost no purpose at all, the dying kids who'd rather protect their killers than talk to the law, the community silence about the kids killing kids, the communities who see the cops as the enemy and the cops who see the communities as the enemy, the front yards and parks and bodegas occupied by drug crews, on and on and on: all of it, obscene.

The shrines that mark the street dead. Walk the hot neighborhoods: The improvised, heartfelt memorials are commonplace. I *loathe* the damned shrines. It's symbol, not substance, I know that, the shrines are the least of it. But the shrines have come to mark for me all the rest of it: our acceptance of it, our unwillingness to act, everybody's open toleration of the obscenity. So many dead black kids that their street memorials are a new urban folk form? Sure, no problem. One in Boston marked where Robert Perry was shot and killed in 2002. His killing has never been solved, though the man the streets thought did it was shot and killed almost immediately. *His* killing has never been solved. Four years to the day after Robert Perry was killed, as his sister, Analicia, a twenty-year-old mother, knelt at his shrine to light a candle to his memory, *she* was shot and killed. She got her own shrine. *Her* killing has never been solved. "She is now in the hands of God," the Rev. William

E. Dickerson, minister at Analicia Perry's memorial service told the young men before him. "I'm just glad she's not in the hands of some of you." There were so many shrines after Operation Ceasefire fell apart in Boston that the city considered *regulating* them.

Twenty-five years ago I stood in Nickerson Gardens and thought, Somebody should do something.

We know how to do it *now*.

Here's the thing about Ceasefire, and the drug-market intervention, and the other concrete, operational work that's flowed from the same basic ideas—I'll have more to say about that in a while. The thing is, they *work*. They cut the killing dramatically, they get rid of the public drug craziness, they keep people out of jail and prison, they repair things between the police and the community. They do that. They *work*. Right now, today.

So we can do the work, right now, today, and we can stop the killing and close the drug markets and start to close the prison pipeline and end the persistent worst of our racially tinged nightmare. It's just that simple. I've got an e-mail in my John Jay mailbox, November 9, 2010. Kelly McMillan, deputy chief in the Salinas, California, police department. Salinas is in central California, near Monterey, small city, about 150,000 people, majority Hispanic, a Norteño/Sureño gang battleground. A horrendous homicide rate, four times the national average, twenty-nine homicides in 2009, every single one a gang killing. Salinas put their version of Operation Ceasefire in place, began the call-ins in January 2010. McMillan's e-mail: homicide down by almost half.

It works. It's not perfect, it's a work in progress. We're trying to make it better, we can see how to make it better: There are big new developments coming. But right now, today, it *works*.

That could be, maybe should be, the end of the discussion. It's so much better than any of the alternatives: What's to talk about, except how to get the work done? In a lot of other areas, it *would* be the end of the discussion. If you went to the doctor and she said, You have pancreatic cancer, it pretty much used to be a death sentence, but we've got a new therapy and it increases survivability by half to two thirds, you'd say, *Thank God*. You would *not* say, and she would *not* say, Well, yes, but I'm really emotionally and professionally committed to the old way of doing things, so think I'll stick with that. You would not say, and she would not say, I don't really like the thinking that led to this new therapy, so I'm not going to use it. You would not say, and she would not say, The way I've thought about medicine doesn't allow for these terrific outcomes, so I'm going to ignore them.

Crime's not medicine. In crime, you deal with all those reactions, all the time. It's predictable, inevitable. I warn people, when I talk in public. This stuff *works*, I say, at conferences, congressional hearings, police departments, community meetings. There's a long track record now. This city, that city, these other cities. Here's the homicide graph from half a dozen places, look at it, it just falls into the basement. Here are the formal evaluations. It *works*. It's a *fact*. But watch, I say. Half an hour from now we're going to be talking about all the reasons it won't work, can't work. We're going to hit the "it works in practice but will it work in theory" part of the conversation.

And the debate about outcomes is in fact the least of it. Our thinking about crime is saturated with *values*: with people's convictions about right and wrong, how people should behave, why people behave the way they do, what will and won't get them to change, what they do and don't deserve, what their obligations are and aren't, what our obligations to them are and aren't. When you go to your doctor with your bad pancreas she's not going to say, That's a *bad* pancreas, it doesn't deserve help, if we help it all the *other* pancreases will get the wrong message. Crime's different. That's as it should be. They're crucial, vital issues, all the values questions. Crime is about what we should and shouldn't do as individuals, parents, ethnic groups, communities, nations, democracies. It's about power, coercion, the laying on of hands. Nobody's going to jump out of a squad car and handcuff you and put you up against a wall and go into your pants to see if your pancreas is healthy. If it turns out it's not, nobody's going to say, Your mother didn't raise you right, this is *her* fault.

So the facts about what works and what doesn't turn out not to go very far on their own. There's a lot more to get through if we're going to get anywhere on this.

The truest thing remains: *We can do this*. We know how, now.

Let's get through why that's so hard to see.

Let's get through why the way we think about crime now almost guarantees failure. Let's get through why the way we think about preventing crime walls away the most powerful approach to prevention we have. Let's get through why this isn't even really *about* crime.

When we think about crime we are almost always thinking about something else, that it's all really *about* something else. It's about bad people with bad character, so we need to change their character, get them to turn their lives around. It's about how they got their bad character, so we need to change their families and communities. It's about racism, so we need to end racism. It's about lack of economic opportunity, so we need to do job development. It's about weak and inconsistent law enforcement, so we need stronger laws, more cops, tougher judges.

To do something about crime, our most central conviction is that we have to go *through other things*.

Let me count the ways in which this go *through other things* thinking dooms us.

One of the standard things I hear in crime discussions is, "We have to eradicate racism." It's a reasonable causal claim. When you unpack it, it carries a lot of freight. It's not just about racism, it's about how racism ripples through the culture, how it leads to neglected communities, leads to bad schools, cuts people off from economic opportunity, gets them unwarranted attention from law enforcement, makes their treatment worse when that attention gets them caught up in the system. It makes a lot of sense. But if we're going to take it as a blueprint for action, it's not just a claim about how we got where we are, about how racism and unequal opportunity and failed schools created the problem. It's not just a claim about a logical arc of causation that would move us from where we are to where we want to be: If we were to change these bad things, we'd get this good result. It's a claim about needing to take concrete operational steps *that will get us from here to there*. It's a claim about how we are actually going to solve the problem. It's an engineering claim. If your brakes don't work, you need to replace the pads.

If we don't have the brake pads, your brakes won't get fixed. It's a medical claim. If you have appendicitis, you need to have your appendix out. No surgeon, you're going to die.

Very good, then.

What's the plan?

How are we going to eradicate racism?

How long will it take?

When's it going to stop the killing?

I move in academic circles where people believe in sophisticated policy-analysis tools: cost-benefit analysis, cost-effectiveness analysis, decision analysis, all sorts of things. For almost everything connected with these issues, you don't need any of that. All you need is ruthless common sense. And when you aim ruthless common sense at these prescriptions, they fail. Miserably.

We've been, in theory, working on racism in this country since the abolition movement began in the early 1830s. The last major turning point was more than forty years ago in the victories of the civil-rights movement. If racism is still so bad that it's driving hellish crime issues, then we haven't gotten very far. What's the plan for accelerating the pace of that change? How are we going to get that plan in place and operating? How long before the changes we make in the culture reach, and change things, in our poorest and most troubled communities?

One of the core operating principles in my work is that, when taking on real issues, no statements of the form *Somebody should do something about that* are allowed. Somebody should do something about the guns. Somebody should do something about the drugs. Somebody should do something about racism. Well, yeah, somebody should. Since we're taking this problem on, that somebody is us. If we think eradicating racism is the way to fix it, that's fine. *Tell me how.* If we don't have a plan, if we don't have the means, if the plan with the means we have available doesn't deliver the results we want, if we won't get those results at a pace that we can live with, then we have *nothing*.

I work with a lot of people who believe the answer is education. That makes a lot of sense, too, for all kinds of reasons. So let's say education reform is the way out. Let's say it'll take fifteen years to completely re-tool the public schools so they work for the most disadvantaged kids in our most disadvantaged communities: wildly optimistic, but let's say. Let's say it'll take another fifteen years to get the first wave of kids through the new schools so they hit their years of peak risk immunized to the violence. That means we live with all this for another *three decades*. At *best*.

That's the plan?

Nearly everything in crime policy, nearly all crime-prevention ideas, fail these utterly common-sense tests. Go through the list. We can't make them happen, we don't have the resources to make them happen, they'll take too long, they won't have enough impact. The federal sentencing disparity that punishes black crack dealers much more severely than white powder cocaine dealers? It's an outrage, fine, get rid of it. Which means that the same number of people will spend time in prison, just not for so long. Impact on the body count? Approximately zero. Get rid of gangs? See above rule re: *form of statements not allowed.* There are no interventions of any kind whatsoever—early childhood, prevention, intervention, enforcement—that have shown any meaningful power to eliminate gangs, prevent kids from joining gangs, or get gang members to leave gangs. Jurisdictions that have eliminated their gang problem as such, anywhere, any time: zero. Early childhood intervention? There are no early childhood interventions that have been shown to have any meaningful impact on lethal violence among our most troubled populations in our most dangerous communities. Bad behavior, yes, bad attitudes, yes, delinquency, yes, homicide, no. There are lots of studies showing cost-effectiveness. They're cost-effective, all right: The programs generally don't cost that much, any serious criminality prevented is hugely expensive, so the costs balance fast and you have almost an entire lifetime for those benefits to accrue. They could hardly *not* be cost-effective. Besieged communities don't want cost-effectiveness. They want their kids to stop getting killed and imprisoned. Examples of any serious community violence, drug, or incarceration problems effectively addressed through prevention:

None.

Maybe new programs could be developed that would be more effective. Maybe we could massively increase the resources to those programs. Back to common sense. What's the likelihood that's true? How are we going to command the resources? How long would it take to get everything operational? How long before we see results on the ground?

A very long time.

This commitment to going through other things turns out to be a major part of why what we usually try to do, the way we usually think, doesn't work. What we think we need to do is so hard, so expensive, and so inherently weak that our commitment to it virtually ensures failure.

It's fascinating, once you start to see this, how different it is from the way we deal with other kinds of problems. You go to the doctor with lung cancer, she's going to think surgery, chemotherapy, there's a pretty good chance she'll save your life. Sure, she's going to try to get you to stop smoking before you *get* lung cancer, and she's going to have colleagues whose life work is trying to get *everybody* to stop smoking. But she and they know not everybody's going to stop. She and they know that some people get lung cancer without *ever* smoking. They're just as committed to saving your life today as they are to working back upstream. It's no kind of stretch for them to look at a very bad thing about to unfold right in front of them and say, *I'm going to stop that from happening.* She and her colleagues are going to be working relentlessly, their whole careers, to get better and better at stopping that thing from happening.

Some disciplines *never* think upstream this way. Nobody stood on the San Francisco side of the bay, looked across at the Marin headlands, and said, We need to be able to get from here to there, I guess we need to reverse glaciation and bring these pieces of land back together. They built the Golden Gate Bridge, which worked pretty well for everybody. Most of us don't think upstream like this in our ordinary lives. We'd be dead if we did. When fall comes and it gets cold, you put on a sweater, build a fire, build a house. You don't go to work on the root causes of winter.

Ridiculous comparisons, of course. Gangs, gang violence, drugs, drug markets, they're not like geology and the weather. They're social problems: We can prevent them. It's different.

Is it?

Saying so is an empirical claim. Saying so means, *We understand how these things come about clearly enough to know how to stop them from coming about, and we have the tools with which to do that.* You need both, not just one. Understanding without tools gets you no-where. We understand the weather a whole lot more than we do gangs: The models are good, the forecasting isn't bad, we've got stations on the ground and satellites in orbit feeding us crucial data. Explain, predict, El Niño, why southern California is about to turn into a toaster? You bet. Can't *do* a thing about it. No tools. No capacity. Another empirical matter: It could change any day, that's possible. Right now, our ability to prevent the weather: zero.

Right now, there's no evidence at all that serious violence and drug issues are any different. We don't understand them very well. The experts can't even agree on what a gang *is*, can't predict why one kid will join when another won't, can't predict why one gang member will kill and the others won't, can't say why one neighborhood has an open drug market and others just like it don't. There's no evidence whatsoever that any going-upstream strategies work. This is not just about causality, about explaining how a problem came to be, why it's in one place and not in another. Yes, communities of affluence and without histories of racism and oppression are virtually without gang and overt drug-market problems. That implies in no way at all that we can act on economic and racial issues in communities with gang and drug-market problems and make those problems go away. Their initial conditions were different, their current conditions are different, we may or may not have the tools to be effective. The evidence to date is that we don't.

There is a core arithmetic inevitability that comes with the commitment to going upstream in these ways. The worst things that go on in the most dangerous communities are done by very, very small numbers of people. When the killing was raging in Boston, there were about fifty "gang" killings a year. All that was needed to prevent those killings was to change the behavior of the fifty people who did them. The next step out was to their gangs: about 1,300 people. Change *their* behavior and you prevent the killings. That's what Operation Ceasefire did. The next steps, the ones that prevention thinking would typically call for? A standard move is *at-risk kids*. Males in their violence-prone years in the most dangerous Boston neighborhoods? About *21,000*. Typical move after that is *families*. Let's say one parent and two siblings for each young man: *84,000* people. Typical move after that is *the community*. Population of the hot Boston neighborhoods, Roxbury, Dorchester, Mattapan, the South End, Hyde Park, Jamaica Plain: about *284,000* people.

Move beyond the kernel of the problem, the math is crushing.

And if you were able to raise the resources, construct the programs, run the interventions, that engaged with all 21,000 young men in Boston, all 84,000 people in their families in Boston, all 284,000 residents in their neighborhoods? Most of those resources, most of your backbreaking work, would be *wasted*. As things stood in Boston, without doing *anything* extra, there were only 1,300 gang members in Boston, only fifty killers a year. The other people your programs touch *don't need them*. Not to keep them out of gangs, not to keep them out of the hardcore population most likely to kill or be killed. *They're not going to go there anyway.*

The same thing goes for law enforcement. Let's say we need to ramp up criminal justice to stop the killing: new laws, mandatory minimums for guns and drugs, tougher sentencing, stricter probation and parole supervision, more prisons. Wasted, nearly all of it. We don't need fancy research or careful models. This is simple common sense. Let's start with the 21,000 at-risk young men in Boston's most dangerous neighborhoods. Let's say half of them have had some kind of criminal justice contact—probably conservative, when half of them are locked up or under court supervision in places like Baltimore. That's 10,500 people. In any given year, fifty killings a year, 10,450 of them won't kill anybody. Over ten years, five hundred killings, a bloodbath, 10,000 of them won't kill anybody. What we do to the rest of them in the name of stopping the killing is pointless.

But, it makes sense to say, it's important work, it's worth doing. People need jobs, racism needs eradicating, families need supporting, probationers need supervising. Absolutely. Decide on the merits. If the work is worth doing for its own sake, for broader reasons, do it. But remember where we started: *We have to do this to stop the killing.* For that, it is fantastically ineffective and inefficient.

This is the geometry of working on rare, extreme events by going upstream. It's inescapable. As you move away from the center, the work grows geometrically, and the likelihood that the work will touch a link to the outcome you're seeking to prevent diminishes geometrically, and the likelihood that you can *actually do it* diminishes geometrically.

The policy conversation about school spree shootings is a classic. That went: The school shootings were driven by social dynamics in big high schools, subtle family dysfunctions, exposure to violent music and video games, rejection by girls and bullying by the cool cliques, access to firearms. Therefore we need to work on those things in order to prevent school spree shootings.

Very good. If we take the universe of high school males who have, say, five of the following seven risk factors—they're in big high schools, their parents have subtle problems, they've listened to violent music, they've played violent video games, they've been picked on by jocks, they've been humiliated by girls they like, they can find a gun at home or at a friend's home or out in the world if they try hard enough—that's . . . pretty much every male high school student in the country. (It's *me* in high school, let me tell you.) To prevent them from shooting up their schools, we therefore need, for *everybody*, to build smaller high schools, treat their parents, eliminate or keep them from violent music, eliminate or keep them from violent video games, completely change youth culture and adolescent sexual politics, and do something about guns in America. And since almost nobody shoots up their school, *on virtually all of this we will get absolutely no return*. That's why there's *been*, basically, no preventive work done around school spree shootings. Schools themselves have taken steps, police departments have changed their tactics, but almost all of it is around students found with weapons and responses to actual shootings. The logic of the prevention analysis makes it effectively impossible to implement.

And we'd better make sure we don't do harm, while we're at it. One not-uncommon consequence of treating low-risk populations for high-risk behavior is that you increase the problem you're trying to prevent. My favorite: the federal government's $1.2 *billion* National Youth Anti-Drug Media Campaign, a massive advertising effort to get parents to police their kids more carefully and to persuade kids not to use drugs that grew out of the famous "This is your brain on drugs" campaign. The National Institute on Drug Abuse evaluation found no evidence of reductions in drug use—and evidence that kids *not* inclined to use drugs were persuaded by the campaign that drug use was normal and smoked more pot.

1.2 billion dollars. Not just wasted: It made things worse.

The deepest commitment to going upstream in ways that don't involve law enforcement comes from people who believe in what's come to be

called prevention: working on root causes, working on racism and economics and education and health care, supporting families, addressing
the risk factors that travel with kids' movement into crime, providing
treatment and counseling and mentoring. It's a commitment with profound personal, professional, and moral salience. It separates social
workers and public-health practitioners from cops and prosecutors, liber-
als from conservatives, those who believe in social accountability and root
causes from those who believe in individual accountability and criminal
justice. It characterizes entire intellectual communities. (How many so-
ciologists does it take to change a light bulb? That's a stupid question:
Changing a light bulb doesn't do anything about the root causes of the
dark.)

The word *prevention* has itself become a term of art. It no longer
means, in this world, what it actually means: *to make something not
happen*. In this world, it has come to mean *not exercising authority*. It
has come to mean *not involving law enforcement*. Working with a kid's
mother to help her run a stable home is prevention. Working to keep her
son in school is prevention. Teaching him anger management in school
is prevention. Teaching him dispute resolution if he does join a gang is
prevention. Sitting down with him and telling him he'll go to prison
if he shoots somebody *isn't* prevention: It's "suppression." Even if it
works, and you don't have to lock him up, and nobody gets shot: not
prevention. Telling all the gangs in town, Don't shoot, they heed, they
like it: *not prevention*.

This conception of prevention is part of a larger and important
morality. It's about not blaming victims, not punishing desperate vulnerable individuals for gross social failures, not bringing the iron boot
of the state down on the necks of the poorest and least powerful. I presented Operation Ceasefire in a lecture at the Kennedy School. One of
the graduate students was *outraged*. "You're going to stop the killing
without doing something about community conditions?" she said. "That's
immoral." That's interesting, I told her. The same community conditions
that are driving the killing are driving infant mortality: historical oppression, current neglect, economic inequality, personal and family and community stress. Doctors know that if they make sure pregnant women get
prenatal vitamins their babies will be born healthy. They're not working
on root causes. They're saving babies. Are *they* immoral?

A very good question. Not a fair question, in one very important way. Doctors don't go through doors, shoot the dog, and handcuff the mothers who don't take their vitamins. Doctors don't go through doors, shoot the dog, and handcuff the kids those mothers have failed by *not* taking their vitamins. Those mothers and their kids don't go to prison in droves for not taking their vitamins. Prevention folks want, correctly, to avoid that kind of thing. Often mixed in with that, barely below the surface, is a visceral distaste for the thugs in uniform. I gave a lecture at UCLA shortly after Operation Ceasefire took hold in Boston, told the story about the gang member who got stopped during the Vamp Hill Kings operation with his assassination kit of gun and gloves and mask. One of the social-work faculty said, I'm not surprised, the kids were getting stopped by the police like that. Uh, no, he wasn't going to shoot a cop, he was going to shoot another *kid*; the cop *saved the other kid's life*.

The cops have their own version. They hear the prevention people call guys they know as homicidal crazies "clients" and roll their eyes, write them off as naïve thug huggers. It's less principled than in the other direction, though. They wouldn't *mind* if this guy turned his life around, they're just sure he won't. About which they are, largely, correct. But it turns out, in this arena, that the cops and prosecutors and all the rest are greatly more broad-minded than the other side. It's rare these days, has been for a long time, *not* to have law enforcement people say, when it comes to gang and drug issues, "We can't arrest our way out of this." Social workers and public-health doctors don't much say, "We can't help our way out of this."

Which has some central implications for the new ways of cracking these problems. One is that there's no place in prevention thinking for a different *kind of use* of law enforcement and state power. Ceasefire, High Point, they're not about locking people up. They're about *not* locking people up. They bend over backward not to lock people up. They're motivated by an understanding of the damage locking people up does to them, their families, their communities. They use law enforcement as a way to shape behavior and get compliance, not to sweep the streets and stuff the prisons. They sit down with likely offenders and say, Here's what we're going to do if you make us, please don't. They use deterrence to protect those most at risk from those most likely to hurt them, to provide a safe way out of hugely dangerous situations. They use clearer and more transparent sanction strategies to make it more appealing to go get help. They use state power to disrupt the dynamics that drive the killing. They put community moral engagement and carefully constructed help in the forefront, try hard to get people to pay attention and take advantage.

Prevention folks should love this. Some do. Some simply can't take it in. In their book *Murder Is No Accident: Understanding and Preventing Youth Violence in America*, Harvard School of Public Health assistant dean Dr. Deborah Prothrow-Stith and her colleague Howard R. Spivak describe Operation Ceasefire as "focused on carrying out federal prosecutions of minors with guns . . ." Among the many ways in which this is howlingly wrong, there were exactly *no* minors prosecuted federally under Ceasefire: The feds don't want anything to do with juveniles, not for homicide or selling guns or carrying guns or moving weight drugs. I've never *seen* the feds take a juvenile; the only one I've ever even *heard* of is the kid who, when he decided to do an arson, made the mistake of torching the shed near Kennebunk, Maine, that held a boat engine belonging to former president George Bush. Him, the feds took.

The Centers for Disease Control put together a handbook for communities on best practices in youth-violence prevention. Operation Ceasefire and its brethren aren't mentioned; *nothing* involving law enforcement is. Lay out the High Point drug strategy for a room full of people, explain how it's designed to switch off the market for good, how it'll stop sucking young men in because it's *gone*, how almost nobody got arrested, how almost everybody who *would* have gotten arrested didn't, how the new status quo replaces enforcement almost entirely with new community norms, and count down for somebody to say it: "What are you doing about prevention?" The insistence that *any* move by law enforcement is "suppression" puts the new strategies out of bounds *by definition*.

The false divide between prevention and law enforcement is not only mistaken but catastrophically misguided. Getting this right is essential to how we need to think, in the most practical terms imaginable, about law and law enforcement, how they engage with troubled communities, and how to address the most severe problems in those communities.

The law is more than just a justification for and a guide to using state power. It's a statement about the values and aspirations of a people. It should and can and does have moral power, particularly in its most central standards. We don't kill. We don't shoot people. We don't destroy communities with drugs. Having to lay on hands and lock people up is a failure of that moral power. The more that power fails, the more the laying on of hands is needed. The law itself, law enforcement itself, is *designed* to do prevention. It says, We the people have decided that we won't do this thing. Having to act means that that prevention has failed.

Ceasefire said: Prevention in law enforcement is deterrence. When we get that right, when we get the right messages to the right people and back them up in the right ways, we get big results. That's still true; it's an important insight. There's always going to be that kind of work to do. Sometimes it's perfectly good enough. Anthony Braga orchestrated the elegant, streamlined elimination of a major shooting problem in Lowell, Massachusetts. His research showed that juvenile Asian gang members were doing the shootings. There's very little that law enforcement can do with, or to, juveniles. Instead, the Lowell Police Department started raiding the neighborhood gambling establishments run by older gang members. Every time they did, they told the older gang members that the raids were because of the shooting. The older guys stopped it cold.

But deterrence is, at its best, a struggle, a tug of war. It's the sheriff facing down the desperadoes with one bullet in his gun. Uneasy but stable, at its very best. It's about formal, open, socially sanctioned threats. Most people don't have to be threatened to do the right thing. Even in the most dangerous neighborhoods, most people do the right thing. Guns are *far* from the preferred method of dispute resolution. Most of even the most serious offenders never kill anybody. When they're tempted, it's usually thinking about the people and the community around them that stops them: informal social control. When that's not going to work, what we want is for the law to work, for its standards and standing to have sway. We want it to work—to prevent—because people believe in it, without *having* to arrest, prosecute, imprison. We want it to have *legitimacy*.

This is *central*.

Legitimacy is a formal idea in the social sciences: It's the standing the authorities have, in the eyes of those regarding them, to say, You should do this, you should not do that. It's been getting a lot of attention lately. Legitimacy scholars like Tom Tyler at NYU home in on the clear fact that most people obey the law most of the time. Even criminals, almost always, don't run red lights, do pay for most of the stuff they get, do resolve disputes peaceably, don't kill people they're mad at. So if they're teetering, wondering whether to kill this person right this minute, wondering whether to tell the cops who killed their friend, it's that standing, that legitimacy, that can make the difference. Think well of the law, think well of the police, and people, even hard-core offenders, are much more likely to do the right thing. Think badly, we've got a vendetta and a body.

Legitimacy turns out to rest on two key supports. One is that people feel that the law is touching them equitably, not as the product of bias or prejudice. One is the quality of that touch, that they're being handled with courtesy and respect. Outcomes turn out not to matter that much. People will accept a result they don't like, as long as they feel that they've been treated with fairness and decency.

Tracey Meares, deputy dean at Yale Law School, is one of the leading figures in the new work on legitimacy. She's a friend, whip-smart, and cops and prosecutors love her. When she was at the University of Chicago she helped the U.S. attorney's office field what became the jewel in the crown of the Justice Department's Project Safe Neighborhoods initiative. She knew the logic behind Operation Ceasefire and crafted a variation focusing heavily on legitimacy.

Parolees with records of gun or gang crime, leaving prison and returning to two of Chicago's most dangerous neighborhoods, were required as a condition of release to attend a call-in. There they heard three messages. The U.S. attorney's office explained to them that as felons they faced at least a five-year mandatory minimum federal sentence if they were caught with a gun. A service provider told them how they could get help. An ex-offender, ex-gang member told how he'd changed his life and that they could do it, too. The call-ins took about an hour. They were held about once a month and became standard operating procedure for the parole authorities and other partners.

As part of the project, Tracey and her colleagues surveyed gun offenders in the neighborhoods, asked them questions designed to get at key issues around police legitimacy, and compared their attitudes with an existing survey of ordinary citizens. The results were fascinating. The offenders respected the law. About three quarters of gun offenders thought people should obey the law even if it goes against what they think is right, slightly *more* than ordinary citizens. What the offenders did not respect was the police. Fully three quarters of ordinary citizens thought that most police treat people with respect; only about a third of gun offenders did. Only about a quarter of ordinary citizens thought most police were dishonest; over half of gun offenders did.

Tracey designed the call-ins to enhance legitimacy: to enhance the moral power of the law and change the streets' view of the police. They were held in what she calls "places of civic importance" in the neighborhood: community centers, community colleges. They were held in the round, everybody on the same level, looking at each other, no special status or power position for the cops and prosecutors. They were calm, matter-of-fact, businesslike. The authorities' attitude and language emphasized the offenders' rationality, that they could make choices, that they were in control of their futures, that the cops and prosecutors respected them and wanted them to have the information they needed to make good decisions, that explaining things to them was only fair.

The outcome was *amazing*.

Homicide in the neighborhoods fell 37 percent. If you were a parolee with a gang record and never went to one of the call-ins, inside five years you were back in prison. A third of gang members who went to the call-ins were still on the street. If you were a parolee with a gun record and never went to a call-in, inside five years you were about 50 percent likely to be back in prison. Almost all the gun offenders who went to the call-ins were still on the street. There was no new enforcement, no service follow-up, no sustained community contact. Most of it was just the meeting. *One hour.*

If you're serious about prevention, legitimacy is the game changer.

Actual enforcement, locking people up, *is* suppression, no question: The prevention people are right about that. Deterrence *is* prevention. It's better, it can be very good indeed, but it's not good enough. Legitimacy is *real* prevention. It means that the neighborhoods trust the law, trust the police, think they're being treated fairly and well, will let the law shape their behavior, will ask the law for help when they need it. Legitimacy is *moral power*.

Legitimacy is what Jimmie Mac was always about: getting the social contract right. In political theory, the social contract is about the people's surrender to the state—to the larger community—of the use of violence. The state of nature is every man for himself: If you're wronged, you pick up your gun and go deal with it. It's personal; it's homicide and vendetta. That way lies madness and destruction. The social contract says, We'll give up that power to the larger community, in exchange for which it will use it well and wisely, and protect us. When that goes right, we've got civil society. But society has to be *civil*. The people have to be protected, the power has to be used well and wisely. Civil society, community, doesn't have to be perfect, it can take all kinds of strain, but it has to be *us*. It can't be *us and them*.

Which throws into even sharper relief how wrong we've got it now. If legitimacy rests on perceptions of equity rather than bias or prejudice, on perceptions of being treated with courtesy and respect—if it rests, fundamentally, on well and wisely—the way we engage with the hot neighborhoods now might as well have been designed to destroy it. Nothing that doesn't transform how broken that is is going to change things.

A few years back, *60 Minutes* called to talk about stop snitching and witness intimidation. I said the same thing to the producers I say to everybody: You're missing the point, you don't get it, the community's not scared, the community is *turning its back*. Unlike almost everybody else, they listened. They went into New York City neighborhoods and talked to people. Anderson Cooper interviewed a black male named Alex.

"Alex, do you trust the police?" he said.

No, Alex said.

Why not? Cooper asked.

"Because there's been numerous times I've been walking," he said, "just being a regular American citizen, and getting stopped by the police for no reason."

Cooper talked to a black female, Tess.

"Anybody who comes forward and talks to the police about something they witnessed, a murder or a crime, are they a snitch?" Cooper asked.

"Yes . . . It's a crime, remember, in our community, to snitch," said Tess.

Alex was *fourteen years old*. Tess wasn't much older. *60 Minutes* found them through the *church group* they belonged to.

We've been convening small, informal groups of black men at John Jay recently, asking them about their experience of being policed. What they say shocks the conscience. My mother taught me not to stand outside on the corner, one said. If I have to stand outside I stay in the middle of the block. The corner is where the jump-out boys—the drug squads—go. The cops just roll up on you, when all you're doing is walking down the street, said another. They follow you in their car, staring, like they want you to do something. I don't go outside my house, said another. It's too much trouble to be in the neighborhood, they mess with you all the time. I stay inside or I go to some other neighborhood.

The most poignant, the most infuriating, to me was the man in his mid-thirties who talked at some length about how he'd never been arrested, never been in handcuffs. This was to him an enormous accomplishment. And so it is, for many black and minority men in many of America's neighborhoods. He has done very well never to have been arrested or restrained. But he also told how he had said the same thing to a police officer who had stopped him, for no reason that he could understand. The officer had scoffed at him. What black man in this place has never been arrested? The check came back clean.

In cities all across the country, people in these neighborhoods aren't talking. You get shot, your friend gets shot, you don't talk. Your best friend gets killed, you don't talk. Nobody talks. Clearance rates for non-fatal shootings in many cities are sinking toward zero. Homicide clearance rates are going the same way. In Boston, David Bernstein, a reporter for the *Boston Phoenix*, looked at clearance rates for homicides involving black victims. For twenty-two killings in 2002, by 2005, *not a single one* had resulted in a homicide conviction. In Baltimore, the state attorney's office *arrests* witnesses to make them show up at trial. Juries won't convict, people don't assume any longer that the cops are telling the truth. People see the people who shot and killed their friends and family walking around and shoot them themselves. Then *their* friends come back at them, and round and round. Vendetta is taking over, all across the country, while we stand and watch. At Analicia Perry's memorial service in Boston, the Rev. Dickerson shouted at the mourners from the pulpit. "If you know who did this, give him up! Give him up! It's not snitching!" Nobody did.

It's not about the cases, the prosecutions, the clearance rates. It's that we can't, and won't, ever get anywhere when the neighborhoods feel like this about the law. No police operation or social program or job-development initiative or sentencing reform can overcome this. If we overcome this—which we can do only by fundamentally changing the way law enforcement deals with these neighborhoods—we can win in very short order.

This is the real significance of what happened in High Point. Nothing important, in our ordinary way of thinking, really changed in the West End. The same people were there. The same cops were there. Nobody had any more money on May 19, 2004, than they did on May 18. Nobody was any more educated, had any more family support; there were no more fathers around, nobody was doing anything extra for at-risk kids. There were no new laws, no criminal justice reforms. Arresting a few drug dealers and talking to a handful more didn't fix the neighborhood. *Nothing changed.*

Except the way the community viewed the cops. Except the way the cops viewed the community. Except that the cops had come up with something that the community could live with that changed what was going on on the ground. Except the changes in the community about what it would and would not tolerate. Changes that had been released by the newly won legitimacy of the High Point Police Department.

If we get legitimacy right, there's a lot less work to do than we think there is. To get where we need to go, we don't really even have to do anything about crime. This isn't *about* crime.

It is, of course. But mostly it's not. It's easier, a whole lot easier, than that.

Crime is *huge*. It's smoking a joint and identity theft and date rape; Bernie Madoff and stealing a car and cheating on your taxes; sleeping with a minor and taking towels from a motel and bribing a congressman; buying an escort and hitting your wife and torching your business; child porn and stalking your ex and drinking and driving; illegal dumping and breaking and entering and hitting a guy in a bar; stealing a television and selling crank and smuggling ivory.

All bad things. Some of them very, very bad things.

Not one of them will destroy a community.

Elliot Spitzer went from being governor of New York to being Client Number 9, made national headlines, humiliated his family, and lost his job. Albany and Washington, D.C., where he committed his crimes, the neighborhood he lived in, never missed a beat. Bernie Madoff destroyed individuals, families, businesses, nonprofits, thieved on a historic scale; the Jewish community he preyed on, the neighborhoods his victims lived in, are fine. I care passionately about domestic violence. I have an intervention I think might work. I've been trying for years to get somebody to try it and I can't, just like I couldn't get anybody to try the drug-market strategy. It looks like High Point's finally going to run with it. If it works, a lot of women, kids, and families are going to be a lot better off. If it doesn't, will we lose their neighborhoods? We will not. There's a lot of domestic violence right this minute in healthy, functioning communities. I hate it, we should all hate it. We don't pay nearly enough attention to it, what we try to do about it doesn't work, and we need something else. Still: For a community, a people, a race, a nation, it's survivable.

What's not survivable is pretty narrow.

America has four inextricably linked problems that converge in its most troubled communities. There's the violence that terrorizes many of its, especially, black and minority communities. There's the chaos that comes with, especially, public drug markets. There's the devastation being wrought on, especially, troubled black and minority communities by our criminal justice response to the first two problems. And there's the worsening racial divide *that's* causing. We can't deal with any of them without dealing with all of them. We deal with them, it's a different country.

We take them on directly, we win, and everything changes. The overwhelmingly good people in our most desperate places get the peace they need to live good lives. They get their streets and parks back. We switch off the engines that are pumping whole generations into prison. We give most of those we've written off as predators a safe way out. We stop the damage to husbands and wives and families and children. We stop acting out the worst racial stereotypes on both sides. We create the calm and the trust and relationships we need to do the deeper work, get the schools working, help families, build businesses, all the things you cannot possibly do when things are as they are now. All we need to do to get there is handle those four problems.

Making it about crime makes it too hard, too big a lift, and it misses the point. There's a lot of crime, bad crime, a lot of seriously bad people, in some pretty good places. When we mapped dead kids in Boston, there were no bodies in the North End, and only a couple in Charlestown. The North End is old ethnic Italian, the seat of the Boston mob. It's dead safe, wonderful restaurants and cafés. Charlestown is old ethnic Irish, seriously tough, breeds bank robbers and armored-car crews, has a huge public housing project and a major heroin problem. Nobody in Boston said, We need to root out crime in the North End, the mob guys are looting Logan Airport, that's not okay, we need to stop all the Italians, kick in their doors. Nobody said, There's heroin in Charlestown, that's not okay, we need to lock down Bunker Hill public housing, stop everybody who lives there and go through their pockets.

Framing this as crime is deeply, *profoundly* unfair to the most dangerous neighborhoods. Their crime problem, as such, isn't much worse than anybody else's. Take away the violence, the public chaos, feel like you have to go after everything else? Fine. Then go after the same things in the white neighborhoods, too. School surveys show that white students are far more likely to use drugs than black students are: Almost 40 percent of whites say they've smoked marijuana in the last year, about a quarter of blacks do. Speed, over 12 percent vs. under 3 percent. Powder cocaine, 5 percent vs. 1 percent. Crack, 2.2 percent vs. 1.2 percent. Heroin, about the same, under 1 percent. About 40 percent of white kids say they've vandalized something, about a third of blacks do. Seventeen percent say they've sold drugs, vs. 13 percent. Carrying a gun? About the same, 16 percent vs. 15 percent. The Substance Abuse and Mental Health Services Administration of the Department of Health and Human Services regularly surveys American households; it's the best data we have on a whole range of drug issues. Year after year after year, the proportion of people who say they use drugs regularly is about the same, by race, as their share of the population. In 2005, the "regular use" breakdown was 69.2 percent white, 14 percent black, when the U.S. was about 76 percent white and 13 percent black. There are shadings here; the specialists all agree that a small proportion of very heavy minority users consumes more than its share. Doesn't change the basic picture. Drug dealing, drug use, as such, is that what we care about?

Lock up one in three *white* men.

A. Rafik Mohamed and Erik Fritsvold showed how it really works in an ethnographic study of white drug dealers at a California college, an article called "Damn, It Feels Good to Be a Gangsta." They quote a "a blonde haired, blue eyed, somewhat preppy-dressed freshman from the Midwest" who deals marijuana and cocaine in volume:

> Everybody—literally every single person—everyone [here] does coke. Everybody, I swear to God I'm not lying. You bust it out at a party, put it on a glass table and just leave it there and everyone will be over there like [sniffs] . . . It is so easy, it's just you can make tons of money.

These dealers don't worry about getting arrested *at all*. Their college has an understanding with the local police department not to come on campus. Administrators know who's dealing and don't do anything. "No one cares that much," says one dealer. "I think a lot of it has to do with the people we are. We don't live in the ghetto."

If we say stopping the killing and the public chaos isn't enough, we need to go after the drugs, go after crime, then we need to go into the white neighborhoods. It would be easy. We know how to do it, we have lots of practice. We could saturate the white high schools and colleges with undercover officers, arrest lots of white kids. We could follow the weed dealers back home, make sure they get in the house, kick in their doors, twist-tie their parents, shoot their dogs, seize their houses, get them and their families evicted from their apartments, make them homeless. Tap their phones, find their suppliers, get everybody on RICO charges, threaten them with federal prison, drop hints about anal rape, flip them on their friends.

Easy.

If this were really about crime, *we'd be doing it*.

It's not about crime from the other direction, either. The guys hustling in the most dangerous neighborhoods don't have to reform for the killing and the chaos to stop. They don't have to, as we say all the time, turn their lives around. That would be great, it's what everybody wants, but we make this too hard, too: far, far too hard. We see two choices: the killing continues, or all the thugs turn their lives around and become middle-class taxpayers. That's not how it works, even in a lot of good neighborhoods. The North End and Charlestown, again: There are a lot of very, very serious criminals there. They just don't kill people, hardly ever. And when they do, it's almost all about business. They don't kill little girls by mistake beefing with their ex-girlfriend's new boyfriend. They hustle, but they hustle, mostly, *quietly*. It's what Eugene Rivers told a roomful of Boston gang members, and which they completely got: If you're going to be a gangster, be a *good* gangster. Be *professional*. It's been maybe the hardest single thing to get people to understand. *The violence isn't about business*. It's personal, beef, street-code nonsense. Even when it is about business, business doesn't have to be done that way. Even the business killings are mostly street-code stuff: You shoot and kill the guy who's operating on your corner because the streets say you have to. There are other ways to deal with it; lots of serious criminals find other ways to deal with it.

It's why not everybody has to get a job for the killing to stop. The record, from Boston on, is not great on this front. Not that many street guys come forward, not that many can stick with the social-service programs designed to help them, not that many can make it even when they really try. They're heavily compromised in awful ways: They have appalling criminal records, street attitudes that are hard to shake, they're shocky, they have terrible work habits. Jobs are hard to get even for people without all those problems. Hardly anybody in any of the successful cities got a good job, relative to the size of the hard-core population. And—and we should be honest about it—our social-service programs for these folks don't work very well at all. But you don't need a job not to shoot people. You don't even need to live a straight life not to shoot people. You just need *not to shoot people*.

The meaning of the social-service side, we came to see, was less about getting people jobs than it was about resetting, creating, legitimacy. It said to the neighborhoods and the streets, The outside cares about you and wants you to succeed. It freed the neighborhoods to say to the streets, Don't tell me you're a victim, there's help for you, if you don't take it that's on you. It meant the streets couldn't say anymore, They won't give us a chance, they hate us. It helped the cops, the neighborhoods, the streets to see that we all want the same thing, even if it's not perfect. It changed things, even if it didn't work very well on its own terms.

We're all trying to do better on the service side. We all want it to work, and we're working hard to figure out how to do that. But the clear fact is that most of even the hard-core street guys don't reform, transform, when the killing tanks and the drug markets go away. They just stop hurting people and tearing the neighborhood apart.

It's not about crime.

Fixing the strained, often poisoned relationship between law enforcement and America's most troubled communities—fixing the crisis of legitimacy—is the key to making those neighborhoods safe and undoing the damage we're doing now. It's the key to restoring our collective sanity. We can do that work and make immediate progress on the core public-safety problems that are tearing those neighborhoods apart. That's all that Operation Ceasefire, the High Point strategy, Tracey Meares's Chicago operation, are. They're concrete, manageable ways of getting that work done. Getting law enforcement together, getting key voices from the community together, getting help together, getting the street guys at the center of things together, finding common ground, and getting big, rapid results.

We saw it happen in Boston as Ceasefire took hold, but we didn't understand it. Cops, prosecutors, gang members, community people, ministers, the feds, the outreach workers all started operating from virtually the same script, were able to talk together and work together, started taking on one another's roles, started stepping outside the roles that had been written for them. Doing the work together, the new relationships, the new ways in which we were engaging one another, led us to a place of respect and common purpose. But we didn't really know what was happening, we weren't explicit about it, we didn't cement it, and when Ceasefire slipped away, we couldn't stay there. We should know enough to stay there now.

We can take on, directly, and in very particular ways, the very few crime problems that are right now tearing apart America's most troubled neighborhoods. We can dramatically reduce those problems, almost right away, and relieve those neighborhoods of the damage they do. Law enforcement can show, as it does so, a respect and caring for the community that undercuts the worst community narratives about law enforcement and restores legitimacy. It can stop doing much of the damage it is now doing. The community can show its moral strength and demonstrate in clear and powerful ways what it does and does not want, undercutting the worst of the law enforcement narratives. Resetting those relationships frees the latent power of community standards and of the law itself, of almost everybody's latent respect for the law. That does a huge amount of the work all by itself. Very, very few people are driving the worst problems. Most of them don't like the situation they're in to begin with. Many will listen to people they respect, and there are lots of people they respect who will talk to them, if we set it up right. We can help them, as much as we can and as much as they'll let us, and that changes things in all kinds of ways. Many will listen to law enforcement when they're approached in the right way, with dignity and respect. When none of that works, law enforcement can often do deterrence, not enforcement. As offenders change how they behave, they undercut the worst narratives law enforcement and the rest of the outside world have about *them*.

We do all those things and we stop stuffing the prisons, stop doing all that harm, there's calm in the neighborhoods, we're not at odds any longer, and we can take a deep breath and get on with the deeper work of community uplift.

Which is where we started.

This stuff works. We can do it.

Cincinnati

Over the speakerphone from his office in late 2006, Mark Mallory said to me, Is this true? This thing that I've been hearing about, it will really bring the killing down?

Yes, I said. And keep people out of prison, and heal the wounds between your police and your community.

We know how to do this.

But that's not what I want to talk to you about. I promise you it will work. We know that now. I'll answer all your questions. I'll give you the evaluations. I'll introduce you to people who've done it; they didn't believe it either, they've seen it, they'll tell you.

I can give it to you, I promise. But I can't keep it for you. *You* have to keep it. That's what I want to talk about, now, from the beginning.

I wanted no more Trina Persads.

Boston, June 29, 2002. Two MIC—Magnolia Intervale Creston streets—guys in a stolen car with a shotgun are gunning for rival Big Head Boyz. They shoot, miss, shoot ten-year-old Trina Persad in the face. She lingers for a couple of days and dies in the hospital. *She* got a street shrine, hung on the park fence. A photograph, a wreath, a stuffed rabbit. She was killed in Jermaine Goffigan Park, named after a nine-year-old who'd been shot dead on his *birthday*, Halloween night, 1994, counting his candy in front of his grandmother's Academy Homes apartment.

It was exactly the kind of thing Ceasefire was designed to prevent, and preventing it was exactly what Boston was no longer doing. Boston seemed willing to do anything *except* put Ceasefire back in place. As the body count rose after Ceasefire was dismantled, police rolled out initiative after initiative, many of them of Paul Joyce's design—Neighborhood Shield, Rolling Thunder, Home Safe. None of it worked.

In his farewell address as mayor of New York in December of 2001, Rudy Giuliani took time to point out that homicides in Boston were soaring while New York's were still coming down. "In the last statistics put out by the FBI," the mayor said, "there has been a sixty-seven percent increase in murder in Boston. During that same period of time, there was a twelve percent decrease in the city of New York. I don't know, which policing theory would you want to follow?" "The Boston model," he went on. "This doesn't have to do with baseball. It has to do with policing." Boston was outraged. "Giuliani's half-baked comparative crime analysis," the *Boston Globe* said in an editorial. "It's easy to take shots when you're walking out the door," Commissioner Evans told the *Globe*. "He has chosen to compare one year, and it's the year most favorable to his city. After the first of the year, he's not accountable."

What nobody said: He's *right*, the bodies are stacking up. And would continue to stack up, at an increasing pace. As the city continued to do anything, everything, except Ceasefire. The Boston Police Department's official line was that it *was* doing Ceasefire, was "taking it to another level," as Evans told *CommonWealth* magazine in January of 2003. If you didn't understand how Ceasefire had worked, why it had worked, it even seemed right. There's a quote from me in the *CommonWealth* story, too. "There is no systematic, interagency response to acts of violence," I said. "The backbone of what worked is gone, it's just that simple." Not so, said Joyce. "According to figures provided by the department, there were 12 cease-fire sessions held last year through mid-December, more than twice the number held all year in both 2001 and 2000."

But there weren't. The department was calling anything it felt like Ceasefire; the new sessions were such things as meetings with each month's "Terrible Twenty," high-risk prisoners about to be released back to Boston. Another initiative the department was wrapping in "Ceasefire" focused on about two hundred people in the perennially hot Grove Hall neighborhood, arresting the very worst and focusing city services on the rest. Not bad ideas, but not what had worked before.

Not, especially, focused on groups and group dynamics, the absolute heart of the strategy. I got call after call as the violence spiraled, reporters trying to make sense of huge lists of "Ceasefire" activity the police provided them. "They say they're doing it," I heard, over and over and over. *It's simple*, I said. *Are they focusing on groups, putting them on prior notice, cracking down on groups that kill, communicating back to the other groups? Backing it up with services and the community?* No, they weren't. *Then they're not doing it.* Joseph Cousins, the MIC banger who killed Trina Persad, had been in one of the new call-ins six weeks before the shooting. *We would have made an example of both MIC and the Big Head Boyz*, I told people. *Has there been any action against either? Has that been marketed back to other groups?* No. *Then they're not doing it.*

I was persona non grata with the Boston police by this point; nobody could afford to be seen talking to me. I had lots of friends there still, they told me what was going on, but it was all sub rosa. Baltimore's politics were the worst I'd ever dealt with, but they were, I will give them, relatively open and direct; you knew pretty much what you were dealing with, they squared off with baseball bats and had at it. Boston's were sullen, secretive, and lethal; they slipped poison into your drink when your back was turned. My relationship with the department had not survived the flood of outside attention. There was a consensual fiction that had been developed in official Boston that all the good work anybody had done in the name of crime prevention had been part of the Miracle. It was a political necessity, I understood it, the mayor and police commissioner had to keep the city together, honor everybody's efforts, keep everybody happy. I did everything I could to play along, had delegations from other cities come to my Kennedy School office and say, *We understand now how this happened in Boston, we've just been with the mayor and he explained how he made it happen, he made all the agencies work together*, bit my tongue.

But I had scholarly obligations as well, and was constantly taking questions from all over the country about what had worked and would work. Our formal evaluation looked at whether the Ten Point Coalition, Operation Nightlight, the public-health campaign, other initiatives, had had any substantial impact on the killing and said no. I'd get calls from cities desperate to stop their killing—How do we launch that probation program that stopped the killing?—and I had to say, *It didn't.* The Kennedy School team said, over and over, *It all probably helped, things*

*could have been a lot worse than they were when the streets were hot,
and most of it ended up playing a crucial role in what became Ceasefire.
We didn't make this up at Harvard, we learned it all from the street guys,
we built it out of what they knew—when it all came together, that's what
worked.* Didn't matter. In Boston, the whispering began. *Kennedy's
claiming credit.* It got bad fast. Nobody ever said anything to me, but the
doors slammed shut. In late 1998, the police department won the Herman Goldstein Award for Excellence in Problem-Oriented Policing, one
of the highest honors in the policing world, for Operation Ceasefire.
Commissioner Evans accepted it in San Diego on behalf of the partnership, bowed to everybody who had been part of it, and then said, and
David Kennedy's here, he did some of the research for us.

I stayed involved with Gary and the Working Group until they were
shut down, and worked behind the scenes to get things going again, but
got absolutely nowhere. I got call after call, was asked everywhere I went,
What's wrong in Boston? *Lack of adult supervision,* I started to say in
private.

When Trina Persad was killed I couldn't stand it any longer and
wrote a *Boston Globe* op-ed: "We Can Make Boston Safe Again." We
know how to do this, it's gone, we can fix it, it said. It was the end; I was
finished in Boston. I'd get calls all the time, have secret meetings with
my old friends, but they were still on the job; in this poisonous atmo-
sphere, none of them could afford to say anything. The killing continued to mount; by 2005, the city had returned to pre-Ceasefire levels of
street violence and had finally figured out that Ceasefire had not been
taken to another level, but gutted. Mayor Menino brought me up from
John Jay to Boston for a secret meeting: *What happened?* It's gone, the
police department killed it, I told him. It's your city, kids are dying, *tell
them to fix it.* His office told the *Globe* about the meeting, and the
Globe published an editorial calling on the city to bring back what had
been "abandoned here about six years ago." The police department,
said new commissioner Kathleen O'Toole, was relaunching Ceasefire.
But it wasn't going to happen. "O'Toole said Joyce's new plan will not
be 'the cookie cutter that used to be Ceasefire,'" the *Globe* reported late
in 2005. "Instead, she said police officials are planning a far broader attack on firearm violence in Boston." My old friend Teny Gross, Streetworker extraordinaire, had left Boston in disgust and was working down
in Providence. He wrote his own *Globe* op-ed in 2006. "There was glory

enough for everybody, but the cooperation turned to competition and control," he said.

There is no polite way to say it: Boston's regression into its old territorial self has translated directly into death. A decade ago a young man in Dorchester told me, "You adults are the real gang members, easy to feel slighted, fighting petty beefs, vying for attention and credit." It is the beefs on the streets that get the headlines. But the beefs in the offices and agencies are now equally to blame for what is happening

I'd learned my lesson—I thought, I hoped—from Boston, Minneapolis, Stockton, Baltimore, all the rest of the successful and then failed cities. I couldn't push this on people who didn't want it. I couldn't make people care enough to do the work. I couldn't magic up peace when the elephants fought, or make dead black kids matter more than politics. I couldn't control the good guys. I needed somebody to control the good guys. I needed adult supervision.

In Cincinnati, Mayor Mark Mallory listened.

When you fly into Cincinnati, you actually fly into northern Kentucky, drive up Interstate 75, cross the Ohio River by Covington—itself a seriously tough town—and bend northeast toward downtown. The view at night from the Brent Spence Bridge across the river is spectacular, the city a crystal sculpture of sparkle and neon. It takes your breath away. Cecil Thomas, the chair of the Cincinnati city council Law and Public Safety Committee, drove me across for the first time late in 2006. (I'd later learn that he spent his own money to bring me in from New York.) From much of what I'd been told, it featured to be my last happy moment in Cincinnati.

I had friends across the country who knew the city well, and many of them had said: *Don't do it.* Just before Timothy Thomas was killed, fourteen separate lawsuits pending against the police—wrongful death, abuse, racial profiling—were consolidated into an ACLU class action. The police department had ended up under federal supervision after the 2001 riot—the Collaborative Agreement, not technically a consent decree but near enough—and the Collaborative Agreement had brought with it a deluge of outsiders, top people in policing, to advise on and monitor mandated reforms. It was an all-star cast: Joe Brann, former director of the Clinton-era DOJ COPS office; John Eck, University of Cincinnati problem-oriented policing guru; my old friend Rana Sampson, who'd been on the ground in police departments all over the world; others. The department did not take kindly to all these people telling it what it was doing wrong and what it should do instead. Rana was thrown out of police headquarters in a dispute with Chief Tom Streicher and his command staff over going on a drug-market ride-along; the special master issued a court order getting her back in. That is not a police department you can work with, one of my circle told me, you'll never get anywhere.

My policing friends, and their fears, were partly right. My standard first move in any new city is to schedule solo meetings with key players—the mayor, city councillors, the police chief, prosecutors, community people, service providers—so they can ask their questions behind closed doors and tell me privately whatever it is they think I need to know. In Cincinnati, I got a pretty good response from almost everybody about actually doing Ceasefire, and then, meeting after meeting, an almost verbatim codicil: *But they*—everybody else—*will never go for it*. And in a lot of cases, *if they know I'm supportive, then they won't be*. The community people told me, *All of Cincinnati's neighborhoods are different, people from outside the neighborhood can't work there, you're going to need a different strategy for every neighborhood*. Cincinnati's politics would turn out to be far from the worst I'd ever seen, but they were without question the pettiest. Rana was in town during one of my early visits and I had dinner with her. She said, *We can't be seen together, it'll kill you dead*. I'd hear it again, from others.

What I saw, though, was a lot of enthusiasm and goodwill. The agencies were all game. Al Gerhardstein, the civil-rights attorney who'd brought the class-action case against the police department that had led to the Collaborative Agreement, quietly took me in hand and walked me through the political and community landscape, helped me figure out what to do and where the landmines were buried; he badly wanted this to succeed. Dr. Victor Garcia, the activist pediatric trauma surgeon whom I was meeting for the first time, was hugely impressive. He'd bootstrapped himself out of his Harlem neighborhood, gone to West Point, been an Army Ranger, studied under C. Everett Koop in medical school. He was soft-spoken, blazingly intelligent, passionate, delighted that things were finally in motion. Chief Streicher, trim, compact, intense, military bearing, was a surprise. We had a long meeting, focused, businesslike, lots of very sharp questions. I don't like this thing about not arresting gang members, he said, we're not going to do that here. Not a problem, I told him, that's part of the drug-market strategy, not part of the gang strategy, it's all about creating certainty. In the gang operation we pull everybody in, say, *Don't be in the next group that kills someone*, it serves the same purpose. He was totally reasonable, said he was in.

Which means he fooled me completely. I have very finely tuned radar for being played, and Streicher slipped under without a ghost of a signal. He makes no pretense now that he thought the whole thing was idiotic, doomed. He saw that it was going to happen and he wasn't going to fight it. He didn't do anything halfway and he'd give it his best, but would it *work*? No. "You are going to tell me that all this time, when we were trying to arrest our way out of this problem, all we had to do is tell these guys to stop what they were doing and offer them another option?" he says. "I just *knew* I could take that back to my cops and sell it right away."

Arrest their way out of the problem, they had indeed tried. Vortex came up, over and over. Vortex was the jump-out squad the police department had put together when the killing got to be too much, sixty officers, hit the streets in the hot neighborhoods—Over-the-Rhine, Avondale, the West End, others—stop everything that moved. The department's own Web site announced Vortex as a "zero tolerance" unit deployed "to seek out and physically arrest both minor and major criminal offenders by enforcing every law available and using every tool at our disposal to inconvenience criminals." Which they did, thousands and thousands of arrests, Timothy Thomas–style. Jaywalk, failure to come to a complete stop, open container, joint, broken taillight. An on-the-street observational study by RAND researchers found that Vortex officers were more likely to make vehicle stops than other officers, twice as likely to search drivers, and that vehicle stops overall were more likely to result in extended detaining and searching of black drivers, particularly so when the officers were white, with white drivers "more apologetic and less argumentative." RAND's careful parsing: "these findings cannot answer whether racial bias does or does not exist, but they do help explain why black Cincinnati residents perceive that it does, which may lead to a more negative attitude in future interactions with the police." Al Gerhardstein started getting calls, black residents whose homes had been hit by warrant teams, *We weren't doing anything, they didn't get anything, there wasn't anything for them to get.* The special master, Saul Green, weighed in repeatedly. He didn't like Vortex, was afraid of what it would do to relations with the black community, which weren't all that great to begin with; he gave a talk on the Collaborative Agreement at a minister's group, said, "We are collaborating with ourselves. The community isn't there."

These sentiments were shared within the Cincinnati Police Department, it turned out. I started circulating inside, meeting more people; some found moments, took me aside: *Can you get them to shut down Vortex?* Not how we do things, I'd have to say, we stay focused on what we need to get done, we can't get tangled up in this kind of internal dispute, it would kill us. I tried to keep my loathing of Vortex-style policing under wraps and suggest, *If we get this other work done, it changes things, we'll get there.* Met the Vortex commander, Dan Gerard, nice guy, civil, not interested, perfectly obvious, hard-core street guy. His worldview, as he would later explain: "Peace through superior firepower."

We'd come back to that, all of it.

I had long talks with Mayor Mallory, Dr. Garcia, Councilman Cecil Thomas. These sessions were not so much about the strategy, though that, too. They were about *keeping* the strategy.

This stuff works, I told the mayor, the others. We didn't used to be able to say that for sure, but now we know. It travels, it's worked with all different kinds of gangs, different settings. It has really big, rapid impact. That's the good part. The bad part is, it's pretty simple, the logic of it, but it's got a lot of moving parts. It takes a lot of keeping together. The drug-market work, it goes drug market by drug market, it turns out to be almost self-sustaining. This citywide violence work we're going to do is more delicate. I want Cincinnati to be the place that shows that cities can keep it going, institutionalize it, sustain it. One person can kill it, we've seen it over and over again now. They try to do that, somebody needs to stop it. It needs high-level attention, at least until the agencies and community really get it and own it themselves. Personnel transitions can kill it. When somebody who really gets it and is keeping things going gets promoted, transferred, goes out of office, retires, it's done. If we don't figure this out, this will be another one that we look back and say, It worked, but it's gone.

They got it. *What will it take?* Mallory asked.

Two things, I said.

I want it vested in the *city*, somehow, I want the city to own it. When the police department goes off track, when the prosecutors or whoever stop playing, when we can't fix it at the day-to-day level, I want somebody who will fix it. I want the city looking at us, at the work, regularly, saying, Is this good? Is it good enough?

And I want a senior, full-time project manager, somebody whose *job* it is to make it happen, somebody with the experience and the standing to be heard where they need to be heard, to be listened to, make things happen. There's no one place where everybody involved is accountable. The police chief answers to the mayor, sort of, the district attorney's elected, probation answers to the court, sort of, the U.S. attorney kind of answers to the Justice Department, parole is state, the community folks do what they want, the service providers can be state or county or city or nonprofit, the churches answer to God. Nobody can tell everybody what to do. It takes persuasion, seduction, shuttle diplomacy, occasional recourse to a higher power. I want *that*.

(It was ludicrous, once we saw it, how necessary it was to have this kind of structure, how we'd never had it, how we'd tried to operate without it, what naïveté and hubris it was to have thought we were smart and agile and *right* enough to make up for it. And, at the same time, how we'd never been in a position to ask for it, demand it. The work had never had the standing and the credibility it needed to make it non-negotiable. I, we, had been going from city to city with a tin cup, in no position to set conditions. I wasn't sure we were there yet.)

They got it. *Okay*, Mallory said. *I can do that.* He, Thomas, and City Manager Milton Dohoney agreed to set themselves up as the governing board for the new project, and to put funds in the budget for a senior, full-time project manager. I was weirdly exultant, felt like George Harrison at the Concert for Bangladesh: *We got Billy Preston!* It was mundane, didn't have the rush of the street action or seeing the big ideas emerge and click together in new ways, but it was a breakthrough, a huge step toward making what we were trying to do businesslike. I hoped.

Things continued to build. It was a wonderfully powerful team that was coming together. John Eck and one of his colleagues, Robin Engel, from the University of Cincinnati Policing Institute, joined in as the local research partner, both of them tremendously strong, both with experience inside the police department. John has done a huge amount of problem-policing work, likes to name things, came up with the Cincinnati Initiative to Reduce Violence, CIRV, pronounced *serve*. It had nice connotations. Vic brought in Ross Love, one of Cincinnati's most prominent black businessmen, to take the lead on the social-service side. We'd never had anybody of remotely his local stature involved. Ross had spent years at Procter & Gamble, one of Cincinnati's leading businesses, and he and Vic got two senior P&G management specialists, Keith Lawrence and Al Spector, focused on CIRV's management and accountability sides. I have no patience for management people, with their pedestrian ideas dressed up in incomprehensible jargon and Power-Point presentations. Keith and Al sat me down, grilled me about how the strategy worked, what had gone wrong elsewhere, and put together crystal-clear charts mapping out where we wanted to go, whose responsibility it was to get there, how we'd measure success and failure, and whose job it was to fix it if it was broken. They were brilliant. *It was our job to keep track of teams working on multimillion-dollar projects*, they said, *they fail in very predictable ways, that's what we do. Most common failure*, they said: *Everybody on the team knows something is wrong, won't take it higher up to get it fixed, by the time they do it's too late.* Makes perfect sense to me, I said, been *there* before.

Be there again, it would turn out, and in not too very long.

CIRV needed some start-up funds to pay for Victor's time, the UC team, the project manager, my time and travel, a few other things. It came to about $350,000 a year. Our team, with Victor in the lead, gave a formal presentation before the city council in mid-January 2007, hit both points hard: the intervention worked, the intervention needed to be sustained. "The challenge," said one of my PowerPoint slides: "Institutionalization, sustainability, accountability." CIRV would pioneer "A corporate model for sustained success and accountability," said one of Victor's. It seemed well received, but the political maneuvering around the project was getting stifling, amped up by the fact that it was an election year for the city council. One sentiment on council was, If we do this, and Dr. Garcia and Children's Hospital are involved, then they're accountable—we're going to write that into the contract. *Uh-uh*, said the hospital, *guarantee up front that we're going to stop street violence citywide? I don't think so.* Robin Engel and UC volunteered to be the fiscal agent.

Another sentiment on council was the desire to demonstrate commitment to the community by pushing funding for additional street-outreach workers—Cincinnati already had some. That money was slated to pass through UC as well, but Robin said, *UC is in no position to supervise ex-gang-member streetworkers.* Council seemed to hear it as *the money is all for law enforcement* and *there will be a second round of requests for community money.* We went back to them, kept saying, *The money's not for law enforcement, we won't be asking for anything else, the project runs on existing assets except for these start-up costs, that's all we need.* It seemed too good to be true, I think; it took forever to get across. The fallout was that we got tagged publicly as all about law enforcement. CIRV came up for formal city consideration and council instead moved funds to expand the street-outreach program.

Existing community groups and violence programs started pushing back, saying that they needed the funding, who was this outsider to tell Cincinnati what to do? Word came to us that one of the key figures at Children's Hospital who could okay Victor's participation in the project was so angry at the mayor he wouldn't talk to him.

We started getting pointed notice of whom particular city councillors would like to see hired for the upcoming project-manager slot. We were homing in on Greg Baker, whom I'd first met at a conference in Wisconsin in his role as director of community relations at the police department. He had an amazing background: public-sector job development, had been with the Cincinnati chapter of the Urban League, had managed department compliance with the Collaborative Agreement. He clearly had Chief Streicher's ear, clearly had the respect of the other law enforcement partners, had a thorough understanding of the city's community dynamics, seemed wonderfully capable, was immersing himself in the operational logic. We only hoped he'd be open to the idea. One of the mayor's senior staff came to Robin Engel and me after getting word that one of the councillors was forcing Greg down our throats. We had no idea where it came from, but told her, *No, we really want him.*

Victor, Robin, John, Greg worked it every day, me in and out from New York, all of us on the phone constantly, the mayor and Cecil Thomas pushing it. We were tight; I'd stay at Victor's house outside the city, sit up late with him and his wife and their dogs, got to know them, came to like them enormously. We made it work.

The city gave the formal go-ahead in early April, 2007, a unanimous council vote. We were in business. Then things blew up all over again. A county commissioner, several council candidates, and a community activist put together what was immediately tagged as a "likely killers list": 1,500 of Cincinnati's "most dangerous criminals," produced from public-access criminal records, people the group said had backgrounds indicating future serious violence. They were going to release the list publicly. There was a huge outcry. "A class-action suit waiting to happen," said Mayor Mallory. We can all focus on these people, the group protested, CIRV can call them in. *It's not our list, criminologists have spent generations trying to do this kind of prediction, it doesn't work, we have nothing to do with this*, we said, over and over. It didn't work. We were constantly getting questions about "the list": who's on it, why are they on it, what's going to happen to them. *There's no list, we have no list*, we kept saying.

Victor had put together a careful plan to design, staff, and implement CIRV that had us going operational—the first call-in—toward the end of 2007. *We'll never last that long*, our team realized, *the politics will tear us apart, we have to grab this back and show what we think it is, what we're doing*. If we kept it simple, we thought, we could have the first call-in by mid-July. That became our overriding goal.

Central to everything else was getting the city's violent groups identified and looking at homicides to see exactly what was happening in Cincinnati. I was in a meeting with Streicher and one of his top people, Lt. Colonel Jim Whalen, to get the reviews set up, said to Streicher, *Your street guys are the experts, we need you to get them together so we can debrief them, this is how we always start, all of the rest of it depends on getting this right*. I saw something shift in Streicher, quick but noticeable. He said, Of course, we can make that happen. Leaving with Whalen, walking down the hallway, he said, do you understand what just happened in there? For years now, ever since the riot, we've had academics coming in here and telling us what to do. For you to say the street cops are the experts? We want to work with them? They know crucial things? That's what Streicher thinks, what real cops think. That was *huge*.

We set up in the department's intelligence "fusion center," a beautiful new building on the edge of the city, full of high-tech communications gear. They're everywhere since 9/11. There must have been sixty cops: narcotics, patrol, homicide, some special units, some street probation and parole officers. Robin and a bunch of her graduate students, me, Streicher, Whalen. Whalen had thrown himself into the Ceasefire ideas, learned them cold, really, really got it. He's a big guy, got the cop's-cop thing going, doesn't wear it on his sleeve like a lot of them do, has an easy manner, he's friendly. In a couple of years a major article would call him "a big bear-like man." I'd get a call from Robin: *Jim says that one more person calls him a big bear and he's going to New York and rip that writer apart.* That day at the fusion center he stood in front of his people and gave a laying-on-of-hands talk that I am morally certain sanctioned CIRV with the working cops in the department and gave it the chance it needed.

I've been looking at this, he said. I've read a lot, and I've talked to cops in other cities who've done it. I've talked to cops who've worked with these people, with us here today. They say this stuff works, they say these are good people, you can trust them. I've looked really hard at this strategy. I'd heard a lot of things about it, that we're going to talk to the thugs and they're going to put their guns down and change their ways, that they all get jobs, turn their lives around. Maybe. Didn't make a lot of sense to me. That's not our part. There's a place in this for what feels to me like really, really good law enforcement work. That's what we're going to do. What we're up to today is we want to get from you what you know about what's going on on the streets. We know you know what the gangs are, what the drug crews are, where they are, what they're doing, who's fighting with who. We're going to get that and build on it. It's going to drive this operation. The way I understand how it works, we're going to identify probationers and parolees from these groups. We're going to call them in to a meeting. There's a community and a service side in that meeting. That's not us. What we're going to say is, We're waiting for the next homicide after this meeting. Whatever group does that homicide, we're going to get together with the DA, the U.S. attorney, the sheriff, probation, parole, the feds. And we're going to rain fire down on their heads, pull out all the stops, scorch the earth. Then we're going to pull the meeting back together, explain what we just did, and warn them again. And we're going to keep doing it until they get it.

It was law enforcement pitch-perfect, nobody at his level we'd ever worked with had ever done anything like it, had ever stepped out in front in the same way. He turned to me, leaning against the wall, off to his right, all the cops at their fusion-center tables in front of us, inert computer terminals in front of them. *Anything you'd like to add?* he asked.

What he said.

His people nodded, asked some questions, gathered around the maps Robin and her team had brought, started pouring out street detail. They were amazing; they always are. We went district by district, one set of officers around a map, the others watching and listening. Pretty soon the teams still to come were clustering together in the big room, comparing notes, working things up. When their turn came they had digests already prepared. Officers brought out their private notebooks and binders; we made notes to go back and collect that information, work it in. We had a similar, separate session and did the homicide review, of eighty-three killings between June 2006 and June 2007.

Answers: sixty-seven groups, about a thousand people, connected as victims or offenders or both with about three quarters of all killings in Cincinnati. Classic patterns of rivalries and alliances. One odd group that operated out of a business that belonged to a little set of much older guys. The main guy, let's call him Spike, was a weight dealer, his crew serious players all: We'd come back to them. One perfectly ordinary group called the Taliband. I'd run into the Taliban name all over the country. There was nothing Islamic about it, the streets had just picked up on the word. These guys couldn't even spell it right. We'd come back to them, too. Robin and her UC team keyed out about 650 of them who were known by name and ran criminal histories. They averaged thirty-five prior charges apiece, about seven and a half felony charges apiece. The Cincinnati Police Department has an officer-safety "approach with caution" tag in its dispatch system; 84 percent had it. All thousand or so group members, combined, represented about three tenths of 1 percent of the Cincinnati population.

As in Boston, Minneapolis, Baltimore, everywhere else, law enforcement had both known this and not known it. The street cops knew it about their own areas, their own groups, their own offenders, not necessarily about other areas and people. It never made it out of their heads, never made it into departmental intelligence or understanding, didn't affect policy or operations. It didn't affect anybody's *thinking*. Now it could. Streicher and Whalen turned out to be of that exceedingly rare category of human being who can look at new facts and say, *I've been wrong*. They got why Timothy Thomas policing didn't work, couldn't work, why ramping up low-level arrests was never going to work. "How do you want to run a police department?" Streicher would later say. "Do you want to go out every day and arrest fifty crackheads with fifty crack pipes and fill up the court system? That's like shooting fish in a barrel. Or do you want to bring in the three tenths of the one percent of the population that were responsible for the homicides?" Whalen looked at the beefs that flared across the network map and thought, That's why working corners doesn't work. "We go to an area after a shooting, the seven guys in that set aren't stupid, they're not going to be standing there," he said. "And if we do arrest the right guy, the guys his crew is fighting with are still across town somewhere. We never reach what's really going on."

The other pieces were falling into place. Ross Love was taking the lead on the social-service side. This was a major theme for our team. I was getting asked constantly how many street offenders were likely to come forward to ask for help when the call-ins started. *Not that many*, historically, I said. We probably don't have to prepare for a deluge, it mostly just hasn't happened that way. And a lot of those who do don't stick with it, or can't make it. The Cincinnati team was determined to do better. It became almost a rallying cry—*nobody's ever taken this seriously before*. No, I kept saying, people have, it just hasn't *worked*. I stopped saying it, there was no point, you pick your battles. The team reached out to a group called Cincinnati Works that had a long history of job training and support work. It had never worked with the hard-core street population CIRV focused on. Their program normally wouldn't take anybody who couldn't pass a drug test. But they were game, too. Ross got others involved—Out of the Crossfire, which worked with gunshot victims; the United Way; the Crossroads Center, which worked with alcoholism and mental illness; others.

Victor took the lead on the community moral-voice side. He was getting to know the outreach workers being run out of the Partnering Center that had been established by the Collaborative Agreement, getting to know the women in Cincinnati's mothers-of-murdered-children group. We had long meetings at Children's Hospital, Victor in green scrubs between operations and rounds, the outreach workers telling their stories of sin and prison and pain and redemption and hope for redemption. Pete Mingo, fiftyish, former gang member, former serial armed robber, now Baptist minister, killing himself to get the young men off the streets, still saying out loud, *I can never make up for what I've done*, haunted. The mothers with their brochures, page layouts of photographs of dead kids, scores of them, each case still unsolved. *If I can tell my story and it will help, yes, of course, I will stand and do it.*

I wanted Cincinnati to be a breakthrough on the community moral-voice side, and on the law enforcement and community side. We needed to map what we'd learned in High Point onto the citywide group violence strategy. We knew it was possible to reset relationships between the police and particular neighborhoods—what we were starting to think of as "reconciliation and truth telling"—but we needed to figure out how to do it citywide. We knew it was possible to identify "influentials" for particular offenders, but not how to do it, in a practical way, for sixty-seven groups and a thousand people. I was sure we could get there; it was time to work it out.

I took Jim Whalen aside at one point. We've had breakthroughs with the community in some places, I told him. The community is furious, alienated, full of conspiracy theories. We've got chiefs going to them and saying, We're sorry, we've done damage, we get it, we're going to change. It's transformative, it's almost unbelievable what happens. Would Streicher do that? *I don't know*, he said, *it would be a stretch*. I talked to Streicher. He heard me out. *I don't know that I'm willing to do that*, he said. Okay, I said, it's your call. One step back from that would be to strike a more-in-sorrow-than-in-anger note in the call-ins. We don't hate you, we're not angry at you, we want you to live, we want you out of prison, we think you'll listen. *I can do that*, he said. To be continued, I said to myself.

And we whipped ourselves into shape organizationally. Greg Baker took the project-manager job as a half-time commitment, worked it more than full time, carried his other police-department responsibilities somehow. The P&G guys continued to be fantastic, made organizational sense out of what we were trying to do and how to systematize it. Chief Streicher and Victor Garcia would be CIRV's "co-owners," representing the law enforcement and community sides. They, with Greg Baker, would run the strategy and implementation team with Whalen, Robin and John from UC, Ross Love, Stan Ross, who managed the outreach workers, the two P&G specialists, and me. Under the S/I team were four working groups: enforcement, services, community, and a "system" group focused on management, performance measures, and accountability. *Over* the S/I team was a governing board to set overall policy, track progress, and if necessary break logjams lower down: Mayor Mallory, Councilman Thomas, and City Manager Dohoney. I was both exultant—*this should crack the sustainability problem*—and embarrassed. *Why did we ever believe we could function without something like this? What were we thinking?*

We missed our deadline, but not by much. On July 31, CIRV had its first call-ins, two back-to-back sessions, almost sixty probationers and parolees between the two groups, at the Hamilton County Courthouse, a couple blocks from City Hall and at the edge of Over-the-Rhine.

Streicher didn't much like the look of the offenders in front of him—he took one look and thought, "Somebody better call the police," he told me later—but he did exactly what he said he would do. "I don't hate you because of what you do or what you've done," he said. "I don't want you to hate me because of what I do or what I've done. Nobody in here wants to be hated"—gesturing to our crowd on our side of the bar—"nobody out here wants to be hated," gesturing to the call-in guys. "What we do want is an opportunity, an opportunity for change, and that's what you're going to hear about today." He gestured to Victor. "Maybe you can even put him out of business," he said. "So he doesn't have to operate on a baby again, because the baby has a bullet hole in it. He doesn't like to do that. We don't like to transport the broken body parts. And I don't think any of you want to be in that position." Whalen, backed up by the rest of the enforcement team, got that core message across with crystal clarity. I'm in charge of what you really don't want, he said. There are two things that you need to understand. One is that this isn't coming from just the Cincinnati Police Department. It's from everybody in law enforcement: city, state, county, federal, northern Kentucky, the sheriff who runs the jail, the attorney general for the state of Ohio is represented here. We've all thrown in together. The other is that it's not about you. It's about the groups. Take it back. Ross Love and the streetworkers were inspirational about how deeply the community wanted the street guys to do well, thought they could do well, what had been set up to help them do well.

Victor and the community people were transcendent.

"I'm here because, it may sound foolish, God loves you, and so do I," Victor said. "I'm a surgeon at Children's Hospital. As a surgeon, should you come to the hospital, regardless of who you are or what you've done, I will take care of you as if you were my brother. But you're here today because of a crisis that we have in our city, a crisis that affects us as human beings, and because of me, as a black man, it's a crisis that affects us as a race. Before you, you have representatives from law enforcement, you have representatives from community services, you have representatives from the community itself. This meeting is not about you. It's about an important message that I'm asking you as a surgeon, who cares for you and your children—and I'm speaking on behalf of the trauma surgeons at University Hospital, as well as the coroner—to listen to what is going to be told to you today. You're all going to go home. And I want you to take what you hear back to the people that you run with.

"*The killing has got to stop.*

"We are doing more harm to ourselves than the KKK has ever done. You think about that. For the first time in history, we as a race are potentially *coming to an end* because of what we are doing to ourselves.

"I want you to take what you hear today back to the group that you run with. Because I don't want to see you in the trauma bay. I don't want to see your children. *My* children. You're my *brothers*. Regardless of what you've done, when you come to the hospital I'm going to do my best to save your life. But God knows I don't want to have to do that. Who knows, I may have taken care of some of you. I want to show you something."

Victor paused, turned to his right, picked up a poster-size graph he'd had mounted on cardboard, turned back, walked to the gold-colored bar that separated the probationers and parolees from the rest of us, his voice increasingly urgent, an edge of anger showing. "I want to show you what *hurts me*, as a black man who grew up in Harlem, in New York City. I want you to look at this graph. I want you to look at this graph, and what this tells us, and what I want you to go back to your brothers and tell them, is that for every one white man that's killed, there are fourteen black men killed in this country, eighteen years of age." He walked along the bar, showing them, their eyes following him. "Can you see that? Do you see it? Do *you* see it? They nodded. "Okay." He put the poster down, went back, picked up another. "That's in this country. This is what's happening in this *city*." The poster showed Cincinnati homicides for the last six years, shooting upward. "We're *destroying* ourselves," Victor said. "I mean, you hear about global warming? Damn, global warming is *nothing*. We're *killing* ourselves. And at this rate we're not going to have babies to carry on. And we're a proud race. We came over on a ship, with no food, in the bottom, we survived hundreds of days. God didn't make junk. But we're *killing ourselves*. And if we're not killing ourselves we're *paralyzed* from the waist down. Or we're paralyzed from the neck down. Or we're on a breathing machine"—gestured to his neck—"or we've got to be *fed through a tube*"—gestured to his abdomen.

"It's got to *stop*. God, it's got to stop."

He put the poster down, picked up a third. "But let me tell you why I'm really here. This is what really scares me. This is why I'm here. This is why a *surgeon at Children's Hospital* is here. This is why I've taken days out of my life to make sure that you get a chance, should you decide. What does this show you?" He spoke to one of the guys in the second row of seats. "Stand up, please. What does this show you? What does that say? Say it out loud to all your brothers."

"Children admitted to Children's Hospital with gunshot wounds," the man said. Victor touched him gently on the shoulder. "Okay, thank you." The man sat down. Victor turned to another. "Stand up for me, please." He did, heavily muscled, tattoos, muscle shirt. "So what happened here in 2001, how many? And what happened here in 2006? All right. Fifty-seven." The man and Victor passed a few quiet words the rest of us couldn't hear, Victor smiling; he sat back down. "Is this good or bad? *Is it good or bad?*" Victor asked them. *Bad*, they said. "It's *children* that are coming to the hospital now. Is that good or bad?" *Bad.* "Bad, man. *We've got to stop the shooting.* How many of you here think it's okay, the average age for a child coming to children's hospital— what do you think, the average age?" he asked a man, his hair in cornrows, in the front tier. *Twelve*, the man said. "That's right," Victor said. "Twelve years old. I mean, that's not right. Do you think that's right? It's not right."

Things are going to be different here from now on, he said. If you understand that this is not right, if you understand that we've been killing ourselves more than the KKK did, you've got to ask yourselves, what can we do differently? He went past the bar, stood in their midst. Law enforcement's going to be doing things differently. But you're also going to be hearing about the community services. I know people have made promises before, said all kinds of things. "What I'm telling you is that things are going to be different. And you're going to hear about that. *But I want you to take it back to the group.*" He spoke to one of the guys in the middle of the group. "Can you do that?"

"Yes," the guy said.

Candace Tubbs stepped forward. She ran a street-outreach organization called the Society for the Advancement of Reforming Felons. Short, intense black woman, close-cropped hair, glasses, paced back and forth while she talked, former drug dealer. "I know a lot of the brothers that are here. I guess I want to first, say, I apologize. I want to apologize for really being the bad example I've been over the years. Some of the brothers from Avondale, Walnut Hills, that I've been knowing since they were really young," she said, holding her palm down by her knee. "I want to apologize on behalf of those of us who did set a bad example.

"Imprisoned before you ever go to a prison," she said. "You all know what I'm talking about, right. Imprisoned right here," she said, tapping her head. "The same prison that caused me to lay up in my bed and have someone come into my apartment and rob me and shoot me." She lifted her blue shirt, showed her abdomen. "This is real. It's real. It's real. I didn't never have no baby. These are bullet holes, right here. Those two wounds are bullet holes. You remember that, don't you," she said to one of the guys. "This is why I'm here today," she said. "Because I'm sick and tired of seeing our babies die. I'm sick and tired of seeing young men go to prison, and go to hell. I'm sick and tired of seeing it before they reach their full potential. You can be whatever you want to be. You can make a decision that nobody, no longer, will dictate the direction that my life will go. You owe a responsibility. I'm here because I owe a responsibility." I was in college, this close to graduating, she said. I told myself the white man would never let me succeed. I turned my dorm room into a drug den, kilos of coke in there. I did it to myself. After so many had sacrificed for me. "Seventy-six thousand black men died in the Civil War for freedom, and here I was, destroying lives, destroying the lives of people I should have been embracing, should have been loving." I broke my mother's heart, she said. But we can fix it, she said. "I am calling on you brothers to help me, to help us, to make this thing a success, because I don't want to see nobody go to prison for the rest of their lives, I don't want to see no more mothers suffer, and most of all, I don't want to see no more babies *die*."

Victor leapt up. "After hearing this, who wants to change," he said. "Stand up. Stand up." A couple of them did, then more, then almost all of them. Our side began to clap. Streicher stood up, Greg Baker stood up, the feds stood up, we all stood up, they were getting a standing ovation. I'd never seen anything like it. Victor was going to them, one on one, man to man. "Are you serious?" he asked. *Yes. Yes.*

Cecil Thomas, the city councilman. Tall, slim, beautifully dressed. "At age eight, the Klan showed up at my house at a rural little town near Birmingham, Alabama, to hang my father," he said. "They showed up. Fortunately he wasn't there. He came up to Cincinnati to get away from that violence, and then sent for the family," he said. "Taken away from my nice, quiet little environment that I thought I had there. Never in my wildest imagination would I ever have thought that the homicides that I see today would have far exceeded anything that the Klan could have done to my father and the rest of the folks in the South. It breaks my heart."

I joined a gang for protection, he said. I was a Walnut Hills boy, I got stabbed right here, he said, tracing a line on his head. I was in jail at eighteen. Getting body searched. One of the guards told me I needed to change my life, that I was headed straight to hell. I listened, he said. I said, I will never, ever go back to jail. There is *nothing* worse than having your freedom taken away. I joined the police force, was twenty-seven years on the job. I've probably locked up some of your family, and it goes on and on, the cycle continues. Your kids are on the same path. It has to stop. My mother died early, I think what I did helped bring that on. I remember her crying and praying over me in the hospital. We're setting you up today, to turn your life around. Let us.

Carla McNeil. Mother of a murdered child. Contained. White pantsuit. Glasses perched on top of her head. She brought a photograph of her son, Jeremy, sitting with his grandfather. He was a good kid, she said, barely able to get the words out. Quiet when he was young, generous, when he got older he gave all his toys away to the little boy next door. Wise. When he was just sixteen, seventeen, I could talk to him like he was thirty. He was my rock.

I want to tell you what it was like to find out that he was murdered, she said.

Something had changed, she said. Jeremy had started staying home a lot, which was fine with her. It had been back in 2001, during the time of the riot, and she wanted to make sure he was safe. In two weeks he was going to get out of Cincinnati, go to Indianapolis, join a Job Corps program, and learn to be a computer technician.

But he went missing, was missing for days. She went to the police, but they were no help. She went to work to make missing posters. She was going to find her son.

"And I get home and his stepfather's on the phone," Carla said. "And it didn't feel right. Tension, I could feel it. And I could hear him say, I can't tell her. You can't tell me what. He was walking through the house, and I was following, you can't tell me what? And that's when someone drove up, I heard the brakes of the car, I went outside on the porch, and they ran up the steps. They said, 'Carla, you remember when you said you saw that body they pulled up yesterday on the news? It was Jeremy.'

"I lost it. I screamed. I could not believe it. Because that was the very day he was supposed to leave to go to Job Corps in Indianapolis. I just knew he was going to make it out of here." She was sobbing and talking at the same time. He'd been killed, thrown behind Dumpsters on the street, and left there for days. He was so badly decomposed she didn't even get to see him one last time. "I was just so totally devastated. I ended up in the psych ward. I ended up on Prozac."

I couldn't take care of his younger brother and sister, she said. I should have, but I couldn't. My daughter is about to have a boy. Maybe he's going to look like Jeremy, I don't know. He's never going to know his uncle. My other son, his older brother's dead, he's never going to know him. They're meeting other brothers, *their* older brothers are dead. "And meanwhile you've got people around here like me, trying to look normal, and act normal, and be normal, got all this pain," she said, now crying openly. "I don't hate you guys. I don't hate you. I *love* you.

Sometimes I see people from the back, you know, their head's shaped like Jeremy's, their walk's like Jeremy's, I imagine it's Jeremy. So think about it. For your mom, your dad, your people."

Most of the probationers and parolees had tears streaming down their faces.

No mother should have to do that, Stan Ross, the head outreach worker, said. This courtroom isn't big enough for all the mothers and fathers who have lost their children to senseless killing.

There was more. Mayor Mallory, his polite public polish temporarily in retirement, letting out a fighter's edge I'd never seen before. There are people in this city who don't understand why I'm doing this, he said. They don't care about you, all they want is for you to be gone. "I'm trying to build something that will benefit everybody in this city," he said. "*Everybody.*"

The mayor and the core team had a press conference that night. Streicher looked like the world had just tilted under him. That was an amazing thing today, he said. He looked at Arthur Phelps of the outreach workers, standing in the room. I used to chase him all over Cincinnati when I was on the street, first on the job, he said. Sometimes he got away, sometimes I caught him. Now we're standing side by side, working for the same thing. He laughed softly. I never would have believed it.

Michael Blass, a career law enforcement officer from the Ohio attorney general's office, went home and wrote a three-page essay. "I saw something profound today," he wrote. His last paragraph:

I walked away from this experience transformed from an observer to a participant, born of a renewed sense of hope and the warmth of a newly sparked inner fire. I believe again—I believe that there is hope for the hopeless, healing for the angry, and justice for the community. I believe that lives are being changed and will be changed. I believe that we—the community in its purest form and finest sense—will prevail, through the certain challenges and general messiness that human interactions create, through the inevitable setbacks, and the new obstacles that success itself will bring. We will prevail; we will be stronger, wiser, and more united as a community and, perhaps, eventually, as a people.

Cincinnati did not go quiet. A dozen people had called the Cincinnati Works hotline by the next day. I was with Streicher when he got the news. He was amazed; I don't think he thought anybody would call, ever. It didn't translate on the streets. August of 2007 was about as bad as it got in Cincinnati, eight of what the team was starting to call Group Member Involved homicides—GMIs. Street law enforcement and the streetworkers both reported the same thing: The streets are buzzing from the call-ins, the message is out, but they don't think you can do it. They don't think you know who they are, and they don't think you can deliver the enforcement. The law enforcement team geared up, under Whalen's direction, and did its job. On October 3, CIRV had its second round of call-ins. Over ninety attendees this time. The social-service and community messages were much the same. The enforcement message was not.

We understand you don't think we can do this, Whalen said. *Well, we can.* He put up, in quick succession, posters on four separate killings. Each had been traced back to a group member. In each, the shooter was in custody for the shooting. In each, most of the rest of his group was also locked up on a range of charges, their pictures on the posters. *They'd all be walking around right now, pretty much, if not for the killing,* Whalen said. *We can do this, and we will.* Oh, he said, and you don't think we know who you are? Check *this* out. He'd put together a PowerPoint presentation of photographs from CPD file surveillance footage—gang members and drug dealers hanging on corners, serving motorists, passing money and drugs back and forth, drinking, smoking. The call-in attendees watched, mesmerized, all front and pretense forgotten, saw themselves and their friends on the screen, poked each other, *Hey, that was you.* I watched one guy lurch into near shock, start to tear up.

Dan Gerard, the commander of the Vortex unit, was in charge of security for the sessions. His men were all over inside and around the courthouse. I was talking to Tom Streicher and some others when it was all over when Dan came over with a huge grin on his face. "I just walked some of these guys down and outside," he told Streicher. "You've got to hear this. I was walking along behind them, listening, and one of them was saying to the others, 'These motherfuckers aren't fucking playing, I'm fucking getting out.'"

Now Cincinnati went quiet.

The graph of GMIs shot downward. It looked just like Boston, Minneapolis, Stockton, Indianapolis, Rochester, all the others. The city ended the year with overall killings down 24 percent, the biggest annual homicide decline since 1991. Top cops from Scotland Yard were coming in to figure out how to take it back home. Gang killing continued to tank; Robin ran numbers in the spring of 2008 showing that since the October 2007 call-ins, when the CIRV message punched through, GMIs were down 60 percent.

The department started to have fun with the new ideas. Whalen sent an officer to talk to Spike. He had to talk himself through multiple locked doors and closed-circuit TVs, but he ended up in Spike's office. You'll have heard about the meetings we've been having with the street crews, he said. We've been telling them they kill anybody, we'll take the whole crew down. Here's how it's going to be with you. We've been dancing around a long time, you've been getting away with it. From now on, anybody you're selling to kills anybody, we'll call the feds, you won't be dealing with us anymore.

Spike spent the next week calling the local crews into his office, telling them to stand down or they'd be dealing with him. The whole neighborhood went quiet.

And it all started to come apart.

We lost Victor.

At the time, I was bewildered. It felt like I, we, were dealing with a completely different man. I didn't recognize him any longer; my friend was gone. From here, now, I believe that was exactly wrong. We were dealing with the same driven, passionate, uncompromising, damn-the-torpedoes man I had known and loved; seeing the same relentless moral fervor that had worked to impose CIRV on the city when nobody would listen to him; seeing, I suspect, the same backbone and fire that had brought him from the streets of Harlem through the Army Rangers to take his place as one of the finest pediatric surgeons in the country. The utter certainty that he was *right*, that he was doing the right thing. I don't know, looking back, how it could have been any different. The man *operated on babies* every day, for God's sake; he couldn't afford to doubt what he was doing.

Only now we were at odds.

Over a lot of things. There was the little matter of the Ku Klux Klan, for example. As leader of CIRV's community moral-voice group, Victor was in charge of figuring out how to mobilize community engagement with our street population, outside the call-ins and the streetworkers and mothers. He fastened on the Klan trope that he'd used in the first call-in, the idea that the black community was doing itself more harm than the Klan ever had. He got some pro bono time from a marketing firm and came to one of the CIRV S/I meetings with a prototype pamphlet—a stop-the-killing brochure, to be handed out in the hot neighborhoods, prominently featuring a graphic of a hooded Klansman. I saw it and froze solid, couldn't believe my eyes. CIRV represents the city of Cincinnati, the Cincinnati Police Department, the U.S. attorney, the University of Cincinnati, all the rest. Greg Baker, Whalen, I, all did our best to explain this, that this was out of the question. Those parties are not going to be passing out, in black neighborhoods that *rioted* not all that long ago, pictures of the *Ku Klux Klan*. I watched Whalen struggle to contain himself, speak very, very carefully: *We've made a huge amount of progress since the riots*, Whalen said. *We'd lose it in a heartbeat. This is not going to happen.* There are things you can do behind closed doors, face to face, that you can't do in public, at a distance, I tried to tell Victor. He would not let it go, kept on coming back to it. We have a moral obligation, he said, over and over, a phrase I would hear a lot in the months to come. At one of the call-ins, along with his regular posters of soaring homicides and shootings, he brought a poster of the Klan graphic into the courtroom. I saw it before we started, froze again, said to him, You *cannot* use that. We are bringing people in on probation and parole, they're here under *court order*, you *cannot* bring black supervisees in here under court order and make them look at *Klansmen*. It'll be fine, he said. I found Whalen and he went to Victor and said, You give me that or I'm taking everybody in law enforcement right out of here. Victor gave it up, but he didn't give up the idea, kept on coming back to it. In the meantime the moral-voice work went nowhere.

There were other things. But mainly, there was services.

Victor had been seized by the idea of personal transformation, the moment in the call-ins when everybody leapt to their feet, the notion that the only way to stop the killing and save the community was to get every offender a job. It's bigger than the gang population, he started to say, we need to work with more than just the group population, we need to work with everybody who might be violent. That's why the other projects, Boston, everything else, failed. Because the service side wasn't there. No, I'd say, they failed because people stopped doing the work. The service side is crucial, for a lot of different reasons, but this is a horribly difficult population to help. It's not just a resource question—we don't know how to do it. And you don't need a job to stop shooting people. Even among people with huge criminal records, hardly anybody shoots somebody.

He didn't buy it. He became more and more focused on the service side. He pulled together a meeting at Children's Hospital with Cincinnati Works, some of the top hospital management, Robin Engel, John Eck, me. We need an independent evaluation of the service side, he said. We need to be able to detail the contribution services make to the violence reduction. *That's not possible*, Robin and John and I all said. It can't be done. All we can evaluate is the overall impact of what we're doing. There's no way to parse out just the impact of services, any more than we can parse out the impact of just law enforcement, or just the moral-voice side. We can look at the outcomes for the guys who are choosing services, but we can't even say that any reductions in their violence are because of services; it's a self-selection problem, like looking at drug treatment: People who choose drug treatment want to quit, you can't compare them to people who *don't* want to quit. We're not doing random assignment of gang members into the services track, we can't make them do anything, so we can't really say what's going on with them. It's part of a package, all we can do is evaluate the package.

Everybody seemed to get it. Then Robin started hearing from around town, *Victor says you guys only care about law enforcement*. It was tearing the team apart, clear divisions forming, Victor and the streetworkers on one side, Robin and me and Greg and the law enforcement folks on the other. I was getting really worried. I gave half my fee back to UC to do some sort of extra study of the service side. Trying to keep everybody happy.

The focus on transformation grew and started to undermine the core logic of what we were doing. Robin and her UC team were systematically fleshing out the list of group members, working with CPD records and officers to identify who exactly was in the street groups. As the list grew, the number of probationers and parolees we could identify grew with it; we were up to over one hundred now. As we repeated the call-ins, some of them had been in several times, and the perfect moments when everybody rose up and promised to change were getting fewer and weaker. *Let's not bring in guys who've been in before,* Victor said, *let's just work with the new ones.* Hold on, I had to say. The call-ins are not about the people in the room, fundamentally—they're about *reaching their groups.* The guys in the room are *messengers.* They can all reform, but if we don't get the messages out to their groups it won't work. That logic, at least, carried the day.

Despite all the tension, it looked like Cincinnati was doing fantastically well on the service side. Huge numbers of people, relative to our experience, were signing up for help. It was wonderful: There was one story of a guy in a call-in going back, dialing Cincinnati Works on his cell phone, signing himself up, then passing the phone around to everybody in his gang; *they* all signed up, a dozen or so of them. The numbers on the service roster climbed. Robin, in her capacity as CIRV's research partner, wrote a report to the city at the end of 2007. Over 160 offenders had signed up; 128 were actively engaged, they had all been assigned an outreach worker to help them out and keep them on track. That amounted to something like 15 percent of the entire core population we'd identified. It was fabulous. The numbers kept growing. *Cincinnati's made a breakthrough,* I started saying elsewhere. Robin reported the numbers to the governing board: Mayor Mallory, City Manager Dohoney, Councilman Thomas. This is extraordinary, I told them, much better than anywhere else. Homicide stayed low, things were fundamentally okay.

Then it all blew up.

June 2008, the federal courthouse. We'd decided to hold a call-in there, impress upon the call-in guys the seriousness of the federal system. Most of them had never seen the inside of a federal courtroom. *You don't ever want to,* we wanted to say. The federal judges were willing, but the court personnel didn't want to hold the multiple small sessions we'd been using, forty or so guys at a time. They'd only allow us one. We assembled 120 or so gang members in a courtroom. Not a good idea, as it turned out.

I wasn't there, didn't see it. Our team lost control of the room, the gang members pushing back, shouting back. There was a girl on the offender side who didn't belong there; she'd come in with one of the guys and we hadn't caught it somehow. *The streetworkers started coming on to her*, Whalen told me later, disgusted. There was no hallelujah moment; these guys weren't leaping to their feet *at all*. Our side pushed harder, got in an argument with the gang members. Some of the streetworkers went *really* street, called them niggers.

I waited for the headlines and the lawsuit: CINCINNATI POLICE BRING BLACK PROBATIONERS AND PAROLEES INTO FEDERAL COURTHOUSE, CALL THEM NIGGERS: ACLU PROMISES ACTION. It didn't happen, somehow. We got word from the other law enforcement agencies. They were on the verge of pulling out, couldn't risk it happening again. Our team was a mess. Victor and the streetworkers thought what had happened was fine, no problem, *You have to talk to people like they're used to being talked to*, they said. For the first time in my work, ever, there was an explicit racial divide forming, Victor and the streetworkers, all black, on one side. Whalen, Robin, me, all white, with Greg Baker, black, on the other. Poor Ross Love was caught in the middle somewhere. *White folks don't like how we talk to each other*, I started to hear. It's not about liking it, I said. We cannot do this. We *cannot* bring supervisees into court, under court order, and call them niggers. The police, the prosecutors, probation, parole, the courts, *will not have it*. If we don't guarantee this will never happen again, we're *finished*.

It rolled off. I think it may have been effective, Victor said. The service calls are coming in.

Services again. Maybe. So were the bodies. Homicide shot up after the June call-in. I can't prove it, but I am virtually certain that we made it happen. We'd assembled over a hundred respect-obsessed men in one place, disrespected them, and turned them loose. The killing climbed to pre-CIRV levels. We were helpless to do anything about it; our team was at one another's throats, and our relationships with our outside partners were hanging by threads.

It got worse. Robin had finished populating the group membership list. For the first time, she had a complete roster of names to compare to the names on our service roster. Of the three hundred people CIRV was working with, only about a fifth, maybe fewer than sixty, were group members. CIRV had not had a breakthrough on the service side; it wasn't even doing very well. Not even the leap-to-your-feet moments in the call-ins, *I'll change*, were translating into service take-up. If all those guys had come forward, they alone would have added up to more real group members than we actually had. They hadn't. Our best efforts weren't succeeding even with the guys we cared about the most. There was next to no talk in our group about what to do to fix *that*, as there should have been, only the debate about expanding the effort. It's the right thing to do, said Victor, there are violent people who aren't in groups, there are people who might become violent, we should expand even further. No, said our side, the whole idea here is focus, it always has been, we don't try to *arrest* everybody, either.

The internal argument became more and more paralyzing. It made less than no sense now, as far as I was concerned. What Victor was proposing was what was being called "reentry": work with offenders and ex-offenders in the neighborhood, get them jobs. People were trying it all over the country, nobody was getting great results even in the immediate sense of moving people into work; absolutely nobody had managed to shut homicide down that way. People had been trying it for decades, in various ways, without much success. Making it work would take an entirely new program structure and massive new funding. It would take years to produce results, if it ever did. It was the kind of thinking CIRV had been developed in *response* to. It was unquestionably a noble ambition, but CIRV was not the vehicle for it.

And while Victor was trying to graft it on, CIRV was hobbled, our work stalled, his crucial moral-voice piece still no further along than it had been eighteen months before. It wasn't true that our side only cared about law enforcement; it *was* true that the law enforcement side of CIRV was the only one in really good shape. I got nowhere, stopped trying—basically Victor wouldn't talk to me anymore, he clearly heard everything I said as, *It's only law enforcement that matters.*

We met with the mayor and the rest of the governing board. They were controlled, heard us out, heard Victor's argument for expanding CIRV's service net to a wider population. Then the mayor laid down the law. We're operating here under a theory that's worked elsewhere, he said. We're sticking with it. This is the city of Cincinnati's project and we will conduct it as we have said we will. The board grandfathered in everybody who was currently getting services and asked Robin to come up with an instrument to help identify serious violent offenders who might not be in groups. They would be allowed in. Others would not.

We had our marching orders. It did not solve the problem within our group. Victor continued to push to expand on the service side. We spent hours and hours and hours in meetings and on conference calls going over it, got nowhere.

We struggled on. Greg Baker worked himself to near collapse repairing our law enforcement partnership and getting us to the point that we could resume the call-ins. It took until early December. I flew in for a rehearsal the week before. Robin took me aside and said, The cops have said that if we have any repeat of what happened last time, that's it, they're done. Will you tell the streetworkers for me? *You get to go home*, we both knew she meant. I did, *still* got pushback. And worse for me personally, Stan Ross said, "I know you don't think much of what we do." I was *enraged*, swallowed it, said, No, it's not that, please don't think that. It didn't mean anything to him, that was obvious.

The call-ins went beautifully. Tom Streicher took me aside and told me that one guy had told him his car got ticketed while he'd been there, could Streicher fix it for him. Streicher said, No, but here, give it to me, I'll pay it for you. He told me another guy had told him he'd been out of prison for a while, he couldn't get work. Streicher said, My brother runs a roofing company, it's hard, nasty work, but if you want it I'll have you on a roof tomorrow. The guy said yes. Streicher did. I wanted to cry.

The killings came right back down.

It didn't help with our group dynamics. Nothing changed. Greg brought me in at one point to talk to people at Talbert House, a Cincinnati nonprofit that worked with the kind of serious offenders we were dealing with. Greg thought they had some insights into changing mindsets and habits that needed to be added to our portfolio. I spent some time with them; they were professional, made perfect sense. As I was leaving, one of their executives took me aside. *It's that doctor that's your problem*, he said.

In May 2009 the city took Victor off CIRV. He went back to being, full-time, one of the best pediatric surgeons in the country. He's still working, as I understand it, on creating job opportunities for Cincinnati's street offenders. I hope he can make it work.

I hated for it to be a triumphant moment, but it was. CIRV was going to survive. What had happened in Cincinnati would have killed any of our other projects. It was the kind of thing that happened, would continue to happen: People brought different convictions, different passions, almost all of them honorable at root, to the work. The work *made* people passionate, you could see it, over and over. There might come a time when the core new thinking we were operating under became its own conventional wisdom, but we were far from there yet. Until it did, the old ways of thinking were going to continue to try to punch through: Send every gang member to federal prison, get every felon a job, lock down every parolee, the gang members are a lost cause but we can work with all their little brothers. In the meantime, we needed support and stewardship.

We'd gotten it. For the first time in what was now almost fifteen years, what we were doing mattered enough to powerful, important people to *keep it*. What we had tried to do to keep it had *worked*. Fitfully, but it had, finally, worked. Greg Baker, the fact that there *was* a Greg Baker, had kept it together, just as we had hoped. Setting up from the beginning so that the city would watch over it meant that the city could, and finally did, act to save it. Either we were right that the work was worth doing, or we were wrong. If we were right, then lack of governance, lack of focus, lack of attention, lack of basic accountability could not be allowed to destroy it. If we were unable to create structures to make that happen, then we had nothing real. Cincinnati had said, this *is* real, it *is* worth it, we *do* mean it, we *will* keep it.

We will keep it.

It *does* work.
It *will* travel.

And while we were consumed with our internal drama, the Cincinnati Police Department was quietly reinventing itself. Dan "Peace Through Superior Firepower" Gerard had looked at the data Robin's people were compiling and basically shut Vortex down. No more doing corners, no more zero tolerance, no more Timothy Thomas policing. Not because it was racist, or alienating, or because he'd stopped believing in hard-core police work. Because it was *dumb*, he saw that now. Arresting jaywalkers and unlicensed drivers and guys with beers wasn't going to reach the groups, wasn't going to reach the vendettas, wasn't going to reach the three tenths of a percent. He turned Vortex into a sharp, focused investigative instrument.

In mid-2008, the most violent group in Cincinnati was the Taliband, what we came to call "the gang that couldn't spell straight." Gerard brought in Robin, Robin brought in her graduate students. The police department that had thrown Rana Sampson out of the building had come to love and trust the UC people. They gave the academics full, no-questions-asked access to their data and people. It is still the only such relationship I know of anywhere. The UC team tore into CPD's systems, pulling information from all over the place—arrest records, case files, field interrogation reports, incident reports, citations, bond histories, court histories, surveillance photographs, tattoo photographs, automated license-plate readers. They built a Web crawler that archived pages from dozens of social-networking sites, thousands of posts about gang crime and photographs of gang members flashing signs and posing with guns and drugs and each other. They built a custom database to hold everything, and used social-network-analysis software to link gang members together and figure out who the impact players were. I was at police headquarters one day when Gerard opened a file folder and started pulling out enforcement simulations: computer runs of what would happen to the network if different patterns of arrests were made. Look at this one, he said. I get these guys and the whole network falls apart. *Zero wastage policing*, I thought. *Zero stupidity policing. Zero collateral-damage policing. Zero offend-the-community policing.*

CPD investigators worked the Taliband for six months, got drugs, money, guns, full automatic weapons, turned it into a ninety-five-count indictment. November 17, 2008, a huge interagency raid team went out after the first forty guys. Dan brought the UC students along and gave them their own raid jackets. They were after the right people. The neighborhood *hated* the Taliband, started calling in tips as word of the sweep spread. CPD had to set up a second Crimestopper phone line to handle the volume. People came outside to cheer as cops went through Taliband doors.

Streicher gave a press conference, explained the operation, and told everybody that this was just the beginning. It was a goof Whalen and Gerard had come up with—there *was* no phase two. They just wanted to rattle the streets. But Vortex had been so surgically precise—gotten so exactly the right, the most serious, people—that they looked telepathic. Street guys started coming out of the woodwork to cop a plea before it was too late. "I've never seen anything like it," Streicher said, a smile of happy wonderment on his face. "We had to start scheduling surrenders at the police station, we couldn't handle everybody." One guy walked in, said, I know I'm next, I'll give you everything. Fine, the cops said. They had no idea who he was. Gerard and Whalen went to a meeting of the Northside Community Council to explain the operation and got a standing ovation.

There are cops coming from all over the country to see how Vortex did it. Dan Gerard just entered a master's program at UC.

Spike's locked up. They finally got to him.

Homicide's down in Cincinnati, gang homicide steady at about a 41 percent reduction. It's not good enough, not close. But we're in motion. Whalen is doing home visits on impact players, visiting them on their street corners, sending a cop and an ATF agent in full fed regalia. We're here because your group's hot and we don't want to have to come down hard, they say. They bring the group's intelligence folder, leaf through it, let the guy see his picture, his boys' pictures, surveillance photographs. Whalen has a chart of shootings in Cincinnati between call-ins. They watch for the spikes, go do the home visits, shootings come right back down. They're doing *voluntary* call-ins in the neighborhoods. They've finally taught us the lesson we missed in the very first Vamp Hill Kings forum in Boston. You don't have to have people on supervision, you don't have to have an arrest hanging over their head. You want them to come sit down with you, *ask* them. Just like Billy Stewart had done, way back in May of 1996. It's working in Cincinnati, too.

The moral-voice work, stagnant for so long, is finally underway. We are mapping, finally, some of the lessons of the High Point work onto the gang work. There's a new woman in charge of that side of CIRV, she's figuring out how to identify influentials for the gangs and the impact players, shooters, how to keep the community voice focused on them: Don't shoot, don't die, don't go to prison, we care about you, we want you to succeed, we'll help. I got a call late last week from city councillor Cecil Thomas. He wants to be part of it, make it work.

We haven't begun the drug-market work in Cincinnati. Cecil Thomas wants to move on that, too.

The ground's prepared, now, for the reconciliation conversation, the larger conversation about how we all see each other and the role race plays in that. People are in different places. Streicher started to make prison visits recently. He's been going, with Stan Ross and Pete Mingo, some of the other outreach workers, to facilities where inmates coming back to Cincinnati are held, having the administration get them together, sitting down with them. What we used to do in Cincinnati didn't work, he tells them. I see that now. "It's nothing personal," he told one group at Lebanon prison, "but how ironic is it that you guys are incarcerated as a result of me being successful in my career?" I see these guys differently now, he said of Mingo and the others. They were strong enough to change, I really respect that. We welcome you back to Cincinnati, he said, we want you to succeed. "We want to help you to get educated and to get the services you need," he said. "No man was ever meant to live in a box." I talked to Streicher a few days ago. "I've been on the job for forty years," he said. "The last couple have turned everything I thought I knew about policing on its head."

Now

We can do this. We are *going* to do this.

About two years ago, January 15, 2009, Dean Esserman from Providence stood in a sixth-floor John Jay conference room with a cup of coffee in his hand, looking west out a window toward the Hudson River a long city block away. Jeremy Travis was there, Tracey Meares was there, Tom Streicher and Jim Fealy were there. Risco Lewis and Meg Reiss from the Nassau County district attorney's office and the Terrace and Bedell operation, my old friend Teny Gross from Boston and Providence, Sherman Mason and Jim Summey from High Point, Anthony Braga. Others from the national community that has grown up around this work. Jeremy and I had pulled them together for two days. We think we may be at a turning point, we said to them. Do we believe in this enough to make a major national push?

On break the first afternoon, looking out the window, Dean went rigid. *A plane is putting down on the Hudson*, he said. He'd seen it gliding south over the river, gear up, so low it was only visible through the gaps between buildings. Crippled US Airways Flight 1549, pilot Chesley "Sully" Sullenberger at the helm, more than 150 people on board. Sully had trained for the moment, executed perfectly, took care of the souls in his charge. The passengers kept their heads, didn't panic, didn't get themselves killed. NYPD scuba divers went into the January waters and pulled people out. EMTs and New York firefighters helped the injured. Coast Guard vessels and a private ferry took passengers off the wings of the sinking aircraft. Emergency evacuation slides, designed to double as life rafts, worked exactly as intended. Everybody lived. They called it the Miracle on the Hudson. And so it was, in the ordinary way we use the word. But, more, it wasn't, any more than Boston had been a miracle. It was professionalism, common sense, common cause. It was work, important work, done well.

It's time to get going, our team said, those two days in New York. This stuff works, we know how to do it, we know how to teach it to people. It's not notional any longer, not an aspiration. It's real. "We who understand this have a responsibility," Dean said. "It's up to us to create the future." Teny ended the two days in his inimitable way, it's why I love him so much. "Knowing what we know now," he said, "if the homicide rate hasn't been cut in half in ten years, I'm filing a class-action suit against the government of the United States."

We launched what we're calling the National Network for Safe Communities. It says, There is too much violence in America; the impact of overt drug markets is unacceptable; there are far too many people in prison; the tension between law enforcement and communities of color is intolerable. There are more than fifty jurisdictions that have signed up, that are committed to those ideas. Our old sites like Cincinnati, High Point, Providence. Boston is back in the fold: A new commissioner, Ed Davis, with whom Anthony had worked when Davis was chief of police in Lowell, Massachusetts, put his foot down and is bringing Ceasefire back; Anthony's a civilian member of the command staff. New sites like Los Angeles, Chicago, Newark. Two states—California and North Carolina—are each doing multiple cities. We're fanning out to help them, to help each other, bringing teams to John Jay, sending people to other cities to teach and learn, writing up innovations, writing up the how-to guides, framing stronger evaluations. Identifying the key issues—sustainability, strengthening the moral voice of the community, helping hard-core offenders, how to do the racial reconciliation work. Moving it along.

What the NNSC is about: resetting the national conversation, the national standard of practice, on gangs, drugs, prison. Cities all over the country have homicide and drug market problems. If they do, they should be doing this. The *country* has a prison problem. It should be doing this. It's just that simple, now.

It's taken almost twenty years, but we've got something basic, fundamental, in hand. All the slowly seen facts on the ground, all the slowly revealed insights, have come together to form something clear, strong, and solid. It doesn't take long to lay it out. There aren't that many things, many crime problems, that will keep a community from being able to function. In the most troubled community, it's a small number of people doing those things, and the core of many of the worst crime problems lie in various kinds of collectivities—gangs, drug crews, drug markets—rather than in individuals. Our official law enforcement response to both the individuals and the collectivities is inconsistent, incoherent, and, on the receiving end, often opaque. A lot of what we take as irrationality, bad character, even self-destructiveness, are in fact reasonable responses to that inconsistency and opacity. A lot more is the result of group dynamics that are both obscure and often unwelcome to the individuals involved. Still more is the unintended *consequence* of our official response. All sides—the neighborhoods, the streets, law enforcement—tell stories about each other that are at their heart deeply mistaken and deeply destructive. But all sides are in deep ways rational, whatever may be appearances to the contrary, and all sides are willing to shift to a new place, if they can see it and find their way there. Everybody, in a very real way, is keeping everybody else going. Everybody can stop.

So in practice, what we need to do is identify those core offenders, which is easy. Then we need to put together a core partnership of law enforcement, service providers, and community voices. If we can add strong figures close to the offenders—parents, elders, "influentials"—so much the better. We need to organize law enforcement so it can provide a clear, crisp, predictable strategic response, particularly to the groups and collectivities at the center of the action. We need to organize the social services and the community voices. We need to build a sustained relationship between the partnership and the streets in which we clearly, crisply, and repeatedly spell out standards, opportunities, and consequences. And in order to do all *that*, we need to undo the worst of the toxic rift between law enforcement and the neighborhoods.

That's it. It takes about ten minutes to explain it. *That's it*, I say. *That's the whole thing. The rest is all details.* It's a little more complicated than the traditional law enforcement story—*just lock them up*— but there's a shrinking constituency for that even in law enforcement: *We can't arrest our way out of this.* Most of that hard-core sentiment comes from politicians, not working law enforcement, and even they're getting tired of paying the jail and prison bills, especially at the state and local level. It's infinitely *less* complicated than the traditional root cause story that we have to fix *everything* to fix crime: the economy, the schools, health care, the families, the culture. That idea still has a lot of appeal to a lot of people, but it comes with one nagging and obvious problem: You can't *do* it. Makes doing something attainable pretty attractive.

We're still learning every day. We're only scratching the surface of the reconciliation and legitimacy work, there's huge additional voltage to come there. We need to figure out how to build up the moral-voice piece, get that out of the call-ins and into the day-to-day work in the neighborhoods. We're working on that, figuring out how to match up community influentials with gangs, groups, impact players. We'll get there, I'm sure of it. There are new variations coming. Steven Alm, a former U.S. attorney and now a judge in Hawaii, has mapped the basic ideas on to probation in something called Project HOPE. He got tired of seeing supervisees who'd failed a dozen drug tests, with no official response, getting hauled before him to get sent back to prison. If I'd raised my kids this way I'd be living on the street, he said. He started telling his probationers, we're going to test you twice a week; you fail a test, or don't show up to your probation meeting, I'm sending the warrant squad out for you and you'll spend two days in jail. His probationers were overwhelmingly meth users everybody had given up on as hopeless addicts; a randomized control trial showed sudden, massive improvements in arrests, incarceration, failed drug tests, and probation revocations. Those who don't do well—not many—self-identify for scarce, expensive treatment resources. In New York, NYPD housing police commander Joanne Jaffe is having her cops sit down with recidivist juvenile robbers and their mothers and saying to them, We're watching you, we want to help you, we want to help your family. She's seeing an 80 percent reduction in robbery. In High Point, they realized a robbery spike was being driven by young gang members; they started calling gangs in and saying, You don't get to shoot people, and now you don't get to rob people; it came back down. They're setting up on domestic violence, now.

They're going statewide in California, with support from the governor's office and private foundations. Stewart Wakeling, who ran the Stockton operation years ago, is heading the support team; it's just a couple of people, but they're active in ten cities. We huddled with him at

John Jay last week. Salinas, violence way down. Oxnard, violence way down. Bakersfield, violence way down. They're doing the same thing in Ohio, modeling other cities on the Cincinnati initiative. I got an update recently. Dayton, violence way down. Canton, violence way down.

This stuff *works*. It doesn't cost much, sometimes it doesn't cost anything, people just need to understand why and how to do it. Garry McCarthy is the police director in Newark, New Jersey, across the river from John Jay, I can get on the train and be there in an hour. He's ex-NYPD, *tough*, got the cop's-cop steel backbone, only in his case it's there to cushion the tungsten carbide core that runs inside. We've been talking racial misunderstanding, history, why the neighborhoods hate stop-and-frisk, why we can do better. He gets it, loves it, is going to Department of Justice meetings and talking about legal cynicism. He had Tracey Meares and me out for a day last week to talk to his department. I gave my race talk, why it's all so awful; Tracey talked legitimacy. Room full of cops, no argument. "The cops used to beat *me* up when I was a kid," said one Hispanic officer. Nobody fought it.

People get this. It makes sense. Jeffrey Rosen, a law professor at George Washington University, looked at Project Hope, High Point, Tracey Meares's Chicago work, Ceasefire. "The relative simplicity of the solutions, it turns out, is at the core of their radical potential," he ended up writing in the *New York Times Magazine*. The country's crisis of crime and incarceration "can actually be solved, practical step by practical step."

Not everybody gets it, and not everybody who gets it likes it. One problem is that it's *too* simple, seems too good to be true. It's too far away from how we think about these issues, the old conviction that they're huge, massive, tectonic, need huge, massive responses. It strains credulity that one-hour meetings can cut homicide in the worst places in Chicago, that five years after the meeting it's still changing the lives of gun criminals. It doesn't seem possible. It doesn't change anything else—or so it seems—doesn't fix the economy or the criminal justice system. The facts help here. There are too many data points now, too many evaluations, all the cities where it's worked, the drug markets that aren't any longer. It's getting harder to say, on principle, *That can't work*. The evolving logic helps, too, our growing understanding of what's driving the violence, what needs to be changed, what the work *does* change. It's true that the Chicago meetings don't change the economy. It's also true that the crisis of legitimacy is as much behind the violence as anything else and that the Chicago meetings are designed to change *that*. Resetting community standards, undoing toxic norms and narratives, fixing legitimacy, is real, very real, change. The more that understanding spreads, the more the work makes sense.

It's still not welcome, in some quarters. It's too soft for some, too hard for others. This is a variation on the theme of enforcement vs. social services, but with philosophical roots. There's the camp that believes in individual accountability, thinks crime is about bad character and bad choices, society has to take a stand about right and wrong. There's that in what we do—*We'll stop you if you make us*—but it's not just that. It means that it doesn't work to say, any longer, *Those are terrible people, hold them accountable, lock them up.* There's the camp that believes in social accountability, thinks crime is about history and neglect and oppression, society has to take a stand about what it has done to troubled communities. There's that in what we do—*We'll help you if you let us*—but it's not just that. It means it doesn't work to say, any longer, *Those people are victims, they're not responsible, they need programs, support.*

The old duality is simple, and it may be comforting, but it's wrong. We need to find a new, more complicated logic, and we have. It's a logic that says no amount of law enforcement will ever work, that law enforcement as we've been practicing it is part of the problem. It's a logic that says no amount of traditional social investment will ever work, that the programs don't help very much, that treating people doing terrible things as "clients" is part of the problem. It's a logic that says, someone can be doing terrible things and still be a victim; someone can have done wrong and still deserve help; someone can have been the victim of history and neglect and it's still right to demand that they stop hurting people. Not even remotely radical ideas: a good parent says, all the time, *You've broken the rules, and I'm going to do something about it, and I love you and of course I will continue to care for you and hold you close.* But radical when it comes to talking about crime, where commitment to accountability seems to crowd out room for caring, and commitment to caring seems to crowd out room for accountability.

It's a logic that says, especially, none of us is without sin here. We have all created this. We cannot look at anybody else, any of the other communities involved, and say, *You change*. This is on us, all of us. We have all done wrong, and must all shift.

There's still the struggle between one way of looking at law enforcement, at policing especially, and another: between a strategy that likes stop-and-frisk and terms like "exile" and "zero tolerance," and one that has police chiefs going to communities and saying, "I'm sorry." It's the old Boston vs. New York fight, at heart. Law enforcement, the public, politics is full of people who look at what we're doing and see hug-a-thug, who can't imagine gang bangers and drug dealers listening, who can't imagine that any conversation with the streets isn't idiocy or a negotiation. It's full of people like Karen Richards, a prosecutor in Allen County, who laughed at us when Janet Zobel and the Urban League tried to bring the High Point strategy to Fort Wayne, Indiana. She wasn't interested in talking to drug dealers, or keeping them out of prison. "Why not slam 'em from the beginning and forget this foolishness?" she told the *Wall Street Journal*. Some people understand what we're about and genuinely reject it. Some don't understand it, see what they think they're going to see, and reject *that*: it's what gets us the POLICE TRY TO SHUT DRUG MARKET BY GIVING DRUG DEALERS JOBS headlines.

But some start out in one place and end up in another. I had a long talk a couple of years ago with Patrick McIlheran, a columnist for the *Milwaukee Journal Sentinal*. The police department was gearing up to do the drug-market operation, and it was clear McIlheran didn't think much of it; he grilled me hard. Then he wrote his piece. And *nailed* it, came up with one of my single favorite lines ever. "The more you learn, any idea that it's about going easy on misunderstood youth evaporates," he said. "It's more like granny wielding the feds as she lays down the law."

It's what happened as we went operational with the gang strategy in Chicago in August of 2010, in Chicago Police Department District 11, West Garfield Park, the most dangerous neighborhood in the city. Half a dozen parolees walked into the call-in, more didn't, didn't bother to show up. Those there heard the messages. The city went crazy: Ludicrous press accounts said police superintendent Jody Weis had tricked the gang members into coming to a secret meeting, had pleaded with them to stop killing people, had negotiated, that the gang members had walked out. Not a word of it was true. The gangs went crazy, held a press conference to argue that they were too disorganized to be held accountable—the irony of organizing a press conference to plead disorganization was apparently lost on them—said they were being given ultimatums, what they needed was jobs, contracts. One of them showed up in a black hat that read MESS WITH THE BEST, DIE LIKE THE REST. The press covered this with a straight face, gave it a lot of attention. What they didn't know about and didn't cover: on the same day, gangs in Garfield Park got together behind closed doors and gang members who had been in our call-in said, I was there, this is what they said, I don't think they're playing, we need to calm down. Gang members started hitting the streets and talking to their own. It's been over seven months now and homicide in District 11 is down over 40 percent. We just had the second call-in. Dozens of gang members attended, listened riveted, hung around afterward and talked to the community people and the cops. People are calling the service line. We're expanding into CPD District 6, will keep going until the violent areas of the city are covered. The new news stories are saying, *It wasn't a negotiation, and it looks like it's working.*

I was in Chicago recently, in a cab going in from O'Hare, the cabbie and I talking about the call-in. "That was a bad idea," he said. Maybe, I said, but it wasn't reported well, here's what really happened. "I was in the life myself," he said. "That'll work. Those guys want to get through the day quiet, just like anybody else."

Why, finally, this is within our reach, why we can change the country, why people are ready to change:
Because *nobody likes what's going on now.*
Nobody.

We can't see it, because we're all too locked in opposition. The cops are writing off the hot neighborhoods, the hot neighborhoods think the cops are race predators, the street guys hate the cops and the people who call the cops, the cops think the street guys are sociopaths, it all goes full circle. Everybody thinks everybody else is doing this because they want to, nobody talks to each other, when we do it's all anger and accusation, it never goes anywhere. It's hiding in plain sight, but we can't see it.
Nobody's having fun.

On the law enforcement side, the cops, prosecutors, probation officers, parole officers, judges, none of them are happy. They know it's not working. The cops, especially. They're desperate, most of them, to stop the killing and make the streets safe. They come to work day after day, year after year, and it all continues. *We can't arrest our way out of this.* They see the bodies, see the dead little girl mistakes, see the shrieking parents, see the viciously angry older brothers heading out to get payback, see the shrines, go through the doors, make arrest after arrest after arrest, make the street stops, see the hate in the eyes of the people they're trying to protect, see the thugs weeping as they get transported to prison, see them shot on the ground screaming for their mothers, try to stop the bleeding, hold them for the EMTs, see them die.

It's not working. They *know* that.

I co-taught a seminar at Yale Law School a year or so ago, invited up by my friend Nancy Gertner, a federal judge in Boston. She brought in Steve Robinson, my old U.S. attorney friend from the New Haven SACSI days; he'd gone on to the federal bench, too. For most of a day, I watched the two of them and a room full of frighteningly bright law students debate two real, but disguised, cases: Boston drug dealers who had been convicted in Judge Gertner's court. What should the appropriate sentences be? The students looked at the defendants, looked at the facts in the cases, looked at the federal sentencing guidelines, looked at sentences in similar cases, looked at reasons to depart from the guidelines. They presented immaculately reasoned arguments leading to hugely different outcomes: a few years, decades, everything in between.

After hours of this, I got my turn. Judge Gertner, I asked, do you feel that any possible sentence you give in these cases will make any difference whatsoever to public safety in Boston? No. Judge Robinson? *You know what I think*, he said. No. I went around the room, asked each student. Every single one of them, *no.*

Everybody knows it's not working.

They'll keep on doing it, all the law enforcement people, if they can't see anything better. *But they don't like it.* They're good, good people, almost all of them. I admire my cop friends more than just about anybody else in the world. They're amazing. Stay on the job a couple of decades, see what that shows you, what almost nobody else in the world sees, keep your balance, find a way not to give in to cynicism and despair, and you come out very, very special. I trust them with my life.

They keep on working, they don't give up, they won't give up. Even in the midst of the horror show, they win major victories. They get a killer off the streets, can go tell a mother that the man who murdered her son is in hand. They lock up the man who's got his ex and her kids hiding in a shelter under a false name. They save the drug dealer bleeding out on the corner. They stop a drive-by before it happens. It's good, good work.

It's *not enough*. They know that. They know that no amount of it will ever be enough. The good ones are deeply, hugely frustrated. They're ready for something else. John Seabrook, who writes for the *New Yorker*, went up to Providence to talk to Dean Esserman about the drug-market strategy. What's it take to be ready to do this, he asked.

Failure, Dean said.

And it's not just not working: It's making things worse. The good cops, the good people in law enforcement, they're ready to see that. They'll take something new if they can see what it is.

The community is in agony. The saturation of pain and misery is paralyzing, once you see it. The steadfastness it takes to carry on, the every day courage, the refusal to give in, the pure *bearing up*, takes your breath away.

I'm working in Pittsburgh with Ricky Burgess, a black man, a minister, a city councillor. We'd been colleagues for over a year before I heard his story. He's behind a Pittsburgh version of Operation Ceasefire. His council district is far and away the most violent in the city. When I was getting started there I did a Net search and found a video somebody had posted of street crews in Ricky's neighborhood. First up were the East Hills boys, dozens deep, outside mugging for the camera, RIP tattoos on their forearms, bragging about their beef with Homewood. In the midst of it one of them racks the slide on a camo pump shotgun: single most chilling sound in the world, it made me freeze up sitting in my living room. The Dallas Avenue Crips, smaller crew, heavily armed: one's brandishing a scoped AK-47, one has a semiautomatic pistol with an extended magazine sticking out of his pocket. RIP T-shirts, two little kids in the group, *I'm eleven*, one says, *I'm thirteen* the other, the eleven-year-old is throwing signs and rapping about AK-47s. One of the guys in the third crew, 1200 Block Hilltop, has an M16 machine gun or an AR15, the semiauto version, I can't tell from the video. ".223," one of the guys says. "Won't no vest save you."

This matters to me more than anything, Ricky said, over and over and over again, as we worked together. This is going on in my neighborhood, these are my people, we have to do something. It was a year before I heard the rest of it, before I heard him, very casually, speak his own piece. When he did I had to ask him to write it down, I couldn't keep up, keep track. This is, word for word, what he told me.

My entire life has been affected by gun violence. It has controlled the direction of my life and has significant consequence on my family. When I was away from home in college, my aunt Shirlene my mother's younger sister, was shot and killed. My mother didn't inform me of my Aunt's death until many months later after final exams. I never got to mourn and bring closure, my Aunt's memory haunts me until this very day. My mother after her sister's murder had a mental break-down from which she never recovered. For the next forty years, my mother was on psychotropic drugs and had to be involuntarily hospitalised over forty times. The mother I knew when I left for college was gone and never returned. My experience from my aunt's murder and my mother's sickness left me searching for life's true meaning. The search for meaning led to me the gospel ministry and for 26 years I have served as Senior Pastor of a church in the same neighborhood I and my wife was born and raised in. The church I pastor is located in one of the most dangerous places in Pittsburgh.

My wife has also been greatly affected by gun violence. My wife's grandfather died of a gunshot wound. Her father was shot in his home by an intruder and afterwards remained permanently disabled. Later her mother was shot and killed in her place of business. Her brother shot and killed a victim during an home invasion and he is still serving part of a 20 year prison sentence. My wife and I have adopted and raised her brother's son. My wife has had several cousins shot and killed.

I too have had many of my cousins shot, two of which were killed by their injuries. Many of my childhood friends were also shot and killed. I have presided over many gun murder funerals. Several of my church members have had family members shot and killed. Two of the children who were members of the church I pastor were shot and killed. My experience with gun violence was so alarming I felt responsible to reduce its deadly incidents and mitigate its devastating effects. I decided to run for City Council because of a deep desire to reduce gun violence in my community.

But law enforcement isn't helping, isn't offering anything wanted, anything that will help. The day he first told me all this, he was with a black woman, we'd just met, I'm not sure who she was, somebody from legal circles in Pittsburgh, I think. She listened, nodding. "I don't talk about this," he said. "It's just how we live." She nodded. "I get stopped by the police all the time," he said. "I put on a suit to go shopping, or I get followed around the store." She nodded. A few days later I was back in New York having dinner with a big group. I got there late, the rest of the group was already seated. I found a chair next to Tracey Meares and Risco Lewis. They were talking. I had an extraordinary conversation the other day, I told them when I had a chance. I'm working with a black minister, a city councillor, in Pittsburgh, one of the most prominent men in the city. He dresses up to go shopping so security won't harass him. Tracey and Risco are black. They stared at me.

We were just talking about how we do that, too, they said.

Glenn Martin is black, was locked up, now has a senior position at the Fortune Society, one of New York City's leading reentry agencies. He moved not long ago from Park Slope, one of the toniest neighborhoods in Brooklyn, to Harlem. He lived in Park Slope for years, was never stopped by the police. He gets stopped regularly in Harlem. He can stand at his window, look down on the street, and see black men getting stopped. I was on a stop-and-frisk panel at NYU with him recently. "The police always say, this is how we bring crime down," he said. "If I had a choice between higher crime and this, I'd choose higher crime." But he doesn't *want* higher crime. Nobody does. Let law enforcement, the outside, offer another way to bring crime down, a way that treats people with respect, doesn't scorch the earth, the community will take it. They're desperate for it.

The community hasn't chosen what's going on. It didn't ask for the violence, for the drugs, for the death, for the prisons, for the stops, for the disenfranchisement, to raise a dead generation's children, for the anger it feels.

Doesn't like it. Doesn't want it. Past ready for a way out.

The guys on the streets don't like it.

They're not getting rich. Seattle shut one of its drug markets down in one of the DOJ-sponsored High Point replications and video of the guys called in ended up on TV. The people who wrote in to comment on a newspaper story in the *Seattle Times* were incredulous: Those can't be drug dealers. "I saw these folks on KING-TV," one said. "They looked homeless." Guess what. Street dealers and gang members *do* look homeless. They don't work steadily, they get robbed, they get arrested and can't sell, they're addicted and that's where all the money goes, it rains and nobody's out buying drugs, the cops are all over and nobody's out, their connection gets busted and things dry up. They're getting hurt and killed at astronomical rates. They've got real enemies after them, trying to hurt and kill them. They get pushed into hurting, killing other people, because that's what the street code says and their friends are watching. They're cycling endlessly through jail and prison. They're on probation and parole and can't do what they want, have to piss in a cup. The police roust them all the time. They're scared for their moms, wives, girlfriends, little brothers and sisters, sons and daughters. Their fathers are absent or locked up, their brothers are dead or locked up or paralyzed. They're saturated with PTSD. Life is like a video game, it keeps on getting harder, they don't know if they can take it much longer.

When they come to their senses when they're twenty-five or thirty, as most do, it's too late. Nobody will give them a chance, they never finished school, they've got no work history, they can't pass a criminal history check, they have bad attitudes they can't get over. It's next to impossible to break through all that.

Some can and do break through, can look at their old worlds from the other side, can see new possibilities. I'm with Tyrone Parker at the Alliance for Concerned Men in Washington, D.C. Tyrone is black, old-school D.C., was a bank robber in the day, went inside in 1966, did twenty-one years, is still on parole. His son was shot and killed in 1989, a mistake. He's a street saint, a relentless indefatigable power for peace and sanity. I adore him. He brokers truces between warring gangs, pulls kids out of the life, runs programs for the D.C. government, goes into prisons and gets the guys inside to squash beefs on the outside, has a little network of old heads from the neighborhoods who do the work together. I've spent the day with him and a couple of them, one an amazing black Muslim woman who helped take care of Muhammed Ali when he was failing. We're thinking on what to do about the killing in D.C.: what they do, where my stuff might fit in. We've been at it for hours and hours. We're finally breaking up, I'm heading out the door, Tyrone's still seated and wearily gathering his papers together, and he looks at the table in front of him and he says, *Everybody's tired.*

I turn back around. What's that? *Everybody's tired*, he says again. What do you mean? Tired of what?

All of it, he says. The killing, the dying, the jail, the scuffling. Everybody's had enough. Everybody's tired.

I know Tyrone Parkers all over the country. They're all unique, and they're all saints, trying to save the world at 2:00 A.M. on the corner, they all live on their cell phones, they're all haunted by their pasts, they all go where practically nobody else will go, and they all say the same thing. They all say, *Everybody's tired.*

I talk to gang members and drug dealers all over the country. I sat with a Mexican Mafia guy in San Diego County, quiet, serious, just out of federal prison. It's right what they say about us, he said. We do run things from inside. Not as much as people think, we don't control everything, but some things, yes. Hits get green-lighted.

But here's the other thing, he said. The guys inside, they're meeting their sons and grandsons on the exercise yard. They've got family they care about, people they love, back in the community, where people are being hurt. They're worried all the time. They hate it. They hate all of it. Could you go to them and say, in the right way, we're trying to make a change, would you use your influence to get the word back to the streets, the craziness has got to stop? Yes, you could. They'd do it.

I go to prisons. Drive out to the country, that's where almost all of them are, down the rural roads into the huge green expanses where the trees have all been cut down to clear sight lines and make escape harder. The prisons have herds of deer grazing at the forest line, it hits me every time, the deer outside and the men locked inside. Leave everything in the car and go into the waiting rooms full of women and children, nobody talks, nobody's eyes meet. Through the metal detectors, get your hand marked with invisible ink, they scan you in and out, through the locked doors and buzzers, down the halls. Look out the windows at the impossibly fit guys staring back at you from the exercise yard. They track your every move, they know you're going back out.

At Graterford state prison outside Philadelphia there's a lifers' group. None of them will ever get out, barring some legal miracle. They've been actively training guys who *will* get out, working through with them the dumb street-code stuff that got them locked up, mobilizing them to fight the violence back in the neighborhoods. It's their own idea. They're passionate about it, they're trying to organize the old heads in the neighborhoods to fight the craziness. We're still influential out there, they say, kids look up to us, we're the street legends, we did terrible things, we need to give back.

Otisville federal prison, upstate New York. Where Freddie Cardoza, one bullet from Boston, is still locked up, as far as I know. Room full of guys from all over the country, that's how federal prison works. They're trying to do reentry, setting up school and housing and work for people getting out. I'm there with Tyrone Parker and one of his partners. I get the floor for a minute. There's a new way of doing things coming together, I say. Some of us think things can be really different, that there's a way of stopping the violence that doesn't rely on locking people up that you guys could play a really big part in. You've got standing, back home. We're working in cities all over the country. Would you be willing to get on the phone at the right time and call home? Say to people, it's got to stop?

I'm from Los Angeles, one guy said. *Tell me when.*

And the others. *Chicago. Detroit. Philadelphia. Washington.*

Tell me when.

It's simple, in the end.

It's taken me twenty-five years to see it, it's been there all along, but it's hard to see, we make it almost impossible to see, all of us.

Standing in the middle of Nicholson Gardens? Thinking

This is not okay?

That's what *everybody else was thinking, too.* The two cops I was with, hyperalert, long minutes from backup, gone in a heartbeat if things went south, working like fiends to take the edge off the community's death spiral. Feeling for the grandmothers, pitying the crack monsters, doing the cool respect dance with the drug boys, little kids running around in the midst of it all, not their fault. The grandmothers locked in their apartments, scared for themselves, their kids, their grandkids, furious at the drug boys: They still don't want them locked up forever, dead forever. The drug boys: life expectancy of mayflies, everything they have can be taken from them in a minute, their friends dead or locked up, their mothers worried sick about them, next to no chance of breaking out and making it big.

I think back to that alley full of drug dealers in Baltimore.

Who's winning?

Nobody.

Nobody's winning. This isn't good for anybody. Nobody likes it.

The last, the core, revelation.

It's not everything. Everybody doesn't want *all* of the same things. The community wants every single gang member to turn his life around; that's probably not going to happen. The cops want every single gang member to stop doing every single crime; that's probably not going to happen. The gang members want the cops to leave them alone; they're not going to get it. But they agree on enough to completely change the way we're doing things.

Here's what everybody agrees on. The cops, the community, the street guys, everybody.

The killing's wrong. The killing's terrible, it's got to stop. Even the street guys, almost all of them, think that.

Those that don't believe that, they've got to go. Even the street guys, there's 5 percent of them the other 95 percent are scared to death of. Take them away.

The worst of the street craziness has to stop. People have to be able to use the streets and the parks, kids have to be able to go to school, the community has to be able to function. Not everybody's going to stop hustling, it's not going to happen. But if you're going to hustle find a way to do it that makes it invisible, takes it deep underground. The *drug dealers* would rather things be quiet and safe, even they don't like the chaos. The cops and the community don't have to approve, don't have to turn a blind eye, don't have to negotiate. But as long as there's violence, public madness, that's where law enforcement should go. The rest of it we can worry about later. Like we do in the white neighborhoods.

Nobody should go to prison who doesn't have to. *We have to stop locking everbody up*. Even the cops agree with that. If the street guys will listen to a warning, listen to the community, put their guns down, keep it on the down low, maybe take help, and it means they don't have to get locked up, fine.

People should get treated with respect. Living in a dangerous place is no reason to get treated like a felon. In the hottest neighborhoods, hardly anybody is driving the worst of what's happening. We should act like it. Even the cops get it, once they see it, they make the shift that Dan Gerard made in Cincinnati.

If the community will step forward, make its voice heard, and that works, that means the cops can step back. That's as it should be. We don't occupy the white neighborhoods, we don't lead with law enforcement there. The cops play cleanup and step in when the community can't handle it. As it should be.

Everybody who wants help should get it, as much as we can. It's not a deal, nobody gets to say, you get me a job, I'll stop killing people. You'll stop killing because killing is *wrong*, that's the end of *that* argument. But if we can help you, will we? Absolutely. The toughest cop would rather see the most seasoned felon paying taxes rather than locked up.

That's it. Everybody agrees. Those who don't, there are a few, there are more of us than there are of them, they lose. We win.

We sit down, we talk to each other, we say how it's going to be, and we do the work. It's not a miracle. It's work.

Time to go to work.

National Network for Safe Communities
www.nnscommunities.org

Acknowledgments

The work described in this book has been an extraordinary collective enterprise. It has proceeded in all of its most important aspects from the ground up; its most central asset has been the willingness of those involved to share their worlds and their work, and to think and to act together. Many of those involved have been named in the book; many, many more have not. I am grateful, beyond my ability to express, to all.

The Kennedy School of Government's Mark H. Moore was my first, and remains my most important, tutor in thinking about crime, criminal justice, and public policy. He and the group that assembled around the Harvard Executive Session on Policing were wonderfully open and welcoming. I am especially grateful to Francis X. Hartmann, Malcom Sparrow, George Kelling, Herman Goldstein, James Q. Wilson, Bob Wasserman, Susan Michaelson, Christine Nixon, and Michael Smith, all of whom were generous beyond reason to an utter neophyte.

Anne M. Piehl codesigned the Boston Gun Project and she and Anthony Braga were at the core of inventing, implementing, and evaluating Operation Ceasefire. It was a magic time, and I am grateful to have been able to be there with them. Anthony has been central, since, in carrying the work forward; I am proud, and lucky, to be his colleague.

Lois Mock at the National Institute of Justice saw possibility when nobody else did. Without her vision and stewardship, none of what followed would have happened. Others at NIJ, particularly Jeremy Travis and Sally Hillsman, were profoundly supportive and protective, for which I am deeply grateful.

The Boston team that assembled around the Gun Project, and ultimately created Operation Ceasefire, was simply extraordinary. Their willingness to make outsiders welcome, teach us, and share with us what they knew and did amazes me still. In addition to Paul Joyce, Gary French, and the others named in the book, central actors included Elizabeth Keeley, John Burke, and Mark Zanini from the Suffolk County District Attorney's Office; Tim Zadai from the Department of Parole; Jeff Roehm, Lennie Ladd, and David Carlson from the Bureau of Alcohol, Tobacco, and Firearms; Joy Fallon and Marianne Hinkle from the Office of the United States Attorney; Ron Corbett from the Department of Probation; Sonya Aleman, Jack Arnold, and Dan Tracy from the Department of Youth Services; and Mike Hennessey of the Boston School Police. Thank you, all.

The firearms trafficking insights and strategies that emerged from the Gun Project became of national significance through the work of a small team of visionaries: the indefatigable Susan Ginsburg, then at the Department of the Treasury; Joe Vince, Jerry Nunziato, Dale Armstrong, and Terry Austin at the Bureau of Alcohol, Tobacco, and Firearms; Glenn Pierce at Northeastern University; and, once again, Anthony Braga. All of you know that never has so much been done by so few with so little.

The Minneapolis work was carried forward by, in addition to those named in the book, Douglas Hicks, Randall Johnson, Dale Barsness, Michael Martin, Jeff Ruegel, Michael Zimmerman, Pat Hoven, Andre Lewis, David Lillehaug, and Chuck Wexler.

The Strategic Approaches to Community Safety Initiative was created and shepherded by an exceptional Department of Justice group. In, again, addition to those named in the book, they included Laurie Robinson, Mary Lou Leary, Julie Samuels, Tom Roberts, Amy Solomon, and Erin Dalton. Many are friends and collegues still; it's been an honor.

In Baltimore, Hathaway Ferebee, Pat Jessamy, Kim Morton, and Jill Myers never gave up. It was hopeless, but it was valiant: I love you guys. Many of the team that tried to implement Operation Safe Neighborhoods continued to try to make the basic ideas work in Baltimore in various ways. One was Baltimore police officer Frederick H. Bealefeld, who is now, as police commissioner, doing a wonderful and effective job.

Walter Holton, who was U.S. attorney for the middle district of North Carolina, embedded the work there in a way that has had not only local but national significance. The fierce commitment of Sylvia

Oberle and Rob Lang was central to its success and institutionalization. Chief Louis Quijas gave the work its first foothold in High Point, for which I am deeply grateful.

The High Point group that took on the drug market strategy is peerless. It included, as central figures, Marty Sumner, Randy Tysinger, Larry Casterline, Lee Hunt, Jim Summey, and others. I admire them as professionals, value them as colleagues, and am proud to call them friends. I am particularly proud of the way they have dealt with each other, their outside partners, and the public attention their successes have brought their way. They have never lost their balance or their focus on what is most important: protecting the communities in their charge, and sharing what they know with others with the same responsibilities.

High Point chief of police James Fealy is in a class of his own. His willingness to take on the toxic issues of racial conflict, tell the truth, and change what he and his officers do makes him, in a very real way, the bravest man in American policing. I needed that, Jim, we all did. Thank you.

In Cincinnati, Tom Streicher, Jim Whalen, Kurt Byrd, Dan Gerard, Robin Engel, and John Eck were central to launching CIRV and making it what it became. Dr. Victor Garcia, despite our later disagreements, was essential to that process and continues to have my respect and admiration.

Steve Perrin, the most dangerous and the sweetest man I know, taught me what I needed when I got tired of being scared on the street— and much more. Well met, brother.

Among academics, a core group has emerged that has taken a lead role in developing the theoretical underpinnings behind the applied work, and supporting it with research, evaluation, and field support to our practitioner partners. Chief among them are Anthony Braga, Tracey Meares, Andrew Papachristos, Ed McGarrell, Nick Corsaro, Tim Bynum, Robin Engel, Terri Shelton, and Alvin Atkinson and the team at the Center for Community Safety in Winston-Salem, North Carolina. Stewart Wakeling, Paul Seave, and Daniela Gilbert have been carrying the work in California. Kahrlton Moore and Lisa Shoaf have been playing the same role in Ohio.

At John Jay College of Criminal Justice, President Jeremy Travis has protected and supported the work, and created a national center of gravity for the growing community committed to it. It has made all the difference. He has, literally from the beginning, made crucial contributions at strategic moments. I particularly, and everybody else who cares about these issues, owe him an enormous debt.

At the Center for Crime Prevention and Control at John Jay, Sue-Lin Wong, Vaughn Crandall, Sibylle Von Ulmenstein, Lisa Marie Vasquez, and Bonnie Sultan are determined to change the world, see no reason to accept anything less, and are acting accordingly. You amaze me. You also made it possible for me to write this book: many, many thanks.

While writing this book, I got special help at key moments from very generous scholars: Mark Kleiman and Jonathan Caulkins regarding the national data on drug selling and drug use; Alex Piquero on the evaluation record on prevention programs; Bruce Western on the impact of incarceration; and Eric Cadora on the concentration of incarceration. Any errors are mine.

I got reading help from my parents, Chris and Jane Kennedy; Lory Newmyer; Susan Herman; Zoe Towns; Vaughn Crandall; Anthony Braga; Stewart Wakeling; Kim Morton; Hathaway Ferebee, Rob Lang, Larry Casterline, Marty Sumner, Jim Fealy; Robin Engel; Greg Baker; Jim Whalen; and Tom Streicher. It helped enormously. Again, errors are mine.

Gail Ross of Ross Yoon believed in this project before I even thought of it; she and Howard Yoon shepherded me through the process of, for the first time in my experience, launching a book somebody might actually want to read. I've loved working with you and hope the results do you justice.

Anton Mueller at Bloomsbury was exactly the gifted, relentless, uncompromising editor I was looking for. I did not expect what I also got: a genuine intellectual partner. His engagement, especially, around the nature of the conflict beween communities this book addresses not only improved the book, it improved my, and my community's, framing of what we are dealing with and how we need to understand and address it. Writing is at some level an intrinsically collective enterprise: Few, and I'm not one, can do it entirely on their own. I've never worked with anyone of close to Anton's caliber.

John Seabrook was good enough to let us use the title of his *New Yorker* article; we couldn't do any better, so we stole it.

And to Alison Johns, who was my first and best reader, who has believed utterly in what I have been doing, and who put up with the selfish, sullen mess this project turned me into, all my love and gratitude.

Notes

Much of the material in this book is drawn from my own firsthand experience. Much of the history and material covered has been addressed in various ways by formal academic evaluations; scholarly qualitative and process accounts; practitioners' documentation, planning and implementation materials; and other kinds of description and analysis. Much of it has been the subject of contemporaneous and retrospective journalistic accounts. It has been the subject of a running conversation among those most centrally involved in developing and implementing the work, a conversation now going back more than fifteen years. I have drawn on all those resources. In addition, for much of the material in the book, I have revisited the site work with some of those most closely involved and drawn on their thoughts, insights, and understandings. The evolving work has also drawn on a much larger scholarly literature from a wide variety of fields.

The notes that follow identify source materials of particular importance. They also suggest a small number of additional sources in key areas that may be of interest to readers wishing to learn more.

Introduction

On Marge Schott, see, for example, John Erardi and Geoff Hobson, "Schott's Was Paradise Lost," *Cincinnati Enquirer*, October 25, 1998. My thanks to my colleague Vaughn Crandall for his recollection of Kenneth Lawson's poster; see also John Johnston, "Junkyard Dog of Justice," *Cincinnati Enquirer*, March 12, 1998.

General background on the Cincinnati riots is drawn from Cecil Thomas's expert testimony before Judge Susan J. Dlott, case No. C-1-99-317, United States District Court, Southern District of Ohio, Western Division; from the Motion by Plaintiffs for a Preliminary Injunction in the same case; from "Mayor Scales Back Curfew After Calm Night in Cincinnati," *New York Times*, April 16, 2001; and Linda Vaccarielo, "Riot and Remembrance," *Cincinnati Magazine*, April 2006. Timothy Thomas's mother's and brother's quotes are drawn from John Larson, "Behind the Death of Timothy Thomas," Dateline NBC, updated April 4, 2004, http://www.msnbc.msn.com/id/4703574, and from Francis X. Clines, "Appeals for Peace in Ohio After Two Days of Protest," *New York Times*, April 12, 2001.

For an introduction to the core ideas behind community policing, see Malcolm K. Sparrow, Mark H. Moore, and David M. Kennedy, *Beyond 911: A New Era for Policing*. New York: Basic Books, 1990. For an introduction to problem-oriented policing, see Herman Goldstein, *Problem-Oriented Policing*. Philadelphia: Temple University Press, 1990. George Kelling's "broken windows" work can be found in George L. Kelling and Catherine M. Coles, *Fixing Broken Windows: Restoring Order and Reducing Crime in Our Communities*. New York: Free Press, 1996.

Historical data on white and black male homicide are drawn from the Department of Justice's Bureau of Justice Statistics, http://bjs.ojp.usdoj.gov/content/homicide/tables/varstab.cfm. Data on recent increases in black male homicide and the 2005 black/white homicide counts are drawn from James Alan Fox and Marc L. Swatt, "The Recent Surge in Homicides Involving Young Black Males and Guns: Time to Reinvest in Prevention and Crime Control," December 2008, http://www.jfox.neu.edu/Documents/Fox%20Swatt%20Homicide%20Report%20Dec%2029%202008.pdf.

Funeral directors in many cities are dealing with retaliation issues. The vignette about Clarence Glover is drawn from Gary Fields, "Violence Roils Black Funeral Parlors," *Wall Street Journal*, March 26, 2008.

David Cay Johnston's article arguing that crime isn't a problem is "It's Scary Out There in Reporting Land," *Nieman Reports*, The Nieman Foundation for Journalism at Harvard University, Winter 2010, http://nieman.harvard.edu/reports/article/102499/Its-Scary-Out-There-in-Reporting-Land.aspx.

The facts about the nature of the 2010 homicide increase in New York City are drawn from Sean Gardiner, "Rise Seen in Black Victims," *Wall Street Journal*, March 9, 2011.

The estimate that roughly one in three black men will go to prison during their lifetime is drawn from Thomas P. Bonczar, "Prevalence of Imprisonment in the U.S. Population, 1974–2001," U.S. Department of Justice, Bureau of Justice Statistics, August 2003. The one in nine current imprisonment rate for black men is drawn from "One in 100: Behind Bars in America 2008," The Pew Charitable Trusts. The extent of criminal justice supervision among young Baltimore black men was documented in Eric Lotke and Jason Ziedenberg, "Tipping Point: Maryland's Overuse of Incarceration and the Impact on Public Safety," Policy Brief, Washington, D.C.: Justice Policy Institute, 2005.

The circumstances of Robert Tate's death were widely reported in Chicago. See, for example, Matt Bartosik, "Dying Teen Takes Killer's Name to Grave," NBC Chicago, April 20, 2010, http://www.nbcchicago.com/news/lo cal/Dying-Teen-Takes-Killers-Name-to-Grave-91610554.html.

The Rev. Jeremiah Wright's quote is drawn from Brian Ross and Rehab El-Buri, "Obama's Pastor: God Damn America, U.S. to Blame for 9/11," *ABC News*, March 13, 2008, http://abcnews.go.com/Blotter/DemocraticDebate/ story?id=4443788&page=1.

Data about escalating violence in Cincinnati after the 2001 riot are drawn from Jennifer Edwards, "Year of Violence: Killings up 52% in City," *Cincinnati Enquirer*, December 29, 2001; the map cited is at http://www.enquirer.com/ editions/2001/09/01/gunfiremap430x567_zoom.jpg. Facts about the renewed crackdown in Over-the-Rhine and elsewhere are drawn from Kevin Osborne, "New Crime Report Is Bleak; Mallory Under the Gun," *CityBeat*, May 10, 2006, http://www.citybeat.com/cincinnati/article-1065-news-deadly-city.html, and from Roger Buddenberg, "A Fresh Grip on Gangs, Gun Crimes," *Omaha World-Herald*, June 27, 2010. Data on shootings of children in Cincinnati were collected and analyzed by the Policing Institute at the University of Cincinnati.

Boston: Street Knowledge, Street Sense

Data on the escalation of youth homicide in Boston are drawn from Anthony A. Braga, David M. Kennedy, Elin J. Waring, and Anne Morrison Piehl, "Problem-Oriented Policing, Deterrence, and Youth Violence: An Evaluation of Boston's Operation Ceasefire," *Journal of Research in Crime and Delinquency* 38 (2001): 197.

The "diffusion" idea that the youth gun problem had grown bigger than the core juvenile criminal population was developed in Alfred Blumstein, "Youth Violence, Guns, and the Illicit-Drug Industry," *Journal of Criminal Law and Criminology* 86, no.1 (1995): 10–36. A very rare and valuable piece of original research into why young people get and carry guns was Joseph F. Sheley and James D. Wright, "Gun Acquisition and Possession in Selected Juvenile Samples," Research in Brief, Washington, D.C.: U.S. Department of Justice, National Institute of Justice, Office of Juvenile Justice and Delinquency Prevention, 1993. My paper on kids and guns would eventually be published, in modified form, as David M. Kennedy, "Can We Keep Guns Away from Kids?" *American Prospect*, June 1994.

The set of ideas that inspired the Tampa, and other, drug-market interventions can be found in Mark A. R. Kleiman and Rebecca M. Young, "The Factors of Production in Retail Drug Dealing," *Urban Affairs Review* 3 (1995). The Link Valley story is told in David M. Kennedy, "Fighting the Drug Trade in Link Valley," Kennedy School of Government Case Program C16-90- 935.0 4-7 (1990); the Tampa story in David M. Kennedy, "Closing the Market: Controlling the Drug Trade in Tampa, Florida," National Institute of Justice, Program Focus series, April 1993.

A good primer on illicit gun markets is Anthony A. Braga, Philip Cook,

•

David Kennedy, and Mark H. Moore, "The Illegal Supply of Firearms," in M. Tonry, ed., *Crime and Justice: A Review of Research, Vol. 29*. Chicago: University of Chicago Press, 2002.

The idea of "superpredators" was popularized by William J. Bennett, John J. DiIulio, and John P. Walters, *Body Count: Moral Poverty . . . And How to Win America's War Against Crime and Drugs*. New York: Simon and Schuster, 1996. Quotes are from pages 26–28. James Alan Fox's analysis of what he called "the young and the ruthless" can be found in James Alan Fox, "Trends in Juvenile Violence: A Report to the United States Attorney General on Current and Future Rates of Juvenile Offending," Northeastern University, March 1996. For an account of how wrongheaded these ideas turned out to be, see Philip Cook and John Laub, "After the Epidemic: Recent Trends in Youth Violence in the United States" in M. Tonry, ed., *Crime and Justice: A Review of Research, Vol. 29*. Chicago: University of Chicago Press, 2002.

The public-health violence prevention approach is best captured by Deborah Prothrow-Stith, M.D. and Michelle Weissman, *Deadly Consequences: How Violence Is Destroying Our Teenage Population and a Plan to Begin Solving the Problem*. New York: Harper Perennial, 1993.

The basic Boston research findings can be found in David M. Kennedy, Anne M. Piehl, and Anthony A. Braga, "Youth Violence in Boston: Gun Markets, Serious Youth Offenders, and a Use-Reduction Strategy," *Law and Contemporary Problems* 59 (1996).

Operation Ceasefire

The quote from Rashad is drawn from Joe Mathews, "Boston Finds Answers to Youth Violence: City's Approach to Crime May Be Model for Baltimore," *Baltimore Sun*, December 27, 1996.

For formal evaluations of the impact of Operation Ceasefire, see Anthony A. Braga et al., "Problem-Oriented Policing, Deterrence, and Youth Violence: An Evaluation of Boston's Operation Ceasefire," *Journal of Research in Crime and Delinquency* 38 (2001), and Anne M Piehl et al., "Testing for Structural Breaks in the Evaluation of Programs," *Review of Economics and Statistics* 85 (2003). On the research finding that Ceasefire's gun-trafficking elements did have an impact on the illicit firearm market, see Anthony A. Braga and Glenn L. Pierce, "Disrupting Illegal Firearms Markets in Boston: The Effects of Operation Ceasefire on the Supply of New Handguns to Criminals," *Criminology & Public Policy* 4 (November 2005).

Building Out I

The first *New York Times* story about the Boston Gun Project was Fox Butterfield, "Federal Program Will Track Sales of Guns to Youths," July 8, 1996. The second was Fox Butterfield, "In Boston, Nothing Is Something," *New York Times*, November 21, 1996.

On the public-health claims about what happened in Boston, see Deborah Prothrow-Stith, and Howard R. Spivak, *Murder Is No Accident: Understanding and Preventing Youth Violence in America.* San Francisco: Jossey-Bass, 2004. On the record of school-based antiviolence curricula, see Daniel W. Webster, "The Unconvincing Case for School-Based Conflict Resolution Programs for Adolescents," *Health Affairs* 12 (1993); of gun buy-backs, Martha Plotkin, ed., *Under Fire: Gun Buy-Backs, Exchanges, and Amnesty Programs.* Washington, D.C.: Police Executive Research Forum, 1996.

The quote about district attorneys acting like "worried parents" is from Blaine Harden, "Boston's Approach to Juvenile Crime Encircles Youths, Reduces Slayings," *Washington Post*, October 23, 1977.

On the academic response to Operation Ceasefire, see Jeffrey Fagan, "Policing Guns and Youth Violence," *Future of Children* 12 (2002); Richard Rosenfeld, Robert Fornango, and Eric Baumer, "Did Ceasefire, Compstat, and Exile Reduce Homicide?" *Criminology and Public Policy* 4 (2005); Charles F. Wellford, John V. Pepper, and Carol V. Petrie, eds., *Firearms and Violence: A Critical Review Committee to Improve Research Information and Data on Firearms*, National Research Council, Washington, D.C.: National Academies Press (2004).

For the early attempts to capture the basic deterrence theory behind Operation Ceasefire, see David M. Kennedy, "Pulling Levers: Chronic Offenders, High-Crime Settings, and a Theory of Prevention," *Valparaiso University Law Review* 31 (Spring 1997), and David M. Kennedy, "Pulling Levers: Getting Deterrence Right," *National Institute of Justice Journal* (July 1998). Reprinted in Malcolm W. Klein, Cheryl L. Maxson, and Jody Miller, eds., *The Modern Gang Reader*, 2nd ed. Los Angeles: Roxbury Press, 2000.

Minneapolis's "Murderapolis" tag came from Dirk Johnson, "Nice City's Nasty Distinction: Murders Soar in Minneapolis," *New York Times*, June 30, 1996. The figures on Operation Safe Street in Minneapolis are drawn from Chris Graves, "Anti-gang Push Nets 9 Bogus Boyz," *Minneapolis Star Tribune*, June 18, 1997. The investigative report on homicide in Minneopolis was Anne O'Connor and Tatsha Robertson, "Chain of Violence," *Minneapolis Star-Tribune*, December 15, 1996. The basic Minneapolis research findings can be found in David M. Kennedy and Anthony Braga, "Homicide in Minneapolis: Research for Problem Solving," *Homicide Studies* 2 (August 1998). Dr. Sterner's quote is drawn from James Walsh, "A Quiet Killing Month," *Minneapolis Star-Tribune*, July 1, 1997.

The Stockton intervention is documented in Stewart Wakeling, *Ending Gang Homicide: Deterrence Can Work*, California Attorney General's Office and California Health and Human Service Agency, February 2003, and in Anthony A. Braga, "Pulling Levers Focused Deterrence Strategies and the Prevention of Gun Homicide," *Journal of Criminal Justice* 36 (2008).

On establishing the Strategic Approaches to Community Safety Initiative, see Veronica Coleman et al., "Using Knowledge and Teamwork to Reduce Crime," *National Institute of Justice Journal* (October 1999). For more on its implementation and impact, see Erin E. Dalton, "Lessons in Preventing Homicide." School of Criminal Justice, Michigan State University, December 2003, and "Paving the Way for Project Safe Neighborhoods: SACSI in 10 U.S. Cities." Research in Brief, National Institute of Justice, April 2008. There is a school of thought that these research-and-practice problem-focused partnerships represent an alternative to traditional "criminal justice system" approaches to crime control; for more, see John Klofas, Natalie Kroovland Hipple, and Edmund McGarrell, *The New Criminal Justice: American Communities and the Changing World of Crime Control*. New York: Routledge, 2010.

Not covered here, but contemporaneous, was a Ceasefire replication in Boyle Heights in Los Angeles, also sponsored by NIJ and Lois Mock, led by George Tita, then with the RAND Corporation and now at the University of California Irvine. See George Tita, Jack K. Riley, and Peter Greenwood, "From Boston to Boyle Heights: The Process and Prospects of a 'Pulling Levers' Strategy in a Los Angeles Barrio," in S. H. Decker, ed., *Policing Gangs and Youth Violence*. Belmont, CA: Wadsworth/Thompson Learning, 2003; and George Tita, Jack K. Riley, and Peter Greenwood, *Reducing Gun Violence: Operation Ceasefire in Los Angeles*. Washington, D.C.: National Institute of Justice, 2005.

The deadly history of the Baltimore corner where Tiffany Smith was killed is from Michael James, "Man Becomes 4th Person Slain in 3 Years at W. Baltimore Corner," *Baltimore Sun*, April 12, 1994.

The quote from the *Lehrer NewsHour* is from a transcript of "Crime Drop," aired April 21, 1997, available at http://www.pbs.org/newshour/bb/law/april97/boston_4-21.html.

The article on the conflict between Boston and New York is Fox Butterfield, "Cities Reduce Crime and Conflict Without New York-Style Hardball," *New York Times*, March 4, 2000.

Baltimore: Politics, Resistance, Obstruction

The dyfunction we experienced in Baltimore law enforcement has been covered extensively. One good survey is "Getting Away with Murder," *Baltimore Sun*, February 14, 1999, available at http://articles.baltimoresun.com/1999-02-14/news/9902230305_1_homicide-rates-baltimore-crack-cocaine. For an account of how serious the rift became between the Baltimore U.S. attorney's office and the Bureau of Alcohol, Tobacco, and Firearms, see Daniel LeDuc, "Md. Attorney Accused of Threats to ATF; Official Livid over Release of Crime Data, Agent Says," *Washington Post*, September 21, 2000.

The distinction between the picture of homicide in Indianapolis drawn by offical police data and that revealed by the SACSI research is drawn from Dalton, "Lessons in Preventing Homicide," cited above.

The basic Baltimore research results can be found in Anthony A. Braga, David M. Kennedy, and George Tita, "New Approaches to the Strategic Prevention of Gang and Group-Involved Violence," in C. Ronald Huff, ed., *Gangs in America*, 3rd ed. Thousand Oaks, Calif.: Sage Publications, 2002.

Formal evaluations of the Indianapolis SACSI intervention can be found in Edmund F. McGarrell, S. Chermak, J. M. Wilson, and N. Corsaro, "Reducing Homicide Through a 'Lever-Pulling' Strategy," *Justice Quarterly* 23 (2006);

and Nicholas Corsaro and Edmund F. McGarrell, "Testing a Promising Homicide Reduction Strategy: Re-assessing the Impact of the Indianapolis 'Pulling Levers' Intervention," *Journal of Experimental Criminology* 5 (2009). Portland's experience is described in Stefan J. Kapsch, Lyman Louis, and Kathryn Oleson, "The Dynamics of Deterrence: Youth Gun Violence in Portland," report to the U.S. Department of Justice, available at http://www.ncjrs.gov/pdf files1/nij/grants/203969.pdf. The finding regarding gun violence in Winston-Salem is drawn from Dalton, "Lessons in Preventing Homicide," cited above; see also Doug Easterling et al., "Evaluation of SACSI in Winston-Salem: Engaging the Community in a Strategic Analysis of Youth Violence," report to the U.S. Department of Justice, available at http://www.ncjrs.gov/pdffiles1/nij/grants/202977.pdf. For New Haven, see Eliot C. Hartstone and Dorinda M. Richetelli, "Final Assessment of the Strategic Approaches to Community Safety Initiative in New Haven," report to the U.S. Department of Justice, available at http://www.ncjrs.gov/pdffiles1/nij/grants/208859.pdf. The 53 percent reduction in gun assaults in Indianapolis's most active neighborhood and the figures for New Haven are drawn from Jan Roehl et al., "Strategic Approaches to Community Safety Initiative (SACSI) in 10 U.S. Cities: The Building Blocks for Project Safe Neighborhoods," report to the U.S. Department of Justice, available at http://www.ncjrs.gov/pdffiles1/nij/grants/212866.pdf, p. 3.

Lynne Battaglia's quote regarding her withdrawal from the Operation Safe Neighborhoods launch is from Peter Hermann, "Crisis in Courts Proves Obstacle to Crime Plan: News Conference Delayed on Campaign to Cut Homicide Rate, U.S. Attorney Backs Out," *Baltimore Sun*, July 21, 1999. The "turf fights and bickering" quote is from a *Baltimore Sun* editorial, "Reducing City Killings Requires Unified Effort," August 1, 1999. See also "Justice Crackdown Has No Room for Rivalries; Joint Mission: Police and Prosecutors Must Set Aside Power Plays to Stem Violence," *Baltimore Sun*, editorial, August 22, 1999; and Peter Hermann, "U.S. Delays Decision on Crime Grant; Baltimore Competing for Funds to Study Patterns of Violence," *Baltimore Sun*, August 11, 1999.

The information about the burial of the dead from the northern Baltimore massacre and the Rev. Horton's comments at their service are drawn from Peter Hermann, "Small Town Buries Baltimore's Dead: N.C. Hamlet Mourns Four Shooting Victims," *Baltimore Sun*, December 13, 1999.

Figures on crime reductions after the Park Heights call-in are from "New Approaches to the Strategic Prevention of Gang and Group-Involved Violence," cited above.

Paul Joyce's comment about rising crime in Boston is drawn from John Buntin, "Murder Mystery," *Governing*, June 2002.

Across the Race Divide

The developing deterrence theory and the treatment of ideas such as direct communication, application to groups, group dynamics, offender norms, informal social control, interaction effects between authorities and offenders, and the like can be found in David M. Kennedy, *Deterrence and Crime Prevention: Reconsidering the Prospect of Sanction*. London: Routledge, 2009. Readers wishing to pursue any of those threads will find many citations. Mark Kleiman explores closely related ideas in *When Brute Force Fails: How to Have Less Crime and Less Punishment*. Princeton, N.J.: Princeton University Press, 2010.

Franklin Zimring and Gordon Hawkin's classic deterrence text is *Deterrence: The Legal Threat in Crime Control*. Chicago: University of Chicago Press, 1973.

Tommy Farmer's quote is from Fox Butterfield, "In for Life: The Three-Strikes Law—A Special Report: First Federal 3-Strikes Conviction Ends a Criminal's 25-Year Career," *New York Times*, September 11, 1995.

The story of the women's sex strike in Periera, Colombia, and the male reaction to it, can be found in "Lose the Gun or Sleep on the Sofa: Men in Violent Colombian Town Denied Sex Unless They Lay Down Arms," *CBS News*, September 14, 2006, available at http://www.cbsnews.com/stories/2006/09/15/world/main2013041.shtml. See also "Colombian Gangsters Face Sex Ban," *BBC World News*, September 13, 2006, at http://news.bbc.co.uk/2/hi/5341574.stm.

The account of how crack dealers came to enforce anti-violence norms in New York is from Bruce Johnson, Andrew Golub, and Eloise Dunlap, "The Rise and Decline of Hard Drugs, Drug Markets, and Violence in Inner-City New York," in Alfred Blumstein and Joel Wallman, eds., *The Crime Drop in America*. New York: Cambridge University Press, 2000. Similar dynamics around gun-carrying in Chicago are documented in Philip J. Cook, Jens Ludwig, Sudhir A. Venkatesh, and Anthony Braga, "Underground Gun Markets," Working Paper No. 11737, National Bureau of Economic Research, Cambridge, Mass., November 17, 2005.

David Matza's classic volume of gang scholarship is *Delinquency and Drift*. New Brunswick, N.J.: Transaction Publishers, 1990.

Robert J. Sampson's and Dawn Jeglum Bartusch's paper is "Legal Cynicism and (Subcultural?) Tolerance of Deviance: The Neighborhood Context of Racial Differences," *Law and Society Review* 32 (1988).

The National Urban League quote on "genocide" is drawn from Michelle Alexander, *The New Jim Crow: Mass Incarceration in the Age of Colorblindness*. New York: The New Press, 2010, p. 6. The Harlem mother's conspiracy conviction is from Timothy Williams, "Mothers Harness Their Grief to Try to Save Others' Lives," *New York Times*, February 3, 2007. Michelle Alexander's comparison of slavery, Jim Crow, and mass incareration is from *The New Jim Crow*, p. 13.

Terrence Hallinan's quote is from Edward Epstein, "Boston Speaker Tells Summit How to End Violence: Hundreds Attend S.F. Session on Crime," *San Francisco Chronicle*, Thursday, March 8, 2001.

The roots of Project Safe Neighborhoods in the previous work are addressed in "About Project Safe Neighborhoods," U.S. Department of Justice, at http://www.psn.gov/about/index.html.

The facts about convict labor in Alabama are from Douglas A. Blackmon, "From Alabama's Past, Capitalism Teamed with Racism to Create Cruel Partnership," *Wall Street Journal*, July 16, 2001.

The growth in black concentrated poverty in Detroit is described in Paul A. Jargowsky, "Sprawl, Concentration of Poverty, and Urban Inequality," in Gregory D. Squires, ed., *Urban Sprawl: Causes, Consequences, and Policy Responses*. Washington, D.C.: The Urban Institute Press, 2002, p. 43. There is a vast literature on this historical shift in the United States, and its consequences; a very good starting point is William Julius Wilson's *The Truly Disadvantaged: The Inner City, The Underclass, and Public Policy*. Chicago: University of Chicago Press, 1990.

The Sherman Griffith story is covered in Allan R. Gold, "Dead Officer, Dropped Charges: A Scandal in Boston," *New York Times*, March 20, 1989.

Figures on current rates of incarceration by age, race, and gender are drawn from "One in 100: Behind Bars in America 2008," The Pew Charitable Trusts.

Figures on New York City's contribution to New York State's prison population are from Peter Wagner, *Importing Constituents: Prisoners and Political Clout in New York*, A Prison Policy Initiative Report, April 22, 2002, available at http://www.prisonpolicy.org/importing/importing.html#_ftn3. Two thirds of NYS prisoners are from NYC. Figures about those prisoners' origins in New York City hot spots are from the "New York City Analysis" of the Justice Mapping Center at http://www.justicemapping.org.

Facts regarding the prison exposure of black men who were in their late thirties toward the end of the last century are drawn from Becky Pettit and Bruce Western, "Mass Imprisonment and the Life Course: Race and Class Inequality in U.S. Incarceration," *American Sociological Review* 69 (2004). Facts about the imprisoned's earning future are from Bruce Western, Jeffrey R. Kling, and David F. Weiman, "The Labor Market Consequences of Incarceration," *Crime and Delinquency* 47 (2001). Facts about marriage and cohabitation are from John Hagan and Ronit Dinovitzer, "Collateral Consequences of Imprisonment for Children, Communities, and Prisoners." *Crime and Justice* 26 (1999) and from Bruce Western and Sara McLanahan, "Fathers Behind Bars: The Impact of Incarceration on Family Formation," in Greer Litton Fox and Michael L. Benson, eds., *Families, Crime, and Criminal Justice: Charting the Linkages*. Greenwich, Conn.: JAI Press, 2000. On the loss of franchise by black men, see Ryan S. King, *Expanding the Vote: State Felony Disenfranchise Reform, 1997–2008*, September 2008, Washington, D.C.: The Sentencing Project. On black children with a parent in prison, and on the impact on their rate of school expulsion, see "Collateral Costs: Incarceration's Effect on Economic Mobility," The Pew Charitable Trusts, 2010. The ripple effect that knowing someone imprisoned has on attitudes toward the police and on community crime prevention is addressed in Dina Rose and Todd Clear, *Incarceration, Reentry and Social Capital: Social Networks in the Balance*. John Jay College of Criminal Justice, 2002. Two good entry points to the impact of mass incarceration are Jeremy Travis, *But They All Come Back: Facing the Challenges of Prisoner Reentry*. Washington, D.C.: Urban Institute Press, 2005; and Todd R. Clear, *Imprisoning Communities: How Mass Incarceration Makes Disadvantaged Neighborhoods Worse*. New York: Oxford University Press, 2007.

Rod K. Brunson's article is "Police Don't Like Black People: African-

American Young Men's Accumulated Police Experiences," *Criminology and Public Policy* 6 (2007).

High Point: Truthtelling and Reconciliation

Findings on PSN's effectiveness in Durham are from M. J. Gathings and James M. Frabutt, *Evaluation of the Durham Police Department's S.T.A.R.S. Notification Program*, Center for Youth, Family, and Community Partnerships, University of North Carolina Greensboro, August 2005.

The 1 in 15,000 prison risk for a cocaine sale is drawn from David Boyum and Peter Reuter, *An Analytic Assessment of U.S. Drug Policy*. Washington, D.C.: AEI Press, 2006.

Background on East Austin and on Operation Rockcrusher is drawn from a number of articles and letters to the editor in the *Austin American-Statesman*: Scott W. Wright, "Curfew Sought in East Austin," December 29, 1992; Daniel J. Vargas, "3 Men Charged in Drive-by Shooting that Killed Girl at East Austin Church," December 30, 1992; Bob Banta and Mike Todd, "City Looking to Cure Neighborhood's Ills," March 8, 1993; Jim Phillips and Chuck Lindell, "Officers Put Dent in Drug Market: Largest Drug Sweep in Travis County Nets 109 Suspects," December 3, 1993; Jim Phillips and Chuck Lindell, "Drug Sweep Arrests Raise Racial Questions," December 4, 1993; Scott W. Wright, "Drug Sweep Gets Mixed Reviews from Neighbors: Did Operation Rock Crusher Make a Dent in City's Drug-Related Woes? The Answers Are Elusive," December 19, 1993; Bill Clark's letter of December 10, 1993; and Jim Fealy's letter of December 24, 1993.

High Point's research partners from the University of North Carolina Greensboro, working with HPPD's Lee Hunt, did a heroic job of documenting the creation of the West End Intitiative. Many of the particulars around implementation are drawn from James M. Frabutt, M. J. Gathings, Eleazer D. Hunt, and Tamela J. Loggins, *High Point West End Inititiative: Project Description, Log, and Preliminary Impact Analysis*, Center for Youth, Family, and Community Partnerships, University of North Carolina Greensboro, July 2004. The formal logic model for the West End Initiative, developed by UNCG, is also in that document.

Melissa Nichols's *Greensboro News & Record* quote is from Mary Best, "Model Police Work," *UNCG Research*, University of North Carolina Greensboro, Spring 2009.

An excellent article on the High Point experience is Mark Schoofs, "Novel Police Tactic Puts Drug Markets Out of Business," *Wall Street Journal*, September 27, 2006. For more, see chapter 9 in *Deterrence and Crime Prevention*, cited above, available at http://nnscommunities.org/Chapter9.pdf; David M. Kennedy, "Drugs, Race and Common Ground: Reflections on the High Point Intervention," *National Institute of Justice Journal* 262 (2009), available at http://www.nij.gov/journals/262/high-point-intervention.htm; and Tate Chambers, "The High Point Intervention: Its Creation, Implementation, and Future,"

United States Attorneys' Bulletin, March 2010, available at http://www.justice
.gov/usao/eousa/foia_reading_room/usab5802.pdf#page=24.

Building Out II

The Winston-Salem intervention was documented in Lynn K. Harvey, *The
New Hope Initiative: A Collaborative Approach to Closing an Open-air Drug
Market and a Blueprint for Other Communities*. Winston-Salem, N.C.: Center
for Community Safety, Winston-Salem State University, 2005, available at
http://152.12.30.96/NR/rdonlyres/1BF7A584-539A-41A6-B860-94EED7C3FD2C/
0/NewHopeBluePrint.pdf. The list of partners in the intervention is drawn in
part from that report.

David Clayton's *Wall Street Journal* quote is from Mark Schoofs, "Novel
Police Tactic Puts Drug Markets Out of Business," cited above.

Amanda Milkovits's stories on the Lockwood operation are "Closing
'Crack Highway': Providence Police Turn to a Unique Initiative to Save a Drug-
Infested Neighborhood," *Providence Journal*, March 10, 2007, and "Calm
Comes to Lockwood Neighborhood: The Police Help Transform Providence's
Lockwood Neighborhood, Once Known for Drug-Dealing," *Providence Jour-
nal*, January 7, 2008. See also David M. Kennedy and Sue-Lin Wong, *The High
Point Drug Market Intervention Strategy*, Washington, D.C.: U.S. Department
of Justice, Office of Community Oriented Policing Services, 2009, which covers
both the High Point and the Lockwood operations.

The formal evaluation of the Rockford drug-market operation, from which
Ted and James are quoted, is N. Corsaro, R. K. Brunson, and E. F. McGarrell,
"Problem-Oriented Policing and Open-air Drug Markets: Examining the Rock-
ford Pulling Levers Deterrence Strategy," *Crime and Delinquency* 20 (2009).

Danielle Lombardo's quotes and the information about Hen-Rock's death
on Terrace Avenue are drawn from Nia-Malika Henderson and Michael Frazier, "Terrace Ave. Residents Have Long Lived with Crime," *Newsday*, January 28, 2008. The drug dealers' quotes are from research conducted by John
Jay College of Criminal Justice master's student Lisa-Marie Vasquez and are
used with grateful permission. Irving Gilreath's quote is from Bruce Lambert,
"Street Known for Drug Crime Is Getting Clean," *New York Times*, January
14, 2009.

The story about the Terrace drug dealer ordering take-out on the corner is
drawn from an ABC *Primetime* piece on the Hempstead drug-market operation. A print version is available, along with some video, as Ke'Yuanda Evans
and K. Michelle Smawley, "New Program Reforms Drug-Torn Neighborhood:
High Point Initiative Bridges the Gap Between Police and Civilians, Gives
Criminals Another Chance," ABC *Primetime*, August 20, 2008, at http://abc
news.go.com/TheLaw/story?id=5612013&page=1.

The impact figures for the Nashville drug-market intervention, and the
resident's quote, are from Nicholas Corsaro, Rod K. Brunson, and Edmund F.
McGarrell, "Evaluating a Policing Strategy to Disrupt an Illicit Street-Level

Drug Market," *Drug Market Intervention Working Paper*, School of Criminal Justice, Michigan State University, July 2009.

Burlee Kersey's speech is drawn from the CHOICE Project Newsletter, Raleigh Police Department, November 2007.

Stopping It

The figures on clearance rates for black male homicide in Boston are from David Bernstein, "The Worst Homicide Squad in the Country," *Boston Phoenix*, August 19, 2005.

The Rev. William E. Dickerson's plea at Analicia Perry's funeral is from Megan Tench, "Mourners Are Told: Give Him Up," *Boston Globe*, July 29, 2006.

Figures for at-risk, family, and neighborhood populations in Boston were calculated from 2000 census data contained in Eswaran Selvarajah and Jim Vrabel, *Census 2000: Key Neighborhood Characteristics, Comparative Data on Neighborhoods and Boston*, Report No. 594, Boston Redevelopment Authority, April 15, 2004, available at http://www.bostonredevelopmentauthority .org/PDF/ResearchPublications//Rpt594.pdf.

The finding that the National Youth Anti-Drug Media Campaign had perverse consequences can be found in Robert Orwin et al., *Evaluation of the National Youth Anti-drug Media Campaign: 2004 Report of Findings, Executive Summary*, Westat, June 2006, available at http://www.drugabuse.gov/about/ organization/despr/westat/NSPY2004Report/ExecSumVolume.pdf.

The quote from *Murder Is No Accident*, cited previously, is from p. 212.

The CDC report omitting all criminal justice interventions is *Youth Violence: Best Practices of Youth Violence Prevention—A Sourcebook for Community Action*, Centers for Disease Control, last updated October 5, 2009, available at http://www.cdc.gov/violenceprevention/pub/YV_bestpractices.html.

Anthony Braga's Lowell intervention is described and evaluated in Anthona A. Braga, Jack A. McDevitt, and Glenn L. Pierce, "Understanding and Preventing Gang Violence: Problem Analysis and Response Development in Lowell, Massachusetts," *Police Quarterly* 9 (2006).

Tracey Meares's Chicago PSN intervention is described and evaluated in Andrew V. Papachristos, Tracey Meares, and Jeffrey Fagan, "Attention Felons: Evaluating Project Safe Neighborhoods in Chicago," *Journal of Empirical Legal Studies* 4 (2007). The individual-level data reported are drawn from Jeffrey Fagan et al., "Desistance and Legitimacy: Effect Heterogeneity in a Field Experiment with High-Risk Offenders," presented at the annual meeting of the American Society of Criminology, St. Louis, Mo., November 2008, and available at http://www2.law.columbia.edu/fagan/papers/Desistance_and_Legitimacy _PSN_Recidivism_2.ppt.

There is a large literature on legitimacy and its impact on crime. Two excellent starting points are Tom R. Tyler, *Why People Obey the Law*, Princeton, N.J.: Princeton University Press, 2006; and Tracey Meares, "The Legitimacy of

Police Among Young African-American Men," *Marquette Law Review* 92 (2009). Robert J. Kane, in "Compromised Police Legitimacy as a Predictor of Violent Crime in Structurally Disadvantaged Communities," *Criminology* 43 (2005), found that in the most troubled communities—the ones this book is about—both overpolicing and high-profile incidents of police misbehavior, which compromised police legitimacy, led to increases in violence.

60 *Minutes*' "stop snitching" story is "Stop Snitchin'—Rapper Cam'ron: Snitching Hurts His Business, 'Code Of Ethics,'" August 12, 2007. It can be found, along with a video including Alex's comments, at http://www.cbsnews .com/stories/2007/04/19/60minutes/main2704565_page2.shtml?tag= contentMain;contentBody.

School survey data on the relative offending rates of black and white students are drawn from Howard N. Synder and Melissa Sickmund, *Juvenile Offenders and Victims: 2006 National Report*, Washington, D.C.: U.S. Department of Justice, Office of Justice Programs, Office of Juvenile Justice and Delinquency Prevention. Substance Abuse and Mental Health Services Administration data on rates of white and black drug use are drawn from Marc Mauer, *The Changing Racial Dynamics of the War on Drugs*, Washington, D.C.: The Sentencing Project, April 2009; 2005 census data are from the U.S. Census Bureau, ACS Demographic and Housing Estimates: 2005–2007, available at http://factfinder.census .gov/servlet/ADPTable?_bm=y&-geo_id=01000US&-qr_name=ACS_2007_3YR_ Goo_DP3YR5&-ds_name=&-_lang=en&-redoLog=false&-format=.

For an account of how violence by even very serious offenders is predominantly not about economic matters, see Andrew A. Papachristos, "Murder by Structure: Dominance Relations and the Social Structure of Gang Homicide," *American Journal of Sociology* 115 (2009).

A. Rafik Mohamed's and Erik Fritsvold's ethnography of privileged white drug dealers is "Damn, It Feels Good to Be a Gangsta: The Social Organization of the Illicit Drug Trade Servicing a Private College Campus," *Deviant Behavior* 27 (2006).

Cincinnati

The *CommonWealth* story from which Paul Evans and Paul Joyce are quoted is Michael Jonas, "Scene of the Crime," *CommonWealth*, Winter 2003. For similar coverage on the collapse of Operation Ceasefire, see Charles A. Radin, "A Shattered Alliance," *Boston Globe*, February 14, 2006; Michael Jonas, "Crime and Puzzlement," *CommonWealth*, February 1, 2006; and Michele McPhee, "Divine Wrath," *Boston Magazine*, December 2006. A scholarly account is Anthony A. Braga, David Hureau, and Christopher Winship, "Losing Faith? Police, Black Churches, and the Resurgence of Youth Violence in Boston," *Ohio State Journal of Criminal Law* 6 (2008).

The *Boston Globe* editorial calling for Operation Ceasefire to be restored is "*Boston's Armistice*," January 28, 2006. The story in which Commissioner O'Toole said that it would not be, in its original form, is Suzanne Smalley, "Talking Tough in Crime Fight," *Boston Globe*, December 7, 2005. Teny Gross's op-ed piece is "Politics, Petty Feuds, and Street Violence," *Boston Globe*, February 12, 2006.

For the process that led to the Cincinnati Collaborative Agreement, see Alphonse A. Gerhardstein, "Can Effective Apology Emerge Through Litigation?" *Law and Contemporary Problems* 72 (Spring 2009).

The RAND Corporation's study of police stops in Cincinnati is Terry Schell et al., *Police-Community Relations in Cincinnati: Year Three Evaluation Report*, RAND Corporation, Santa Monica, 2007, available at http://www .rand.org/content/dam/rand/pubs/technical_reports/2007/RAND_TR535.pdf.

Saul Green's comment regarding the lack of collaboration in the Collaborative Agreement was quoted in a sermon by the Rev. Sharon K. Dittmar, First Unitarian Church, October 8, 2006, available at http://www.firstuu.com/Sunday_ Services/Sermon_Archive/2006/10-8-06.pdf.

Mayor Mallory's comment about the "likely killers list" comes from Jane Prendergast, "Mallory Says List Makes It Hard for Ex-criminals to Go Straight," *Cincinnati Enquirer*, April 25, 2007.

The core Cincinnati research findings, CIRV's operational and administrative structure, and results according to a range of process and outcome measures can be found in Robin Engel et al., *Implementation of the Cincinnati Initiative to Reduce Violence (CIRV): Year 1 Report*, University of Cincinnati Policing Institute, April 2008, available at http://www.uc.edu/ccjr/Reports/ Cincinnati_CIRV_YR1_Report_FINAL.pdf, and in Robin Engel et al., *Implementation of the Cincinnati Initiative to Reduce Violence (CIRV): Year 2 Report*, University of Cincinnati Policing Institute, available at http://nnscom munities.org/pdf/CIRV_2NDYEAR_REPORT.pdf.

Michael Blass's essay, "The CIRV Call-In: Reflections on a Profound Experience," can be found at http://www.jjay.cuny.edu/centers/crime_prevention_ and_control/Blass_essay.pdf.

A case study of Cincinnati's prison call-ins, "Lebanon Correctional Institutional Call-In," written by Sibylle Von Ulmenstein, is available at http://www .nnscommunities.org/Lebanon_Correctional_Facility_Call-In_FINAL(1).pdf. Tom Streichers's comments at the prison call-in are drawn from it.

An excellent article on the Cincinnati experience is John Seabrook, "Don't Shoot," *New Yorker*, June 22, 2009. The quotes from Dan Gerard about superior firepower and the description of Jim Whalen as a big bear are from John's piece.

Now

The National Network for Safe Communities is supported with funding from the Office of Community Oriented Policing Services of the U.S. Department of Justice and from the MacArthur Foundation. The gang violence work in Chicago is also supported by the MacArthur Foundation. Both have our deep gratitude.

Information on Hawaii Hope can be found in "Hawaii's Opportunity Probation with Enforcement (HOPE) Program," Coalition for Evidence-Based

Practice, Newsletter Summary, February 2011, available at http://coalition4evi dence.org/wordpress/wp-content/uploads/HOPE-Program-Feb-2011.pdf. The description of the NYPD's Juvenile Robbery Intervention Program, or JRIP, is from Joanne Jaffe. The sketch of an approach to domestic violence can be found in chapter 10 of *Deterrence and Crime Prevention*, along with an argument and supporting evidence that domestic violence is not as significantly different from other kinds of violence as is generally believed.

Jeffrey Rosen's article is "Prisoners of Parole," *New York Times Magazine*, January 10, 2010.

Karen Richards's quote is from Mark Schoofs, "Novel Police Tactic Puts Drug Markets Out of Business," *Wall Street Journal*, September 27, 2006.

The quote from Patrick McIlheran is from "How to Let People Do Heroes' Work," *Milwaukee Journal Sentinal*, July 12, 2007, available at http://drugmar ketinitiative.msu.edu/07-12-2007_Milwaukee_Journal_Sentinel_Ar.pdf.

John Seabrook's "failure" quote of Dean Esserman is from "Don't Shoot," cited previously.

The video of gangs in Ricky Burgess's Pittsburgh neighborhood is "Tour Inside Gang Neighborhoods Of Pittsburgh, PA (Including East Hill Bloods, Hilltop 581 Crips & Dallas Ave Crips With Even 11-Year-Olds Joining In)," no author given, http://www.worldstarhiphop.com/videos/video800.php?v=wshh V6HGG206K5ml2Om2&set_size=1.

A Note on the Author

David M. Kennedy is the director of the Center for Crime Prevention and Control at John Jay College of Criminal Justice in New York City. Previously, he was a senior researcher and adjunct lecturer at the Program in Criminal Justice Policy and Management at Harvard University's Kennedy School of Government. He is the author of *Deterrence and Crime Prevention: Reconsidering the Prospect of Sanction* and coauthor of *Beyond 911: A New Era For Policing*, and he has been called on as an adviser on troubled communities, illicit drug and firearm markets, youth and domestic violence, and deterrence theory for the Justice Department; the Department of the Treasury; the Bureau of Alcohol, Tobacco and Firearms; the Office of National Drug Control Policy; and the White House, as well as government bodies in England, Scotland, Canada, Brazil, Australia, Japan, and elsewhere. His Operation Ceasefire intervention has been deployed in scores of cities, and his High Point approach to eliminating drug markets has also been implemented in a number of cities nationally, including nineteen sponsored by the Justice Department. His work has received two Webber Seavey awards from the International Association of Chiefs of Police, two Innovations in American Government awards from the Kennedy School of Government, and a Herman Goldstein Award for Excellence in Problem-Oriented Policing. He received the 2010–2011 Hatfield Scholar Award for scholarship in the public interest. Kennedy lives in Brooklyn, New York.

Questions for Discussion

Questions for Law Enforcement

Questions for Citizens/Members of the Community

Questions for Students

Questions for Law Enforcement

1. While policing Over-the-Rhine, why do you think police couldn't or didn't differentiate between the hapless, the serious criminals, and everybody else?

2. When were the ideas of community- and problem-oriented policing introduced in your agency? Did they provide a more effective way to go after important crime problems? Do you have any success stories of your own?

3. When describing the community of law enforcement, the author discusses the notion that one of the problems affecting America's poor and crime-riven neighborhoods is institutional racism. Do you encounter this idea in your own work? What do you think of it? How do you respond to it?

4. The author states that our response to crime has become part of what is sustaining it. How so? Do you agree?

5. Another revelation, one the author describes as hiding in plain sight, is about how the community of law enforcement and the community of the most dangerous neighborhoods see, influence, and drive each other. Can you think of some of the dynamics of these relationships and how they affect citizens, law enforcement, and crime?

6. What would you say to a member of a poor black community who told you that the problems of poverty, violence, and drugs they experience are directly caused by a white conspiracy?

7. What are some of the merits of the researchers' approach to collecting information, including immersing themselves in the street culture, surveying at-risk kids, conducting ethnography in cities' hot neighborhoods, and interviewing police officers and others dealing with this problem?

8. The idea of violent youth as "superpredators" gained much traction nationally and led to wholesale changes in state juvenile justice systems and laws about charging and trying juveniles as adults for violent crimes. How has this idea affected juvenile justice policies in your own state?

9. The fear that gang members experience in poor, crime-riven neighborhoods was a common theme in Operation Ceasefire's Working Group discussions. Knowing that gang members are "soaked in trauma and PTSD" (48), is a harsh law enforcement response to the problem of gang violence appropriate?

10. Police legitimacy is a central theme in the ideas behind the interventions created: "Legitimacy is *real* prevention" and "legitimacy is *moral power*" (222–23). Would you agree? Has the issue of police legitimacy affected you in your work?

11. Focused deterrence is a central part of the interventions created. What are the advantages of taking this approach? Are there any disadvantages?

12. Prior to reading about Operation Ceasefire and its counterparts, would you have thought that forums with gang members would be successful in stopping gang violence? Why do you think they were/are successful?

13. The author describes a competition between the two big national success stories on crime reduction, Boston and New York. The de-

bate was over strategy: The new NYPD was heavily relying on zero-tolerance policing, while Boston had implemented Operation Ceasefire. What are some of the differences between the two methods of crime reduction?

14. When describing what he encountered in Baltimore, the author states that the streets were nothing compared to the offices, and the gang rivalries were nothing compared to the political ones. This is shocking, considering that Baltimore was viewed as a proof test ("If we could handle Baltimore, we could handle anything," [97]) due to the fact that its gangs and drug markets were "insanely" active. Have political rivalries affected your own work? If so, how?

15. After the success in Boston, a common criticism of and concern with Operation Ceasefire was that it would not travel, that each city was too different. Would you agree? After discovering that it actually does travel and can be done, would you advocate for this approach to be taken in response to your neighborhoods' gun and gang problems?

Questions for Citizens/Members of the Community

1. What were your first thoughts when reading that Timothy Thomas ran from a police officer and was shot and killed? What were your thoughts when reading that Timothy Thomas ran because of outstanding warrants for traffic offenses and was not armed? Finally, what do you think about Ms. Leisure's statement "If you are an African male, you will run" (3)?

2. Prior to reading this book, did you know that even though the homicide rate has been steadily decreasing nationally, it has increased for black men? What do you think about these figures?

3. Do you agree with the author's statement that the argument that the crack epidemic created a moral panic misses the mark? Why?

4. Do you know any police officers? Why do you think they joined law enforcement? What would they say if you asked them?

5. "Thug love" is a central concept in the lives of young men in the community of the streets. Is it important for young individuals to be members of groups? Why?

6. The author discusses the views of the members of the three core communities involved in the crime problem. Can you see the rationality

behind the understandings and misunderstandings of members of the law enforcement community, the poor black neighborhood community, and the community of the streets? How has America's racial history affected these views?

7. The author argues that the core of the problem, and the key to the way out, lies in community. Why are communities so important?

8. A common finding in all the cities where Ceasefire and its counterparts were implemented was that a small number of individuals in gangs were accounting for a large part of serious crime. Does this surprise you? How does it shape your view of "troubled" neighborhoods?

9. The book states that the popular perception of violent black youth as "superpredators" was in fact misleading and without evidence. Why was this idea so attractive?

10. The fear that gang members experience in poor, crime-riven neighborhoods was a common theme in Operation Ceasefire's Working Group discussions. Gang members are "soaked in trauma and PTSD" (48). How did this finding affect the interventions? How does it affect your view of "bad kids?"

11. When reading the discussions that took place in the formal meetings with gang members held in each city, how did you feel? Would you have expected them to be so successful in stopping the violence? Why were they successful?

12. One concern with the proposed interventions was the possibility of applying draconian federal sanctions to gang members, such as those enforced on Freddie Cardoza. Was this a legitimate concern? How did the author respond to this concern?

13. Prior to the Cincinnati Initiative to Reduce Violence (CIRV) being implemented in Cincinnati, the police response to gang violence and homicide was to "arrest their way out of the problem" (238). This was done especially through the use of Vortex and their aggressive,

zero-tolerance policing methods in hot neighborhoods, resulting in thousands of arrests. What is your opinion of zero-tolerance policing? How can such methods affect relations with the black community?

14. Why is it important that citizens trust the police? Can there be a direct link between "legal cynicism" and crime?

15. A basic tenet of the interventions proposed by the author is that drug dealers and gang members are rational beings. Is this something we can easily accept?

Questions for Students

1. When visiting Over-the-Rhine, Harry Belafonte declared it a third-world country. Was this statement warranted? Do you agree?

2. Timothy Thomas had incurred twenty-one traffic charges in less than a year and a half, getting four tickets in one day. What was the intent of such persistent law enforcement?

3. What is a "moral panic"? How does the moral panic argument affect policies regarding drug use and drug markets? Can you think of any other situations that have been viewed as creating a moral panic?

4. The author asserts that he had a good view of the policy conversation around the crack epidemic in law enforcement, government, and scholarly circles and concludes that it was all nonsense. Which dominant discourses in each field is the author referring to? Why were they missing the mark?

5. The author and his partners' approach to the problem, beginning with a diagnosis that would lead to a then unknown intervention, was very different from standard academic research proposals. In fact, their National Institute of Justice (NIJ) proposal was initially rejected. Why do you think that was the case? What are the merits

of taking a new approach, such as the one taken by the author and his team?

6. The common ideology in all of the public, policy, and political attention to the homicide epidemic was the core conviction that the problem was huge, amorphous, and deeply rooted. Thus, it needed a similarly huge response. What are some problems with such an approach?

7. A clear theme coming from Operation Ceasefire's Working Group discussions was that gang members had imperfect knowledge of the legal risks they faced. How does this affect deterrence?

8. In the book, the author refers to Hobbes and the concept of the social contract. Why is the social contract important here?

9. When discussing crime, the issue of displacement frequently comes up. What is the evidence for displacement? Is there any evidence that crime was displaced to other neighborhoods from the neighborhoods where Operation Ceasefire and its counterparts were implemented?

10. The forums held with gang members were viewed as providing them with an "honorable exit" and "a way to step back without losing face" (71). Why was this successful in many cases? Why wasn't it in others?

11. After the "Boston Miracle" and the international interest in Operation Ceasefire, the academic literature and debate still tended toward the conclusion that nothing had happened, or if it had, it wasn't Ceasefire that had made it happen. What was the academic reaction based on? What are your own conclusions?

12. What are some differences between a strategy like Operation Ceasefire and methods such as zero-tolerance policing?

13. The author refers to David Matza's work *Delinquency and Drift*. How did this book affect the author? Why are the concepts of

drift, pluralistic ignorance, and fundamental attribution error important?

14. Why wasn't CIRV an appropriate vehicle for "reentry" work?

15. The author and his team described their work in High Point as "reconciliation and truth telling" (247). Is this an appropriate characterization? Why?